GENEALOGIES OF TERRORISM

NEW DIRECTIONS IN CRITICAL THEORY

NEW DIRECTIONS IN CRITICAL THEORY

Amy Allen, General Editor

New Directions in Critical Theory presents outstanding classic and contemporary texts in the tradition of critical social theory, broadly construed. The series aims to renew and advance the program of critical social theory, with a particular focus on theorizing contemporary struggles around gender, race, sexuality, class, and globalization and their complex interconnections.

For a complete list of titles in this series, please refer to
cup.columbia.edu/series/new-directions-in-critical-theory.

GENEALOGIES
OF TERRORISM

REVOLUTION,
STATE VIOLENCE,
EMPIRE

VERENA ERLENBUSCH-ANDERSON

Columbia University Press
New York

Columbia University Press
Publishers Since 1893
New York   Chichester, West Sussex
cup.columbia.edu

Library of Congress Cataloging-in-Publication Data
Names: Erlenbusch-Anderson, Verena, author.
Title: Genealogies of terrorism : revolution, state violence, empire / Verena
Erlenbusch-Anderson.
Description: New York : Columbia University Press, [2018] | Includes
bibliographical references.
Identifiers: LCCN 2017053625 (print) | LCCN 2017057123 (e-book) | ISBN
9780231547178 (e-book) | ISBN 9780231187268 (hardcover) | ISBN
9780231187275 (pbk.)
Subjects: LCSH: Terrorism—Social aspects. | Terrorism—History.
Classification: LCC HV6431 (e-book) | LCC HV6431 .E744 2018 (print) | DDC
363.325—dc23
LC record available at https://lccn.loc.gov/2017053625

Cover design: Chang Jae Lee
Cover image: © Jung Jihyun, Demolition Site 01 Inside, 2013

FOR L, M, AND P

La première tache de la liberté, plus souvent conquise qu'acquise, est d'aller à la longue quête du passé parce qu'il pèse de tout son poids sur le présent et que c'est sur lui que l'avenir se greffe.

—Mouloud Mammeri[1]

The allure of the archives entails a roaming voyage through the words of others, and a search for a language that can rescue their relevance. It may also entail a voyage through the words of today, with the perhaps somewhat unreasonable conviction that we write history not just to tell it, but to anchor a departed past to our words and bring about an "exchange among the living." We write to enter into an unending conversation about humanity and forgetting, origins and death. About the words each of us uses to enter into the debates that surround us.

—Arlette Farge, *The Allure of the Archives*[2]

A critique is not a matter of saying that things are not right as they are. It is a matter of pointing out on what kinds of assumptions, what kinds of familiar, unchallenged, unconsidered modes of thought the practices that we accept rest.

—Michel Foucault, "Practicing Criticism"[3]

CONTENTS

ACKNOWLEDGMENTS

This book has been a long time in the making, and I have incurred many debts along the way. At the University of Salzburg, Professor Clemens Sedmak made me love philosophy. Professor Theodor W. Köhler introduced me to the world of archives and taught me how to read carefully—in medieval Latin shorthand writing, no less. Without the mentorship of Professors Michaela Strasser and Sonja Puntscher Riekmann, I would have never pursued a career in academia. The unwavering support of Professor Heinrich Schmidinger allowed me to pursue graduate work under exceptional conditions thanks to a prestigious DOC Fellowship from the Austrian Academy of Sciences. I owe them all much more than they know.

At the University of Sussex, Gordon Finlayson and Darrow Schecter taught me to think and write in a language and discipline in which I am only now beginning to feel more at home. Bill Scheuerman and Tarik Kochi provided invaluable feedback that made this book conceivable. I am thankful to Tom Akehurst, Chris Allsobrook, Szu-hung Fang, Andrei Gómez-Suárez, Phil Homburg, Shamira Meghani, Simon Mussel, Chris O'Kane, Miguel Rivera, Katya Salmi, Gunjan Sondhi, Nadine Voelkner, and Yuliya Yurchenko for their friendship and intellectual companionship. I had the great fortune of reading Foucault's lectures with Tom Flynn at Emory University. For his generosity and care, both as a scholar and mentor, I remain profoundly grateful. For making a wonderful semester at Emory University possible, I thank Colin McQuillan and John Stuhr, as well as Gordon Finlayson.

This book has been made possible by an incredible community of friends and colleagues. I owe a particular debt to Colin Koopman, whose own work and engagement with mine have created the space in which what I do becomes possible and meaningful. For making me think harder, more clearly, and more fearlessly and for always being there, I am deeply grateful. To be able to think and write alongside Mary Beth Mader truly is a dream come true. Her genius, guidance, unwavering support, and, above all, friendship have been formative for my intellectual and personal development. I am also thankful for a wonderful friendship with the brilliant Maia Nahele, whose generosity, intellectual and otherwise, has been a source of inspiration. I thank Andrew Dilts for being an amazing friend and interlocutor. His insight on questions of method, reading practice, and activist scholarship has been invaluable not only for writing this book but also for my thinking about the role of theory in political struggles. My deepest thanks are due also to Mathias Thaler, whose clarity of thought and writing I hope one day to emulate and whose perspicacity and encouragement helped me tie this project together.

For their happy refusal of disciplinary border policing and their steadfast commitment to philosophical pluralism, I thank my colleagues at the University of Memphis: Luvell Anderson, Stephan Blatti (now at the University of Maryland), Remy Debes, Shaun Gallagher, David Gray, Bill Lawson, Mary Beth Mader, Mike Monahan, Tom Nenon, Hoke Robinson, Tim Roche, Kas Saghafi, Lindsey Stewart, John Tienson, Deb Tollefsen, and Somogy Varga. I am grateful to have experienced the warmth and wisdom of Pleshette DeArmitt; I miss her greatly. For taking such good care of me, I thank Connie Diffee and Cathy Wilhelm. I am grateful to current and former students at the University of Memphis for their curiosity and antidogmatism. Special thanks go to Bilge Akbalik, George Andrews, Shouta Brown, Lorena DeFrias, Josh Dohmen, B. Tamsin Kimoto, Jordan Liz, Chris Lucibella, Alberto Bejarano Romo, and James Zubko, as well as Skipper Boatwright, Robert Bowden, Allison Escobar, Chimene Okere, and Hunter Rhodes.

I am grateful to my fellow genealogists and to the speakers at the 2016 Spindel Conference for generously sharing their work, trying out ideas, and helping me think through hard problems of method and archival practice. Thanks to Amy Allen, Natalie Cisneros, Stuart Elden, Simon Ganahl, Rob Gehl, Stephanie Jenkins, Ladelle McWhorter, Thomas Nail, Kevin Olson, Brad Stone, Tuomo Tiisala, and Perry Zurn. I thank Tobias Klass for discussions of French philosophy during an unusually pleasant Memphis fall and for reading an early draft of the manuscript. Audiences at the University of Memphis, the University of Oregon, the California Roundtable on Philosophy of Race, the 2016 ECPR Joint Session in Pisa, the Critical Genealogies Workshop, and the 2016 Graduate Student Summer Institute in Rhetoric and Public Culture at Northwestern University provided critical feedback on various parts of this project. I thank all of them, and especially Penelope Deutscher, Dilip Goankar, Matthias Kaelberer, Alexander Livingston, Mihaela Mihai, Sharon Stanley, Mathias Thaler, and Yves Winter. I greatly benefited from discussions with Gerry Berk, Nicolae Morar, Chris Penfield, and Dan Rosenberg in a workshop on Colin Koopman's current project, and I thank the students in Colin's Data Genealogies seminar and participants in a workshop on what is now chapter 6 of this book for their exceptionally thoughtful engagement with my work.

At Columbia University Press, Amy Allen and Wendy Lochner saw something in this project before there was much there to see. I am grateful beyond measure for their faith in this book and my ability to write it, as well as for their steadfast support and patience. I also thank the production team at Westchester Publishing Services, especially Maura Neville and Charles Eberline, for their hard work turning the manuscript into this beautiful book.

Research at the Service historique de la Défense in Vincennes was made possible by the generous support of a Faculty Research Grant awarded by the College of Arts and Sciences at the University of Memphis. Presentation of a draft of chapter 3 at the ECPR Joint Session in Pisa was supported by a College of Arts and Sciences Travel Enrichment Award. Final revisions of the manuscript were completed during a Professional Development Assignment supported by the College of Arts and Sciences in the spring and summer of 2017.

For being the best friends I could ask for, I thank Katya Salmi and Patrick Liebl. For everything, I thank Luvell and my parents, Hannelore and Wilhelm Erlenbusch.

Parts of chapters 2 and 3 were previously published in "Terrorism and Revolutionary Violence: The Emergence of Terrorism in the French Revolution," *Critical Studies on Terrorism* 8, no. 2 (2015): 193–210. Earlier versions of some parts of chapters 1, 2, and 3 appeared in "The Place of Sovereignty: Mapping Power with Agamben, Butler, and Foucault," *Critical Horizons: A Journal of Philosophy and Social Theory* 13, no. 1 (2013): 44–69; "Terrorism: Knowledge, Power, Subjectivity," in *Critical Methods in Terrorism Studies*, ed. Jacob L. Stump and Priya Dixit (London: Routledge, 2016), 108–120; and "From Race War to Social Racism: Foucault's Second Transcription," *Foucault Studies* 22 (2017): 134–152.

1

THE TROUBLE WITH TERRORISM

DO WE KNOW WHAT WE SEE?

We seem to have a good sense of what terrorism is. We are pretty adept at discriminating between things that are terrorism and things that are not, and we generally know when the term applies and when it does not. Although scholars, lawyers, politicians, and laypeople are unable to agree on a definition of the term, and there are some hard cases in which it is less clear whether something is terrorism, more often than not, we are able to use the term without much difficulty. It seems that our intuitions about what is terrorism and who is a terrorist are so reliable that definitions are unnecessary.

Great Britain's United Nations representative, Jeremy Greenstock, gave voice to this claim when he famously argued that "there is common ground amongst us all on what constitutes terrorism. What looks, smells and kills like terrorism is terrorism."[1] But it is not obvious that Greenstock is right.

Consider, for example, drone strikes. They certainly look, smell, and kill like terrorism when they are viewed from the perspective of their victims, but they are justified by their perpetrators as military operations intended to end, precisely, terrorism.[2] Or take gun violence in the United States. Even though incidents of gun violence are usually described as mass shootings or rampage killings, the identity of the perpetrator gives rise to vastly different descriptions of identical forms of violence. An event in December 2015 in San Bernardino, California, for instance, was initially described as a mass shooting but quickly became an act of terrorism when the suspects were identified as an American citizen of Pakistani parentage and a Pakistani-born permanent resident who had pledged allegiance to Daesh on their Facebook accounts.[3]

These examples indicate that phenomenally identical actions are perceived rather differently depending on the identity of the perpetrator and the perspective from which these actions are described. They raise doubt about (1) the reliability of phenomenal qualities of certain actions—what they look, smell, and kill like—in determining whether something is terrorism; (2) the "we" whose intuitions are taken to be universally shared; and (3) the idea that the concept *terrorism* picks out a stable and readily identifiable thing in the world. How, then, ought we to proceed to figure out what terrorism is?

We can identify three general approaches to this question in the academic field of terrorism studies. First, we can explicate the implicit assumptions that underpin the dominant understanding of terrorism expressed, for instance, in Greenstock's dictum. I call this the *descriptive* approach. On this view, terrorism is simply the set of actions, conducts, practices, individuals, and other entities to which the term extends, regardless of whether there is, or whether we are able to identify, a property or organizing principle that unites the members of the set we call terrorism. A more critical version of this view insists that attributions of terrorism are biased and that one person's terrorist is another person's freedom fighter, as the saying goes. Consequently, we must provide a fuller survey of the conceptual landscape, attending to a range of dominant and subordinated meanings of the term *terrorism*. Terrorism, then, is the maximal class of things that have been, are, or could be identified as terrorism.[4] Second, we may supplement such descriptive approaches with an attempt to situate terrorism within a taxonomy of political violence. Think of characterizations of terrorism as a form of insurgency as an example of this approach.[5] Such a *classificatory* approach asks whether our vocabulary of terrorism refers to a more general type and provides criteria that distinguish terrorism from other types of political violence. Third, it is possible to stipulate a definition that meets certain desiderata determined by reference to a particular goal. I call this the *normative* approach. Tamar

Meisels explicitly advocates this view as the basis for moral evaluations of terrorism. She notes, "If terminology is to contribute to ethical judgment, the definition itself ought to highlight the characteristic normative category in question." Meisels further argues that because *terrorism* is a derogatory term, we must assume that the distinguishing features of terrorism "are bound to be at least objectionable if they are to bear any connection with ordinary speech."[6]

Notice, though, that these approaches are only analytically distinct. In practice, there are significant overlaps. For example, much of the literature on terrorism appears to adopt a descriptive approach but actually builds normative judgment into description by virtue of the cases selected for consideration.[7] To prevent such manipulative or partisan uses of the term, Anthony Richards advocates for a normative definition of terrorism for critical purposes and suggests an understanding of terrorism as "the use or threat of violence or force with the primary purpose of generating a psychological impact beyond the immediate victims."[8] But although Richards's proposal is interesting in its own right as an ameliorative project,[9] it nevertheless draws attention to a fundamental problem with definitional attempts to determine what terrorism is.[10] This is the problem of incorrigible positions, which are unacknowledged suppositions that correlate with a particular epistemic standpoint or cultural system. In short, when we try to determine what terrorism is, our answers are inevitably shaped by unquestioned and implicit assumptions about what we already recognize as terrorism.

To avoid this circularity, this book elaborates a methodology for studying terrorism that is keenly aware of the limitations of our own forms of thought. This method is genealogy, or the study of the empirical—material or discursive—conditions of the emergence of terrorism. Rather than prioritizing or even universalizing contemporary modes of understanding terrorism, genealogy attends to the historically specific conditions under which terrorism emerges, as well as the contextually specific modes of understanding those phenomena we uncritically identify as terrorism. Drawing inspiration from the work of Ludwig Wittgenstein and Michel Foucault,[11] among others, the genealogy developed in this book rests on the premise that an adequate and fruitful account of terrorism must begin with a consideration of the contexts within which terrorism is embedded and becomes meaningful.[12]

TERRORIST LANGUAGE GAMES

In his *Philosophical Investigations*, Wittgenstein likened the process by which we come to understand the meaning of a concept to that of a spectator unfamiliar with the rules of chess trying to figure out what *checkmate* means by observing a game.[13] The spectator, Wittgenstein argued, cannot work this out simply by looking at the move that puts the king in check. No matter how diligently she might study that one move, her observations will tell her little, if anything, about the meaning of *checkmate* because she knows nothing about the objective of the game and the different moves of the pieces permissible in pursuit of that objective. Knowledge of these things is necessary, however, to understand why the move that puts the king in checkmate amounts to winning the game. Because checkmate is made possible by a series of rules and moves that precede and lead up to the final move, knowing what *checkmate* means requires us to take account of the context of the game in its entirety. In the same way, Wittgenstein intimated, concepts can be understood only by considering the larger context in which they are used and acquire meaning.

Wittgenstein drew attention to the historicity and contextuality of concepts, to which we must attend if we want to avoid anachronism, an impoverished understanding of historical examples, ideological bias, mere exercises in lexicography, or further obfuscation of an already difficult concept. As Ian Hacking argues, "If one took seriously the project of philosophical analysis, one would require a history of the words in their sites in order to comprehend what the concept was."[14] The crucial methodological implication of these claims is that if we want to understand what terrorism is, we must first determine what the term means, how it functions in a given context, and how it is operationalized as an element in different discursive and nondiscursive practices.

As an illustration of what I have in mind, take the so-called *sicarii*, a commonly cited early example of terrorism. The *sicarii* were a religious sect that engaged in resistance against the Roman occupation of Palestine in the first century C.E. According to the Jewish-Roman historian Flavius Josephus, the *sicarii* were robbers whose name derived from the weapon they carried, a small curved dagger called a *sica*. Josephus specifically referred to them as robbers (*lēistai*) and explained that the term *sicarii* was "the name for such robbers as had under their bosoms swords called Sicae."[15] Josephus's precise description of the *sicarii* suggests that he understood them as a particular type of robbers who could be distinguished from other robbers by reference to their specific weapon. Indeed, Josephus described the *sicarii* as "another sort of robbers" who emerged in Jerusalem in the 50s C.E.[16] Even if the methods used by the *sicarii*, who were masters of disguise and conducted public and symbolically charged attacks, resemble present-day terrorist methods, describing them as terrorists obscures how they were understood by their contemporaries. Moreover, it privileges our own categories over those used at the time— in my view, without good reason. After all, we do not call al-Qaeda a band of robbers either. What it means to be a robber or a terrorist is determined according to a set of contextually specific norms that give regularity to and thus determine the meaning of the words. Terms like *terrorist* or *robber*, in other words, do not refer to a natural kind that exists in the world independently of human thought and practice. Rather, their meaning is conventional and determined by their use within discursive formations.

A number of scholars have drawn attention to the significance of words in disputes about the meaning and interpretation of violent acts, or what they call *the politics of naming*.[17] Michael Bhatia, for instance, argues that in the context of violent conflict, "names, words and discourse are viewed as objective representations of fact" when in fact they are victories in contestations over interpretation. Once a particular interpretation has been established through an act of naming, "the process by which the name was selected generally disappears and a series of normative associations, motives and characteristics are attached to the named subject." For Bhatia, in other words, names conceal the interests of those doing the naming, as well as the particular perspective that is thereby presented as objective. By rendering objects or phenomena knowable and known in specific ways, names also make possible "certain forms of inquiry and engagement, while forbidding and excluding others."[18] The *terrorism* label, for instance, serves as a means to deny the legitimacy of some forms of violence while affirming the necessity of others. As a consequence, paying attention to who names, who is named, how names are assigned and contested, and which names stick opens up possibilities for mapping both the discursive terrain and the political landscape on which conflicts over meaning and interpretation take place. In short, names or labels serve as what Foucault calls *"analyzers* of power relations."[19]

To insist that acts of naming something *terrorism* are impositions of power is not to say that there is no merit at all in conceptual clarity, descriptive or normative definitions of terrorism, or taxonomies of political violence. Rather, it is necessary to emphasize the importance of the complex web of social, political, legal, cultural, and historical practices within which distinctions between what is and what is not terrorism become possible and meaningful. Recall the example of the San Bernardino shooting. It is unhelpful to insist that because the incident fails to meet even some minimal conventionally accepted criteria of terrorism (such as intimidation or coercion of a civilian population or government), the proposition that it is an act of terrorism is false. What is important is that the shooting triggered a variety of sanctions, discourses, practices, beliefs, and judgments that suggest that it was terrorism in the relevant context. It was clear in public discourse that the shooting was an act of terrorism, and law enforcement opened a counterterrorism investigation. Even Daesh claimed that the shooters were "soldiers of the caliphate" acting on behalf of the organization.[20] There is no good reason, in my opinion, to privilege particular definitions of terrorism over the understanding operative in social, political, legal, military, and other practices. In fact, if we really want to understand terrorism, we must attend to these practices and examine the role terrorism plays within them.

HOW TERRORISM WORKS: A CASE STUDY

Over the past fifteen years, a growing number of scholars have heeded this insight and have increasingly focused on how terrorism works rather than what it is. Specifically, the transformation of the global political landscape after 9/11 has resulted in a growing and multidisciplinary concern with real-world effects of appeals to terrorism.[21] Here I examine the work of two prominent legal theorists, Leti Volpp and Muneer Ahmad, who are part of a larger attempt by critical scholars of race to draw our attention to the centrality of discourses of terrorism in the production of citizenship and national identity through the racialization of terrorism.[22] Their contributions are particularly useful because of their focus on the function of terrorism as a mechanism for excluding particular subjects from the social body.

Ahmad's main claim is that "the hate violence and racial profiling directed against Arabs, Muslims, and South Asians and the apparent African American and Latina/o support for the profiling of these communities provide an important example of how racial positions in the United States have been reordered by September 11, and how the citizenship status of all people of color has been further degraded." [23] He argues that 9/11 engendered a new mode of excluding certain communities from citizenship through the production of a new identity category, the "Muslim-looking person." Ahmad explains that according to a logic of fungibility, particular phenotypic characteristics, as well as nonphenotypic signifiers such as cultural garments, beards, and other visible markers of religious or cultural identity, are associated with being Muslim.[24] Being Muslim is then equated with being a terrorist. The result is that individuals who are perceived to share certain phenotypic characteristics or cultural markers are regarded as terrorists. That is, the Muslim-looking construct "captures not only Arab Muslims, but Arab Christians, Muslim non-Arabs (such as Pakistanis or Indonesians), non-Muslim South Asians (Sikhs, Hindus), and even Latinos and African Americans, depending on how closely they approach the phenotypic stereotype of the terrorist."[25]

Moreover, regardless of legal citizenship, the identification of individuals or communities as terrorists also serves to disidentify them as citizens and exclude them from the social body. By casting the Muslim-looking person as a terrorist and positing the terrorist as the noncitizen, the construction of American identity and the determination of who is American take shape in distinction from the Muslim-looking person. As Volpp explains, "The 'imagined community' of the American nation, constituted by loyal citizens, is relying on difference from the 'Middle Eastern terrorist' to fuse its identity at a moment of crisis."[26] However, the racialization of terrorism in terms of the Muslim-looking individual—and, in turn, the identification of certain communities as terrorists—operates not only as a mechanism of excluding some people of color from the national body but also as a means of bringing others into the fold of the nation-state. As Ahmad suggests, the enlistment of some communities of color to support the subordination and exclusion of others serves to maintain white supremacy behind a veneer of color blindness. After all, if those most harshly affected by racial profiling speak out in its support, "racial profiling is no longer racist." [27] Adding nuance to this analysis, Jasbir Puar sheds light on the complex interplay of race, sexuality, gender, class, and nation in the production of "terrorist look-alike populations" and illuminates the ways in which the production of racialized and perversely sexualized terrorist identity allows for the normalization and inclusion of "proper" or "patriotic" sexual identities.[28] On this view, the term *terrorism* is an instrument in an elaborate strategy of dividing and conquering communities of color and stigmatized sexual identities in an effort to shore up white supremacy and ensconce a racist, sexist, heteronormative, and, as Puar shows, homonormative national identity.

Although the production of citizenship as distinct from its "alien" and racialized other is by no means a new phenomenon,[29] critical analysis of the racialization of terrorism and the identification of a particular community as terrorists highlights the function of terrorism as a mechanism of exclusion, disidentification, and social control. Nevertheless, much of this literature remains limited to post-9/11 political realities in an (Anglo-)American context. But the operation of terrorism as a mechanism of exclusion and social control predates 9/11. It is a central thesis of this book that terrorism emerged at the end of the eighteenth century as the correlate of a new economy of power whose concern with the investment and improvement of life brought into being an entire series of technologies that served the purpose of social defense.

RIGHT OF DEATH AND POWER OVER LIFE

Foucault famously argued that since the seventeenth century, new technologies of power have emerged that differ sharply from practices of sovereign power typical of a state.[30] According to Foucault, the classical privilege of sovereign power is the "right to *take* life or *let* live"; sovereignty manifests itself as a right to kill when the sovereign's existence is in danger.[31] Consider, for example, Foucault's claim in *Discipline and Punish* that the public spectacle of torture and execution constitutes not primarily a juridical procedure but a political ceremony by which sovereign power is asserted. Because the law represents the will of the sovereign, a violation of law is simultaneously an attack on the sovereign. It follows that those who break the law are not merely transgressors who must be punished for their offense. Instead, insofar as they attack the authority and existence of the sovereign, they are enemies of the state and must be prosecuted as such. That is, they enter into bellicose relations with the sovereign, and punishment serves as an act of war in defense of the sovereign.[32]

Foucault argued that in the seventeenth and eighteenth centuries, new forms of power appeared that contrasted sharply with the repressive mode of power manifest in the sovereign right to kill. These new forms of power, which Foucault named *biopower*, pursued the management, optimization, and increase of life and took shape in two distinct forms. The historically first were the disciplines, or what he described as an anatomo-politics of the human body that targeted the bodies of individuals to make them docile and extract their forces. In contrast to individualizing disciplinary mechanisms, a biopolitics of the population focused on the collective body of the human species by means of regulatory controls intended to manage vital processes, such as reproduction, mortality, morbidity, and life expectancy.

Foucault took care to point out that the two technologies of biopower supported each other and were closely connected through diverse practices and relations. For example, in the interest of decreasing the mortality rate associated with a given disease, states deployed disciplinary mechanisms to influence individuals' hygiene and dietary habits and ensure immunization. Foucault also insisted that the emergence of disciplinary and regulatory forms of power did not lead to the disappearance of sovereignty. He cautioned that "we should not see things as the replacement of a society of sovereignty by a society of discipline, and then of a society of discipline by a society, say, of government."[33] Foucault instead showed that modern societies implement and integrate sovereign, disciplinary, and regulatory techniques.

This integration of different and, in fact, incompatible forms of power is facilitated at the level of political practice through a technique of power I will call *mechanisms of social defense*. Note that Foucault himself controversially and, in my view, unhelpfully opted for the word *racism* to describe mechanisms of power by which killing is justified in defense of the social body and the state's power to kill is made subservient to a larger project of the administration and regeneration of life.[34] Although there are historical and linguistic reasons for Foucault's rather unconventional use of the term *racism*,[35] it is important to emphasize that he did not mean by this an "ethnic racism" but a biologizing racism against the abnormal that is quite different from "traditional, historical racism."[36] Contrary to common usage, racism in Foucault's sense is not a mode of oppression directed against other races external to a social body but a "principle of exclusion and segregation" deployed to protect the health of the population from abnormal elements within.[37] Its aim is not the repression and enslavement of classes to be exploited, but an investment and improvement of life.

Foucault thus proposed a functional (rather than cognitive, behavioral, attitudinal, or even structural) account of racism as a technology of power that allows for the integration of different and even conflicting forms of power in a single regime. For him, racism was a justificatory operation by which the state's right to kill could be preserved and deployed in the name of the defense of society. To be sure, such an understanding of racism highlights the often-overlooked interconnection and shared purpose of different kinds of biopolitical regulation and normalization. That is, Foucault's notion of a racism against the abnormal draws our attention to the common goal of ethnic racism, sexism, ableism, homophobia, transphobia, Islamophobia, and other forms of exclusion in the production of a pure and immaculate social body, purged from all the dangers born in itself. But subsuming all these different mechanisms of exclusion under the banner of racism also results in a certain imprecision in distinguishing different ways in which exclusion is realized in political practice. For reasons of clarity and precision, as well as to underscore the functional character of Foucault's account, I therefore call the set of mechanisms by which the state internalizes and justifies killing for biopolitical ends *mechanisms of social defense* rather than *racism*.[38] Unless noted otherwise—for instance, by speaking of "racism in Foucault's sense"—I use the term *racism* as it is commonly used by Anglo-American scholars of race and racism to characterize dispositions, behaviors, and structures that discriminate against individuals believed to be members of certain racial groups.[39]

TERRORISM AS A *DISPOSITIF* OF SOCIAL DEFENSE

Against the background of Foucault's account of the modern economy of power, this book argues that terrorism functions—and has functioned since the eighteenth century—as a mechanism of social defense that is deployed when biopolitical concerns about the life of the population and the survival of the nation come into tension with traditional sovereign interests. In the name of defending society against the threat of terrorism, the use of violence is justified as necessary for the protection of life. In this sense, terrorism is best understood as a larger historical formation in which discursive and nondiscursive practices, laws, institutions, political decisions, military measures, architectural forms, and mentalities are joined together. This is what Foucault called a *dispositif*:

> What I try to locate with this term is, first, a thoroughly heterogeneous ensemble consisting of discourses, institutions, architectural forms, regulatory decisions, laws, administrative measures, scientific statements, philosophical, moral and philanthropic propositions—in short: the said as much as the unsaid, these are the elements of the dispositif. The dispositif itself is the network that can be established between these elements. Second, what I would like to locate in the dispositif is precisely the nature of the relation that can exist between these heterogeneous elements. Thus, a particular discourse can sometimes appear as a program of an institution, sometimes, by contrast, as an element that allows for the justification and masking of a practice, which itself remains silent, or the secondary reinterpretation of this practice, giving it access to a new field of rationality. In short, between these elements, discursive or not, there is a sort of play, changes of position, modifications of functions, which can themselves differ vastly. Third, by dispositif, I mean a sort of, say, formation, which, at a given historical moment, has as its major function to respond to an urgency. Thus, the dispositif has a dominant strategic function. This could have been, for example, the reduction of a mass of floating people, which a society with an essentially mercantilist economy found burdensome. There was a strategic imperative, which served as the matrix of a dispositif, which gradually became the dispositif of control-subjugation of madness, mental illness, neurosis.[40]

For Foucault, in other words, a dispositif is a historical formation that has a particular strategic purpose, but it is simultaneously functionally over-determined and permanently readjusted or modified. That is, although a dispositif responds to a particular problem or urgency, it produces effects that enter into new relations with other elements of the dispositif and engender new and unintended consequences that are co-opted for other ends. Foucault gives as an example the dispositif of imprisonment, which resulted in an acceptance of detention as the most rational means of addressing criminality. But at the same time as it was intended to reduce criminality, it produced a milieu of illegality, which was seized on by the state to be reintegrated, exploited, and made profitable. Consider, for instance, prostitution, which serves to "bring back to capital itself, to the normal circuits of capitalist profit, all the profits that can be extracted from sexual pleasure" through a threefold movement of criminalizing sexual pleasure, allowing it to take place, and exposing it to surveillance and power.[41]

I suggest that we ought to understand terrorism in the same way, namely, as a dispositif or surface network of heterogeneous elements that responds to historically specific urgencies. At the same time as the dispositif of terrorism provides a framework within which bodies of knowledge, norms of behavior, forms of resistance, and modes of being a subject are formed and acquire meaning, it also generates unforeseen effects that are integrated into new political practices and reused for new ends. Consider, for instance, the National Security Strategy (NSS) of the United States of September 2002, which acknowledges the opportunities afforded by measures introduced under the pretext of combating terrorism:

> Emergency management systems will be better able to cope not just with terrorism but with all hazards. Our medical system will be strengthened to manage not just bioterror, but all infectious diseases and mass-casualty dangers. Our border controls will not just stop terrorists, but improve the efficient movement of legitimate traffic.[42]

I will return to the post-9/11 American dispositif of terrorism in chapter 5. Here it suffices to emphasize that strategies implemented under the pretext of combating terrorism have effects that, whether by design or by accident, serve ostensibly unrelated ends like border control,[43] lead to a transformation of the science and practices of mental health,[44] and facilitate the transfer of public money to corporations through the privatization of warfare and postwar reconstruction in the so-called war on terror.[45]

Methodologically, such a historical account of terrorism as an apparatus of social defense has important implications. If terrorism is best understood as a dispositif whose main function is to respond to an urgency, it follows that we cannot give a general description of terrorism as such. Instead, we must excavate the historically specific conditions under which terrorism emerges as an apparatus of social control. To this end, we have to attend to the function of terrorism in specific contexts and its operationalization in different rhetorical, political, legal, and militaristic frameworks. That is, a more reliable and accurate understanding of terrorism is to be found not in a grand metaphysical theory but in an analysis of particular contexts in which it is deployed.

This is not to suggest that no general insights about terrorism are possible because a historical description of statements and practices merely records particular claims that have been made and particular things that have been done about terrorism. Rather, the challenge in studying terrorism as a historical formation or dispositif is to overcome the problems associated with the search for a universal theory or definition of terrorism while at the same time avoiding the relativism of an empiricist analysis of its politically, historically, socially, and culturally determined representations.

A GENEALOGY OF TERRORISM

The tradition of critical philosophy since Kant offers a rich repository of tools that can help us navigate between the Scylla of speculative theory and the Charybdis of positivist empiricism in building an empirically grounded and conceptually robust analytic framework appropriate for studying contemporary terrorism. Kant proposed a transcendental critique of a priori conditions of possibility of the cognition of objects, but the understanding and practice of critique elaborated in this book is largely Foucauldian. For Foucault, the philosophical project of critique was best described as a "historical ontology of ourselves," that is, a "historical investigation into the events that have led us to constitute ourselves and to recognize ourselves as subjects of what we are doing, thinking, saying."

> In that sense, this criticism is not transcendental, and its goal is not that of making a metaphysics possible: it is genealogical in its design and archaeological in its method. Archaeological—and not *transcendental*—in the sense that it will not seek to identify the universal structures of all knowledge or of all possible moral action, but will seek to treat the instances of discourse that articulate what we think, say, and do as so many historical events. And this critique will be genealogical in the sense that it will not deduce from the form of what we are what it is impossible for us to do and to know; but it will separate out, from the contingency that has made us what we are, the possibility of no longer being, doing, or thinking what we are, do, or think.[46]

Accordingly, the method developed here is an archaeological and genealogical investigation into the historical conditions of emergence under which terrorism appears in a range of specific contexts.[47] One of the central claims of this book is that contemporary formations of terrorism are ensembles of and have their conditions of possibility in different historical discourses, institutions, devices, methods, tactics, and technologies of terrorism and counterterrorism. That is, today's deployment of terrorism is not merely a repetition of historical precedents but their reinvention for new and changing purposes.

This book excavates the history of various conceptual and practical uses of terrorism and maps concrete conditions that make possible their revision and rearrangement in a contemporary dispositif of terrorism that includes terrorism as state violence, or *systemic terrorism*; terrorism as ideologically motivated violence, or *doxastic terrorism*; terrorism as violence associated with particular persons, or *charismatic terrorism*; terrorism as violence associated with a certain religious or political identity, or *identarian terrorism*; terrorism as the use of violence as a political strategy, or *strategic terrorism*; terrorism as an illegal act, or *criminal terrorism*; and terrorism as a new kind of war, or *polemic terrorism*. Today, these different notions of terrorism coalesce in what I call *synthetic terrorism*.[48]

This book examines these different modes of understanding terrorism, as well as the discourses, practices, tactics, strategies, and institutions they make possible, across a range of contexts with the aim of showing that the emergence and continuous rearticulation of terrorism are closely tied to historically distinct attempts to reconcile sovereign, disciplinary, and regulatory technologies of power. By articulating contextually specific and variable forms of enmity, historical formations of terrorism serve as dispositifs of social defense that justify the exercise of the sovereign right to kill for the defense and protection of the nation, the class, or humanity against internal and external enemies.[49]

Although the emergence of a specifically synthetic concept of terrorism can be traced to the rise to prominence of neoconservatism in the United States in the late 1980s, we can follow its genealogy further, to the year 1794, when terrorism emerged in the French Revolution. Thus, chapter 2 turns to the French Revolution as the moment when core components of the scaffolding onto which contemporary synthetic terrorism is grafted were first installed. I offer a fresh perspective on a well-rehearsed origin story about the emergence of terrorism and show that the French Revolution constituted a template onto which additional layers of meaning and practice were successively superimposed. Through a close examination of the discourses and practices of key revolutionary actors, such as the Jacobin Maximilien Robespierre, the Thermidorian Jean-Lambert Tallien, and the radical egalitarian journalist François-Noël Babeuf, in the period between 1794 and 1797, I challenge dominant accounts of revolutionary terrorism as the name for excessive violence used by a state and its representatives in pursuit of political goals. Instead, I show that terrorism was understood in at least four ways: (1) as the rule of a particular person, namely, Robespierre, or *charismatic terrorism*; (2) as a system of government, or *systemic terrorism*; (3) as a political philosophy, or *doxastic terrorism*; and (4) as a political identity to be cultivated, or *identarian terrorism*.

In addition to mapping the conceptual space of terrorism between 1794 and 1797, I inquire into the relations of power and political rationalities that make different modes of understanding and conceptualizing terrorism possible. This analysis reveals that terrorism emerges when a political concern with the life and health of the population requires new justifications of traditional forms of sovereign power. Robespierre's defense of sovereign terror against foreign enemies as the virtuous foundation of the Republic in times of crisis was thus replaced by a concept of terrorism that both permitted and compelled the exclusion of dangerous elements within the population.

Chapters 3 and 4 examine processes of co-optation, revision, and superimposition of French revolutionary concepts and practices of terrorism as they traveled to late imperial Russia and colonized Algeria. In chapter 3 I examine how the French revolutionary heritage of terrorism was taken up and transformed in the context of late imperial and early Bolshevik Russia. Here a new strategic notion of terrorism was superimposed on charismatic, systemic, doxastic, and identarian conceptions and added to the conceptual armature of contemporary terrorism. Drawing on a close reading of the discourses and practices of Russian social revolutionaries, Bolsheviks, and representatives of the tsarist regime, I challenge comparative accounts of French revolutionary terrorism and Bolshevik state terrorism. I show that despite some similarities, the Jacobin Reign of Terror and Bolshevik terrorism not only had vastly different histories but also arose from distinct political rationalities. Against the background of an emerging biopolitical rationality, social revolutionaries accused the tsarist regime of representing the ruling class and oppressing the peasant and working classes, who constituted the state's source of wealth. In light of the state's disregard for the well-being of the proletariat, social revolutionaries thus articulated a revolutionary justification of violence against the class enemy, which gave rise to a systematic theory of terrorism as a tactic or strategy of class war, or *strategic terrorism*. Despite the regime's attempt to appropriate the rhetoric of terrorism to assert its sovereignty by means of antiterrorist emergency legislation, terrorism remained firmly in the hands of social revolutionaries. With their rise to power in the Russian Revolutions, their discourse of terrorism was incorporated into the machinery of the Bolshevik state and transformed into state terror. But even as an institutionalized state practice, Bolshevik state terror was understood in strategic terms as a tactic of class war.

Chapter 4 follows the trajectory of terrorism from the French Revolution to Algeria in order to explore its imperial dimensions. By focusing on the complex relationship between terrorism and colonialism in the context of French colonial history in Algeria, I examine how nineteenth-century French imperialism, which served as a response to the social, political, and economic turmoil caused by the French Revolution, came to shape the conditions of possibility of the twentieth-century dispositif of terrorism during the Algerian Revolution. In contrast to descriptions of twentieth-century French counterterrorism during the famous Battle of Algiers (1956–1957) as a repetition of military strategies of colonizing Algeria in the early nineteenth century, I argue that seemingly identical military practices were understood and justified in new and different ways. To this end, I offer a reading of Alexis de Tocqueville's writings on Algeria to reconstruct a science of colonial war, which specified a set of military strategies intended to subjugate Algeria's indigenous population in the name of France's national salvation. Drawing on documents of the Algerian Revolution in French military archives, I then show that practices of twentieth-century counterterrorism did not serve to conquer foreign populations but instead functioned to secure internal order against formally French subjects who sought Algerian independence. The justification of state violence against the state's own subjects was facilitated by a new theory of revolutionary war and a concomitant concept of terrorism as a new kind of war, or *polemic terrorism*, distinct from a legal notion of *criminal terrorism*.

The new concept of polemic terrorism, as well as the practices of counterterrorism it engendered in twentieth-century French Algeria, figures as a "primer for American imperial politics" in many contemporary analyses of terrorism.[50] In fact, the U.S. Pentagon explicitly invoked French tactics of counterterrorism during the Battle of Algiers as a model for American counterinsurgency operations in the Middle East in the early twenty-first century. In chapter 5, I complicate this understanding of the relationship between French and U.S. counterterrorism to suggest that the contemporary dispositif of terrorism is not a simple replica of French discourses and practices. Rather, it is a heterogeneous set of practices, discourses, institutions, methods, devices, tactics, and strategies that have a much longer history, a significant part of which is traced in chapters 2 to 4. Chapter 5 examines how these historical discourses and practices have been given new unity by a synthetic concept of terrorism, which has its conditions of possibility in a political rationality that posits American-style liberal democracy and a free-market economy as the only viable political model. In this context, various conceptions of terrorism, such as state violence, doctrine, identity, crime, and form of war, coalesce to form a concept of terrorism that portrays any opposition to American interests as a threat to the nation and—since these interests are said to be universal demands of human dignity—to humanity. The strategies, technologies, and practices that are put into circulation in the name of defending the nation and humanity against these threats produce, at the same time as they rely on, normative ideas about citizenship and humanity that authorize killing for humanitarian ends.

This brief overview highlights that the genealogy offered in this book explores the powerful French heritage of contemporary terrorism. The focus on this specific lineage is motivated by the attempt to give an account of terrorism that is particularly relevant for understanding our historical present, that is, terrorism's current configuration in an era of American imperialism and Western political, economic, cultural, and military hegemony. Nevertheless, the selection of cases and contexts examined here may raise questions about the omission of other cases. Although the following chapters include alternative histories (chapter 3) and subaltern contexts (chapter 4), the overall narrative still gives an admittedly Western-centric, one might say French, account of terrorism. I have little to say here about the Black Jacobins in Haiti, the Revolutionary Armed Forces of Colombia, the politics of terrorism in Sri Lanka, Turkish discourses about the Kurdistan Workers' Party (PKK), and many other cases. Similarly, readers will note the absence of the history of terrorism in Israel and Palestine, Northern Ireland, or Spain, which all figure prominently in the current literature on terrorism.[51] The omission of these cases is not intended to suggest that they do not matter. On the contrary, the focus on a set of common reference points in the academic, especially the historical, literature on terrorism allows me to highlight the radical contingency of even those cases about which there is general agreement. In this way, I hope to lay the groundwork for a more nuanced appreciation of the complex interplay between power and forms of resistance, which produce and are produced by apparatuses of terrorism.

Moreover, there are important considerations of methodology, readability, and coherence that impose constraints on the contexts, cases, and time periods that can be examined. Importantly, a set of skills and resources is necessary in order to carefully and rigorously execute the kind of empirical work required for the genealogical analysis developed in this book. Some of these resources, like accessible archives, pertain to particular sites of inquiry, while others, such as historical knowledge, sufficient command of the language of an archive, and time, are specific to the individual researcher. Consequently, this book has its archive—understood both as a collection of records, documents, and artifacts that are the stuff of historiography and as a technical Foucauldian term designating a domain of statements characterized by specific discursive regularities—in the French revolutionary lineage of terrorism.[52] I examine a heterogeneous set of published and unpublished political speeches, pamphlets, theoretical treatises, policy documents, maps, news sources, and other documents produced by representatives of the state, political theorists and activists, revolutionaries, and resistance fighters. Many of these sources are familiar points of reference; others are barely legible shreds of evidence of lives and events tucked away in library basements. The primary languages of this archive are French and English. This is true even for the writings of Russian revolutionaries, who often published their works in French or English before translating them into Russian, as well as for members of the Algerian resistance movement, who used the language of the colonizer to avoid the suspicion and scrutiny with which Arabic and other native languages were met.[53]

Finally, I have attempted to give as much autonomy as possible to the archives. Following Arlette Farge's insight that extracting meaning from an archive requires that archival work take place within the "conditions of appearance" of statements, I have paid attention to the contexts in which words appear in order to reconstruct patterns and regularities of their use.[54] For Farge, statements are never just expressions of individual experiences, beliefs, or intentions but rather point us to collective imaginaries, shared modes of understanding, discursive formations, and relations of power that make them possible. Thus, she insists, instead of simply reading archival statements and providing positivist commentary on them, we must "look deeper, beyond their immediate meaning, and interpret them further, at the heart of the circumstances that permitted and produced them."[55] My guiding interest in approaching source material, then, was not to establish the truth of a statement or the truthfulness of its expression but to understand how it came to be articulated—in short, to excavate the conditions of its possibility. The various concepts of terrorism I identify in this book should, accordingly, be understood as descriptive categories, not ideal types, intended to flag, explicate, and track different

rules of use implicit in the archive. They are not abstractions from political struggles over the meaning and use of the term but indicate distinct
and distinguishable ways in which the word *terrorism* is used in such
struggles. In other words, they describe the many different things *terrorism* means depending on the concrete context in which it is used. Because
I have let the archives themselves guide the work of historical and conceptual analysis, the methodological emphasis is more archaeological in
some chapters, focusing on discursive conditions of appearance, while
others are more genealogical in their attention to the methods, devices,
and relations of power that permit and require different concepts and
practices of terrorism.

All these considerations give rise to the specific account of terrorism
presented in this book. I do not and cannot offer an exhaustive history
of terrorism, nor do I want to suggest that the genealogy of terrorism
sketched here is the only one to be written. My aim is both more modest
and more ambitious in that I seek to develop an empirically informed
critical history of terrorism that yields a robust conceptual armature useful for contemporary analysis. By means of an examination of four paradigmatic dispositifs of terrorism in their concrete historical contexts of
emergence, I map the conceptual space of terrorism and identify its general political function. On one level, then, the account developed here is
incomplete, not only because it can be supplemented with other cases and
different contexts but also because the empirical material under consideration can always be taken up according to different periodizations, examined on different registers of discourse and practice, and passed through
alternative normative frameworks. In addition, genealogies are, in a sense,
multiple. That is, a genealogy of terrorism connects in important ways
with other genealogies, for instance, of political legitimacy, government,
reason of state, liberalism, and deviance.[56] On another level, however, the
genealogy I present in this book is complete insofar as it performatively
constructs an analytic model appropriate for studying the historical formation or dispositif of terrorism.[57] A defense of the validity and relevance of this model, as well as an explication of the normative strategies
it yields, is the task of chapter 6 of this book. Suffice it to say at this point
that my aim and hope are that the kind of engaged critique offered here
may loosen the grip of habitual frameworks of thought and help articulate
strategies for political transformation.

2

THE EMERGENCE OF TERRORISM

The concept of terrorism did not exist before 1794, when it was introduced by the Thermidorian Jean-Lambert Tallien in a speech at the National Convention to denounce Robespierre's infamous Reign of Terror. Although Tallien's coconspirator Bertrand Barère first characterized Robespierre's reign as a "system of terror" the day after Robespierre's execution,[1] it was Tallien who conceived of the Terror as a system of power—a system he called *terrorism*. But although Tallien coined the term as a political concept, there is some evidence that the word *terrorism* was used even earlier by Immanuel Kant in *The Contest of Faculties*. In this text, Kant called "moral terrorism" a view of history that saw humanity as continual regression and deterioration. Kant rejected this "terroristic conception of human history," for it could not go on infinitely.[2] To be sure, *The Contest of Faculties* was first published in its entirety in 1798, and thus after Tallien's description of Robespierre's system as terrorism. However, Kant had tried unsuccessfully to publish the three parts separately in 1794 and 1797 and referred to the work in a 1793 letter to Johann Gottfried Kiesewetter.[3] Thus, his may actually be the earliest confirmed use of the term *terrorism*.

Be that as it may, a specifically political concept of terrorism emerged in the French Revolution in the context of contestations among different factions of a popular movement, as well as various political clubs, over the source and form of legitimate political authority.[4] Amid fierce debates among defenders of the monarchy, populist republicans who called for a government that represented the will of the people, and more liberal supporters of a republican system in which government authority was limited by individual rights defined and protected by general laws, the absolute monarchy of the ancien régime was first transformed into a constitutional monarchy in 1791 and, in 1792, replaced by a republican government under moderate Girondin leadership. A parliamentary coup in 1793 allowed the populist Montagnards, the most radical Jacobin faction under the leadership of Robespierre, to seize power, install a revolutionary dictatorship, and establish a system of terror against alleged enemies of the Revolution.[5] A conspiracy against Robespierre, as well as his deposition and subsequent execution in the Thermidorian Reaction in 1794, led most notably by Robespierre's former ally Jean-Lambert Tallien, paved the way for the introduction of the term *terrorism* into the political vocabulary of the Revolution.

When it was first used in 1794, the term *terrorism* functioned like descriptions such as "Hitler's Germany," "Stalin's Russia," or "the Bush administration" as the name for the rule of a specific person, namely, Robespierre. I call this *charismatic terrorism*. Within the subsequent four years, the term *terrorism* was first decoupled from the person Robespierre and attributed to any system of government that relied on terror as a means of exercising power. In addition to describing Robespierre's regime, terrorism now also functioned like *monarchy, democracy*, or *tyranny* as the name for a system of government, or *systemic terrorism*. Second, the *terrorism* label began to be understood in a different sense, namely, as a political philosophy. As *doxastic terrorism*, the concept operated much like *liberalism* or *republicanism* in that it described a philosophical doctrine that specified principles of political organization and justified certain political practices and beliefs.[6] Third, because the term *terrorism* picked out those who endorsed certain principles, it was possible to call individuals terrorists. Further, there were some who argued that since these principles were republican principles, being a terrorist was actually a good thing. Arguing that the government's use of the word implied that *terrorism* meant patriotism and allegiance to the Revolution, some political commentators attempted to appropriate the term in a self-referential and affirmative way. Terrorism here functioned as a political identity, analogous to being a Republican or a Democrat in the context of U.S. politics. As *identarian terrorism*, terrorism constituted a social identity that could be assumed and cultivated by way of an active commitment to certain beliefs, values, and principles.

The French Revolution thus occupies a central place in a genealogy of terrorism. Indeed, many scholars identify the French Revolution as the birthplace of terrorism. On the one hand, there are those, primarily intellectual historians, who regard the Revolution as an important moment in the history of terror, the moment at which terrorism is articulated as a new idea in distinction from the older notion of terror. Consider as an example Gerd van den Heuvel's claim that the modern concept of terrorism has its origins in the French Revolution.[7] Similarly, Mikkel Thorup argues that the French Revolution introduced a break between an older concept of terror as "the barbaric or deterrent use of state violence, the psychological dispositions of individuals, religious and social fear, etc.," and a new concept of terrorism as "non-state violence aimed at the state or the citizens which the state is obliged to protect." On this view, the French Revolution constitutes a point of rupture between a concept of "terror as state practice" and a concept of "terror as terrorism."[8] On the other hand, scholars concerned with concrete practices rather than conceptual uses of terrorism attribute its origin to Robespierre's Reign of Terror. Citing Robespierre's defense of terror as "prompt, severe, inflexible justice,"[9] they either argue that Robespierre embraced terrorism as an instrument to enforce the general will or observe that Robespierre's Terror was the referent of the neologism *terrorism*, which was introduced by his opponents as a term of moral opprobrium.[10] On both conceptual and phenomenal accounts, *terrorism* emerged in the French Revolution as the name for a particular form of violence. Specifically, it designated the excessive and arbitrary use of force for political goals, exercised by a state and its representatives.

In this chapter, I offer a fresh perspective on this origin story in pursuit of two goals: to identify and examine a range of conceptual uses of *terrorism* elaborated in the French Revolution, and to embed this explosion of discourse within an account of the emergence of a biopolitical rationality. My aim is to show that the proliferation of discourses and practices of terrorism in the short period under consideration set the stage for a continuous reworking of the French revolutionary heritage of terrorism that would eventually lead to our own historical present. To this end, I first pursue an archaeological approach and analyze discourses of terror and terrorism in order to identify various conceptual uses of the term *terrorism* during the French Revolution. Although it is true that *terrorism* entered the political vocabulary as the name for a system of government, and thus state violence, an archaeology of terrorism in the French Revolution forces us to expand the conceptual space in which the term is understood. Taking the Thermidorian Jean-Lambert Tallien and the radical egalitarian and journalist Gracchus Babeuf as my guides, I distinguish at least four different concepts of terrorism that were put into circulation during the period between 1794 and 1797: charismatic terrorism, systemic terrorism, doxastic terrorism, and identarian terrorism.

Second, I offer a genealogical account of terrorism in order to show that terrorism emerged in the French Revolution as a mechanism of biopolitical social defense. I contend that terrorism came into being precisely at the point at which a sovereign political rationality, which I identify in the populist republicanism of Robespierre, ran up against a new political rationality, paradigmatically articulated in Tallien's defense of a system of general laws that limited the government's power, which was concerned with the protection of the nation from internal threats. Robespierre's sovereign defense of terror as the just and virtuous foundation of the Republic in revolution was replaced by a concept of terrorism, introduced by Tallien and soon taken up and transformed by others, that referred to dangerous elements within the population and allowed for their exclusion. It was in the transition from a political rationality steeped in the theory of sovereignty to a new rationality of biopower that terrorism came into being as a dispositif of social defense that reconciled the old sovereign right to kill and new techniques of disciplinary and regulatory power under the pretext of defending the nation from its deviant and terrorist elements.

ACTS OF VIOLENCE, PRACTICES OF TERRORISM

Before I turn to an examination of the conceptual and practical emergence of terrorism against the background of changing political rationalities in the French Revolution, I briefly consider a possible objection to the central role of rationalities in my analysis. It might be argued that what really is important to account for the conditions of possibility of what became known as terrorism is the history of violent actions, such as guillotinings, drownings, or beheadings. It is certainly possible to study the history of these techniques, which goes back to the Middle Ages and perhaps even further. Consider, for instance, Edgar Quinet's monumental work *La Révolution*, a critical history of the French Revolution first published in 1865. The work contains a chapter titled "The Historical Precedents: How the Old France Has Provided Models for the Terror" ("Les précédents historiques. En quoi l'ancienne France a fourni des modèles à la terreur"), in which Quinet showed that the Terror of 1793 found its model in the "declarations and ordinances of Louvois in the Revocation."[11] The Marquis de Louvois was French secretary of state for war during the revocation of the Edict of Nantes, which had granted the Huguenots freedom of religion. In 1685 the edict was revoked because, as Louvois explained, "his Majesty [Louis XIV] wishes the worst harshness on those who do not partake of his religion."[12] Quinet cited the subsequent drownings of Huguenots in the Loire, proposals to throw them into the sea, and threats that entire populations would be put to the sword as models for the Terror. Although he insisted that the Terror of 1793 was not the Terror of 1687—there was not the same patience in the henchmen, torture did not last as long, and executions were not drawn out for entire days for spectators to enjoy—torture did not disappear at the end of the eighteenth century. A century after the persecution of the Huguenots, the gallows still "marked the days."[13] Quinet wrote,

> Thus, the Terror was the fatal legacy of the history of France. The weapons of the past were gathered to defend the present. The iron cages and [Provost of the Marshals] Tristan l'Hermite of Louis XI, the scaffolds of Richelieu, the mass proscriptions of Louis XIV, those are the arsenal from which the Revolution drew. Through the Terror, and unbeknownst to them, new men all of a sudden became old men again.[14]

Quinet's diagnosis of a genealogical relation between the Terror and older practices of torture derived from the Inquisition was supported by Pierre Victorien Vergniaud, one of Danton's associates, who feared "the establishment of an inquisition a thousand times more formidable than that of Venice."[15] Similarly, the journalist and radical egalitarian François-Noël Babeuf, whose writings I will consider in detail later in this chapter, argued that the terror was merely a reversal of the violence of "the wheel, the stake, and the gallow" that had been inflicted on the people and was now used against the people's enemies.[16] In addition, Quinet maintained that the measures deployed during the Terror were reminiscent of the torture of Robert-François Damiens, who, like Robespierre, had been born in Arras and had attempted to kill Louis XV in 1757.[17] The historian Jules Michelet, too, was reminded of "Damiens, quartered, tortured, and sprayed with molten lead" by the "barbaric procedures and even more barbaric judgments" of popular vengeance.[18]

These references show that it is certainly possible to study forms of public torture and determine at what point they were mobilized for the purpose of accomplishing the Revolution. But there is a more general and more intricate history of behaviors, methods, tactics, and devices that draws our attention not only to the techniques but also to their contextually specific function. As Foucault suggested in his discussion of penalties like fines or capital punishment in *The Punitive Society*, that we can find these particular "operations, tactics, strategies" across a range of societies often works to conceal that such "apparently constant penalties do not at all perform the same role, do not in fact correspond to the same economy of power in different systems." The fine, for example, "does not exist as a penalty in the same way in different systems" but rather constitutes "a procedure whose tactical role is entirely different according to the punitive regimes within which it figures." Similarly, Foucault noted that "even if it seems that, in the end, there have not been many ways of dying," the tactical function of the death penalty in different systems of punishment varies such that "there are, precisely, many ways of dying."[19] Consequently, we can and should distinguish between ostensibly similar acts of violence that serve rather different purposes depending on the context in which they are deployed. As Arnold Davidson points out, such distinctions are important for analytic and historiographical reasons even though different forms of understanding are often indistinguishable in the archives.[20] Consider that although the guillotine was by no means a new form of punishment, there was nevertheless a different understanding of public executions and their purpose once they were integrated into the Reign of Terror.[21] That is, the political rationality motivating the Jacobin Terror also framed how older techniques of punishment and state violence were endowed with new meaning and stabilized as new practices of terror.[22] Attention to these techniques and to the ways in which they were understood and justified thus enables us to bring into view varying relations of power that were put into play by seemingly constant tactics, strategies, methods, devices, and behaviors.

Note, however, that not every new mode of understanding also constitutes a new political rationality. Following Arnold Davidson's distinction between modes or forms of explanation and styles of reasoning,[23] I distinguish modes of understanding, sense making, or justification from political rationalities. For Davidson, these two categories belong to two different analytic levels, namely, those of conditions of validity and conditions of possibility, or what Foucault described as *connaissance* and *savoir*, respectively. While conditions of validity help determine whether a particular statement is true or false within a particular body of knowledge (*connaissance*), conditions of possibility refer to a more fundamental level at which the existence of statements as candidates of truth or falsehood is regulated (*savoir*).[24] Putting it differently, we might say that an utterance has to be intelligible as a statement before it can be judged as a statement that is true or false. Whereas Davidson's inquiries are guided by an archaeological concern with the formation of conceptual spaces by different styles of reasoning, I am more broadly interested in both the conceptual and political configuration of the space in which something like terrorism becomes possible and intelligible as a phenomenon of cultural history, on the one hand, and an object of discourse about which we can utter true and false statements, on the other. My use of the syntagmata "mode of understanding, sense making, or justification" and "political rationalities" throughout this book is intended to flag this twofold interest.

With regard to the present chapter, then, a focus on both modes of understanding and political rationalities reveals that in the years between 1794 and 1797, terrorism acquired meaning within four main modes of understanding, as *charismatic terrorism*, *systemic terrorism*, *doxastic terrorism*, and *identarian terrorism*. The contestations over these meanings—that it was possible, for example, to deny that terrorism was the government of Robespierre or that terrorists were honest patriots—indicate that despite their differences, various concepts of terrorism were part of the same grid of intelligibility. That is, these four modes of understanding terrorism were part of a larger political rationality that issued from a new economy of power bent on the investment of life. The emergence of terrorism had its conditions of possibility in a biopolitical rationality that relied on mechanisms of social defense for the protection, optimization, and management of life.

A GRID OF INTELLIGIBILITY FOR TERRORISM

The emergence of terrorism as a mechanism of social defense was made possible by the formation of a new biopolitical rationality that concerned itself with the elimination of abnormalities and irregularities within society in order to guarantee its regular and natural functioning. Foucault argued that this biopolitical rationality emerged out of a crisis of the classical model of sovereignty in the sixteenth century. In the theory of sovereignty, political government formed part of a theological-cosmological continuum that provided both authorization and standard for the exercise of sovereignty. On this view, political sovereigns were good sovereigns if they imitated God's rule over creation and ensured the common good in the way shepherds cared for their flock or fathers for their families. With the foundation of the classical episteme between 1580 and 1650, however, this continuum was broken.[25] New scientific practices revealed completely regular, immutable, universal laws of nature and resulted in a loss of the traditional view of an all-powerful, interventionist God as the model of sovereign power.[26] Because the continuum among God, nature, and politics was severed, a new space had to be carved out for politics, which was left without a model and had to articulate a new rationality for governing human beings.

Foucault argued that this new rationality entered into the reflected thought and practice of the *politiques*, a group of political thinkers, at the beginning of the seventeenth century under the banner of *raison d'État* (reason of state).[27] In *Security, Territory, Population*, Foucault offered an intricate account of the historical emergence of this rationality, which took shape in a military-diplomatic apparatus and the police and had as one of its major effects the state in the modern sense of the term.[28] To briefly summarize his main observations, Foucault maintained that the chief concern of *raison d'État* is the preservation of the state, and that *raison d'État* is absolutely immanent in the state in four ways. First, *raison d'État* does not refer to anything other than the state itself; it specifies what is necessary and sufficient for the preservation of the state on the basis of knowledge of the state. Second, *raison d'État* is both the essence or vital force of the state and the knowledge necessary for its preservation. Third, *raison d'État* is conservative in the sense that it seeks to preserve the state (*l'État*) in its condition (*en état*). Fourth, the purpose of *raison d'État* is the state itself. Because *raison d'État* makes the question of government absolutely immanent in the state, it cancels out problems of origin, foundation, legitimacy, or teleology. It presupposes that we are within a state, whose preservation must be ensured by whatever means necessary, including the suspension of the law.

Foucault argued that the theorists of *raison d'État* regarded laws as an instrument of which the government should avail itself as long as they were useful for the preservation of the state. *Raison d'État* usually yields to the law, not because of some moral, natural, or divine force inherent in the law, but simply because it recognizes that laws are useful for its own game. This is to say that obedience to the law is no longer an end in itself, but that the law has purely instrumental value as a tactic employed to serve the purpose of preserving the state. As a consequence, the law must be suspended when necessity demands it. In times of crisis, the salvation of the state makes it necessary to "brush aside the civil, moral, and natural laws that it had previously wanted to recognize and had incorporated into its game."[29] The *politiques* called this suspension of law in times of necessity *coup d'État*.[30] The *coup d'État*, Foucault noted, is "the self-manifestation of the state itself" and the purest manifestation of *raison d'État* that "asserts that the state must be saved, whatever forms may be employed to enable one to save it."[31]

Foucault further suggested that the functioning of *raison d'État* was guaranteed on the political level by the police, which implemented a set of disciplinary mechanisms intended to increase the state's forces, and by a military-diplomatic apparatus. In the seventeenth century, the term *police* referred to a set of mechanisms that ensured the state's splendor, such as the education of children, the regulation of professional choices, public health, the regulation of agriculture and the circulation of goods, and infrastructure. The aim of the police was "that living, better than just living, coexisting will be effectively useful to the constitution and development of the state's forces."[32] To this end, it had to deploy mechanisms of disciplinary regulation, whose localized manifestations in prisons, schools, hospitals, and other institutions had to be understood within a wider context of a "general disciplinarization, a general regulation of individuals and the territory of the realm in the form of a police."[33] Whereas the police was concerned with the internal order of states, the relationships between states were maintained by military-diplomatic techniques that sought to ensure peace through a balance of independent states.[34] These two technologies of the police and a military-diplomatic apparatus gave rise, on the economic level, to a mercantilist system, whose aim was to "ensure maximum economic development through commerce within a rigid system of sovereignty."[35]

Foucault argued that in the eighteenth century, the rationality of *raison d'État* was modified in important respects and gave rise to a new rationality, namely, *raison économique*, which he identified as the beginning of Western liberalism because *raison économique* sought to maximize the state's prosperity by telling the government to leave alone (*laisser faire*) the natural processes inherent in society and the economy. While *raison d'État* had privileged the sovereign will over the regularity of laws by subordinating law to the preservation of the state, *raison économique* made the sovereign subservient to the laws immanent in society, the population, and the economy. Society emerged as a domain with its own natural processes that government must take into consideration. The subject of this society was not a multiplicity of individuals but the population, that is, "a reality that has a natural density and thickness that is different from the set of subjects who were subject to the sovereign and the intervention of the police."[36] Individuals must no longer be subject to minute disciplinary regulation, but insofar as they formed a population with its own natural processes, such as mortality and fertility, they must be managed through biopolitical technologies. To this end, government must have knowledge of a sphere that was external to the art of government. Governing was no longer a problem immanent in the state itself, but an art that depended on knowledge of a different domain that was society. This knowledge was political economy. Finally, the separation of society and government entailed a fragmentation of the old mechanism of the police, from which the economy was carved out as a space that must not be regulated and that, in fact, told government what to do and gave it its rationality. The function of the police was henceforth limited to the repression of all forms of disorder, delinquency, and illegality that threatened the freedom required for a maximization of the state's forces. Instead of the unlimited and continuous intervention of the police state within a framework of *raison d'État*, government now found its limits within its own nature and purpose—namely, in the specific nature of the "objects of governmental action," which it had to respect on pain of jeopardizing the enrichment and well-being of the state.[37]

I offer this rather detailed reconstruction of Foucault's historical account of the transformation from a sovereign rationality of *raison d'État* to an emerging biopolitical rationality of *raison économique*, or "liberal reason,"[38] because it yields critical insights about the background rationalities that facilitated the emergence and stabilization of practices of terror and terrorism in the French Revolution.[39] To be sure, Foucault maintained that *raison économique* was firmly established by the middle of the eighteenth century and thus well before the outbreak of the French Revolution and the establishment of the Reign of Terror. But Foucault is not usually known for equating the emergence of new phenomena with the disappearance of old ones. In fact, his genealogical method serves the purpose of demonstrating that new practices rely for support on older practices out of which they develop. Resisting notions of replacement and obliteration, Foucault emphasized interpenetration and superimposition. At various points in his work, for example, he insisted that the two great technologies of power in modernity, sovereignty and biopower, did not replace but were "superimposed" on each other.[40] Similarly, he argued that *raison d'État* was not completely effaced, suppressed, or obliterated by *raison économique* but persisted and continued to exercise significant influence on political thought and practice in the final decade of the eighteenth century. Robespierre's defense of terror as a form of government appropriate for times of crisis demonstrates this with exceptional clarity.

SOVEREIGN TERROR

The contours of Robespierre's political rationality, which motivated a form of government that would come to be identified as terrorism, come into view in his position on the problem of scarcity.[41] To combat rampant food shortages in France, the monarchy had issued edicts in 1753 and 1764 that established complete freedom of grain. Maintaining that scarcity was a result of overregulation and lack of freedom of circulation, the king's advisers hoped that the problem would go away if nature were left to take its course. Driven by supply and demand, farmers could sell at a price that would allow them to save enough grain to sow to avoid shortages. A good harvest would then decrease the price for grain, further minimizing the risk of scarcity. Although some people might still die of starvation under such conditions, these deaths were acceptable in light of the elimination of scarcity as a social problem. These claims are indicative of the strong presence of a biopolitical rationality well before the beginning of the Revolution. Nevertheless, sovereign models of government exerted influence late into the eighteenth century and motivated Robespierre's adoption of terror as a principle of government. As "prompt, severe, inflexible justice" and as a means for founding the republic in times of revolution, terror was the only means of establishing a legitimate form of government that would rid France of the causes of scarcity.[42]

Robespierre argued that scarcity was a problem that required government intervention and regulation. Although he accepted the principle of free trade with regard to "foodstuffs that are in no way essential to life," he rejected free trade with regard to basic goods necessary for the survival of the people. Nonessential goods, he argued, "can be left to untrammelled speculation by the merchant" because "any momentary scarcity that might be felt is always a bearable inconvenience." Shortage of grain, however, was not merely an inconvenience but a serious threat to people's lives. So although it was "acceptable in general that the unlimited freedom of such a market should turn to the greater profit of the state and some individuals," he held that "no man has the right to amass piles of wheat, when his neighbour is dying of hunger." For Robespierre, in other words, free trade in nonessential goods was acceptable not because natural fluctuations of production and trade would eliminate scarcity, but because scarcity was tolerable with regard to goods that were not essential for survival and whose unavailability was merely inconvenient. "The lives of men," however, "cannot be subjected to the same uncertainty."[43]

Moreover, Robespierre rejected the idea that there was anything natural about scarcity. For him, scarcity was an entirely artificial problem in a rich and fertile country like France. Rather than resulting from natural circumstances, he argued, scarcity "can only be imputed to defects of administration or of the laws themselves; bad laws and bad administration have their origins in false principles and bad morals."[44] What was worse for Robespierre was that free trade had not, in fact, brought about freedom of the people. Instead, it had led to a condition where "everything is against society" and "everything favours the grain merchants."[45] Since the majority of the people were starving, it did not make sense to speak of freedom of the people in any meaningful way. What was necessary to achieve freedom and prosperity for the people was, therefore, not less government but better government and more effective regulation:

> Let the circulation of goods be protected throughout the whole Republic, but let the necessary measures be taken to ensure that circulation takes place. It is precisely the lack of circulation that I am complaining about. For the scourge of the people, the source of scarcity, is the obstacles placed in the way of circulation, under the pretext of rendering it unlimited.[46]

Because the principles of free trade actually inhibited circulation, Robespierre thought that government had an active and important role to play in economic matters. Against the lack of transparency and freedom of the free market, he demanded a detailed record of production, harvests, and supplies of grain, as well as laws against monopolies.[47] In short, Robespierre envisaged a governmental rationality that was entirely different from that of the ruling Girondins, who, in the words of historian Jonathan Israel, "preferred not to infringe upon the basic principle of economic freedom by imposing sweeping price controls, or taking the draconian measures against hoarders and speculators urged by [the Montagnards]."[48] Because government was guided by a dangerous rationality that jeopardized the people's freedom, Robespierre argued that a new legitimate form of political authority had to be established.

The question of legitimate government had plagued the revolutionaries for some time. The different positions can be illuminated by examining their uptake of the political thought of Jean-Jacques Rousseau, which constituted an influential point of reference in these debates.[49] On the one hand, the Girondins drew on Rousseau's theory of popular sovereignty to argue for a universalist notion of the general will, anchored in reason rather than virtue, as the basis of human rights. Put differently, they claimed that universal reason constituted the source and basis of political sovereignty.[50] On the other hand, the Montagnards proposed a populist rather than rationalist reading of Rousseau, firmly rooted in a belief in the virtue of the common people. In particular, Robespierre invoked Rousseau's notion of the general will, understood in terms of the necessarily just judgment of the common people.[51]

Robespierre's position on the fate of the king clearly articulates this view. Although democratic republicans argued that the king had to be subjected to juridical process, and any measures taken had to be approved by popular referendum, Robespierre, who had famously declared his opposition to the death penalty,[52] rejected a referendum and insisted that Louis ought to be executed without trial. Why?

In his famous speech "On the Trial of the King," Robespierre argued that the demand to put the king on trial was incoherent; a trial was obsolete because a judgment had already been made. The fact that the Republic existed, he argued, meant that the king had already been tried and found guilty by the people. The very foundation of the Republic through popular insurrection was a manifestation of popular judgment of the crimes the king had committed against the nation. Putting Louis on trial, however, amounted to nothing less than a presumption of his innocence. But if the possibility of Louis's innocence was granted, the legitimacy of the Republic was denied. In Robespierre's words, "Louis was king, and the Republic is founded: the famous question you are considering is settled by those words alone. . . . Louis cannot be judged; either he is already condemned or the Republic is not acquitted."[53]

Robespierre's theoretical justification for this claim was articulated in contractarian terms. He argued that because the king had not consented to the social contract that founded the Republic, he was in a state of nature with regard to the social body. From this followed two important conclusions: first, the laws that applied to the body politic, including legal procedures such as criminal trials, did not apply to the king. "Courts and legal proceedings," Robespierre claimed, "are only for members of the same side."[54] Second, Louis was not only not a citizen but also a traitor and conspirator who was in a natural state of war with the social body. As such, he was an enemy against whom society had to be defended by any means necessary. As a consequence, Robespierre declared, "there is no trial to be held here."

> Louis is not a defendant. You are not judges. You are not, you cannot be anything but statesmen and representatives of the nation. You have no sentence to pronounce for or against a man, but a measure of public salvation to implement, an act of national providence to perform.[55]

Because the salvation of the Republic required the elimination of all "enemies of the homeland," Robespierre insisted that "Louis must die, because the homeland has to live." His execution was not only justified but "necessary for the security of individuals or the social body."[56]

Robespierre's rejection of a trial for the king was thus framed in terms of the classical theory of sovereignty in its contractarian form. Arguably, Robespierre was inspired by Rousseau's doctrine of popular sovereignty. In *On the Social Contract*, Rousseau had argued that the social contract unites a multitude of individuals in a perfect union, thereby giving rise to a social body whose individual members cannot be harmed without attacking the entire body. Attacks on the social body, however, are not a matter of civil relations between private individuals but relations of war between the state and its enemies.

> Every malefactor who attacks the social right becomes through his transgressions a rebel and a traitor to the homeland; in violating its laws, he ceases to be a member, and he even wages war with it. In that case the preservation of the state is incompatible with his own. Thus one of the two must perish; and when the guilty party is put to death, it is less as a citizen than as an enemy. The legal proceeding and the judgment are the proofs and the declaration that he has broken the social treaty, and consequently that he is no longer a member of the state. For since he has acknowledged himself to be such, at least by his living there, he ought to be removed from it by exile as a violator of the compact, or by death as a public enemy. For such an enemy is not a moral person, but a man, and in this situation the right of war is to kill the vanquished.[57]

For Rousseau, in other words, the appropriate course of action against enemies was not civil law but exile or death, which was a demand of the salvation of the state.

Robespierre endorsed the same form of reasoning when he defended the characteristic right of sovereignty to take life whenever the existence of the social body was in danger. In such situations, those who presented a threat must be prosecuted as enemies of the state by means of war. Since the king was not a member of society but a threat to the social body, he could not legitimately be put on trial but rather had to be prosecuted as a public enemy.[58] Moreover, Robespierre argued that the category of enmity applied not only to the king but also to his supporters.

> There are no citizens but republicans in this Republic. Royalists and con-spirators are foreign to it, or rather they are enemies. Is not the terrible war waged by liberty on tyranny indivisible? Are not the enemies within allies of the enemies without? Assassins who ravage the homeland from the inside; intriguers who buy the consciences of people's representa-tives, and the traitors who sell them; mercenary scribblers bribed to dis-honor the people's cause, to kill public virtue, to stoke the flames of civil dissension, to clear the way for political counter-revolution with moral counter-revolution; are all these people less culpable or less dangerous than the tyrants they serve?[59]

By portraying all supporters of the king as enemies of the people, Robes-pierre set the stage for an institutionalization of violence as a requirement of national salvation. "Revolutionary government," he argued, "owes good citizens full national protection; to enemies of the people it owes nothing but death."[60] Put differently, revolutionary government had to wage war against enemies of the body politic, and this war took the form of systematic and institutionalized terror. Consider Robespierre's infa-mous justification of terror as virtue in his speech of February 5, 1794, as a forceful statement of this view:

> If the mainspring of popular government in peacetime is virtue, the mainspring of popular government in revolution is virtue and terror both: virtue, without which terror is disastrous; terror, without which virtue is powerless. Terror is nothing but prompt, severe, inflexible

justice; it is therefore an emanation of virtue; it is not so much a specific principle as a consequence of the general principle of democracy applied to the homeland's most pressing needs.[61]

Emphasizing the exceptional context in which the Republic had to be founded, Robespierre regarded the use of violence against its opponents as necessary, just, and virtuous. Arguing that "it has been said that terror was the mainspring of despotic government," Robespierre invoked Montesquieu in order to then subvert his categories.[62] In *The Spirit of the Laws* (1748), Montesquieu had identified virtue as the principle of republican government, whose nature is popular sovereignty, whereas terror is the principle of despotism, whose nature is the caprice of a single individual.[63] By rearticulating virtue as terror in times of emergency, Robespierre effectively collapsed Montesquieu's distinction between despotism and republican government, suggesting that "the revolution's government is the despotism of liberty over tyranny."[64] Robespierre then introduced a distinction between good terror, whose purpose it was to rid the Republic of its enemies, and bad terror, which was used by tyrants like Louis to maintain their power.[65] For Robespierre, revolutionary terror appeared as the only possibility to institutionalize virtue in the form of legitimate law that would guarantee true freedom for the people. It was "supported by the holiest of all laws: the salvation of the people; by the most indisputable of all entitlements: necessity."[66] Constitutional government could be established only once the Republic was founded, since its goal was not the foundation but the preservation of the Republic.

Robespierre's speeches are a remarkable expression of a political rationality moored in the traditional model of sovereignty. Three main themes appear in these texts that support this claim. First, the salvation of the Republic takes priority over legality. Second, the salvation of the state depends on violence. And third, the salvation of the Republic is not yet a matter of its preservation but its foundation.[67]

These themes echo the sovereign rationality discussed earlier, particularly as it was expressed in *raison d'État*, as well as the form the latter took in times of crisis, namely, *coup d'État*. Robespierre's defense of the Republic's foundation in revolutionary terror relied on the radical separation of legality and legitimacy, a view of violence as necessary, and a theatrical staging of terror. For Robespierre, the law was purely instrumental for the purpose of the preservation of the state. "The law," he argued, "can only forbid what is damaging to society: it can only order what is useful to it."[68] Because of his distinction between legality and legitimacy, Robespierre also insisted on the incommensurability of law and justice, and he disputed the notion that freedom was a sphere of nonintervention demarcated and protected by law. Instead, he proposed an understanding of freedom as "the power that man has to exercise all his faculties at will. Justice is its rule, the rights of others are its borders, nature is its principle, and law its safeguard."[69] In addition, Robespierre articulated his defense of revolutionary terror against the background of an understanding of politics in terms of war. The salvation of the people required an act of war against its main enemy, the king, who constituted a threat to the social body. Once the Republic was established, this war was preserved in form of revolutionary terror against enemies of the Republic. By virtue of their opposition to the Republic, these enemies were cast as noncitizens and nonmembers of the nation and thus external threats that had to be eliminated in the name of public safety.

In sum, Robespierre's justification of terror derived intelligibility and meaning from a political rationality characterized by the traditional model of sovereignty. Against his defense of sovereign terror against enemies external to the social body, the Thermidorians mounted a condemnation of terrorism that ushered in measures of social defense aimed to protect the nation from dangerous elements within.

CHARISMATIC TERRORISM

On August 28, 1794, exactly a month after Robespierre's execution, the leading Thermidorian Jean-Lambert Tallien coined the term *terrorism* to denounce Robespierre's Reign of Terror. Tallien had been a former leader of the Terror in Bordeaux, but his moderation—only 104 counterrevolutionaries had been guillotined under his watch—put him at risk of having to face the blade. To avoid this fate, Tallien conspired with other moderate Montagnards. On 9 Thermidor (July 27, 1794), Robespierre and other members of the Committee of Public Safety were arrested, sentenced to death, and executed the following day.[70] A month later, Tallien delivered a speech at the National Convention in which he offered his reflections on appropriate principles of revolutionary government. He did so by distinguishing revolutionary government from Robespierre's system of terror, which he named *terrorism*. I call Tallien's notion of terrorism as the name for the rule of a specific person *charismatic terrorism*.

Tallien objected to terror on both moral and pragmatic grounds. To begin with, he argued that terror produced a generalized state of fear that compromised human nature. Terror, he claimed, "is a habitual, general shiver, an external shiver that affects the most hidden fibers, that degrades man and makes him resemble a beast; it is the shock of all physical forces, the commotion of all moral faculties, the disorder of all ideas, the inversion of all affections; it is a real disruption of the soul, which, by only giving it the capacity to suffer, deprives it both of the gentleness of hope and the resources of despair in its own misery." Tallien further observed that the dehumanizing force of terror had important implications for political practice. Because it was "an extreme affection," he diagnosed, "terror is not susceptible to either more or less."[71] Rather, a government that relied on terror to control its subjects must permanently increase threats and actual violence. As Tallien noted, "Nothing has been achieved cutting off twenty heads yesterday if today one does not cut of thirty, if tomorrow one does not cut off sixty." The continuous escalation of violence was necessary to maintain domination in light of "resentments that flare up in the minds every day."[72] Finally, Tallien argued that terror was necessarily totalizing in scope and temporality. It had to target all citizens because "if the government of terror pursues some citizens over presumed intentions, it alarms them all; and if it restricts itself to monitoring and punishing actions, it is no longer terror that it inspires" but "the healthy fear of retributions that follow crime."[73] It also had to be permanent because of terror's inability to generate freedom and instill in people a sense of liberty.

All the reasons that explained terror's tight grip, however, also led to its fragility as a political system. Tallien diagnosed a "profound aversion against cruel and unjust beings that nature has put at the heart of men," which made a government of terror precarious.[74] As a consequence, he argued, finally giving a name to this "infernal system" to which "they now give the name of Robespierre"[75] and which he had described in such detail, "when terrorism has stopped for a moment to terrify, it can only be terrified itself."[76] Since it was clear, for Tallien, that "this system has been that of Robespierre," his concept of terrorism was a charismatic one associated with a single person.[77]

In a spectacular display of the politics of naming, Tallien imposed a particular interpretation of Robespierre's system that served to delegitimize and reject the latter as a viable form of revolutionary government. Consequently, Tallien outlined a different kind of government that was appropriate in times of crisis. Noting that the problem for any revolutionary government was to determine how to govern justly under conditions of emergency, he argued that there was no consensus on "what is revolutionary without being tyrannical, and terrible without being unjust." The task at hand, then, was to clearly determine "what is to be understood by revolutionary government. . . . We must remember the principles, and place them like milestones that must direct our march on the revolutionary road we have to travel."[78] What, according to Tallien, were these principles, and how did he identify them?

First, Tallien maintained, it was necessary to clarify what was meant by revolutionary government, and he offered two possible answers. On the one hand, revolutionary government might mean a government able to accomplish the revolution. On the other hand, it might refer to a government acting in the manner of the revolution. To act in the manner of the revolution, he elaborated, was "to imitate the popular movement in the act of revolution." But because the revolution had put "under the foot of the people the throne that weighed on its head" through an act of "open war against the tyranny and its henchmen," governing in the manner of the revolution amounted to nothing less than an understanding of government as a continuation of war.[79] It meant "to continue to treat France like a battlefield, to act for the people, through the people, as if it were in insurrection, that is to say, leaders of armed legions pursuing declared enemies."[80] This, however, was precisely what characterized terrorism. Tallien insisted, by contrast, that the declared enemies of the people had been overthrown. Therefore, it was no longer necessary to govern in the manner of the revolution and wage open war against the monarchy and its agents. In the current situation, he argued, "it is not about pursuing declared enemies, but about discovering hidden enemies: so we need the justice of the judge and not the force of the warrior."[81]

Let me pause for a moment to take note of a significant shift in the discourse of enmity evident in Tallien's program of revolutionary government. As we saw in the previous section, Robespierre had defined the enemies of the people as those who opposed republican values and thus were not members of the nation. On Robespierre's view, being a citizen was identical with being a republican; therefore, royalists, aristocrats, and other opponents of the Republic were by definition outside the bounds of the civil sphere. Hence they were in an important sense external enemies—not because they were citizens of another country or foreigners in any geographic sense, but because they were not regarded as members of the body politic. The aim of revolutionary terror was to eliminate these enemies, who threatened the Republic from outside. Tallien, by contrast, saw the identification of internal enemies as the task of revolutionary government. For him, the greatest danger to the Republic came from within. This displacement of danger from external to internal enemies had its conditions of possibility in a new political rationality, which centered on an understanding of the nation as the universal subject of political representation.

Tallien's elaboration of a political system that allowed for universal representation was situated within a larger context in which ideas of the nation as the universal political subject circulated. Consider, for example, the Abbé de Sieyès' famous pamphlet "What Is the Third Estate?"[82] In this text, Sieyès argued that the Third Estate performed all functions necessary to maintain a nation, such as agriculture, handicrafts, and military duties. In fact, he asserted that the Third Estate was the only estate able to execute all the tasks that were required to secure the existence of a nation. But although the Third Estate effectively constituted the French nation, it had not been given the political status of the nation. As a consequence, Sieyès argued that the Third Estate must be given political representation that recognized and corresponded to its national totality. In short, Sieyès demanded nothing less than the supplementation of the Third Estate's national totality with political universality.

In the same vein, Tallien asserted the universality of the nation and argued that universal political representation could be achieved only by way of a system of clear, objective, egalitarian principles—that is, laws—that protected a set of fundamental rights specified in the *Declaration of the Rights of Man and the Citizen.* The only kind of fear that was acceptable for Tallien was "the fear of the law for actions against the law."[83] Rather than "threatening *people*, threatening them always and for everything, threatening them with all cruelties one can imagine," a system of legal norms ensured "surveillance of bad *actions*, to threaten them and to punish them with proportionate pains."[84] In sum, Tallien argued for a system that exhibited key features of what we now call the rule of law, that is, a system in which general laws demarcated the sphere of legitimate governmental intervention, fear was acceptable only as punishment for those who violated these laws, and laws were enforced by "a police that watches over their observation."[85]

Tallien's denunciation of terrorism and his defense of a system of universal laws as an alternative form of revolutionary government feature a number of elements that clearly distinguish his political rationality from Robespierre's. These elements include, first, Tallien's definition of the role of the police as enforcement of law and repression of illegality rather than the increase of the state's splendor. Second, he identified government as "the complement of the essential order of political society; it must be a severe institution, but above all it must be sufficiently just to arrange for the benefit of a free constitution."[86] In other words, government must adapt to the needs of society, which told government what to do. Society was that for which government was responsible and which it must regulate. Finally, Tallien endorsed an understanding of freedom as a sphere of nonintervention delineated by general laws. Crucially, these laws no longer represented the will of the sovereign who ruled over the people. As the formal expression of the universality of the nation, the law's primary function was instead to limit the actions of a government whose task was the political representation of national totality. Put differently, the law functioned as a principle of limitation derived from the nature and purpose of government itself. Although Tallien availed himself of the familiar framework of law, he did so to constrain, rather than to make manifest and buttress, the government's power. In contrast to Robespierre's sovereign reason, Tallien's articulation of law as an instrument of the self-regulation of government is thus characteristic of *raison économique* or liberal reason.[87]

This discussion suggests that elements of *raison d'État* continued to exist in productive tension with *raison économique* and engendered new uses and justifications for older strategies of power. Nevertheless, the differences between Tallien's and Robespierre's accounts of revolutionary government indicate that Tallien's political rationality was no longer of the order of sovereignty but of biopower. This transformation in the register of political rationality helps explain, first, the new concept of enmity operative in Tallien's speech. In contrast to Robespierre's understanding of enemies as external threats, Tallien argued that enemies of the Republic emerged from within the nation itself. Enemies of the nation were not foreign elements attacking an otherwise-vigorous nation from outside but members of the nation itself who threatened its very makeup. As a consequence, as a French newspaper succinctly stated, the guns had to be turned "on the French people in order to make it better."[88]

Second, the presence of a biopolitical rationality, which we can identify in Tallien's thought, also forms the background of the subsequent development of the discourse of terrorism, by which the term became a sign of deviance and danger and a justification for state violence. The concept of terrorism, as well as the discourses, laws, practices, institutions, and knowledge to which it gave rise, underwent a series of transformations before they finally achieved a sort of unity that permitted the portrayal of terrorists as threats to the nation, as well as their violent removal from the body politic in the name of defending society.

DOXASTIC, SYSTEMIC, AND IDENTARIAN TERRORISM

Although the concept of *charismatic terrorism* had allowed Tallien to firmly tie the term to Robespierre's Reign of Terror, it became dissociated from the person Robespierre and attached to the new Thermidorian government under Tallien's leadership in a matter of weeks. The pamphlets of the journalist, political activist, and radical egalitarian François-Noël Babeuf, better known by his pen name Gracchus, present a clear elaboration of this transformation and illustrate the contestations over meaning and interpretation of the *terrorism* label. Babeuf initially argued that in addition to being a tyrant, Robespierre had also been a righteous and honorable patriot. He declared that one had to "distinguish between two persons, that is to say, Robespierre the sincere patriot and friend of principles until the beginning of 1793, and Robespierre the ambitious tyrant and most profound scoundrel since that time."[89] Second, Babeuf maintained that Robespierre the patriot had supplied the weapons to fight the legacy of the Terror, namely, the rights and liberties guaranteed by the constitution of 1793, which Robespierre and the Jacobins had supported. At the same time, however, in an attempt to curb dissent and political opposition, Robespierre had restricted these very rights by imposing censorship and suppressing all newspapers, publications, and theatrical performances that were not in line with Montagnard ideology. Babeuf's distinction between the good Robespierre who had adhered to revolutionary principles and the bad Robespierre who had committed atrocious actions prepared the ground for new conceptual uses of terrorism as a political philosophy and, later, a particular form of action. Babeuf implied that Robespierre stood for a particular philosophical view, namely Jacobinism, which ought to be preserved, while his actions were reprehensible and ought to be denounced.

I will examine the concept of terrorism as a particular kind of action in detail in chapter 3. Here I want to focus on Babeuf's claim that Robespierre's actions represented a mode of governing that was not particular to Robespierre. First, this move paved the way for the conceptual transformation of terrorism into the name for any political system that relied on the use of particular measures, or *systemic terrorism*. Second, it allowed for an understanding of terrorism as a political philosophy, or *doxastic terrorism*. And third, it gave rise to an appropriated use of the term to describe a political identity, or *identarian terrorism*.

The notion of systemic terrorism had already been implicit in Tallien's characterization of terrorism as the government of Robespierre, but it was Babeuf who explicitly divorced terrorism from Robespierre and articulated a concept of systemic terrorism. Given Robespierre's dismantling of constitutional rights, Babeuf argued that it was necessary to return to that form of Jacobinism that had supported revolutionary principles and to restore freedom of expression, which he regarded as the condition of possibility of public liberty. "I open a forum [*une tribune*] to plead for the rights of the press," Babeuf declared,[90] and he was full of hope that "10 Thermidor marks the new term in which we work for the rebirth of freedom."[91] However, his hopes for a return to the rights of the 1793 constitution were soon disappointed. On 6 Vendémiaire An III (September 27, 1794), just three weeks after the first issue of his *Journal* had appeared, Babeuf complained that even though 10 Thermidor had been called a revolution, "the people noticed that it was nothing but the revolution of a dead man, a tyrant, if you will, but that this so-called revolution did not get rid of tyranny—the latter merely fell into other hands."[92] The society of 9 Thermidor, he argued, "has not changed [Robespierre's] system. The same means, the same way of government continue after his death. . . . What does it matter to abolish a tyrant but not tyranny?"[93]

This passage reflects Babeuf's first subtle reworking of the concept of terrorism. By decoupling it from Robespierre, he proposed an understanding of terrorism as any government that undermined civil rights, constrained freedom of speech, and demanded, "like the tyrant Robespierre, that the blood flow in wide streams, that in the name of security and private property an immense number of peaceful individuals be sacrificed."[94] Babeuf thus sought to achieve a certain generalization of the concept in order to then apply it to any government that abrogated constitutional rights and controlled public opinion by fear and intimidation. The term *systemic terrorism* is meant to capture this idea.

The notion of systemic terrorism clearly underpins Babeuf's interpretation of the actions of the Thermidorian government. For instance, when the president of the National Convention, André Dumont, dismissed a popular petition to proscribe the Thermidorian government, Babeuf interpreted this as a return to terrorism. "You threaten the people in the name of the Convention," Babeuf accused him; "you make it take up the language of terrorism by making it say that it knows how to save the people, by striking those who want to agitate against it."[95] Moreover, Babeuf criticized Tallien and the journalist Stanislas Louis Fréron, former Montagnard and acolyte of Marat who became a prominent critic of the Terror, and demanded that they be guillotined as terrorists, drinkers of blood, destroyers, and incendiaries (*terroriste, buveur de sang, démolisseur, incendiaire*).[96]

For Babeuf, the Thermidorian government was ultimately not much different from Robespierre's Reign of Terror. Its violation of the rights of man, which it justified as "the certain and only guarantors of freedom,"[97] meant, for Babeuf, that the Thermidorian regime itself met the definition of "terrorism, the government of blood, the government of Robespierre, the tyranny of Robespierre, the despotism of the committees, and all the subsequent atrocities, the *guillotinades*, the shootings, the drownings, oppression, despair, all forms of squalor, deprivation and misery."[98] Babeuf maintained that the real terrorism (*le vrai terrorisme*) was the "Thermidorian terrorism" (*le terrorisme Thermidorien*) of the government,[99] which "pretended to want to kill another [terrorism]."[100]

Note that Babeuf accomplished the transition from charismatic to systemic terrorism by way of a subtle shift that left the explicit meaning of the term intact. Specifically, he argued that the violation of the rights of man committed by the National Convention meant that it engaged in terrorism by its own lights. That is, Babeuf took Tallien's description of terrorism as a particular type of government at face value and suggested that the new political leadership conformed to its own understanding of terrorism.

Moreover, Babeuf claimed that terrorism had been legalized with the establishment of the Thermidorian government on 22 Thermidor. "Is it really true," he asked, "that we have done nothing but change terrorism" from that of Robespierre to that of the current revolutionary leadership?[101] For Babeuf, the Thermidorian Reaction had brought "the most revolting of miseries, the insulting triumph of the aristocracy, terrorism, and the most excessive oppression against patriots."[102] As a consequence, his journal ran a section on the "terrorism of the counterterrorists" (*le terrorisme des anti-terroristes*) on 9 Pluviôse An III (January 28, 1795). Here Babeuf observed, "The enemies of the people have established terrorism against the patriots, . . . massacres of whom have been openly preached."[103] For Babeuf, it was clear that the Thermidorian government had itself become a terrorist government. Calling it anything else was a "logogriph," an anagrammatical charade that forced people to speak "une langue d'argot," a secret code intended to conceal reality.[104]

Babeuf's first modification of the concept of terrorism, by which he abstracted from Robespierre's government and generalized the term to accommodate any government that violently infringed on individual rights, prepared the ground for another, more substantial conceptual transformation. The notion of systemic terrorism came to be supplemented by a concept of terrorism as a political philosophy, or *doxastic terrorism*.[105] By this I mean that the term *terrorism* no longer functioned only as the name for a system of government, even though it continued to operate in this way, but was also understood as a set of normative principles of political organization. Therefore, the use of the term *terrorism* as a form of government, analogous to concepts like *tyranny, monarchy,* or *despotism,* came to be supplemented by its use as a name for political commitments, like *republicanism, populism,* or *royalism.*

To be sure, this new use of the term did not replace previous discourses. Rather, the concept of terrorism now operated as a name for Robespierre's rule, a system of government more broadly, and a set of political commitments. Thus, charismatic, systemic, and doxastic notions of terrorism circulated at the same time, informing, supporting, and keeping one another in existence.

To illustrate the new concept of doxastic terrorism, consider the response of the National Convention in the face of rising food prices at the beginning of 1795, which lent support to radical sans-culottes and royalists.[106] To avoid riots, the Convention, by now decidedly anti-Thermidorian and dominated by Girondins, articulated the need to "make unremitting war on both *royalistes* and *terroristes*" as "twin dangers" to the revolution.[107] Eager to stabilize the Revolution, the revolutionary leadership knew that it had to draft a new constitution that suppressed not only authoritarian populism but also royalism. For this purpose, the 1795 constitution, which established the Directory with the aim of reconciling revolutionary principles with a liberal democratic order, implemented safeguards against the risk that direct democracy would be hijacked by authoritarian populists, on the one hand, and the danger of a return to monarchy, on the other.[108] Individual rights formed the basis of legitimate political authority, determined the boundaries of government intervention, and limited the rightful use of force to cases where the law was violated. Accordingly, government was legitimate as long as it acted in accordance with law, freedom ended where it violated the rights of others, and violence was permitted for punishing such violations. As François Antoine Boissy d'Anglas (1756–1826), member of the Committee of Public Safety after Thermidor, eloquently argued, this punitive use of violence against illegal activities was necessary, for "if the people make bad choices and opt for monarchism, terrorism or fanaticism, the Republic will be lost!"[109]

In his history of the French Revolution, the historian Albert Soboul notes the association of the term *terrorism* with a normative system of values that served to justify governmental violence against political opponents:

> Anti-terrorism and the extirpation of militant sans-culottes from the sections—which together comprised an embryonic version of the White Terror—progressed throughout the winter of 1794–1795, from Frimaire to Ventôse Year III. No longer a question of purges in the true sense of the term, like that which had followed directly after 9 Thermidor—for the terrorist cadres had already been eradicated—the element of personal vengeance now predominated. After having first turned against the main terrorists, the repression widened its scope to include the whole of the former sectional personnel. As it did so, it acquired a social complexion, attacking in the former militants a whole system of republican values.[110]

It was clear by the fall of 1795 that a doxastic understanding of terrorism had been firmly established in the discourse of the government. Far from describing, first and foremost, a particular system of government, as well as political actions and institutions, the term *terrorism* now designated a political stance one could choose. Although a system of terrorism might eventually result from people's bad choices, the choices themselves were motivated by a set of underlying normative political commitments and attitudes. Just as the triumph of royalism was presumed to result in a restoration of absolute monarchy, doxastic terrorism was regarded as the ideological foundation of and road map to a terrorist government.

Noting this new use of the term, Babeuf observed that the name *sans-culotte* had been turned into an insult and that the term *terrorist* had become an accepted epithet of the same order as *royalist* and was "synonymous with patriot and friend of the principles."[111] In the same way, Philippe Buonarroti, an early socialist and chronicler of Babeuf's Conspiracy for Equality, observed that *terrorism* had become a synonym for *republicanism*.[112] By denouncing republicans, patriots, and friends of the Revolution as terrorists, the government effectively used the constitution to portray their actions as illegal transgressions of individual rights. As a consequence, Babeuf sharply criticized the 1795 constitution as a "work of crime" and declared that it made "terror against the people the order of the day" (*la terreur contre le Peuple est à l'ordre du jour*).[113] For Babeuf, in other words, the constitution of 1795 represented a significant step backward from the rights guaranteed by the constitution of 1793, which, sadly, had never been put in force.

Babeuf had already registered his disagreement with such a limitation of rights for the purpose of preserving freedom in October 1794. The logic by which the "violation of all your rights, . . . the most audacious oppression that they cover under the name of necessarily strict measures, under the name of measures for the general security, are the only certain guarantee for your liberty," Babeuf asserted, was twisted and relied on faulty reasoning.[114] In addition, Babeuf pointed out that *terrorism* had become a term of opprobrium against sans-culottes and Jacobins and thus against those who, for him, were actually patriots and true supporters of revolutionary values.[115] On Babeuf's view, then, the government attempted to eliminate political opposition and increase its power by disseminating two falsehoods: first, it argued that the only way to preserve freedom was through the restriction of rights; and second, it portrayed those committed to the Revolution as terrorists and a threat to national security.

It was in response to the second maneuver, that is, the denunciation of patriots as terrorists, that Babeuf mounted a two-pronged response. First, he argued that the government's understanding of terrorism did not describe actual terrorism but was merely a means to denounce those committed to revolutionary principles. Second, he introduced the term *furoriste*, derived from the Latin word *furor* for anger or frenzy, to distinguish republicans from royalists and other enemies of the people. He did so in order to condemn what he regarded as the real enemies of the people while at the same time reclaiming the term *terrorism* and endowing it with a positive valence.[116]

Babeuf's comments in an exchange with Jean-Baptiste Armonville, one of the few sans-culotte deputies in the Convention, illustrate this move. Babeuf expressed his hope that at least part of the Convention had "opened its eyes to the ferocious conduct of the *furoristes*, and that it has repeatedly declared itself protector of the patriots who are oppressed under the name terrorists, which is given to all republicans, even to the soldiers of liberty. It has been proven that the *furoristes* do not know anything but terrorists, those who have scared the *emigrés*, the kings, the royalists, the papists, the plungers, the wholesale buyers, eventually, all enemies of the people."[117]

In contrast to his earlier efforts to retain a systemic understanding of terrorism as a tyrannical system of government and apply it to the Thermidorian government, Babeuf now argued that the government's actual use of the term effectively changed its meaning.[118] If terrorism was indeed the demand for freedom, the rights of man, democracy, justice, and equality, then surely it was desirable to be a terrorist. On this account, terrorism constituted not merely a political philosophy but a form of understanding oneself and a mode of being a subject—in short, a political identity one could and, in fact, should assume and cultivate. I call this *identarian terrorism.*

The normative force of Babeuf's attempt to establish an identarian concept of terrorism, however, was undercut by the practical consequences of being labeled a terrorist. Being denounced as a terrorist, Babeuf observed, was "the equivalent of being branded on the forehead."[119] Objecting to the violent assaults the ultraroyalist Companions of Jehu committed against Jacobins under the pretext of terrorism, he admonished the government for *laisser faire le royalisme.*[120] Agreeing with Babeuf, Alexandre Legot, member of the National Convention from 1792 to 1795, expressed his dismay at the failure of the "true friends of the *patrie* to take care that the hot and energetic patriots who had carried out and consolidated the Revolution were not sacrificed under the pretext of terrorism, Robespierrism, etc."[121] In the same vein, Paul vicomte de Barras, an opportunist politician and military strategist with a talent for conveniently siding with the dominant political faction, reported, "They have hunted down the best patriots with the help of a word as insignificant as terrorist."[122] The *Moniteur Universel*, the main Parisian revolutionary newspaper, reported that "the assassins of the counterrevolutionary regime slit the throats of those they call terrorists in prisons, in the streets, and even in private residences, and men without passion made sure that more than a good citizen perished in these massacres."[123]

These observations demonstrate that at the level of political practice, charismatic, systemic, doxastic, and identarian notions of terrorism were merged to create a deflationary concept of terrorism that functioned as an effective rhetorical weapon against critics of the political establishment. Consequently, anyone who opposed the Thermidorians was liable to charges of terrorism, regardless of whether he or she endorsed Jacobinism, held certain political opinions, engaged in subversive actions, or self-identified as a terrorist-patriot. As Babeuf, who was himself "impris-oned for eight or nine months as an apostle of terrorism,"[124] observed, those branded terrorists were condemned "to bread and water, to rotten straw, to the most despicable darkness, to the horror of having to exist for a number of months in this subterranean place where the floor was covered a foot deep in putrid and infected water [and] where they stayed for many days without food; and instead of consolation, they received nothing but abuse and death threats from the soldiers of Jesus of Douai."[125] For Babeuf, this treatment was not legal punishment for a crime stipu-lated by the constitution but rather outside the law (*hors la loi*). Drawing attention to the double standard of the government, which failed to ex-ecute the constitutional procedures it had itself implemented, Babeuf charged:

> In your mind and according to the letter of your acts, you have already judged and condemned me in advance. If I have the misfortune to fall into your hands, I firmly believe that by virtue of your full authority you will scoff at my good reasons and deliver me to the judges that you choose at your pleasure.[126]

Babeuf was wrong that his fate was to be determined outside the law,[127] but his and others' reflections on the abuse of terrorism as a justification for antiterrorist violence are nevertheless significant. They attest to the fact that terrorism functioned as a "magic word" (*un mot magique*) to jus-tify the persecution of political opponents in the name of the salvation of the republic.[128]

What critics of the discourse of terrorism picked up on was that rather than being a primary given in relation to which laws, institutions, admin-istrative measures, and juridical decisions were arranged, terrorism was a means of justifying preexisting interests and practices of power. It served as a way of exercising the sovereign right to kill in a context in which the health and protection of the population became increasingly important. Under these conditions, terrorism was one marker of devi-ance, which had to be removed lest the existence of the nation be jeopar-dized. As Baczko notes, "The Republic had of necessity to purify itself, to get rid of the 'impure,' of traitors, intriguers, careerists, vile profiteers, elements unworthy of the Republic, not to say its worst enemies, hidden and dissembling."[129] To this end, "*exclusion* swiftly became the regulatory mechanism of the political game; the adversary was excluded in the very name of the fundamental unity of the Nation, of the People, or of the Republic."[130] Under the pretext of terrorism, the government justified its exercise of the old sovereign right to kill for the defense and protection of the nation against dangerous terrorists. In this sense, the concept of terrorism and the practices, laws, institutions, and judgments that it made possible must be understood as a mechanism of social defense.

In conclusion, although the short period between the Thermidorian Reaction in July 1794 and Babeuf's execution in 1797 saw a veritable explosion and polyvalence of the discourse of terrorism, the stabilization of new forms of biopower ultimately led to the consolidation of a dispositif of terrorism as a mechanism of social defense characteristic of biopolitical societies. The apparatus of terrorism was one way of discriminating between good and bad citizens, between those who could live and those who must die to ensure the health and salvation of the nation. Whereas Robespierre had endorsed terror as the proper instrument to eliminate enemies who threatened the Republic from outside, the dispositif of terrorism functioned in the service of a state that sought to protect, strengthen, and improve the body politic by removing its own deviant, abnormal, and dangerous terrorist elements. The French Revolution thus saw the inauguration and proliferation of concepts and practices of terrorism that were subsequently taken up, transformed, and overlaid with new meanings and uses in other contexts. In the following chapters, I trace these processes of transformation and superimposition in the context of late imperial and early Bolshevik Russia and colonized Algeria before examining, in chapter 5, the convergence of this legacy in our contemporary dispositif of terrorism.

3

STATE TERRORISM REVISITED

n chapter 2, I argued that the term *terrorism* emerged in the French Revolution as the name for a system of government before being used to describe a political philosophy and political identity. A little more than a century later, with the rise of the totalitarian regimes of the twentieth century and Bolshevik state terrorism, in particular, the term seemed to have been restored to its initial meaning and to function as designating a distinct kind of political system. In his 1944 study of Nazi Germany, the Frankfurt School legal theorist Franz Neumann, for instance, identified terror as the basic principle of National Socialism. Specifically, he suggested that the Nazi regime lacked political structure and instead used terror as a means to manipulate the masses.[1] Building on Neumann's analysis but opposing his claim that totalitarian regimes lacked political structure, Hannah Arendt famously argued in *The Origins of Totalitarianism*, first published in 1951, that Nazi Germany and Soviet Russia were the first regimes in history to elevate a particular ideology—racism and the classless society, respectively—to a new form of rule by means of terrorism. Arendt claimed that this systematic use of terrorism is what distinguishes totalitarian regimes from their authoritarian cousins.[2] In the same vein, in their book *Totalitarian Dictatorship and Autocracy*, first published in 1956, Carl Friedrich and Zbigniew Brzezinski described terror, especially terrorist police, as the principal feature of totalitarian regimes such as Nazi Germany and the Soviet Union.[3] These analyses reflect a return to a systemic understanding of terrorism that corresponds to its earlier conceptual use as the name for the Jacobin Reign of Terror. Like the Jacobin system of government, totalitarian regimes are distinguished from other political systems by their use of terror as a principle of government.

The conceptual connection between totalitarian terrorism and Jacobin terrorism operative in the analyses of these scholars finds empirical support in the self-description of technicians of terrorism. To explore their relationship, this chapter focuses on the case of Russia in the late nineteenth and early twentieth centuries, when an oppressive tsarist regime and an inefficient feudal economic order gave rise to various political movements that pushed for social change. While nobles and members of the military class called on the tsarist regime to implement reforms that imitated European liberalism, a diverse revolutionary movement, influenced by egalitarian, socialist, anarchist, and nihilist ideas, advocated for the abolition of autocracy and a return to the collectivism of traditional village communities.[4] These social revolutionaries explicitly endorsed the use of terrorism as a means of deposing the ruling classes and situated this strategy in continuity with the Jacobin terror of the French Revolution. In the 1860s, the revolutionary Alexander Herzen, for instance, called for a "Russian Jacobinism" in the tradition of "the great terrorists of the 1790s."[5] Four decades later, Lenin argued that for a consideration of Bolshevik state terror, "the example of the Jacobins is instructive."

> It has not become obsolete to this day, except that it must be applied to the revolutionary class of the twentieth century, to the workers and semi-proletarians. To this class, the enemies of the people in the twentieth century are not the monarchs, but the landowners and capitalists as a class.[6]

For the orthodox Marxist Karl Kautsky, however, this appeal to the French Revolution to justify terrorism was no more than a propagandistic and ideological misuse of history. Moreover, Kautsky argued that the establishment of a historical continuity that tied Russian terrorism to Jacobin terror obscured important differences between the two regimes. An adequate understanding of terrorism, the historical materialist insisted, required careful analysis of the material conditions out of which it arose. On the basis of an examination of the French Revolution and the Second Paris Commune, Kautsky argued that terrorism had to be understood as the effect of a misalignment between the political claims of a certain social group and the stage of its economic development. Whenever the political interests of a class were ahead of concrete economic conditions, these interests could be realized only by way of terrorism. While in the French Revolution the bourgeoisie resorted to terrorism in order to enforce political liberalism and a capitalist economic system, Russian terrorism was the effect of the proletariat's untimely push for socialism and proletarian political rule under unsuitable economic conditions. For Kautsky, in other words, Jacobin and Bolshevik terrorism were diametrically opposed. Whereas the former was an instrument of the bourgeoisie to implement capitalism, the latter was a proletarian tactic of socialist revolution. Nevertheless, Kautsky regarded terrorism in both cases as the product of an incongruence of political demands and economic conditions. Jacobin and Bolshevik terrorism were opposed not with regard to concrete actions and behaviors but by virtue of the class identity and political aims of the technicians of terrorism.[7]

In this chapter, I follow Kautsky in challenging the idea that Bolshevik terrorism was a continuation of Jacobin terror, but I propose an account of their relationship that differs from Kautsky's historical-materialist analysis. Specifically, I aim to show, through an archaeological and genealogical analysis of Bolshevik state terror, that the Jacobin Reign of Terror and Bolshevik terrorism were different, albeit not dialectically opposite, practices characterized by different modes of understanding. My central claim is that while the dispositif of terrorism served bourgeois interests and the establishment of liberal rule in the French Revolution, its Russian counterpart was a tactic of class war, or what I call *strategic terrorism*, waged by the proletariat in its effort to secure a communist state.

I showed in chapter 2 that terrorism came into being in revolutionary France during the emergence of a biopolitical rationality that deployed mechanisms of social defense to protect the social body from its own unhealthy elements. The political injunction to defend the nation against its abnormal and dangerous members justified the exercise of the sovereign right to kill within an economy of biopower. In this chapter, I argue that the dispositif of terrorism that took shape in late nineteenth- and early twentieth-century Russia was formed against the backdrop of different configurations of power. Embedded within an emerging biopolitical rationality, Russian social revolutionaries began to elaborate a defense of revolutionary violence in the 1860s and 1870s that gave rise to a systematic theory of terrorism as a tactic of revolutionary warfare against tsarist sovereignty in the 1880s. With the accession to power of revolutionary forces in 1905 and 1917, the revolutionary discourse of class war was inscribed in the discursive, institutional, and political architecture of the Bolshevik state. The Bolshevik dispositif of terrorism functioned as a mechanism of social defense against the class enemy. Thus, Bolshevik state terror was neither a straightforward repetition of Jacobin terror nor its diametric opposite, but an effect of processes of superimposition underneath which traces of older meanings and uses remained. Concepts and practices of terrorism inaugurated in the French Revolution spiraled away from their site of emergence to new places and contexts, where they were taken up, transformed, overlaid with new meaning, and inserted into different political calculations and power relations.

FROM RACE WAR TO CLASS STRUGGLE

The new concept and practice of terrorism as a tactic of class warfare and, specifically, a weapon against the class enemy had its historical and conceptual conditions of possibility in an understanding of social relations as bellicose relations between classes, which was itself a modification of a historical discourse of race war described by Foucault in "*Society Must Be Defended.*" To summarize briefly, Foucault argued that a historical discourse of race war emerged in the sixteenth and seventeenth centuries in political struggles in England and France as a way to challenge sovereign power. In opposition to justification of the unity and legitimacy of the state by the juridical theory of sovereignty, this discourse of race war contended that the state was the product of invasions, conquests, and a war that was preserved and continued in all mechanisms of power. What appeared as right, law, and obedience from the perspective of the victors was domination, violence, and enslavement from the vantage point of the vanquished. This logic was based on an understanding of race that "is not pinned to a stable biological meaning" but rather "designates a certain historico-political divide."[8] On this view, races were groups united by language, religion, geographic origin, or custom. It was possible, as a consequence, to conceive of society as divided by a binary of two races, like Normans and Saxons in England or Franks and Gauls in France.

During the eighteenth and nineteenth centuries, this discourse underwent two transcriptions, which Foucault understood as two distinct series of historical transformations by which the discourse of race war was adapted to newly emerging biopolitical rationalities. Whereas the first transcription was an openly biological one that gave rise to a discourse of a battle between the human race and those who threatened its biological integrity,[9] the second transcription "tends to erase every trace of racial conflict in order to define itself as class struggle."[10] This social modulation of the discourse of race war reworked the notion of race in terms of class and conceived of society as stratified by relationships of class domination. The outcome of this process was what Foucault described as socialist racism and what I have described as mechanisms of social defense, that is, the state's exercise of the right to kill in the name of defending society against its (class) enemy.[11]

According to Foucault, this development was made possible by two distinct operations. First, the historical discourse of race war was transformed into a revolutionary discourse of class struggle. Second, this revolutionary discourse was then inscribed in the workings of the Soviet state.

A paradigmatic example of this view of politics as a war between social classes was articulated by Lev Tikhomirov, a member of the Executive Committee of Narodnaia Volia (People's Will), the self-proclaimed terrorist branch of the revolutionary movement, who drastically changed his political views and became one of Russia's canonical conservative thinkers.[12] His monumental political history of Russia, titled *Russia, Political and Social*, was written in 1885 and first published in French a year later. The work is interesting for a critical history of Bolshevik terrorism because it performs the transcription of a historical discourse of race war into a revolutionary discourse of class war and firmly anchors Russian terrorism in an understanding of social relations as relations of class domination.

Tikhomirov argued that the social, political, and economic difficulties that plagued Russia in the second half of the nineteenth century were due to the illegitimate authority of a ruling class, which had its origin in a conquering race. By races, he meant groups of people differentiated by a distinctive "*modus vivendi*" that comprised language, customs, tales, and songs.[13] Historically, the Russian race inhabited "Russia proper," which was surrounded by a "large belt of three million square kilometers, peopled to the number of at least twenty-four millions by subjects of foreign races," such as the Finnish, Lithuanian, and Polish races."[14] The Russian Empire was thus populated by different races, whose presence was the result of a history of conquest and invasion. Most notable were the Tartar invasions in the thirteenth century and conquests by Sweden and Poland in the seventeenth century because they led to the enslavement and domination of the Russian people by foreign races.

Tikhomirov here clearly spoke a discourse of race war that reveals political sovereignty as the product of invasions, conquests, and war, which are preserved in all mechanisms of power. But while this historical account located the origin of sovereign power in conquest, Tikhomirov had to explain how the illegitimate rule of a foreign race gave rise to social relations of class domination. To do so, he argued that social classes had their roots in different races that were forced into distinct social occupations in the wake of conquest. Specifically, the Tartar invasions of the thirteenth century geographically isolated Russia proper and forced the Russian race, which inhabited this territory, into agriculture. The Russian race became a people of peasants, and farming became "the lot of all the land, and only yields to all men means of subsistence uniformly poor."[15]

At the same time, the Tartar invasions upset the balance of power in the region. In 1283 the princes of Moscow established the Duchy of Moscow (or Muscovy), the predecessor of the Tsardom of Russia proclaimed in 1547, by cooperating with the Mongols. Its greatest rival was the Kingdom of Lithuania, which had been formed in 1251 and by 1320 had conquered most of the lands between the Baltic and Black Seas. In the late fifteenth and early sixteenth centuries, Muscovy initiated a series of battles to regain Russian lands. Lithuania, facing a threat to its survival, united with Poland in the Polish-Lithuanian Commonwealth in 1569. This event was crucial in the development of the Russian aristocracy because it gave rise to a rapid process of polonization, by which the Polish language and Polish customs and political conventions replaced those of

Russia as the dominant influences among the ruling classes in all territories under Lithuanian rule. Tikhomirov wrote,

> The constitution of Poland was absolutely aristocratic; all rights, intel-
> ligence, wealth, were concentrated in the ranks of the . . . nobility. As a
> consequence, Poland only attracted the sympathies of the upper classes,
> but these latter everywhere very rapidly became Polish. This was the
> highest point of Poland's political development. In the 16th century,
> the Baltic provinces, of their own accord, unite themselves to her. In
> the 17th, Poland comes near to conquering all Muscovite Russia. But the
> exclusive preponderance of the nobility is hollowing out an abyss
> doomed to engulf the country.[16]

What is important about Tikhomirov's claims here is not their historical accuracy but their function in translating a historical discourse of race war into a discourse of class struggle. The Russian nobility was illegiti-mate, on this view, because it originated in a foreign race. As the Tartar invasions turned the Russian race into a class of peasants, they also cre-ated the conditions of emergence of a nobility that was Polish. Tikhomirov clearly did not mean to suggest that the Russian nobility was ethnically Polish, but that nobles were members of the Polish race to the extent that they adopted the Polish language and Polish customs in order to gain ac-cess to the privileges granted by the Polish constitution. The notion of race as heritage, which coded racial membership in terms of tradition, language, and custom, allowed for an easy transformation of race into class. By connecting social relations of class domination to a history of race war and conquest, Tikhomirov was able to argue, first, that the Russian nobility was foreign to the Russian people, and second, that the nobility's power was illegitimate. The racial distribution of social occupations and the origin of political privileges in racial membership gave rise to social classes and reinscribed the hierarchy of conquering and conquered races in social relations characterized by class domination.

Tikhomirov's understanding of politics as a form of war underpinned his subsequent account of the historical development of Russian social relations, which he regarded as a series of changing political alliances that the peasants made to gain protection from aristocratic oppression. Yet every step toward the liberation of the peasants engendered new forms of oppression, which in turn gave rise to new coalitions. It was in the context of this trajectory that Tikhomirov understood widespread popular support for the Tsardom of Muscovy in 1547, which wrested power from aristocrats by means of expropriation, public executions, and other means of political repression in a policy known as *oprichnina*.[17] But the end of aristocratic oppression meant the beginning of autocratic despotism and, over the course of the first half of the seventeenth century, the formation of a new noble class, the *dvoryanstvo*, which staffed Russia's quickly expanding bureaucracy. In return for their service, these bureaucrats received privileges such as land rights, serfs, and hereditary property. These developments consolidated the domination of the peasant class, which was sealed with a new comprehensive legal code in 1649. This law established serfdom and gave landlords complete power over their serfs. It was in the social conditions of serfs that resulted from these measures that the elaboration of a theory and practice of terrorism as a tactic of class struggle became possible.

Peasant uprisings occurred throughout the second half of the seventeenth century and persisted throughout the eighteenth. Weakened by foreign policy debacles such as Russia's defeat in the Crimean War, as well as the fact that Russia's economy was increasingly lagging behind those of Western European countries, Tsar Alexander II implemented a series of reforms, known as the Great Reforms, in the 1860s. The first measures were the emancipation of the serfs and a land reform in 1861, which Alexander regarded as necessary to avoid an escalation of peasant violence. The purpose of the reforms, however, was not the liberation of the peasants but the protection of the ruling classes. "It will be better to abolish serfdom by a measure coming from above," the tsar declared, "than to wait for the time when it will abolish itself from below."[18] The Great Reforms, in other words, were intended as a means of pacifying the peasants and securing the property and status of the upper classes rather than as a good-faith attempt to lessen the serfs' oppression. In keeping with this goal, the Emancipation Manifesto decreed the compensation of lords, allocated insufficient amounts of land to emancipated serfs, and distributed land in such a way as to give the nobles the means of maintaining their economic and political power. It is thus hardly surprising that social unrest persisted and ultimately gave rise to a revolutionary movement.

Yet the principal actors of this revolutionary movement were not the peasants but a subgroup of a newly emerging proletariat that included intellectuals such as Tikhomirov, liberated serfs, former nobles who had been unable to consolidate their economic and political power, and other dispossessed individuals. This revolutionary stratum of society formed the so-called intelligentsia, which was dominated by a segment of the educated nobility whose education and exposure to new ideas had led them to become aware of "the ineptitude, the perfect illegality, and the want of solidity of the *régime* of the nobility."[19]

> All of the nobility that are in the least degree educated give up of their own accord the memory of their past. A new type is appearing, that the newspapers call "the repentant noble"—a most accurate name. These are the nobles that are trying to atone for the faults of their class by becoming good sons of the fatherland. . . . A large number of these repentant nobles tried to become one with the people. They joined the ranks of the revolutionists and of the socialists.[20]

The intelligentsia became a hotbed of revolutionary ideas and, acting on behalf and in the name of the oppressed classes, criticized serfdom, opposed the privileges of nobles, and called for a state organization that would secure popular representation. "Throughout the nineteenth century," Tikhomirov wrote, "all the attempts at political disturbance in Russia are due to the initiative of the intelliguentia [*sic*], and that not in the interests of a class but of the whole people."

> This is the cause not infrequently of an apparent contradiction in the agitations set on foot by the upper classes—a contradiction that Count Rostoptchine formulated with as much acuteness as injustice when the Decembrist outbreak took place. "I can understand," said the count, "the French *bourgeois* bringing about the Revolution to get his rights, but how am I to understand the Russian noble making a revolution to lose them?" The count's mistake and the key to the enigma are in this—that the noble who aimed at this revolution was not the noble that had remained

true to his class, but the noble who had gone over to the ranks of the intelliguentia [sic].[21]

According to Tikhomirov, in other words, the repentant nobles who formed the intelligentsia betrayed their own class interests and instead joined the proletariat, whose status as the universal subject of politics they affirmed. To do so, the intelligentsia drew on the historical narrative exemplified in Tikhomirov's thought, according to which race and class were congruent. Because the proletariat suffered oppression at the hands of ruling classes that had their origins in the illegitimate power conferred on foreign races by conquest and invasion, what was needed was the abolition of the ruling classes and the establishment of the proletariat as the universal class. That the proletariat constituted the nation and represented the interests of humanity as a whole was clear to Tikhomirov. Echoing the Abbé de Sieyès's claim that in France, the Third Estate was the only estate able to secure the existence of the nation because it alone performed all the functions necessary to maintain a nation, Tikhomirov argued that in Russia, the proletariat was the nation.

> In France, the third estate was everything; it was the nation. The most notable minds of the age were on its side. Its principles seemed to open up a new era in the life of humanity. . . . The third estate, in working for its own interests, served at the same time humanity as a whole. To how small an extent is this a portrait of our nascent industrial class! From its dawn almost, the most notable minds of Russian society oppose the interests of the mass of the laboring population to those of the industrial class. Tchernychevsky, the most popular of Russian writers, and moreover the only Russian economist of note, is an adept in socialist doctrines. His friend Dobrolioubov, the most eminent Russian critic, lays bare in his celebrated "Reign of Obscurantism" the corruption and gross ignorance of the bourgeoisie. In a series of articles he contrasts with them the working people, full of strength and life. The best writers, the most eminent observers of the life of the people, constantly insist upon the necessity of maintaining the rural commune, of encouraging and developing the local branches of industry that are in the hands of the producers and not of the capitalists—measures in direct contradiction to the interests of the bourgeoisie.[22]

We can see here the positing of the working class as the universal class or nation, whose interests corresponded to all of humanity. The working class harbored the country's productive forces and constituted the source of the state's wealth. While it was thus the proletariat who ought to be given representation in the state, the tsarist regime pursued its own interests and sought to cement the privileges of the ruling classes. For Tikhomirov, the real tragedy of this state of affairs was not only that the institutions of power preserved domination and war, but also that the regime's actions were simply bad government. Asserting that a country's vital force lay in its people, he argued that Russia's "deplorable economic state is in great measure the fault of the political government, which for thirty years past had, by its clumsy interference, brought endless confusion into the economic conditions of the country."[23] Instead of working with the country's natural riches—fertile soil, favorable climate, abundant metallurgic products, and a people full of life and strength—the oppression and exploitation of the Russian people had resulted in "an artificial state of things, out of correspondence with the natural development of productive forces,"[24] and an "abnormal condition of the productive forces of the country."[25]

Tikhomirov's opposition to the tsarist regime was couched in language that indicates the presence of a political rationality that emphasizes the naturalness of socioeconomic relations and regards governmental intervention in economic processes as sovereign overreach. On this view, government is an art that works with the organic processes of the country and its people to maximize the state's forces. It is an art of government that recognizes the economy as a sphere that guides and limits sovereign power. We encountered this rationality in chapter 2, where I located its development in France within the apparatuses of the state in the form of *raison économique*. Recall that *raison économique* was articulated in France in the seventeenth and eighteenth centuries in response to the problem of scarcity. It advocated respect for the natural processes of the economy and society as best suited to maximize the state's forces. On this view, governmental intervention was not only inefficient but also constituted a sort of sovereign overreach that signified the government's refusal to submit to the forces of the economy and the population. In Russia, by contrast, *raison économique* formed the backbone of an antisovereign revolutionary discourse elaborated by opponents of the tsarist regime.

Based on a historical understanding of Russian social relations as relations of class war and domination, the revolutionary critique of tsarist sovereignty constituted the rationality that allowed for the articulation and stabilization of a concept and practice of terrorism as a weapon against the class enemy. The tsars' stubborn refusal to give up sovereign power jeopardized the well-being of the proletariat and, thereby, the progress of humanity itself. As a consequence, the proletariat had a right and obligation to depose the ruling classes. With the historical discourse of race war thus completely transformed into a revolutionary discourse of class struggle, the stage was set for the elaboration of *strategic terrorism*, that is, a concept and practice of terrorism as a tactic of class war.

TOWARD A STRATEGIC CONCEPT OF TERRORISM

I have examined Tikhomirov's political history of Russia in some detail because it presents the clearest elaboration of what Foucault described as the second transcription of a historical discourse of race war into a revolutionary discourse of class struggle. The latter formed the political rationality within which social revolutionaries began to develop a theory of terrorism as a tactic of class war. This theory was underpinned by a concept of terrorism that differed significantly from earlier charismatic, systemic, doxastic, and identarian notions of terrorism that had emerged during the French Revolution. To see how terrorism became conceptually available for Russian revolutionaries in the second half of the nineteenth century, we must for a moment step back in history to take stock of a number of conceptual transformations that the term *terrorism* underwent in the years after the French Revolution. A new agential or strategic understanding of the term allowed for its use in a range of different contexts where it no longer described a system of government, a political philosophy, or an identity but a variety of behaviors and actions. *Terrorism* first became a term of moral opprobrium against a variety of political groups; second, it began to circulate outside France and was increasingly disconnected from the context of the French Revolution; and third, it was applied to groups who perpetrated phenomenally similar acts of violence. I argue that these developments at the level of the concept, which the subsequent archaeological analysis will clarify, constitute the conceptual conditions on which the theory and practice of terrorism as a tactic of revolutionary class war, or *strategic terrorism*, was elaborated in the second half of the nineteenth century.

In chapter 2, I examined some of the contestations over the term *terrorism*, which Jean-Lambert Tallien had introduced in 1794 as the name for Robespierre's system of terror. We saw that the radical egalitarian Gracchus Babeuf challenged this charismatic concept of terrorism by articulating systemic, doxastic, and identarian alternatives. In addition, Babeuf argued as early as 1795 that "in order to govern justly, one must terrify the villains, the royalists, the papists, and those who starve out the public, and that one cannot govern *democratically* without this terrorism which alone is permitted and legitimate; otherwise, there is nothing but injustice and famine; there is nothing but the most terrible tyranny and servitude for the good citizens, just like it has been exercised for too long."[26] Implicit in this claim is an understanding of terrorism that differs from earlier charismatic, systemic, doxastic, and identarian versions. Specifically, terrorism is conceived as an action, something one does in order to fight against the enemies of the good citizens. Here we see the origins of a concept of terrorism that dominates our present thinking and, regardless of its moral status, conceives of terrorism in terms of means and ends and as a strategy, method, or tactic of political struggle. How did this new concept of terrorism come about?

By the end of the eighteenth century, the word *terrorism* had become interchangeable with a number of other terms, such as *anarchist, Jacobin*, or *Babouvist*. As Babeuf noted in his defense in court, his own name had "acquired the odious distinction of designating a sect which includes all republicans, all patriots, and which is charged with preparing them all for the establishment of a new reign of terror. Gone are the epithets of Robespierrist, Terrorist, Anarchist, and Jacobin: *Babouvist* has taken their place."[27] Regardless of whether Babeuf was right about the waning importance of the terms *terrorist, anarchist*, and *Jacobin*, the important implication of his observation concerns the essentially synonymous use of the words *Robespierrist, terrorist, anarchist*, and *Babouvist* as terms of moral opprobrium against a rather diverse group of people. This interpretation is supported by a range of archival sources, such as a report of the Bureau Central of Paris of April 29, 1799, which cautioned that an inflationary use of these words by royalists masked the real danger posed by anarchism. "The parties which the force and above all the agreement of the constitutional powers have been depriving of all means of open revolt," the report stated, "seem today to wake up, gain hope and prepare new troubles."

> The impotence to act, the profound memory that the disastrous epochs had left in the mind, the only idea of disorganization, of troubles and of murders that presents the horrifying word *anarchy*, reduce for the moment to silence and to inactivity the followers of this horrible party. It is certain that, if there were only the hatred of the true friends of the Constitution of the Year III, [anarchism] would be better appreciated and consequently more fearsome; but unfortunately, the horror that it instills in the sincere republicans is accompanied by that which it causes in the crowd of royalists; in the eyes of these latter, all those who cling to republican institutions, all those who embrace with interest the principles of maintaining the existing order of things, or who ardently intercede for the defense and prosperity of the Republic are anarchists. For a partisan of the old regime, *patriot* is equally synonymous with *anarchist* and *terrorist* and, by dint of reverberations, a certain class of incorrigible reactionaries grows and extends this illustrious and often misunderstood word *anarchy*.[28]

The problem, according to this report, was an undifferentiated use of a variety of terms that obscured important differences between opponents of the revolutionary government and the French constitution of 1795.

In addition to the conflation and generalization of *terrorism* and *anarchism* as umbrella terms for diverse political commitments, these labels began to circulate outside France in the final years of the eighteenth century. At first, the connection between terrorism and the French Revolution, and in particular Robespierre, remained intact. For instance, in the fourth of his *Letters on a Regicide Peace*, a series of letters in opposition to the British prime minister's effort to seek peace with France, the Irish philosopher and critic of the French Revolution Edmund Burke criticized the Thermidorian government for issuing the amnesty law of 4 Brumaire An IV (October 26, 1795). Burke argued that the law, which the

revolutionary government had passed in a desperate effort to garner support against the royalists,[29] ensured that "thousands of those Hell-hounds
called Terrorists, whom they had shut up in Prison on their last Revolution, as the Satellites of Tyranny, are let loose on the people." Burke further argued that the Directory "differed nothing from all the preceding
usurpations" but was, in fact, "strengthened with the undisciplined power
of the Terrorists." Although his use of the word *terrorist* echoed the Thermidorian use of *terrorism* as a term of opprobrium against Jacobins,
sans-culottes, and egalitarians, it is important to note that Burke also
understood terrorism in its systemic sense as a form of government, emphasizing the continuity between the Jacobin Terror and the Directory.
Denouncing the latter as a regicide government, Burke argued that its
hatred of royalism led it to ally with "irregulars" and "robbers."[30] In a
similar vein, the German poet Christoph Martin Wieland endorsed a systemic notion of terrorism and was convinced that only Napoléon's coup
in September 1797 had saved France from being "thrown back into all the
horrors of anarchy, terrorism and the most ferocious civil war."[31]

Others, however, such as the leading German Jacobin Matthias Metternich, objected to the inflationary and indiscriminate use of the words
anarchism and *terrorism*. Metternich complained that "whenever a republican plucked up the courage to show the abyss toward which this anarchic
system would lead, he was branded a Jacobin, a terrorist, an anarchist—
and proscribed."[32] For Metternich, in other words, *terrorism* and *anarchism*
had become smear words against anyone who was critical of the political
establishment, regardless of the former's political views and the latter's
ideological and institutional makeup.

It was this use of terrorism as a rhetorical weapon against political opponents that paved the way for a decoupling of the term from the French
Revolution throughout the first half of the nineteenth century. As Rudolf
Walther observes, until the mid-nineteenth century, "only here and there
had the term 'terror' been detached from the French Revolution and applied to other events and constellations."

This was to change in situations of political and social crisis when the
political enemy and his praxis could be described with the term....
"Terrorism" now served to qualify every political opponent who advocated

radical claims—independent of his history, his praxis and his other aims. . . . Whenever the term appears in the political sphere, it carries negative connotations.[33]

By 1848, *terrorism* was firmly established as a term of opprobrium for nonstate political actors who exercised excessive, illegitimate, and illegal violence.[34] Aided by the invention of dynamite and hearkening back to Babeuf's understanding of terrorism as a form of political action designed to intimidate, terrorism was increasingly regarded as a carefully orchestrated attempt to create fear by causing maximum public impact.[35] On this view, the word no longer named a system of government, political philosophy, or political identity but described a particular form of violent action articulated in terms of means and ends. Terrorism was now primarily (but not exclusively) understood as a strategy of revolutionary struggle against illegitimate and tyrannical governments—what I call *strategic terrorism*. Russian social revolutionaries began to take up this notion of terrorism in the 1860s, but a full elaboration and stabilization of a concept and practice of terrorism as a tactic of revolutionary class war took two more decades.

STRATEGIC TERRORISM

It is commonplace in the contemporary literature on terrorism to think of 1880s Russia as the birthplace of modern terrorism, and of various anarchist, nihilist, and revolutionary movements as its midwives.[36] But the explicit and systematic use of terrorism as a strategy of class war in the 1880s emerged out of a set of discourses and practices of revolutionary violence against the ruling classes endorsed by the revolutionary movement in the 1860s and 1870s. The evangelization for terrorism in the 1880s was in large measure a campaign that gave coherence and structure to these earlier actions and ideas.

One of the first calls for revolutionary violence against the ruling classes was issued by two students, Peter Zaichnevsky and Pericles Argiropulo, in the pamphlet *Young Russia*, distributed in the streets of Moscow in 1862.[37] They situated their demand for violence within a discourse of class war between the popular masses and the ruling or imperial class. The oppression of the people, they claimed, had brought Russia to the point where it "is entering the revolutionary stage of its existence," which "must change everything down to the very roots."[38] The salvation of the Russian people and the future of the country required nothing less than the complete destruction of the ruling classes. Their subsequent defense of revolutionary violence is notable for introducing two elements that were to become defining characteristics of the use of terrorism by Russian social revolutionaries. On the one hand, Zaichnevsky and Argiropulo clearly understood society as bifurcated into those who may live and those who must die. "Anyone who is not with us," they declared, "is against us, and an enemy, and . . . every method is used to destroy an enemy."[39] On the other hand, they accepted the inevitability of collateral damage. The end of defending society against the class enemy justified means that required that "even innocent victims will perish."[40]

The nihilist Sergei Nechaev radicalized the program articulated in *Young Russia*. In his 1868 manifesto "The Catechism of the Revolutionary," Nechaev offered a vigorous defense of violence as a means of popular revolution against the class enemy. Nechaev's "Catechism" advances two key points that are of particular interest for the subsequent development of terrorism in Russia. First, he described Russian society as divided into the people and its class enemy. Like the authors of *Young Russia*, he regarded society as divided into two mutually exclusive classes, which had been formed by a long history of conquest, invasion, and domination. Contemporary social relations, Nechaev argued, had their roots in the Tartar invasions and the foundation of the Muscovite State, which institutionalized the war between the Russian race and a race of foreign conquerors as relations of class domination. In short, Russian society in the second half of the nineteenth century was characterized by the domination of a ruling class whose power over the people was the outcome of war and violence and was thus illegitimate. As an institutionalized form of illegitimate power, the state was an instrument of oppression and, as such, must be destroyed. For Nechaev, then, everyone who was not a member of the popular class was by definition a class enemy. This implied that there was really only one class, the people, and that this class was the legitimate basis of political representation. Victory over the class enemy would result in the universalization of the popular class and the emergence of a classless society. The salvation of the people could thus be achieved only by means of a revolution that "will eliminate all state traditions, orders, and social classes in Russia."[41] How was this to be achieved?

Nechaev's answer to this question entails a second important theme. Although he argued that the destruction of the state and the elimination of the ruling classes had to be brought about by any means necessary, the most effective strategy of class war was the perpetration of acts of revolutionary violence by heroic individuals who dedicated themselves entirely to the cause. The revolutionist, he wrote, was "a doomed man. He has no interests, no affairs, no feelings, no habits, no property, not even a name. Everything in him is wholly absorbed by a single, exclusive interest, a single thought, a single passion—the revolution."[42] Nechaev dedicated a significant portion of the "Catechism" to an elaboration of a revolutionary asceticism, whose purpose was to instill in the revolutionary an uncompromising discipline and commitment to the struggle. By cultivating an ascetic ideal, the revolutionary should become merciless toward himself and others.

> A single, cold passion for the revolutionary cause must suppress within him all tender feelings for family life, friendship, love, gratitude, and even honor. For him there exists only one pleasure, one consolation, one reward, and one satisfaction—the success of the revolution. Day and night he must have one single purpose: merciless destruction. To attain this goal, tirelessly and in a cold-blooded fashion, he must always be prepared to be destroyed and to destroy with his own hands everything that hinders its attainment.[43]

The success of the revolution, according to Nechaev, thus depended on acts of terrorism committed by individuals who subordinated their lives to class struggle.

By the early 1870s, a number of ideas had been brought into circulation among the social revolutionaries that came to shape subsequent developments: (1) an understanding of social relations in terms of class war as a continuation of a historical process of conquest and invasion; (2) a notion of the state as an instrument of illegitimate power and class domination; (3) a demand for ending popular oppression by means of revolutionary violence; and (4) the effectiveness of individual terrorism as a tactic of revolutionary class struggle. In the late 1870s and 1880s, a growing self-proclaimed terrorist movement synthesized these ideas in a doctrine of "armed struggle with the government."[44] Because the ruling classes were waging war against the people, these revolutionaries advocated terrorism as a form of popular self-defense. Writing under his pseudonym Tarnovski, Gerasim Romenanenko, for instance, described terrorists as "the defenders of the people" in a war against "a gang of worthless louts exploiting poor, hungry Russia, writhing in a wild frenzy on ground spattered with the blood of its finest people."

> At its head is the czar, without heart or reason, who has made it his aim to stifle all those who show signs of life. . . . For the good of the homeland we have to sacrifice this foreign way of life and not stand too much in awe of our own way of life.[45]

The ruling classes were foreigners, "crowned vampires, kings, and czars," who oppressed the Russian people and condemned them to "social slavery."[46] Similarly, in a letter to Tsar Alexander III in 1881, the Executive Committee of Narodnaia Volia defended terrorism as necessary against a regime whose existence was "evidence of a complete usurpation." The government sought to preserve its illegitimate power by all means necessary. Even political reforms, the committee wrote, "result merely in a more perfect enslavement and a more complete exploiting of the people. . . . The protection of the law and of the Government is enjoyed only by the extortionists and the exploiters, and the most exasperating robbery goes unpunished."[47] Echoing Nechaev's hope for a classless society, the committee argued that the liberation of the people required the abolition of classes and a complete reorganization of social relations. This could not be achieved by reform from above but only, barring a voluntary transfer of power to the people, through a revolutionary deposition of the usurpers. For the revolutionaries, in other words, the material conditions of tsarist rule required popular self-defense by means of terrorism, which appeared as nothing but "a pointed manifestation of the abnormalities of social relations in Russia."[48]

Two insights follow from this understanding of terrorism as a product of historically and socially specific conditions. First, nothing short of a change of social conditions would put an end to terrorism. As the Executive

Committee wrote, "Revolutionists are the creation of circumstances of the general discontent of the people—of the striving of Russia after a new social framework. It is impossible to exterminate a whole people—it is impossible by means of repression, to stifle its discontent."[49] Only the termination of class war and the liberation of the people through the abolition of social classes would end popular discontent and terrorism.

Second, the revolutionaries' highly contextualized understanding of terrorism as a tactic of class war against the oppressors of the people, or strategic terrorism, imposed important constraints on the legitimate use of terrorist violence. To begin with, they argued that terrorism ought to target only those responsible for the suffering of the people. Moreover, they maintained that terrorism was unjustifiable under different conditions. In the fall of 1881, for instance, Narodnaia Volia denounced the assassination of U.S. president James Garfield because, it wrote, "in a land where personal freedom gives an opportunity for an honest conflict of ideas, where the free will of the people determines not only the law but also the personality of the ruler, in such a land political murder as a means of struggle presents a manifestation of that despotic spirit which we aim to destroy in Russia."[50] In short, the legitimacy of terrorism was determined by the social context in which it occurred. As a consequence, it had to be tailored to the specific conditions in which it was used. For this purpose, terrorism had to become a scientific form of revolution.

Nicholas Morozov's 1880 pamphlet "The Terroristic Struggle" is one of the clearest articulations of such a scientific account of terrorism. His aim in "The Terroristic Struggle" was "to summarize theoretically and to systematize practically this form of revolutionary struggle" and to establish terrorism as a "rich, consistent system."[51] He thought that this was necessary because the success of terrorism in bringing about social revolution depended on its large-scale adoption as a theory and practice of class struggle. Only if the "future terroristic struggle becomes a deed of not only one separate group, but of an idea, which cannot be destroyed by people," he wrote, can the struggle become "popular, historical, and grandiose."[52]

Morozov explicated the tactical requirements of revolutionary terrorism, which were determined by the conditions of the tsarist regime. The power of the government, he claimed, could be opposed only by a network of small terrorist groups that operated in secrecy. Secrecy, in particular, afforded a set of critical tactical advantages. First, in contrast to Nechaev's claim that spectacular acts of individual terrorism required heroic rebels willing to sacrifice themselves, Morozov wrote, "Contemporary terroristic struggle is not like this at all. Justice is done here, but those who carry it out remain alive."[53] Secrecy allowed terrorists to escape retaliation and increased their chances of survival. Thus, the problem of constant recruitment of martyrs was avoided. A second benefit of secrecy, according to Morozov, was that it protected the revolutionary movement from open confrontation with the state's military force. "Secret assassinations" gave the terroristic struggle "exactly this advantage that it can act unexpectedly and find means and ways which no one anticipated."

> All that the terroristic struggle really needs is a small number of people and large material means. This presents really a new form of struggle. It replaces by a series of individual political assassinations, which always hit their target, the massive revolutionary movements, where people often rise against each other because of misunderstanding and where a nation kills off its own children, while the enemy of the people watches from a secure shelter and sees to it that the people of the organization are destroyed. The movement punishes only those who are really responsible for the evil deed. Because of this the terroristic revolution is the only just form of a revolution.

For Morozov, then, the surgical precision with which terrorists were able to strike their targets was an effective response to a problem identified by Zaichnevsky and Argiropulo. While the authors of *Young Russia* justified the death of innocent bystanders as an unfortunate but necessary upshot of the injunction to eliminate the class enemy, the precise targeting of those responsible for oppression advocated by Morozov minimized collateral damage. As a result, terrorism was the most just and the "most convenient" form of revolutionary action.[54] Rather than terrorizing the people and creating a climate of fear and suspicion, terrorism effectively pursued the "final disorganization, demoralization and weakening of government for its actions of violence against freedom."[55] This revolutionary conception of terrorism in strategic terms, as well as the practice of terrorist violence it motivated, presented a great threat to the tsarist regime, which sought to assert its power by means of counterterrorism. In an attempt to protect tsarist sovereignty, the state represented terrorism as a threat to the security of the Russian people and defended autocratic domination as the only possible means to maintain order.

SOVEREIGN COUNTERTERRORISM

The writings of Konstantin Pobyedonostseff (1827–1907), adviser to the tsars, advocate of autocracy, and leading supporter of reactionary policies, provide a remarkable record of the tsarist regime's political rationale for counterterrorist policies.[56] In particular, Pobyedonostseff's work *Reflections of a Russian Statesman*, first published in Russian in 1896 and translated into English in 1898, illustrates the tsarist regime's strategic use of the rhetoric of terrorism for the purpose of asserting tsarist sovereignty. Pobyedonostseff rejected liberal values such as constitutional rights and liberties, democratic institutions, popular sovereignty, and secularism. Like the social revolutionaries, he regarded terrorism as an effect of the abnormal development of Russian social relations, but he fundamentally disagreed with the revolutionaries about what constituted abnormality. Appealing to the need to submit to a "law of life," he located the cause of terrorism in the disintegration of the "organic relations of public and family life" in Russia, which was brought about by the democratic propaganda of certain social groups.[57] While the revolutionaries regarded terrorism as a strategy to establish a democratic system appropriate for the natural constitution of the Russian people, Pobyedonostseff claimed that the Russian character called for another kind of government. "Among the falsest of political principles," he argued, "is the principle of the sovereignty of the people, the principle that all power issues from the people, and is based upon the national will."[58]

The reason that Pobyedonostseff opposed democracy was that he regarded the formation of the requisite national will as impossible in a heterogeneous country like Russia. For democracy to function, a single will and, consequently, a homogeneous population were necessary. Pobyedonostseff predicted that because of the racial mixture of Russia's population and the lack of assimilation of "separate races,"[59] a push for democracy would give rise to a system in which parliamentarians would pursue "personal ambition, vanity, and self interest." Tsarist autocracy would be replaced by a significantly inferior form of administrative autocracy, in which the national will would no longer be "embodied in the person of the sovereign, but in the person of the leader of a party; and privilege no longer belongs to an aristocracy of birth, but to a majority ruling in Parliament and controlling the State."[60] In Russia, then, the single will required for government could not be a national will but must be the personal will of a sovereign, which alone was able to synthesize competing interests "not alone by means of force, but by the equalisation of rights and relations under the unifying power."

> But Democracy has failed to settle these questions, and the instinct of nationality serves as a disintegrating element. To the supreme Parliament each race sends representatives, not of common political interests, but of racial instincts, of racial exasperation, and of racial hatred, both to the dominant race, to the sister races, and to the political institution which unites them all. Such is the unharmonious consequence of parliamentary government in composite States, as Austria, in our day, so vividly illustrates. Providence has preserved our Russia, with its heterogeneous racial composition, from like misfortunes. It is terrible to think of our condition if destiny had sent us the fatal gift—an All-Russian Parliament! But that will never be.[61]

It is perhaps unsurprising that a defender of autocracy would avoid the revolutionary discourse of class struggle and instead cast Russian social relations in terms of a war between races. But the discourse of race war played a crucial role in Pobyedonostseff's narrative because it allowed him, in classical Hobbesian fashion, to paint a picture of democratic government as a nightmarish war between races that could be avoided only by investing a sovereign with supreme power. In *Leviathan*, Hobbes famously argued that a condition without government would take the form of a war of all against all because human beings, who were relatively equal in their faculties of body and mind, shared equal hope to secure limited resources necessary for self-preservation. Since such a condition of war, however, made self-preservation difficult, Hobbes advocated the establishment of a sovereign whom individuals invested with the right to govern them. They promised to obey the sovereign in exchange for protection of their lives.[62] In the same vein, Pobyedonostseff defended tsarist sovereignty by resurrecting a discourse of race war, which, he argued, could be suppressed only by a sovereign ruler. As a consequence, he opposed the legal reforms of the 1860s, which, in his assessment, opened the door to an erosion of absolute tsarist sovereignty. This trend continued in "new theories and practices of legislators," who increasingly thought of law as a tool for "the regulation of external action, the preserver of mechanical equilibrium of the diverse operations of human activity in their juridical relations."[63] Such a formalistic understanding of law undermined its essential nature as the command and expression of sovereign will.

A different way of understanding Pobyedonostseff's argument is to read it as an expression of anxiety of a political actor whose firm mooring in a sovereign political rationality was challenged by newly emerging forms of biopower, in which laws ceased to be expressions of sovereign will and instead served as instruments to maintain conditions under which a free play of economic interests was possible. It is clear that Pobyedonostseff endorsed a notion of law as the manifestation of the will of the sovereign, which worked in the mode of prohibition, distinguished between the licit and the illicit, and had as its instrument the threat of punishment. In this context, the rhetoric of terrorism functioned as a means to assert and retain traditional techniques of sovereign power against the encroachment of new forms of biopower.

It is important at this point to underscore a critical difference between the operation of terrorism as a dispositif of the state in late imperial Russia and in revolutionary France. I argued in chapter 2 that the Thermidorian government during the French Revolution implemented a dispositif of terrorism in order to reconcile techniques of sovereign power and biopower within a single governmental regime. Terrorism allowed the state to move toward disciplinary and regulatory forms of governing the population while at the same time preserving the old sovereign right to kill in the face of perceived threats to the social body. By contrast, the tsarist regime in Russia did not seek to reconcile techniques of sovereign power and biopower but rather pursued a particular politics of naming certain practices *terrorism* to resist the subordination of tsarist sovereignty to other forces. This is evidenced by an explosion of emergency legislation passed under the pretext of fighting terrorism in the 1880s and 1890s.

The tsarist government had already begun to repeal crucial parts of the Great Reforms in the late 1860s, particularly in response to the attempted assassination of Tsar Alexander II by Dmitry Karakazov in 1866.[64] In addition, in response to the assassination of Tsar Alexander II by members of Narodnaia Volia in 1881, his successor, Alexander III, enacted the so-called Statute on Measures to Safeguard State Security and Public Order, better known as the Security Law, on August 14 of the same year.[65] The statute gave broad discretionary powers, such as summary search, arrest, imprisonment, exile, and trial by courts-martial, to government officials. Intended for a period of three years, the Security Law was continuously renewed until the collapse of tsarist autocracy. As the historian Nicholas Riasanovsky explains, the result was that "Russians lived under something like a partial state of martial law."[66] Under the pretext of public safety, the Security Law authorized measures of reinforced protection when "public order in an area is disturbed by criminal infractions against the existing state structure or against the security of individuals and their property or by the preparation of such acts," and it further justified extraordinary protection when "these infractions have put the local population into a disturbed state, making it necessary to take exceptional measures to urgently restore order."[67] Notice that the law did not define what counted as a disturbed state, or when precisely the disturbance was significant enough to warrant intervention. Thus, the law was sufficiently vague to expose virtually everyone to state violence. As the revolutionary Sergei Kravchinski, better known under his alias Stepniak, observed, the consequence was that "the merest suspicion led to arrest."

An address; a letter from a friend who had gone "among the people;" a word let fall by a lad of twelve who, from excess of fear, knew not what to reply, were sufficient to cast the suspected person into prison, where he languished for years and years, subjected to all the rigour of the Russian cellular system. . . . The sentences of the exceptional tribunal, which was simply a docile instrument in the hands of the Government, were of an incredible cruelty. Ten, twelve, fifteen years of hard labour were inflicted, for two or three speeches, made in private to a handful of working men, or for a single book read or lent. Thus what is freely done in every country in Europe was punished among us like murder. But not satisfied with these judicial atrocities, the Government, by infamous secret orders, augmented still more the sufferings of the political prisoners, so that in the House of Horrors—the central prison of Karkoff— several "revolts" took place among them in order to obtain equality of treatment with those condemned for common crimes.[68]

Stepniak's description draws our attention to the precarious legal status in which everyone, not only those who threatened the regime, found themselves. Under the pretext of fighting terrorism, the rights of all citizens were undermined. By means of exceptional tribunals and secret orders, the judicial system was turned into an instrument for the assertion and expansion of sovereign power.

At first, the regime's extraordinary measures appeared to be effective in shoring up tsarist sovereignty. But the geographic expanse of the Russian Empire meant that the regime had to rely on a massive bureaucratic apparatus for the exercise of sovereign power. Instead of implementing and strengthening the tsar's rule, however, local bureaucrats ate away at the central power of the sovereign. The German social theorist Max Weber's reports on the Russian Revolution of 1905 provide a remarkable description of this process.

Weber drew attention to the dilemma in which the tsarist government found itself. On the one hand, growing popular unrest forced the tsar to implement a series of liberal reforms. On the other hand, we saw earlier that the tsar's motivation for these reforms was not concern about the demands of the people or the public good. Rather, the government pursued its own interest, arguing that reforms imposed from above were less threatening to sovereign power than changes enforced through revolutionary violence from below. To retain absolute power, the government thus implemented reforms only nominally and suppressed any actual use of ostensibly granted rights. Weber vehemently criticized "the insincerity by which liberties are officially granted, and at the moment when one is about to avail oneself of them, are taken away again with the other hand."[69]

Weber further identified the key role terrorism played in the regime's justification of emergency legislation, bureaucratic expansion, and growth of administrative power. He observed that in order to conceal its attempt to "restore its lost 'prestige' by remorseless police tyranny," the government "blames the activities of terrorists for the police's insane rule of tyranny." The imposition of martial law, however, did not end terrorism. Rather, it "has caused these activities to *increase* and created sympathy for them."[70] In short, the government's efforts to contain and manage terrorism aggravated the problem and effectively escalated terrorism, thereby justifying ever more repressive measures of tsarist counterterrorism. In this situation, a number of possible solutions to the problem of terrorism came into view. Some representatives of the government called for real liberalization, democratization, and a program of capitalist development modeled on Western Europe as the solution to revolutionary terrorism.[71] For Weber, however, Russia's historical trajectory had led to social conditions that made such a project impossible.

> The imported ultramodern forces of big capitalism run up against a subterranean world of archaic peasant communism and unleash, for their part, such radically socialist feelings among their work-force (which they then meet with equally uncompromising "antifreedom" organizations of the most modern character) that one can scarcely imagine what kind of development is in store for Russia, even if—as is overwhelmingly probable—the "sanctity of property" ultimately gains the ascendancy over the Socialist Revolutionary peasant ideology.[72]

Weber here pointed to an incongruity between Russia's internal socioeconomic conditions and capitalist development abroad. As a consequence, the ruling classes' attempt to increase their wealth and influence by means of economic liberalization failed to recognize that socioeconomic conditions in Russia were not ripe for an import of capitalist elements. Rather than increasing productivity, the introduction of capitalist economic forces created tension between the economic interests of the ruling classes and the workforce. For Weber, socialist radicalization was thus made possible by a conflict between class interests exacerbated by economic interventions that were out of step with Russian development.

This kind of analysis was shared by the Bolsheviks, who argued that conflicting class interests and the continued domination of the working class required revolutionary social change. It is in this context that the Bolshevik position on terrorism comes into clear view. Leon Trotsky's and Vladimir Lenin's reflections on revolutionary violence are conspicuous examples in this regard and throw into sharp relief several themes that indicate an important transformation in the concept and practice of terrorism. These are (1) a view of terrorism as a means to resolve contradictions between class interest and material conditions; (2) a rejection of individual terrorism for pragmatic reasons; (3) an endorsement of terrorism understood as class struggle; and (4) the disappearance of the language of terrorism from official discourse. Before I turn to the leading Bolsheviks' discussion of terrorism, however, I must first reconstruct their assessment, articulated most clearly by Trotsky, of Russia's economic development as the background against which they evaluated terrorism as a means of social change.

BOLSHEVIK TERROR AS SOCIAL DEFENSE

In *History of the Russian Revolution*, first published in 1930, Trotsky presented perhaps the clearest assessment of the socioeconomic conditions that, in his view, made socialist revolution possible and necessary.[73] He argued that Russia's historical development was vastly different from that of capitalist countries such as England or France. As a result, Russian social relations were also dramatically different from those in Western Europe. Russia's uneven development compared with that of capitalist countries, however, did not prevent it from combining elements of capitalism pioneered abroad with Russian economic conditions. The paradoxical consequence of this uneven and combined development was that Russia implemented capitalist elements when socioeconomic progress in the country was not yet ready.[74] The result was significant incongruity between Russia's social relations and the development of its productive forces. Moreover, in the absence of an economically powerful capitalist class, Russian capitalists depended on foreign support. Foreign investors, however, relied on the autocratic regime of the tsar, which imposed heavy taxes on the peasants to pay its international debt and guarantee a return on foreign investment. Trotsky thus concluded that the Russian people were subjugated by a state that represented the interests of international capital. The appropriate response to this state of affairs was proletarian revolution, and it is in this context that Trotsky's position on terrorism comes into clear view.[75]

In his 1909 pamphlet "The Bankruptcy of Terrorism," Trotsky identified the incongruity between the proletariat's class interests and the material conditions of Russia's economic development as the background against which terrorism appeared as a useful strategy. The proletariat "had their thinking revolutionized before the economic development of the country had given birth to serious revolutionary classes."[76] The import of capitalist elements, which was made possible through foreign support, had made the wealth of the ruling classes independent of the Russian economy. As a consequence, the revolutionaries fell prey to the illusion that the state was "a purely external organ of coercion, having no roots in the social organization itself." This misconception led them to believe that the state was a merely "extraneous superstructure" that could be blasted "into the air with dynamite." The "very idea of destroying absolutism by mechanical means" was, for Trotsky, a product of a certain misalignment of revolutionary ideas and revolutionary forces . It derived from a failure to recognize the necessity of a revolutionary class to bring about social change.[77]

Moreover, Trotsky rejected individual terrorism such as that the social revolutionaries had practiced during the second half of the nineteenth century. In his 1911 polemic "The Marxist Position on Individual Terrorism," he cited three reasons for this opposition. First, he argued that individual acts of violence against representatives of the ruling classes led only to a temporary disruption of the system, which absorbed momentary disturbances by increasing repression. Further, individual representatives of the regime who fell victim to terrorist assassinations were quickly replaced, and the machine continued unabated. Individual terrorism was thus rather inconsequential for the ruling class as such, even if it was undesirable for some of its members. Second, Trotsky argued that individual terrorism was incoherent as a tactic of class war because the use of individual terrorism, while intended for the liberation of the proletariat, achieved the opposite effect: it not only was unable to match the destructive power of the state but also led to increased police repression, thereby compounding the oppression of the proletariat. Third, Trotsky argued that "individual terror is inadmissible precisely because it *belittles the role of the masses in their own consciousness*, reconciles them to their powerlessness, and turns their eyes and hopes toward a great avenger and liberator who some day will come and accomplish the mission."[78] By establishing what Trotsky later denounced as a "'hero' cult" and presenting the acts of heroic individuals as sufficient for social change, individual terrorism had a detrimental psychological effect and undermined the proletariat's disposition for self-organization.[79] Trotsky maintained that "the anarchist prophets of the 'propaganda of the deed'" had proved that the more spectacular the acts of individual terrorism, the more they encouraged the proletariat to abdicate its responsibilities in the class struggle.[80] Similarly, Trotsky remarked in response to the assassination of Bolshevik leader Sergei Kirov ordered by Stalin in 1934, "Individual terrorism in its very essence is bureaucratism turned inside out. Bureaucratism has no confidence in the masses, and endeavors to substitute itself for the masses. Terrorism behaves in the same manner; it wants to make the masses happy without asking their participation."[81] Therefore, individual terrorism was opposed to the aim of revolution, which Trotsky understood as the "direct interference of the masses in historical events."[82]

Notice, though, that Trotsky's rejection of individual terrorism was not motivated by moral considerations. In fact, he denounced the "bought-and-paid-for moralists who, in response to any terrorist act, make solemn declarations about the 'absolute value' of human life" while readily sending people to war in the name of national honor.[83] But neither did he want to minimize the feeling of vengeance that drove people to individual acts of terrorism. Rather, he claimed, "If we oppose terrorist acts, it is only because *individual* revenge does not satisfy us."

> The account we have to settle with the capitalist system is too great to be presented to some functionary called a minister. To learn to see all the crimes against humanity, all the indignities to which the human body and spirit are subjected, as the twisted outgrowths and expressions of the existing social system, in order to direct all our energies into a collective struggle against this system—that is the direction in which the burning desire for revenge can find its highest moral satisfaction.[84]

Trotsky's objection to individual terrorism was based entirely on its inability to create the conditions of its own success. That is, because individual terrorism only momentarily disrupted the system, increased repression of the proletariat, and alienated the working class from its revolutionary task, it could not accomplish the goal of proletarian revolution—namely, the absolute destruction of capitalism and all its supporting structures.

This left open the possibility of a different form of terrorism as a collective strategy. Trotsky admitted that if terrorism meant "all the activities of the proletariat directed against the class enemy's interests," then terrorism would essentially be synonymous with class struggle.[85] Understood in this way, as an institutionalized system of proletarian mass insurrection, terrorism was not only acceptable but also necessary.[86] This, however, was a rather unusual notion of terrorism that broke with accepted use at the time. In addition, the Bolshevik rise to power in the revolution of 1917 made the concept of terrorism, a term primarily associated with antistate violence of the social revolutionaries, ill suited to describe Bolshevik state violence against the class enemy. With their integration into the Bolshevik state apparatus, the preferred term to describe practices of revolutionary violence previously known as *terrorism* became *terror*.

Lenin's evaluation of the necessity of terror for the class struggle illustrates these claims. For Lenin, the question of terror was an issue of tactics rather than principle, and its usefulness as a strategy of class struggle depended on concrete conditions of proletarian revolution. Thus, he wrote in "Draft Programme of Our Party" in 1899, "We will make the reservation that, in our own personal opinion, terror is not advisable as a means of struggle at the present moment, that the Party (as a party) must renounce it (until there occurs a change of circumstances that might lead to a change of tactics) and concentrate all its energy on organisation and the regular delivery of literature."[87] Such a change of tactics was inaugurated by the 1905 revolution. In a series of texts written that year, Lenin observed that "individual terrorism . . . is gradually becoming a thing of the past," being replaced by "military operations *together with the people.*"[88] Echoing Trotsky's rejection of individual acts of terrorism, Lenin maintained that the success of revolution depended on a proletarian mass movement. As a consequence, he now endorsed an understanding of terror as armed struggle perpetrated by a revolutionary army. Although he warned of "disorderly, unorganised and petty terrorist acts" of a handful of heroic individuals, which would "only scatter and squander our forces," Lenin insisted that "to launch attacks under favourable circumstances is not only every revolutionary's right, but his plain duty."[89] Once a conception of terror as a necessary means of proletarian revolution was in place, the stage was set for an incorporation of revolutionary terror against the class enemy into the state apparatus.

In "The State and Revolution," written in the summer before the Bolshevik takeover of political power in the October Revolution of 1917, Lenin's endorsement of revolutionary terror as a means of class struggle transformed into a demand for state terror against the bourgeoisie. Criticizing common misreadings of the Marxist account of the relationship between the state and proletarian revolution, Lenin presented a detailed reconstruction of what he took to be the correct interpretation of Marx's views on this matter. He began by offering a view of the state as the product of a struggle between classes, in which one class relied on the state to oppress another class. The state was only apparently a means of maintaining order; it actually served to legitimize, regulate, and perpetuate relations of domination. The state, for Lenin, was thus properly understood as a "special coercive force," that is, the organized use of force of one class against another, and it was made necessary by irreconcilable class antagonisms that threatened the interests of the oppressor.[90] As a consequence, freedom and equality required, in Friedrich Engels's famous dictum, the withering away (*Absterben*, dying away) of the state.[91]

Lenin took care to lay out the complexity and protracted nature of this process. The transition from capitalism to communism could not happen in one fell swoop; rather, the proletariat must first seize state power in a socialist revolution. Although this constituted the abolition of the bourgeois state, the state apparatus remained in modified form as an organ of oppression in the hands of the proletariat. In this first or lower phase of communist society, Lenin argued, the state persisted as a "'special coercive force' for the suppression of the bourgeoisie by the proletariat."[92] He continued:

> The state is a special organisation of force: it is an organisation of violence for the suppression of some class. What class must the proletariat suppress? Naturally, only the exploiting class, i.e., the bourgeoisie. The working people need the state only to suppress the resistance of the

exploiters, and only the proletariat can direct this suppression, can carry it out. For the proletariat is the only class that is consistently revolution-ary, the only class that can unite all the working and exploited people in the struggle against the bourgeoisie, in completely removing it.[93]

The state apparatus therefore could not wither away completely until the suppression of the bourgeoisie was no longer necessary. To be more pre-cise, Lenin argued that the state disappeared when "a *special force* for the suppression of a particular class" was no longer needed because it was re-placed by "the suppression of the oppressors by the *general force* of the majority of the people."[94] That is, once the state actually represented so-ciety in its entirety, it ceased to be an organ of class oppression and thus a state. Yet although the abolition of the state was the ultimate goal of proletarian revolution, Lenin was clear that the material conditions of the transition from capitalism to communism required a temporary or tran-sient proletarian state in order to achieve this aim. Because communist society emerged out of bourgeois, capitalist society, it must gradually transform the institutions of capitalist oppression until they were ren-dered unnecessary. In this process, Lenin argued, the state was of critical importance because it "first welds together the class that wages a revolu-tionary struggle against capitalism—the proletariat, and enables it to crush, smash to atoms, wipe off the face of the earth the bourgeois, even the republican-bourgeois, state machine, the standing army, the police and the bureaucracy and to substitute for them a *more* democratic state machine, but a state machine nevertheless, in the shape of armed work-ers who proceed to form a militia involving the entire population."[95] Because the emergence of communist society required the suppression of the bourgeoisie by the proletariat and because the oppression of one class by another was the state, a proletarian state was a "necessary *step* for thoroughly cleaning society of all the infamies and abominations of cap-italist exploitation, *and for further progress.*" It was the only means by which the working class could "exercise control over the parasites, the sons of the wealthy, the swindlers and other 'guardians of capitalist tradition.' "[96]

Lenin underscored the necessity of actual violence against the class enemy in "Letter to American Workers" of 1918. He rejected criticisms of the destruction and terror deployed by the Bolsheviks as hypocritical and pedantic, and he dismissed the notion that the class struggle could be overcome by agreement, collaboration, and reconciliation as "philistine utopia." For Lenin, the class struggle against the bourgeoisie was a struggle for the existence of the proletariat; it was a civil war that was "inconceivable without the severest destruction, terror, and the restriction of formal democracy in the interest of this war."[97] Moreover, the responsibility for violence was not the proletariat's. Rather, Lenin argued, the bourgeoisie had forgotten that "terror was just and legitimate when the bourgeoisie resorted to it for their own benefit against feudalism."

> Terror became monstrous and criminal when the workers and poor peasants dared to use it against the bourgeoisie! Terror was just and legitimate when used for the purpose of substituting one exploiting minority for another exploiting minority. Terror became monstrous and criminal when it began to be used for the purpose of overthrowing *every* exploiting minority, to be used in the interests of the vast actual majority, in the interests of the proletariat and semi-proletariat, the working class and the poor peasants![98]

Lenin's analysis here is interesting not only for its explicit advocacy of terror as state policy but also for its clear articulation of state terror as a means of social defense. Lenin clearly situated Bolshevik state terror in a history of war between classes, in which the state had been an instrument of domination of an oppressive minority against the proletariat. The state was nothing other than the organized use of force for the oppression of one class by another, and this purely formal understanding of the state allowed Lenin to call for the proletariat's seizure of state power as a means of warfare in its struggle for existence against the bourgeoisie. Moreover, his emphasis on the transience of a proletarian state throws into relief his understanding of the proletariat as the universal subject of political representation. The state was necessary as long as there was a capitalist class to be suppressed, and it would wither away as soon as genuine freedom and equality were established through the universalization of the proletariat and the elimination of class society. Even though Lenin thus justified state terror as a means to suppress the class enemy, it is worth emphasizing that the aim of Bolshevik state terror was the creation of communist society, purged of all capitalist enemies that threatened it. The attempt to create a new society of communist individuals by means of terror thus suggests that Bolshevik state terror had a primarily productive rather than repressive function.

Such an interpretation of Bolshevik terror might seem preposterous or cynical, but some contemporaries advanced it. The Bolshevik revolutionary and theorist Nikolai Bukharin, for instance, noted, "Proletarian coercion in all its forms, from executions to labour service, is, however paradoxical this may sound, a method of creating a communist mankind from the human material of the capitalist epoch."[99] Further, the historian Peter Holquist insists that Soviet terror served as a means of population politics.[100] It played a key role in the engineering of a homogeneous sociopolitical body, whose internal enemies it prophylactically removed to ensure the health and productivity of the population. Policies such as administrative resettlement, de-Cossackification, dekulakization, anti-insurgency campaigns, and operations against counterrevolutionaries and anti-Bolshevik agents of the state were ultimately efforts to "foster an idealized image of the politicosocial body by excising those elements determined to be harmful."[101]

This interpretation of state terror as a form of social defense against society's unhealthy and dangerous—that is, nonproletarian—elements also operated in official state discourse and practice. Consider as an example the following description of the purpose of concentration camps by Rychkov, head of the Tambov and Borisoglebsk camps. In response to demands that the class enemy be completely annihilated, Rychkov responded:

> That is an entirely incorrect error, we've heard it repeatedly. It wouldn't take long to shoot them—unlike the bandits, we'd have enough cartridges. But to turn our recent, inveterate enemies into good, strong friends— that's what we need to do. Of course, if any barons or other wealthy sorts ended up there, they'd soon be a head shorter. Also, if a fervent, murdering bandit does not respond to political enlightenment, insists on his own way, his song won't last very long. But we must have an absolutely different approach for those who fell into error and deeply repent. Not for nothing did we, on orders from above, release an entire echelon back to their homes. . . . No, we destroy some, others—those who are able— we reeducate, turn to our side. Such are the conclusions we've come to in our camp.[102]

Yet while it may seem that for Rychkov, concentration camps were not extermination camps but spaces of discrimination and correction, where redeemable individuals were isolated from incorrigible individuals and subjected to reform and reeducation through labor, it is worth noting that he considered certain groups inherently incorrigible and ineligible for correction. Nobles and the wealthy, for instance, were subject to prompt execution upon their arrival at correction camps because their incorrigibility was deemed inherent in their class identity. A secret police periodical from 1918 affirmed this point, declaring that "we are not waging war against individual persons."

> We are exterminating the bourgeoisie as a class. During investigation, do not look for evidence that the accused acted in deed or word against Soviet power. The first questions that you ought to put are: To what class does he belong? What is his origin? What is his education or profession? And it is these questions that ought to determine the fate of the accused. In this lies the significance and essence of the Red Terror.[103]

These claims cast doubt on a view held by some historians, as well as the Bolsheviks themselves, that the Red Terror is distinguishable from its Nazi counterpart by virtue of its nontotalizing nature.[104] Although it is true that the Bolsheviks, unlike the Nazis, did not justify state violence as a means of social defense against individuals who were said to threaten the purity of the race, the logic of exclusion was functionally identical: at stake was the protection of the proletariat against its class enemy. Despite important differences with respect to the particular identity in reference to which enmity was defined (the proletariat as a social class versus the Aryan race as an ostensibly biological category), as well as concrete means of extermination (mass murder, correction, reeducation), both Bolshevik and Nazi terror served as mechanisms of social defense.

It is because of this similarity between Nazi and Bolshevik terror that Kautsky was able to maintain that the bourgeoisie "appears in the Soviet Republic as a special human species, whose characteristics are ineradicable. Just as a negro remains a negro, a Mongol a Mongol, wherever he shows up and however he dresses, so the bourgeois remains a bourgeois even if he becomes a pauper or lives off his work."[105] An understanding of state terror as a "supreme measure of social defense" in "the final, decisive struggle" against "anti-Soviet elements" also explains why the Bolsheviks abandoned the language of terrorism in favor of the slogan Red Terror.[106] On the one hand, the necessity of state terror against the class enemy ran counter to a powerful revolutionary tradition that regarded terrorism as acts of individual violence against the state. On the other hand, terrorism became increasingly understood as violence intended to "intimidate the opponent through the violation [*Vergewaltigung*] of the defenseless."[107] This led to the use of the language of terrorism by critics of state violence. As a consequence, Bolsheviks reactivated the old Jacobin notion of terror to describe their use of terror as a necessary means of proletarian self-defense. As we saw at the beginning of this chapter, Lenin explicitly situated Bolshevik terror in continuity with the French Jacobins and insisted that Jacobin terror "has not become obsolete to this day, except that it must be applied to the revolutionary class of the twentieth century, to the workers and semi-proletarians. To this class, the enemies of the people in the twentieth century are not the monarchs, but the landowners and capitalists as a class."[108]

The analogy posited by Lenin is, however, misleading. For Lenin, Jacobin and Bolshevik terror differed only in the social identity of the enemy but were otherwise identical practices of violence. In both cases, various forms of state violence, such as executions, detention, and banishment, were used to protect the people against elements that threatened its existence. But the same actions do not constitute identical practices. It matters for an evaluation of terrorism as a practice that we are dealing with different revolutionary subjects who were motivated by different political aims and, consequently, made sense of violence in different ways. Violence that served bourgeois interests and the establishment of liberal rule in the French Revolution is not the same practice as violence as a means of class war waged by the proletariat in its effort to secure a communist state. The meaning and function of these conducts were characterized by different modes of understanding, which arose from the emergence of biopolitical rationalities under very different social, political, historical, economic, and cultural circumstances. These provided the frameworks within which similar forms of violence became distinct political practices.

In the French Revolution, terrorism emerged as the name for Robespierre's system of government, which relied on the use of state violence against a monarch whose power resulted from conquest and invasion. A process of conceptual transformation that gave rise to doxastic and identarian notions of terrorism made possible its integration into the institutional and discursive apparatus of the state. By representing opponents of liberal values as threats to the new bourgeois republic and, therefore, terrorists, the state was able to justify its old sovereign right to kill in the name of defending society. In Russia, by contrast, the development of a dispositif of terrorism followed a different and, indeed, inverse historical trajectory. First, the transformation of a historical discourse of race war into a revolutionary discourse of class struggle formed the political rationality within which social revolutionaries articulated a theory of terrorism as a tactic of class war. Second, the revolutionaries had access to a new strategic concept of terrorism that differed significantly from earlier charismatic, systemic, doxastic, and identarian notions of terrorism that had emerged during the French Revolution. After a period of tsarist counterterrorism, which resulted in an increase rather than the elimination of terrorism, the Bolshevik Revolution and the seizure of state power by the Bolsheviks led to an appropriation and modification of revolutionary strategic terrorism by the state, where it functioned as a mechanism of social defense against the class enemy. Notice, however, that even though terror here became an institutionalized state practice, it was still understood in strategic terms as a tactic of class war.

In sum, then, the historical development of terrorism from the French Revolution to Bolshevik Russia did not come full circle but rather spiraled away from its point of emergence without ever returning to or coinciding with it. Rather than straightforwardly identifying Bolshevik state terror as the systemic terrorism of a nation-state, we must understand it as strategic terrorism adapted to the needs, if you will, of a class-state. The taking up of older concepts and behaviors in a new social and historical context by different political subjects, as well as the co-optation of these behaviors for different political projects, effects a continuous displacement and reworking of meanings and practices of terrorism. This chapter has traced this spiral movement in the conceptual and political development of terrorism after the French Revolution and over the course of the nineteenth century, which made possible a new practice of state terrorism in Bolshevik Russia.

4

TERRORISM AND COLONIALISM

W e saw in chapters 2 and 3 that the French Revolution, in particular the Reign of Terror and the Thermidorian Reaction, led to social, political, and economic turmoil in France and other European countries. With regard to France's internal political situation, the stabilization of liberalism as the dominant political program, accomplished for a brief period through the Thermidorian Reaction, was interrupted by Napoléon's coup of 18 Brumaire, his establishment of a military dictatorship and empire, and the Bourbon Restoration of 1814; resumed in the revolutions of 1848; reversed by Louis-Napoléon's coup in 1851 and his self-proclamation as the emperor of France; and revived in the Paris Commune of 1871. France suffered an economic downturn in the first decades of the nineteenth century that was more serious than the troubles that had led to the Revolution of 1789 and spurred the rise of a large and rebellious underclass.[1] With regard to foreign politics, the fall of the French Empire in 1814 severely compromised France's position among the great European powers, and the country's position in the Concert of Europe was tenuous.[2] In this situation, colonization emerged as the ideal solution to France's internal and external troubles. As a measure of foreign policy, colonization promised to secure France's reputation as one of Europe's leading powers.[3] As a means of domestic politics, it appeared as an efficient means to rid French society of its troublesome and unruly elements.[4]

Nowhere is the central role of colonization as a means of national salvation more evident than in French debates about the so-called Algerian
Question in the first half of the nineteenth century. Consider, for instance,
the French socialist politician and historian Louis Blanc's plea for conquering Algeria as a "glorious necessity" intended to purge French society
of those elements that constituted a threat to the social body.[5] The advantage of colonization, Blanc argued, was not only that it extended French
influence to North Africa, thus making the Mediterranean French and
expanding France's sphere of economic relations, but also, and more
important, it opened Algeria "to the overflow of paupers that threatens our
European societies with speedy and deadly inundation."[6] For Blanc, the
resettling of the indigent part of French society in its colonies directly benefited the life and health of the social body. But French society also profited
indirectly because Algeria was "the precious ground on which trial might
be made without danger of those attempts at social renovation, which the
habits, prejudices, and political and industrial complications of our old
Europe cause to appear so menacing."[7] On Blanc's view, in other words,
the colonization of Algeria was necessary for France's internal well-being
and external reputation. Similarly, the conservative liberal François Guizot
argued that colonial domination was necessary to create the conditions of
possibility for ridding France of its underclass and resettling it in Algeria.
But since Algeria's native population did not voluntarily relinquish the territory France desired for its settlements, "the effective conquest of Algeria
had become the condition of our establishment at Algiers and on the
coast."[8] In this lens, colonial war against a foreign population appeared as
a precondition of the internal social defense of French society.

A century after the conquest of Algeria, colonial history appeared to
repeat itself. Confronted with a growing nationalist movement that demanded Algerian independence through armed resistance, the French colonial state relied on many of the measures of colonial war pioneered in the
nineteenth century in the name of maintaining public order and defending society against what it described as acts of terrorism. According to the
historical sociologist Marnia Lazreg, French state violence in Algeria during the Algerian Revolution of 1954–1962 was a "repetition of nineteenth-
century colonial history."[9] Lazreg argues that the systematic use of
violence against terrorist acts perpetrated by the Front de Libération Nationale (FLN, National Liberation Front) was informed by the theory of

revolutionary war that French military officers had elaborated in colonial wars in the mid-twentieth century, notably in French Indochina (1945–1954). But it was the history of colonialism in Algeria, for Lazreg, that provided the technologies of revolutionary warfare, such as torture and internment. Moreover, she argues that the colonial army's military tactics served to establish a "climate of terror" that was a "reenactment of a historical precedent," namely, the revolutionary Reign of Terror of the late eighteenth century.[10] This interpretation of colonial violence as a reenactment of the Great Terror leads Lazreg to characterize the actions of the colonial state in Algeria as state terrorism and torture as one of its primary techniques. On her view, the colonial state's portrayal of nationalist violence as terrorism was a pretext intended to justify state terrorism as counterterrorism.

Lazreg's analysis not only mobilizes a systemic concept of terrorism, according to which terror was a principle of French colonial government, but also suggests a certain continuity among the Jacobin Reign of Terror, nineteenth-century French imperialism, and French counterterrorism during the Algerian Revolution. Although she is certainly correct to emphasize the similarity of measures, tactics, and devices of state violence, too narrow a focus on continuity obfuscates important differences between nineteenth- and twentieth-century colonial violence.[11] Specifically, new modes of understanding and justifying state violence led to the transformation of the dispositif of colonial war of the nineteenth century into a dispositif of terrorism in the twentieth, even though both shared phenomenal similarities and were embedded within a biopolitical rationality that permitted and required state violence as a means of social defense.

To develop this argument, I first reconstruct in some detail what I call, following Alexis de Tocqueville, the nineteenth-century *science of colonial war*, that is, a systematic theory for the military subjugation and domination of Algeria's indigenous population. I then examine the apparent reactivation of practices of colonial war during the infamous Battle of Algiers, a military conflict between Algerian nationalists and French forces in the Algerian capital from late 1956 to late 1957. By mapping the conceptual space of terrorism during this period, I show that a reduction of nineteenth-century colonial war and twentieth-century counterrevolutionary war to state terrorism obscures the political salience of the concept of terrorism that circulated at the time. The category of

state terrorism not only fails to adequately track the way in which terrorism was understood in twentieth-century colonial Algeria but also is
unable to take account of various political practices and strategies a
complex dispositif of terrorism made possible.

An archival focus on how seemingly constant methods, devices, tactics,
and strategies of state violence were understood reveals that in the
nineteenth century, state violence against Algeria's indigenous population,
authorized by the science of colonial war, was justified as necessary for the
improvement and regeneration of French society. The elimination of external enemies was thus understood as a precondition for internal social defense. In the twentieth century, by contrast, state violence was implemented
under different circumstances and characterized by different modes of explanation, even though it continued to serve the purpose of social defense.
Rather than subjugation of a foreign enemy, the defense of society required
the maintenance of internal order, which was threatened by a nationalist
movement that sought Algerian independence from France. Moreover,
Algerian combatants fought what the French regarded as a new, irregular
kind of war, whose suppression required equally new and irregular antisub-
versive strategies. This understanding was reflected in the concept of
terrorism that French military officers articulated during the Battle of Algiers, namely, as a new kind of war. I call this *polemic terrorism*. The elaboration of a polemic notion of terrorism facilitated and indeed required the
preservation of techniques of colonial war in a dispositif of terrorism. By
making tactics and operations of state violence the primary focus of analysis, we thus see that these older strategies did not have the same strategic
function in the twentieth century. As techniques that were understood in
terms of counterterrorism, they now allowed the colonial state to use violence against its own subjects. This new mode of understanding older techniques, as well as the new tactical role to which it gave rise, also generated
new practices of resistance against the colonial state that Algerian nationalists justified as forms of self-defense in a war started by France in 1830.

THE SCIENCE OF COLONIAL WAR

The political situation in late eighteenth- and early nineteenth-century
France was fertile ground for a political push for colonization. Under

conditions of internal and external social and political upheaval, colonization was portrayed, on the one hand, as a political necessity intended to restore France to its rightful position among the great European powers. On the other hand, it was seen as a social necessity and the only means to halt the decay of France and the degeneration of its population. The occasion for invading Algiers came in 1827 in the form of a diplomatic incident between the dey of Algiers and the French consul. The casus belli was the so-called *l'affaire de l'éventail* (the "fan affair" or "fly whisk incident"), in which the dey of Algiers allegedly hit the French consul with a fly whisk over unpaid debts France had owed since 1799. After a three-year blockade of the port of Algiers, which hurt French merchants but was skillfully evaded by the dey, France invaded Algiers and set up a civil administration. French military forces began to acquire land and offered subsidies to European settlers. A veritable land rush ensued in the years immediately after the invasion, and by 1848, almost 110,000 Europeans, mostly poor farmers from southern Europe, had settled in Algeria. In 1834, France annexed Algeria's Mediterranean regions and placed them under the control of the Ministry of War. In 1848, Article 109 of the Constitution of the Second Republic (1848–1851) formally declared Algeria "French territory" that was to be "ruled by particular laws until a special law placed them under the regime of the present constitution."[12] Algeria was officially French, albeit under a special statute, and its inhabitants were French subjects.

From the 1830s on, however, the French presence in Algeria was threatened by armed indigenous resistance. There was widespread popular opposition to colonization, and indigenous leaders inflicted several significant losses on the colonial army. In France, growing concerns over the costs of colonization emerged and sometimes even led to calls for abandoning Algeria. But withdrawal from North Africa did not just pose a threat to France's political status in Europe and the world; colonization was also an existential question of national salvation. As a supreme necessity for the *salut public* of the country, colonization had to be achieved by all means necessary. Ending indigenous resistance and subjugating Algeria's native population were thus of utmost priority. To this end, the French colonial army elaborated and implemented a science of colonial war, that is, a systematic theory of military techniques adequate to the task.[13]

Alexis de Tocqueville's writings on Algeria provide one of the clearest statements of the science of colonial war. In addition to being a notable political thinker, Tocqueville was a prominent parliamentarian and had significant political influence as one of the chief experts on the Algerian Question. His assessment of colonization is not only symptomatic of widely held beliefs among French politicians across the political spectrum but also a prime example of an understanding of colonialism and a concomitant justification of colonial war as mechanisms of social defense.

Tocqueville's fierce defense of colonialism in his writings on Algeria is perhaps surprising in light of his admiration of American democracy, but he was not the first liberal to take a stand for imperialism and colonization. In *On Liberty*, for instance, John Stuart Mill advocated despotism as an appropriate form of government for "barbarians, provided the end be their improvement and the means justified by actually effecting that end."[14] In contrast to Mill's rather paternalistic defense of colonization for the benefit of the colonized, however, Tocqueville regarded colonization in general and the colonization of Algeria in particular as necessary for France's internal well-being and external reputation. Specifically, colonies served as spaces for the settlement of the poor, unruly, and criminal in an effort to improve and regenerate the French social body.

Tocqueville offered a particularly clear statement of this idea in an appendix to *On the Penitentiary System in the United States and Its Application in France*, in which he considered penal colonies to claim that the purpose of having colonies was to protect society from its dangerous members. He argued that the widespread support of penal deportation among French politicians and the public was due to the social situation in France, "where the number of criminals is on the rise and among which already breeds a people of delinquents." In these conditions, penal colonies had the great advantage that "of all punishments, that of deportation is the only one that, without being cruel, delivers society of the presence of the criminal." In contrast to prisoners who remained a threat to society after having served their sentence or upon escaping from prison, the criminal who was deported hardly ever returned to France. "With him," Tocqueville maintained, "a fertile germ of disorders and new crimes is taken away."[15] For Tocqueville, then, deportation offered permanent protection from criminal elements, who threatened social order and security.

There is plausible evidence that Tocqueville regarded settler colonies as functionally related to penal colonies. For instance, he considered settler colonies in his 1833 text "Some Ideas About What Prevents the French from Having Good Colonies," which he had written for inclusion in *On the Penitentiary System*. His coauthor, Gustave de Beaumont, deemed "Some Ideas" outside the scope of the analysis offered in *On the Penitentiary System* and published the majority of Tocqueville's text in the latter's *Oeuvres complètes* in the section on the journey to America. However, a two-page summary of "Some Ideas" appeared in an appendix to the first French edition of *On the Penitentiary System*.[16] In addition, Tocqueville explicitly connected his discussion of settler colonies in "Some Ideas" to the problem of penal colonies, whose foundation, he argued, was even more vital than the establishment of settler colonies. Thus, while Tocqueville considered penal colonies detention sites for France's criminal population, settler colonies were to be populated with the country's indigent classes. Indeed, Tocqueville's characterization of European settlers paints a picture of destitute people taken from the underclass of society. In his "Second Report on Algeria" of 1847, for example, he variously described Algeria's European population as indigents "who, even in Europe, were among the rabble of the population;"[17] who were "from the dregs of European society, that their vices equaled their misery;"[18] and who were a class that was "less regular in its mores, less stable in its habits" than the French population in France.[19]

From the vantage point of French society, colonization was thus instrumental in ridding France of the delinquency and pauperism of its lower classes. But this internal regeneration of French society by means of colonization required the subjugation of indigenous populations, who were cast as inferior races reflecting an earlier stage of social development. Considerations of class and race thus converged in a dispositif of social defense that justified the conquest of foreign races as a means to improve French society by eliminating dangerous elements within.

Tocqueville argued that the successful establishment of a colony in Algeria required an appropriate form of government over the country's indigenous peoples.[20] Adequate knowledge of the territory and its resources, climate, and population was thus central to determine "the true and natural limits of our domination in Africa, what must be the normal state of our forces there for a long time to come, the instruments we need and the appropriate form of administration for the peoples who live there, what we may hope of them, and what it is wise to fear."[21] In his

early writings on Algeria, Tocqueville argued that the colonial administration of Algeria required tolerance and a plurality of legal and political
systems for different races in hopes of bringing about the amalgamation
of Arabs and French settlers. The safest way "to make French the country
around us," he argued, was to follow the rules and customs of the natives
for a time so as to earn their respect and slowly intermix the French
and Algerian populations.[22] After 1841, however, Tocqueville's writings
reflect a striking change of position. Convinced that the native population's fierce resistance to colonization made amalgamation impossible,
Tocqueville now called for military domination and a strategy of colonial
war that enabled France to "replace the former inhabitants with the conquering race."[23]

Tocqueville's turn to advocacy of military domination was precipitated
by a journey to Algeria in 1841, during which he observed interactions
between European settlers and the native population. What he saw was
not peaceful cohabitation that would ultimately lead to amalgamation of
the races but resistance, conflict, and violence on both sides. He concluded that under such conditions, France's military superiority was "almost useless," serving "to conquer, but not to retain under our laws" the
native population.[24] The challenge of colonization, he thus argued upon
his return to France, lay in the fact that France "faced not a real army, but
the population itself."[25] Because "the quarrel is no longer between governments, but between races," native resistance could not be crushed by traditional means of warfare.[26] If France wanted to ensure that European
settlers would find "a perfect image of their homeland" in Algeria, constant
and active intervention was necessary.[27] The concrete forms intervention
had to take, he further maintained, were determined by the characteristics
of the indigenous population.

Accordingly, the cornerstone of the science of colonial war was a hierarchy
of races that prescribed concrete techniques of colonial government and
served to justify violence against ostensibly inferior indigenous races. Already in his "First Letter on Algeria" of 1837, Tocqueville had offered a
theory of social stages as the basis for classifying the civilizational status
of the two native races, Kabyles and Arabs. He argued that Kabyles, sedentary Berbers of the Atlas Mountains, were the most European of the
Algerian races, even though they were at an early stage of social development.[28] On a purely physiological register, they looked more European,

with light skin, green eyes, and cranial measurements that approximated those of the European race. This physical similarity found social expression in the fact that Kabyles were sedentary, cultivated land, had houses made of brick and mortar, and lived in monogamous relationships. Accordingly, Tocqueville argued that Kabyles were more advanced than and, therefore, preferable to Algeria's Arab population. Tocqueville contrasted Kabyles with Arabs or Muslims, terms he used interchangeably throughout his writings. He considered Arabs a race of "singular savages" who failed to "resemble civilized man entirely."[29] He continued,

> Like all half-savage peoples, they honor power and force above all else. Putting little stock in the life of men, and scorning trade and the arts, like those others, they love war, pomp, and tumult, above all; defiant and credulous, subject sometimes to an unreflective enthusiasm and sometimes to an *exaggerated* despondency, they fall and pick themselves up again without trouble, often excessive in their actions and always more willing to feel than to think.[30]

The civilizational state of the Arab race, Tocqueville argued in the 1841 "Essay," corresponded to a stage of "social development very much like that which took place in Europe at the end of the Middle Ages."[31] This backwardness was said to find expression in lifestyle: Arabs were more nomadic, lived in tents, and cultivated only some of the land, using the rest as pastures for their herds. Even the architecture in Arab parts of Algeria, Tocqueville observed during his 1841 journey, "depicts needs and mores."

> The architecture here does not merely result from the heat of the climate, it also marvelously depicts the social and political state of the Muslim and oriental populations: polygamy, the sequestration of women, the absence of any public life, a tyrannical and suspicious government that forces one to conceal one's life and keep all affections within the family.[32]

Tocqueville's discussion of Algerian races is characterized by three noteworthy features. First, it exhibits a distinctly modern, biological concept of race in terms of development. Briefly, the formation of biology as a science in the nineteenth century gave rise to a new understanding of organisms as functional systems. In contrast to the structural ordering of living beings typical of natural history, the science of biology was organized around processes of life, such as respiration, reproduction, and circulation. These functional processes could be measured in a way that allowed for the identification of normal development. On this view, human beings formed a species by virtue of resemblances in biological functions. But just as it was possible for individuals to deviate from normal development (as, for instance, in cases of madness or delinquency), a new biological style of reasoning also led to a new notion of race as a marker of development.[33] By introducing the concept of development, Tocqueville was thus able to (1) present Algerian races as developmentally delayed in comparison with a European norm; (2) maintain the unity of the human species while insisting on the inferiority of non-Europeans; (3) characterize inferiority as a temporary condition on the path to civilization; and (4) justify colonial war not only as the appropriate form of government over inferior races but also as a civilizing instrument.[34]

Second, the biological concept of race as a marker of development allowed for the persistence of an older understanding of races as communities united by cultural, religious, and linguistic practices, which were interpreted as visible signs of biological inferiority. This explains the equivalence of Arabs and Muslims in Tocqueville's writings, as well as in colonial legal discourse. At first, colonial law established distinct categories for Muslims, Arabs, indigenous people, and Jewish Algerians. Between 1830 and 1848, this legal classification led to a division of the country into three administrative territories: the civil territory, inhabited mostly by Europeans and ruled by French common law; the mixed territory, populated by Europeans and Muslims; and the so-called Arab territories, inhabited by indigenous peoples and placed under the so-called *régime de sabre* (government of the sword or military rule). The legal category "Arab" specifically referred to people in territories under *régime de sabre*. By 1870, however, it had been completely subsumed under the legal category "Muslim," which henceforth comprised people of Arab, Kabyle, and Berber origin.[35] The legal term Muslim had been formalized by an act of the French Senate of 1865 that granted French nationality, though not citizenship, to Algerian Muslims, who became a subject people under French rule but subject to Muslim law. In 1881, the Code de l'indigénat (Code of Indigenous Status) further cemented the exclusion of Muslims by relegating them to second-class status with special judicial procedures such as administrative tribunals, internment, and torture.[36] This was markedly different from Algeria's Jewish population, to whom the so-called Crémieux laws of 1870 had granted full French citizenship.[37]

Third, the theory of social stages posited by Tocqueville and the hierarchy of races to which it gave rise yielded concrete guidelines for governing Algeria's indigenous population. Tocqueville recommended that the more advanced and European Kabyles not be ruled by force but made dependent on French goods through trade. This position was further supported by pragmatic considerations because Kabyles lived in impenetrable mountain regions and had a reputation of killing any foreigner who came into their territory. Even the Turks, Tocqueville remarked, who had ruled Algeria before French colonization, "never managed to make their sovereignty recognized" by the Kabyles.[38] For "backward," "imperfect," and half-civilized Muslims, who had become outright "barbarous" through colonization, by contrast, Tocqueville regarded rather different means as necessary.

In the 1841 "Essay" and the "First Report on Algeria" of 1847, Tocqueville detailed the requisite techniques for establishing domination over Algeria's Muslim population. Although it was clear to him that war was the appropriate means for governing Algerian Muslims, it was less obvious what "type of war we can and must wage on the Arabs."[39] Tocqueville's answer to this question came into view as distinct from two commonly held positions, which he rejected. The first, which Tocqueville described as government in the "Turkish manner" because of its similarity to Turkish rule over Algeria, was held primarily by soldiers who advocated the total extermination of the Muslim population. In Tocqueville's estimation, "this manner of conducting war seems . . . as unintelligent as it is cruel."[40] It was cruel because France risked becoming more barbarous than the Muslims. It was unintelligent because even if France matched the Turks in barbarity, it would still be regarded as an inferior, because Christian, despot.

The second position on the nature of war in Algeria, by contrast, rejected the brutality of France's colonization effort.[41] Tocqueville explained that this view, held by "men in France whom I respect, but with whom I do not agree," proposed that it was "wrong that we burn harvests, that we empty silos, and finally that we seize unarmed men, women, and children." For Tocqueville, such categorical opposition to these measures was naively humanitarian because it failed to realize that they were "unfortunate necessities . . . to which any people that wants to wage war on the Arabs is obliged to submit."[42]

Between the demand for an inhumane war of extermination and a humanitarian rejection of war against Algerian Muslims, Tocqueville elaborated a military strategy that he saw as appropriate for the inferior developmental state of the Muslim race and the specific conditions of colonization in Algeria. As a consequence, he defended practices that he regarded as generally unnecessary in wars between advanced European nations. He further argued that "our troops would have to be almost as numerous in times of peace as in times of war" because the colonization of Algeria was "less a matter of defeating a government than of subjugating a people."[43] In sum, the establishment of a settler-colonial state in Algeria required an abandonment of any aspiration to rule over Kabyles, on the one hand, and permanent war against Algerian Muslims, on the other.

It is worth underscoring that even though Tocqueville had clearly abandoned his earlier endorsement of tolerance, peaceful cohabitation, and eventual amalgamation of European and Algerian races, he did not understand permanent war in terms of extermination. Rather, he sought to formulate a science of colonial war "whose laws are known to everyone and that can be applied almost with certainty" in such a way as to subjugate enough but not too much, to exert domination over Algerian races while at the same time making them profitable for European development.[44] To this end, Tocqueville outlined a set of practices of colonial war that allowed the colonial army to repress native resistance without compromising the productivity and profitability of Algeria's Muslim population.

In his 1841 "Essay" and the "First Report on Algeria" of 1847, Tocqueville articulated a set of practices intended to allow for a more efficient use of French resources in Algeria. First, to effectively govern nomadic and barbarian Muslims, the colonial army had to "cover the country with small, light corps that could overtake populations on the run, or who, placed next to their territory, would force them to remain there and live in peace." High mobility and the possibility of military intervention at the slightest sign of resistance were to be achieved through sequestration of the territory. A tight network of "storage outposts, placed at distant intervals," made it unnecessary for soldiers to carry large amounts of provisions and ammunitions. In this way, troops became "as mobile as the armed Arab" and moved "more quickly than a tribe on the march." Moreover, Tocqueville argued, it was necessary to survey the territory in order to strategically place military camps near centers of native resistance so as to "prevent or suppress their revolts." The aim was to cover the territory "as if by an immense net whose mesh, tightly woven in the west, will loosen to the degree that it extends to the east"—that is, away from hotbeds of Muslim resistance.[45] Finally, it was necessary to determine where to establish European settlements by means of enclosure and fortification. This would ensure that "Muslim society and Christian society do not have a single tie" and instead "form two bodies that are juxtaposed but completely separate."[46] Consequently, the native population was confronted with the constant "proximity of a mobile force that may descend on them unpredictably and at any moment."[47]

In addition, Tocqueville recommended that the colonial army randomly "seize harvests, capture herds, and arrest people."[48] He explained that one of the most important means to subjugate Muslim tribes was to lay waste the country: "I believe that the right of war authorizes us to ravage the country and that we must do it, either by destroying harvests during the harvest season, or year-round by making those rapid incursions called razzias, whose purpose is to seize men or herds."[49] Such occasional demonstrations of force served to create a permanent display of colonial power that made regular intervention unnecessary. Nevertheless, the colonial state had to create a pervasive network of power that would allow for continuous surveillance to detect early signs of native resistance. For this purpose, Tocqueville recommended a form of colonial administration that exploited existing local forms of government. The exercise of colonial power, he argued, "must seek to rely on already existing influences" and ensure that "secondary powers of the government" were "exercised by the inhabitants of the country." Native officials, who served as "intermediaries" employed to "administer . . . the Muslim populations," were subject to "more or less detailed surveillance, and we become more or less closely involved in monitoring their activities; but almost no part of the tribes are administered by us directly. It is our generals who govern; their principal agents are the officers of the Arab bureaus."[50] These claims show that colonial rule was made possible, supported, and amplified by indigenous intermediaries who served as relays of colonial power. What linked these intermediaries to the center of power were so-called Arab bureaus, which consisted of Arabists and military officers tasked with the accumulation of knowledge about and administration of indigenous society.

Tocqueville's sketch of the dispositif of colonial war is characterized by technologies of power that are best understood in terms of discipline. We saw in chapter 1 that Foucault described disciplinary power as the first of two technologies of biopower that emerged in the seventeenth century. Its primary aim was the production of docile bodies, which was achieved by inserting individuals in a specific spatial arrangement designed to make power highly visible but render its actual exercise unverifiable. Consider as an example Foucault's discussion of Jeremy Bentham's panopticon, which functioned on the basis of a spatial arrangement that confronted inmates with an ever-present watchtower but made it impossible for them to know whether they were under surveillance at any given moment. This architectural form served to "induce in the inmate a state of conscious and permanent visibility that assures the automatic functioning of power. So to arrange things that the surveillance is permanent in its effects, even if it is discontinuous in its action; that the perfection of power should tend to render its actual exercise unnecessary."[51] The mere possibility of observation, coupled with the threat of sanctions in case of misconduct, would cause inmates to act as if they actually were under permanent surveillance and thus to spontaneously exercise power on themselves. As Foucault noted, "This enclosed segmented space, observed at every point, in which the individuals are inserted in a fixed place, in which the slightest movements are supervised, in which all events are recorded, in which an uninterrupted work of writing links the centre and periphery, in which power is exercised without division, according to a continuous hierarchical figure, in which each individual is constantly located, examined and distributed among the living beings," would elicit a sort of self-policing on the part of prisoners.[52] Prisoners would become the executors of the very power to which they were subject by means of a strict spatial partitioning, ceaseless inspection, and a system of permanent registration.

These principles are operative in Tocqueville's description of the deployment of colonial war. A particular spatial ordering resulted in a compartmentalization of the territory, to use Frantz Fanon's terminology, in which a European and a native sector confronted each other in a logic of mutual exclusion.[53] It also made possible the permanent surveillance of native populations and the harnessing of indigenous knowledge and structures of power. But while the dispositif of colonial war served to repress native resistance, it was integrated into overall political strategies that were also productive. The deployment of colonial war was, above all, a means to create the conditions necessary for the improvement and regeneration of the French social body. This meant that native Algerians were collateral damage in an effort to make Algeria inhabitable by French settlers. The goal was to sanitize the European sector to make it "healthy and habitable" and to cultivate "ways of living, of fighting, of being healthy" appropriate for the colonized territory.[54] For Tocqueville, the science of colonial war was as much concerned with the identification of principles of government over native races as it was with determining "under what laws [the European population] must live and what must be done to hasten its development."[55] More precisely, the subjugation of Algeria's indigenous population was a precondition for the salvation of the European race, both at home and abroad. On this view, colonial war was the corollary of a struggle for life and the improvement of life.

This view of colonization persisted throughout the late nineteenth century and the first half of the twentieth. In 1923, for example, the French minister for colonies, Albert Sarraut, explicitly declared that colonization was "an episode in the struggle for life, of the great contest for life" (*une épisode du combat pour la vie, de la grande concurrence vitale*) and an "enterprise of personal interest, unilateral and selfish, accomplished by the stronger over the weaker."[56] On this account, legal inequality between French citizens and indigenous subjects was merely the formal expression of natural inequality and the sign, as Émile Larcher had put it in 1902, of "a victorious race, imposing its yoke and its domination on a vanquished race."[57] Until the end of the Third Republic (1870–1940), Algerians were denied social and political equality, as well as basic civil rights, while at the same time being subjected to all the duties and obligations of citizenship, including military service. In response, a nationalist movement emerged in the first half of the twentieth century that demanded, first, equal rights for and assimilation of Algerian Muslims; second, cultural and political autonomy under French rule; and third, Algerian independence and sovereignty. Legal reforms implemented after World War II formally granted French citizenship to all Algerian Muslims but failed to extend rights of citizens. As a consequence, on May 8, 1945, Algerians organized a protest in the eastern city of Sétif to demand Algerian independence. The French police fired shots at the protesters that led to riots and attacks on European settlers; 103 *pieds-noirs* were killed.[58] The ensuing retaliation of the colonial army and individual violence against the Muslim population resulted in thousands of Algerian deaths and galvanized massive support for a nationalist movement that had been simmering since the 1920s.[59] Encouraged by French losses in the Indochina war, the Front de Libération Nationale (FLN, National Liberation Front) and its military arm, the Armée de Libération Nationale (ALN, National Liberation Army), launched a series of attacks on military and civilian targets on November 1, 1954, that killed eight people. A manifesto in which the FLN took responsibility for the events called for an independent Algeria by any means necessary.

What followed was a two-pronged effort on the part of the colonial state to preserve French Algeria. First, France implemented a series of legal and political reforms intended to integrate Algerian Muslims and ensure that Algeria would remain French.[60] Second, the colonial state unleashed a military campaign to end armed resistance that bore a striking resemblance to nineteenth-century practices of colonial war. But unlike in the nineteenth century, when colonial war was justified as a means of subjugating a foreign enemy for the benefit of the French nation, twentieth-century armed resistance came from formally French citizens and thus from within. That is, France's century-long effort to establish Algeria as an extension of French national territory made necessary a new mode of making sense of military intervention. This justificatory framework was provided by a new theory of revolutionary war and a concomitant new concept of terrorism as a new kind of war, or *polemic terrorism.*

FROM SCIENCE OF COLONIAL WAR TO REVOLUTIONARY-WAR THEORY

France's assertion that Algeria was French made Algerian independence inconceivable. To be sure, France feared damage to its international reputation and global influence. The socialist prime minister Guy Mollet, for instance, warned in December 1955 that without Algeria, "France would become a small power, in the second or third rank, deprived of its world role."[61] More important, however, Algeria's secession would violate the integrity and internal order of the country. As Mollet's successor, Pierre Mendès-France, declared, "One does not compromise when it comes to defending the internal peace of the nation, the unity and the integrity of the Republic."

> The Algerian departments are part of the French Republic. They have been French for a long time, and they are irrevocably French. . . . Between them and metropolitan France there can be no conceivable secession. . . . Never will France—any French government or parliament, whatever may be their particularistic tendencies—yield on this fundamental principle. . . . *Ici, c'est la France!*[62]

The declaration "Algeria is France," as François Mitterrand, then minister of the interior and later president of France, put it, had important consequences for how the problem of nationalist resistance was understood.[63] Most important, nationalist resistance was conceived as a problem of internal order. Traditionally, problems of internal order are police matters and do not fall within the purview of the military. Algeria's police forces, however, were impotent in the face of escalating violence.

Here I will focus specifically on the so-called Battle of Algiers, an episode of guerrilla warfare between French forces and the FLN and its military arm, the ALN. In the context of increasing international attention (the Algerian Question was to be heard at the United Nations in 1956) and increasing violence against Muslim Algerians perpetrated by *pied-noir* "ultras," extremist European settlers determined to keep Algeria French, the FLN first carried out attacks against Europeans, sparing women, children, and elders. After peace talks between the Mollet government and the FLN leadership broke down in the fall of 1956, the FLN adopted a bombing campaign against Europeans to inflict on France its Algerian Dien Bien Phu.[64] The French government issued a set of special powers and ordered elite divisions of its military to Algiers to tackle the problem posed by nationalist violence. Executive power was transferred to the resident minister of Algeria; the executive obtained the right to govern by decree; military tribunals replaced civil and administrative courts; and police powers were conferred on the army. On January 7, 1957, police powers were delegated to General Jacques Massu and his 10th Parachutist Division (10e DP or paras), paratroopers used for counterinsurgency operations. The responsibility to maintain order was thereby transferred "to the military authority, which will exercise . . . police powers normally vested in the civil authority."[65]

The transfer of police powers to the military was made possible by a new theory of revolutionary war that French officers had developed in the 1950s during colonial wars in Indochina.[66] According to revolutionary-war theory, a new pattern of warfare had emerged after World War II in which ill-equipped guerrilla fighters relied on irregular methods to hold hostage technologically superior conventional armies. The theory held that these new wars were essentially subversive; that is, they sought to destroy not only the political order established through colonization but also the moral order associated with it. The notion of subversion, as Lazreg succinctly puts it, must be understood as an ideological move that allowed colonial authorities to raise "the specter of an insidious revolutionary movement bent upon the destruction of French qua 'Western' values, and implicitly shored up colonial rule as a bulwark against an immoral and shadowy adversary."[67] In this way, the true motivations of resistance fighters could be effaced, and their actions could be presented as a threat, both real and ideological, to France and French values. To repress this new kind of war, the architects of revolutionary-war theory argued, it was necessary that conventional armies establish complete control over recalcitrant populations by means of constant surveillance and the continuous threat of violence. In short, military activity had to be transformed into a permanent exercise of police power.

The theory of revolutionary war and the merging of techniques of military and police power it facilitated bear all the hallmarks of a development that the German jurist Carl Schmitt described as the emergence of a generalized "peace-enforcing function of the state."[68] Traditionally, the state's function of peace enforcement comprises two analytically and practically distinct spheres, the maintenance of internal order through policing and the protection of a state and its citizens against external threats through military force. This is not to say that the distinction between internal and external enemies disintegrated, nor that these two forms of peace enforcement are entirely independent of each other. As we saw in the case of the science of colonial war earlier, military pacification of enemies external to France's population served the purpose of maintaining order within the French social body. Moreover, Tocqueville's discussion of colonization suggests that settler colonies were understood in clear continuity with penal colonies as means of maintaining internal order. Nevertheless, nineteenth-century practices of colonial war were, conceptually speaking, firmly anchored in the external sphere of military power and were justified in terms of warfare.

The distinction between military and police powers, according to Schmitt, became increasingly blurred after World War I, when attempts to abolish war through its criminalization rendered internal order and external peace analytically and practically indistinguishable. Schmitt contends that whereas the juridical formalization of warfare as legitimate conduct between equal sovereigns characteristic of the European public law had led to a "rationalization and humanization—a bracketing—of war," the criminalization of war characteristic of modern international law made any aggressor a criminal.[69] As a consequence, states no longer fight wars but pursue "police action against troublemakers, criminals, and pests." On Schmitt's view, then, military and police powers collapse into a generalized function of peace enforcement. He further adds that the need to justify police violence against troublemakers requires "ideological phenomena" that must measure up to "the industrial-technical development of modern means of destruction."[70] In other words, the increasing harm done by modern technology necessitates ever more intricate mechanisms of justification. Such justification is provided by political and moral condemnation of the aggressor and his cognate, the terrorist, as an enemy of the nation or, to anticipate a central claim of the next chapter, humanity.

In light of Foucault's genealogy of modern biopower, we can ascertain the conditions of possibility of the emergence of the peace enforcement Schmitt diagnoses. Recall that according to Foucault, the sovereign right to kill was supplemented in the seventeenth and eighteenth centuries by two new forms of power. Whereas an anatomo-politics of the human body seeks to discipline the body of the individual, a biopolitics of the population deploys regulatory controls to manage life processes, such as reproduction, mortality, morbidity, and life expectancy. Foucault insisted that these two forms of biopower not only rely on each other but also have to come to grips with extant forms of sovereign power, which do not disappear once biopower emerges. In societies concerned with fostering and managing life, the sovereign right to kill thus must be made subservient to a larger project of the administration and optimization of life. In short, killing can be justified only if it serves the protection and defense of a population's life. I argued in chapter 1 that the determination of those who must be killed so that the population can live is accomplished through mechanisms of social defense. What follows from this generalized need to defend society from everything that threatens its life and health is that the distinction between internal and external enemies becomes superfluous. It does not matter whether aggressors menace society from within or outside; both are threats to the life and health of the social body that must equally be eliminated. On this account, the disappearance of the distinction between internal and external and between military and police power appears as an effect of the emergence of modern biopower's investment in life. Under conditions of biopower, formerly distinct practices of police action against internal disorder and military intervention against external threats are transformed into a new practice of peace enforcement. Along with scientific, medical, psychiatric, and economic means to protect society, new peace-enforcing practices of state conducted previously within the purview of separate spheres of war and public order serve the purpose of social defense. It was as a functional requirement of a system of social defense that the colonial army's elaboration of polemic terrorism, that is, a concept of terrorism as a problem of the peace-enforcing function of the state and thus a new kind of war, became possible and intelligible.

CRIMINAL AND POLEMIC TERRORISM

The concept of polemic terrorism was neither a French invention nor exclusively a response to anticolonial resistance. Rather, the deployment of this notion was made possible by developments in international law by which terrorism became embedded within legal norms for dealing with political crimes across national borders.[71] A more refined genealogy of the currently dominant legal concept of terrorism is beyond the scope of this book; it suffices here to note that the historical conditions of possibility of this concept originated in nineteenth-century debates over the distinction between ordinary crimes and political offenses and thus an understanding of terrorism in terms of crime. I call this *criminal terrorism*. According to the European public law, perpetrators of crimes classified as political crimes—such as attacks on heads of government or espionage—were protected from extradition to the jurisdiction of the state harmed by their crimes. The distinction between ordinary and political offenses was complicated by states' opposition to the principle of nonextradition. In particular, an attempt to assassinate Napoléon III in 1854 triggered international debates that eventually resulted in the enactment of the Belgian attentat clause in 1856, which exempted certain political crimes from the protection of nonextradition.[72]

The attentat clause is significant in the history of the legal conceptualization of terrorism because it exempted certain politically motivated offenses from the category of political crimes. This move allowed for a two-pronged international effort to contain terrorism in the interwar period, when a series of international conferences for the unification of penal law focused on the streamlining of national legislation against terrorist acts, on the one hand, and furnished international debates on terrorism with the perspective of criminal jurisprudence, on the other.

A string of proposals concerning the criminalization of terrorism took up the exemption of certain political crimes from the principle of nonextradition set forth by the Belgian attentat clause and suggested that terrorism be legally conceptualized as a set of "offences punishable 'as ordinary crimes.' "[73] In this way, crimes classified as terrorism would no longer be protected by the principle of nonextradition and instead would be opened up to legal sanctions. But despite these demands to criminalize terrorism, the League of Nations failed to systematically implement any of these recommendations. It was not until the assassination of Austrian chancellor Engelbert Dollfuss, Romanian minister Ion Duca, and King Alexander I of Yugoslavia in 1934, which caused fear of a repetition of the assassination of Archduke Franz Ferdinand in 1914 and another world war, that the league was forced to take action.

The decisive event was the assassination of Alexander I, who was killed on a state visit to France. The suspects escaped to Italy, a jurisdiction that did not recognize the Belgian attentat clause. When France demanded their extradition to bring them to justice under French law, the Italian court handling the case ruled, "The assassination of a sovereign is a political crime if it is prompted by political motives" and refused to extradite the assassins.[74] In fear of another world war, the League of Nations noted the deficiency of national law in combating political crime and declared, "The rules of international law concerning the repression of terrorist activity are not at present sufficiently precise to guarantee efficiently international co-operation."[75] To make cooperation possible, states either had to uniformly accept the attentat clause or agree on a new legal category, distinct from ordinary and political crimes, that allowed for an effective response to terrorism.

Pursuing the latter option, the league created the Committee for the International Repression of Terrorism (CIRT), which was tasked with drafting a convention to prevent crimes that had a political or terrorist purpose. Instead of merely exempting certain crimes from the category of political offenses, thereby removing the protections afforded by this classification, CIRT introduced a new and distinct category for acts of terrorism. Specifically, CIRT distinguished between political crimes that fell under the nonextradition clause and political crimes with a special character that were not covered by the clause.

The introduction of a new category of terrorism as a special political crime was made possible, first, by the Fifth International Conference for the Unification of Penal Law in 1935, which had called for the punishment of some crimes as "special offences apart from any general criminal character which they may have under the laws of the State, whenever such acts create a public danger or a state of terror, of a nature to cause a change in or impediment to the operation of the public authorities or to disturb international relations, more particularly by endangering peace."[76] Second, the League of Nations Assembly had passed a resolution in 1936 that defined terrorism as attacks on "the life or liberty of persons taking part in the work of foreign public authorities and services."[77] In combination, these two developments gave rise to a new legal category of terrorism as a special offense directed against state representatives, which justified intervention because it resulted in a state of terror and threatened peace. This category not only fixed the meaning of terrorism as antistate violence but also created a significant amount of flexibility and discretion for states to identify terrorism on an ad hoc basis depending on whether they felt that peace and order were in danger. It is here that we can identify a distinction between the notion of criminal terrorism, which conceives of terrorism as a matter of law and (public or international) order, and an understanding of terrorism in terms of war, or polemic terrorism.[78]

These developments provided the conceptual framework for the French army's construction and regulated use of a polemic concept of terrorism as an effect of the peace-enforcing function of the state. Consider as an example General Massu's systematic elaboration of polemic terrorism in his memoirs, *La vraie bataille d'Alger* (1971). Massu situated terrorism within a taxonomy of various forms of peace enforcement, each of which was regulated by a specific set of norms. More specifically, he regarded terrorism as a new problem of peace enforcement and distinguished it from common crimes, military conflict, and irregular warfare. The latter three were entirely within the purview of traditional forms of either police action or military intervention.

Massu explained that as the proper object of policing, *common crimes* were wholly immanent in the civil or internal sphere. They were subject to a system of clear, publicized, stable, just, and general laws, whose enforcement was the task of the police. Because crimes were constituted by the violation of these laws, they triggered a sanction that was predetermined by the norms that were transgressed. Common crimes pertained to the relationship between the delinquent individual and the state and thus to the internal sphere of public order. This sphere, Massu argued, was governed by a system of norms that specified "a well-defined procedure of criminal investigation, employed without difficulty" and "can achieve healthy justice, all while respecting the rights of individuals and those of society."[79]

In contrast to common crimes, *military conflict* took place in the external sphere of war between sovereign states. In military conflict, soldiers' actions formed part of a military relationship between combatants, which was regulated by the laws of war. These laws were known to, were accepted by, and applied equally to both sides in a conflict.

Whereas crime and war are easy cases that clearly belong to traditional areas of the state's peace-enforcing function, the problem of irregular fighters such as guerrillas, partisans, and franc-tireurs appears to be more difficult. Schmitt, for instance, claims that the laws of war are ill equipped to respond to irregular fighters and that the problem of the partisan "demonstrates that a normative regulation [of irregular warfare] is juridically impossible."[80] For Schmitt, then, it is unclear whether irregular warfare is subject to military or police power or whether there are any norms at all that apply to the conduct of irregular fighters. In sharp contrast to the legal theorist Schmitt's assessment, however, the military strategist Massu firmly located irregular fighters within the external sphere of military intervention. He maintained that they clearly were soldiers who belonged to the domain of war. Because irregular fighters attacked soldiers, they knowingly entered into a military relationship governed by the laws of war. Indeed, they sought to gain advantage by selectively eschewing the constraints of these laws. Massu explained, "As for the guerrilla or franc-tireur . . . who attacks a regular army, the fact that he transgresses the laws of war by fighting without a uniform, thus avoiding the risks he would run by wearing a uniform, takes away the protection of these same laws. Captured arms in hand, he is shot on the spot."[81] By choosing not to accept the duties imposed by the laws of war, irregular fighters thus also relinquished the protection they offered. As a consequence, irregular warfare was not a new problem that required new forms of peace enforcement but a form of war that sought to exempt itself from the laws of war.

Terrorism, however, was an altogether different matter. Drawing a sharp distinction between terrorism as a particular kind of violence and the systematic application of such violence as a means of warfare, Massu argued that "terrorism is not a new weapon,"[82] but "the use of terrorism as a weapon of war is a new fact." In the past, revolutionaries had used terrorism for very limited purposes. Only since 1954 had the deployment of terrorism as a tactic of warfare become a systematic strategy. "Even in Indochina," Massu maintained, "where guerrilla warfare reached a remarkable development that has definitively allowed the rebels to take home victory, terrorism was not used."

The rare notable incidents always had very limited impact (terrorist attacks by explosive in Saigon that had the most victims were not acts of the

Viet Minh). The maintenance of peace and security in the big cities we occupied never posed a particular problem to the command.[83]

As we have seen in chapter 3, Massu was wrong to deny that terrorism had been used as a tactic of warfare before 1954. But what is important about his account is not its factual accuracy but the concept of terrorism it articulates. Specifically, Massu understood terrorism (1) in terms of the systematic rather than occasional use of violence; (2) in reference to the identity of the perpetrator; and (3) with regard to the state's ability to maintain peace and order. On his view, terrorism was properly understood as the systematic use of a particular kind of violence as a tactic of warfare employed by revolutionary forces to create disorder. What kind of violence did Massu have in mind?

Massu observed that the specific characteristic of terrorist violence was that the terrorist "never attacks people ready to defend themselves but always peaceful and unsuspecting passers-by, often women and children, always innocents."[84] In contrast to irregular fighters, who attacked opponents trained and prepared for battle whose "weapons are equal, methods similar," terrorists engaged in indiscriminate killing of "women, children, defenseless individuals, who had always been protected by the laws of war." Modern laws of war required soldiers to wear uniforms or bear other distinctive signs, carry weapons openly, and abstain from harming noncombatants, but the terrorist "not only does . . . not have a uniform, but he generally attacks unarmed persons, who are unable to defend themselves."[85] Thus, terrorism was a form of violence that broke altogether with the laws of war. "What characterizes the terrorist and what constitutes his essential strength," Massu wrote, "is that, acting in a system of well-defined laws, he does not take any of the usual risks run by ordinary criminals, soldiers on the battlefield, or even guerrillas and francs-tireurs who face regular troops."[86] Neither criminals nor regular or irregular combatants in war, terrorists acted outside any coherent system of rules by which their conduct could be judged. Terrorism was thus "a new form of war"[87] and "war of a new kind,"[88] which was neither legal nor illegal but "outside the law" (*hors-la-loi*).[89]

Massu asserted, "If, in the past, it was admitted that the laws of war no longer protect the franc-tireur who transgresses them, today it must be admitted that our current laws are maladjusted to terrorism for the simple reason that this form of aggression had never been envisaged."[90] There was, he maintained, a "grave lacuna . . . in our legal arsenal," which terrorists used to their advantage. In fact, the strict application of existing legal norms, both criminal and military, would make it impossible to apprehend terrorists. As a consequence, "the forces charged with the maintenance of order" could either accept their impotence and "leave the field open to the terrorists," or they could "transgress the law normally accepted to ensure the fulfilment of a mission, the protection of their fellow citizens, which has been entrusted to them as their essential task."[91] In the name of public order and security, Massu demanded a set of special norms, which he specified as follows:

1. Any individual entering a terrorist organization, or knowingly facilitating the action of its elements (propaganda, aid, recruitment, etc.), is liable to capital punishment.
2. Any individual belonging to a terrorist organization and falling into the hands of special law enforcement will be interrogated on the spot, without break, by the same forces who arrested him.
3. Any individual suspected of belonging to a terrorist organization may be arrested at home and taken for interrogation by special law enforcement at any hour during the day or night.
4. A special jurisdiction will be set up to judge terrorists; sentences will be executed within 48 hours.
5. These measures come into force once several characteristic terrorist attacks have been committed in a town or a given territory, at the request of the authorities responsible of maintaining order, addressed to the government, which retains the decision of application.

Massu was explicit that although these norms were not legal norms, they were nevertheless efficacious and ought to be given the "force of law."[92] Note the justificatory work done by the concept of terrorism in Massu's defense of such exceptional norms that have the force of law. His appeal to terrorism and the need for "politico-military work" necessary for "defending . . . the population" authorized special measures such as summary executions, torture, expedited trials by military tribunals, and the suspension of basic protections against state power.[93] These practices could be implemented against terrorists and terrorist suspects under conditions of repeated acts of violence identified as terrorism in order to prevent further terrorist attacks. French military practices during the Battle of Algiers illustrate the consequences of implementing these norms.

THE DISPOSITIF OF TERRORISM
IN THE BATTLE OF ALGIERS

Confronted with escalating violence during an episode of the Algerian Revolution known as the Battle of Algiers (1956–1957), Massu's paras were tasked with and given special power to ensure "the 'maintenance of order' in the worst of disorders."[94] To this end, they began to set up a system that bore all the marks of the disciplinary apparatus of colonial war. A strict spatial partitioning was achieved through the compartmentalization of space into a native and a European sector. Native space was further sequestered, placed under military occupation, and crisscrossed by colonial power in the form of *quadrillage* (grid arrangement), *chevaux de frise* (barricades), roadblocks, and patrols. The archives on Algeria conserved by the Service historique de la défense in Vincennes bear witness to these practices. We can find, for example, a *plan de bouclage*, a sort of lockdown map that specifies both the means and the exact locations for sealing off the native sector in the northwestern city of Mascara, as well as a *plan de protection*, on which military strongpoints throughout the city are marked.[95] Newspaper clippings show pictures of *harkis*, Algerian Muslims who served the colonial state, patrolling the streets of the casbah, Algiers's old town, inhabited by the native population.[96] Using barbed wire and patrols, the military cordoned off Arab quarters, turned roads into one-way streets, and placed radio cars at every intersection to control the movement of the native population.[97] In this way, the territory was transformed into a wholly compartmentalized and sequestered space. As Zohra Drif, an Algerian combatant, explained:

> On one side, the Arab city and neighborhoods, and on the other, the European city and neighborhoods, separated by an immaterial and impassable wall and de facto apartheid. . . . The European cities and

neighborhoods bathed in a tranquility that was revolting compared to the terrible repression imposed on the indigenous civil population.[98]

Native space, Drif continued, had been turned into an "open-air concentration camp," a "ghetto subject to curfew, surrounded and locked behind *chevaux de frise,* barbed wire, and various patrols."[99] The casbah, FLN leader Saadi Yacef recounted, was "an immense concentration camp" in which "for twenty-four hours per day, patrols and raid regiments (about 2,000 men for surrounding a neighborhood) searched systematically house by house, corner by corner."[100]

This sequestered space allowed for the ceaseless inspection of its inhabitants. As soon as the paras had sectioned off native quarters in Algiers, Massu took a census in the casbah, issued identity cards to each of its inhabitants, and covered the citadel with guards, who reported all suspicious activities. Every Algerian was identified by reference to his or her place in a complex network of genealogical, geographic, and professional relations. Consider as a striking example a police report of Saadi Yacef's interrogation on September 29, 1957. The report specifies the individuals in attendance: Captain Jacques Allaire of the 3rd Marine Infantry Parachute Regiment, Gendarme Nogueira, and Saadi Yacef, "29 years old, baker, resident at 3, rue des Aberrames in the Casbah of Algiers. Born January 20, 1928, in Algiers, son of Mohamed and of Boualem, Kheltouma Bent Mohamed. Married, one child. Nationality French. Detained at the sorting center [*centre de triage*] in the subsection *Centre* since September 24, 1957."[101]

In addition, the paras conducted raids and searches, preferably at night. Deploying methods of "absolute lockdown and the work of special teams," they were charged with the official mission of "blow[ing] up the terrorist hive by attacking its main lair, the Casbah."[102] We can see the application of these methods in General Massu's description of the paras' effort to prevent a general strike organized by the FLN in January 1957. Massu intended to make as many arrests as possible in order to "apprehend those who, according to still very fragmentary intelligence in our possession, are in a position to play a more or less important role in the launch and subsequent unfolding of the strike."[103] Because arresting suspects was not enough, they had to be detained in internment camps. During their stay in such "sorting centers" (*centres de triage*), where suspects could be held for up to a month, they were subject to "detailed interrogation."[104]

The information gathered through ceaseless inspection was fed into a system of permanent registration from which no scrap of evidence, no matter how trivial, escaped. The archives burst with police reports; intelligence briefings; statistics; tables of terrorist attacks ordered by date, region, and identity of the victims; newspaper clippings; letters intercepted or recovered from dead resistance fighters; testimonies of informants; confessions; maps; plans; graphs; organigrams; photographs; propaganda material; guidelines for improving military morale; and instructions for disarming bombs. Tens of thousands of *fiches de renseignement* (information cards) recorded every bit of information by number, origin, and reference and identified its source in agents, informants, recovered documents, or interrogations. Information was filtered, quantified, and processed statistically to identify the normal distribution of terrorist activity.[105] By far the most popular technique of intelligence gathering, especially in urgent cases, was torture. Reflecting on the French campaign against the FLN in the Algerian capital, for instance, the French general Paul Aussaresses claimed, "The best way to force a terrorist who refused to disclose what he knew was to torture him."[106] Lieutenant-Colonel Roger Trinquier advised, "If the prisoner gives the information requested, the examination is quickly terminated; if not, specialists must force his secret from him."[107] Torture was necessary, according to Massu, because "it was a matter of urgently obtaining operational information, on which depended the life of innocent beings."[108]

In spite of these avowals, however, what stands out is the archive's silence about concrete acts of nationalist violence that were prevented because of torture.[109] Consider the *fiches de renseignement*, which attribute each piece of data to its source. Information was procured from informers (*informateurs*), agents (*agents*), prisoners (*prison.*), suspects (*suspect*), interrogations (*interrogatoire*), intercepted documents, and media sources such as the Egyptian radio station Voix des Arabes. These *fiches* show that good—that is, true, critical, and timely—intelligence came from informers and double agents, as well as from FLN correspondence intercepted or recovered from arrested or killed combatants. Interrogation and torture, by contrast, produced information that was either untrue or, if true, uninformative, irrelevant, not critical, or untimely. Here are some examples:

> No. 61: The FLN intends to effect a large-scale attack in [the north-western city of] Tlemcen on Easter Sunday. Public places will be targeted. Similar actions are possible in other cities.
>
> No. 65: The HLL [*hors-la-loi*, outlaws] publicized that an offensive will be launched at the start of June 1957.
>
> No. 507: The political commissaries of region 3, zone 7, Abounadja and Si Mohamed, informed the leaders of the O.P.A. of their intention to harass the centers, the night before or after the referendum.[110]

The information obtained in these and other cases of torture was so obvious that it was entirely lacking in value for the colonial army. Moreover, the colonial army was aware of this fact. Colonel Marcel-Maurice Bigeard, for instance, determined that "infiltration [and] information spontaneously obtained from the population are the most useful methods."[111] Memoirs of French soldiers who tortured in Algeria further support the claim that the army knew about the inefficacy of torture techniques.[112] Why, then, did the colonial state continue to rely heavily on torture?

A plausible answer is that torture did not primarily serve to produce knowledge. Rather, "one of the objectives of the use of torture was to remind Algerians that, by definition, they were considered accomplices of the FLN."[113] An entry on "the technique of interrogation" recorded on December 27, 1960, in a *fiche de renseignement* explains that "tortures are used when the interrogated individual does not want to talk, or even a priori when it is known that the interrogated individual has to die."[114] In other words, torture was not principally an instrument of intelligence but a key element in a larger disciplinary apparatus intended to elicit spontaneous submission to colonial power from the native population.[115] By subjecting native Algerians to "the rhythm of raids of troops, army and police combined, daily arrests by the hundreds (every indigenous person being suspicious), summary executions and condemnations to death by guillotine," the colonial power sought to induce a sense of permanent visibility and uncertainty.[116] According to testimonies of French soldiers, the aim of the paras was to create a sense of permanent threat and to make every native Algerian fear that "within an hour, men will perhaps be knocking at my door to take me away forever."[117] Colonial discipline, which was based on spatial sequestration, continuous surveillance, and permanent registration, served to contain and eliminate suspect populations so as to maintain internal order and security. Although the means for doing so certainly resembled practices of colonial war, there was nevertheless an important difference between the disciplinary techniques deployed during the Algerian Revolution and the practices of colonial war elaborated a century earlier. To be sure, what was at stake in both contexts was the defense and protection of society. But in contrast to practices of colonial war, which were portrayed as a necessary means to secure space for relocating France's indigent population, the exercise of colonial power in the twentieth century was justified in terms of counterterrorism. That is, a new mode of understanding made intelligible and gave stability to techniques of colonial domination as practices of counterterrorism.

An entire system of relations was thus established around terrorism that imposed mechanisms of repression but also produced new bodies of knowledge, new clusters of power relations, and new modes of being a subject. A new concept of polemic terrorism as the systematic use of indiscriminate violence against innocents as a tactic of warfare used by revolutionary forces to create disorder stipulated specific rules according to which attributions of terrorism to particular acts of violence became possible and meaningful. It also allowed for statements about terrorism to be judged as true or false and gave rise to the formation of a body of knowledge about terrorism that was reflected in statistics, graphs, and other forms of compiling information. In addition, knowledge about terrorism served as the basis of a set of norms that guided the counterterrorist actions of the French army just examined. Finally, knowledge about terrorism, as well as normative frameworks generated on its basis, made possible specific subject positions in relation to the problem of terrorism. Most important, it allowed for a clear distinction among terrorists, innocent civilians, and agents of counterterrorism. Terrorism during the Algerian Revolution might thus plausibly be understood as a historically specific construct, or dispositif, that facilitated the pursuit of French imperial interests by generating new forms of knowledge, power, and subjectivity.

But the dispositif of terrorism deployed in Algeria by the French colonial state also generated new forms of resistance. Recall that according to revolutionary-war theory, conventional armies must mimic the methods of their adversaries in order to combat irregular war. Indeed, a number of scholars attribute the invention of terrorism in the Algerian Revolution to frontists and regard French military action as essentially reactive to the specific forms of what they describe as FLN terrorism.[118] In what follows, I show that the discourses and practices of Algerian combatants suggest that rather than understanding colonial violence as a mimesis of frontist violence, we should reach the opposite conclusion.[119] The methods of armed resistance were responsive to and determined by the techniques of peace enforcement implemented by the colonial army. However, these tactics were integrated into an understanding of the conflict not in terms of internal order but as an episode of war, which the French had begun in 1830. Hence, the frontists understood terrorism as both polemic and strategic. It was polemic insofar as terrorism was not a historically new kind of war but the classic form of insurrectional war. It was strategic to the extent that terrorism was a particular tactic that characterized this type of warfare. This alternative mode of understanding the conflict resulted in practices of resistance that subverted the French deployment of terrorism as a nexus of knowledge, power, and subjugation by opposing it with a modified set of rules of veridiction, norms of behavior, and modes of being a subject.

TERRORISM AS THE CLASSIC FORM OF INSURRECTIONAL WAR

Against the French representation of the events in Algeria as a problem of internal order, frontists insisted that the conflict was a matter of war in the traditional sense. This interpretation was framed in continuity with France's own nineteenth-century discourse of colonial war. That is, frontists and combatants resurrected an earlier understanding of French-Algerian relations in terms of warfare between two communities distinguished by heritage, language, and tradition.[120] The frontists claimed that they were fighting a war that France had initiated with the conquest of Algiers in 1830. Thus, the terms of war had been determined by the colonizer. Consider, for instance, Zohra Drif's response to Danielle Michel-Chich, a victim of the famous FLN bombings of the Milk Bar on place Bugeaud and the Cafeteria on rue Michelet in September 1956, who accused Drif of being a war criminal responsible for the deaths of children. Drif replied,

> The French army waged total war against the Algerian people. The clear objective was to terrorize the Algerian people to make it lose confidence in the capacity of the FLN to fight and protect them. It is not me you have to hold responsible for this bomb, but the French powers who have enslaved the Algerian people since 1830 by using the most barbarous methods. Of what were the millions of Algerians guilty who have died since 1830? Of what were the "napalmed" villagers [*les villageois "napalmés"*] guilty? Of what were the victims of total war guilty, which had been waged in the small villages with the means of the fourth largest army in the world and the support of NATO? I was not born to kill, I got no personal pleasure from throwing that bomb, but we were in a state of war, a war that had been imposed on us since 1830.[121]

For Drif, armed resistance against the colonial state was not "on the register of a problem internal to the French state" but an episode in a long history of war initiated by France.[122] As a consequence, the frontists and their supporters vehemently denied that anticolonial violence was terrorism as defined by French military personnel. Instead, they argued that it was a legitimate form of "self-defense" whose concrete tactics were determined by the material conditions of colonial domination.[123] As Saadi Yacef emphasized in his memoirs of the Battle of Algiers, it was due to "ultracolonial terrorism" that the revolutionary leadership had to "show to the people that we were in a position to dispose of weaponry as terrible as that of the enemy."[124] For him, the actions of FLN combatants were a means of "counterterrorism" against the violence of the colonizer.[125] As a consequence, their use of violence was not a simple repetition or imitation of colonial violence but a subversive attempt to turn the colonial power's system of peace enforcement back against itself.[126]

Frantz Fanon's account of the Algerian Revolution, *L'an V de la révolution algérienne*, serves as a productive point of entry for a consideration of the interplay among a subversive understanding of terrorism, practices of frontist counterattack, and new forms of subjectivity. Fanon's analysis of terrorism is couched in the language of strategic terrorism. Specifically, Fanon argued that what the French called *terrorism* was, in fact, the last resort of a colonized people in the face of terror inflicted by the colonizer:

> Having to respond in quick succession to the massacre of Algerian civilians in the mountains and cities, the revolutionary leadership sees itself forced to adopt forms of struggle that had up to then been ruled out to avoid letting terror take hold of the people. There has not been sufficient analysis of this phenomenon; there has not been sufficient emphasis on the reasons that lead a revolutionary movement to choose the weapon that is called *terrorism*.[127]

Fanon identified the conditions of colonialism as the reason that Algerian combatants turned to terrorism. He argued that "new forms of combat" were necessary to compensate for the "advantage the enemy derived by pursuing the path of terror."[128] If the FLN was fighting a new type of war, it was because it was responding in kind to a war started by the colonizer.

With respect to the phenomenon of terrorism, Fanon emphasized its strategic dimension and denied that it constituted a new kind of war initiated by the FLN. Rather, it was a tactic of warfare that France itself had used and deemed legitimate in the past. Concretely, he insisted that on a purely phenomenal level, acts of terrorism such as "individual or collective attempts by means of bombs or by the derailing of trains" were identical to actions undertaken by French soldiers during the Résistance. The "technique of terrorism" was the same in both cases.[129] Moreover, the intentions of Algerian combatants appeared to be entirely indistinguishable from those of French soldiers fighting Nazi Germany. In both contexts, terrorism was justified by its perpetrators as a means of resistance against an illegitimate occupation. By explicitly connecting armed resistance in Algeria to armed resistance during the Résistance, Fanon sought to appeal to a shared experience of illegitimate occupation. He highlighted the similarities of the tactics used by French and Algerian resistance fighters to justify them as legitimate means of warfare, on the one hand, and defend them as the only form of struggle appropriate to conditions of domination, on the other.

Fanon's analysis, albeit with some modifications, reverberates in Zohra Drif's recollections of the Algerian Revolution, *La mort de mes frères* (1960) and *Mémoirs d'une combattante de l'ALN* (2014). Drif, a member of the infamous Réseau bombes (bomb network) organized by Saadi Yacef in Algiers, insisted that the actions taken by the FLN "were determined by the objective conditions of the terrain, and the forms of struggle were dictated by the conditions that the colonial power imposed on us for the benefit of the Europeans."[130] In order to fight the colonial state, combatants had to "counterattack [*riposter*] by using their methods."[131] On Drif's view, bombings and other acts of violence were "a response and a counterattack, absolutely necessary but not premeditated, to the bombings perpetrated by European civilians against ours, especially as the war and its carnage was only experienced by our people and in our neighborhoods while the Europeans continued to live the sweet life in 'their city,' protected by an armada of soldiers and police officers."[132] The particular form these means of counterattack took, however, depended on the specific conditions under which armed struggle took place.

> In the *djebels* [mountains], our men took part in war as soldiers, they were part of the National Liberation Army, which also existed in the cities. And if the combatants of the *maquis* could fight in uniform, those of the cities evidently could not fight in uniform in the streets of Algiers, Oran, Constantine. The form the war took in the cities, to counter the strong concentration of enemy troops, is the classical form of insurrectional war: terrorism.[133]

Moving between strategic and polemic terrorism, Drif held that the use of particular strategies made terrorism a specific kind of war. The kind of violence the French called *terrorism* was simply the form of war appropriate for urban centers. Drif further suggested that it was the very techniques and conditions of colonial discipline that made regular warfare inexpedient and dictated other forms of anticolonial resistance. Conditions of domination also generated new forms of agency and subjectivity, which took advantage of the colonial authorities' lack of knowledge and prejudiced perceptions of the indigenous population.

Consider, for instance, the combatants' response to constraints imposed by a strict spatial partitioning of colonized space, which prohibited the native population access to the European sector. Taking the struggle to the colonizer thus required strategies of infiltration that enabled combatants to move freely between native and European spaces. This was achieved by exploiting the very actions, traditions, and forms of subjectivity that the colonial state regarded as a sign of native submission to colonial power. Specifically, the FLN increasingly relied on Algerian women, who assumed a Westernized embodiment in order to perpetrate attacks on agents and places of colonial power.

As Fanon explained, the importance of Algerian women in the liberation struggle directly reflected the importance the French authorities attributed to them in their colonization effort. The French authorities believed that underneath the patriarchal structures of indigenous society was a matrimonial essence that gave the Algerian woman significant social power. Consequently, they thought that "to convert the woman, to win her over to foreign values, to wrest her from her status, this is at the same time attaining real power over the man and possessing practical and efficient means to destructure Algerian culture."[134] The colonial authorities thus undertook massive efforts to Europeanize women, and the veil became the symbol of their success. Every unveiled woman was regarded as a sign of French victory. But it was precisely this investment of the veil with political meaning that generated possibilities of resistance. Fanon wrote,

> We find here one of the laws of the psychology of colonization. Initially, it is the action, the projects of the colonizer that determine the centers of resistance around which a people's will to survive is organized. It is the white who creates the Negro. But it is the Negro who creates negritude. To the offensive of the colonialist around the veil, the colonized opposed the cult of the veil. What used to be an undifferentiated element in a homogeneous ensemble acquired the character of a taboo, and the attitude of the Algerian women with regard to the veil was constantly related to her general attitude with regard to the foreign occupation. The colonized, faced with the emphasis the colonizer put on this or that area of their traditions, reacted in a very violent manner. The interest in modifying this area, the inverse affectivity of the colonizer in his pedagogical

work, his prayers, his threats, weave around the privileged element a veritable universe of resistances. To stand up to the colonizer on this precise element is to inflict on him a spectacular failure; it is most of all to maintain conflict and latent warfare as dimensions of "coexistence." It is maintaining the atmosphere of armed truce.[135]

Fanon drew attention to the fact that the colonizer's racial prejudice and lack of knowledge of native culture transformed tradition into a site of resistance. He identified three phases of struggle, each of which was characterized by a distinct mode of subversive deployment of the veil. In the first phase, Algerian women insisted on wearing the veil as a symbol of victory over the colonizer. The veil signaled a refusal to accept colonial power. But with an intensification of the political conflict in 1956, Algerian women adopted what Fanon called an "absolutely incredible offensive tactic": by unveiling themselves, they appeared to submit to colonial power so as to carve out new spaces of resistance.[136] By transforming into European women, unveiled Algerian women were able to pass freely between native and European sectors of the city, thus becoming a "woman-arsenal" for the revolution.[137]

> Carrier of revolvers, grenades, hundreds of false identity cards or bombs, the unveiled Algerian woman moves like a fish in Western waters. French soldiers and patrols smile at her in passing, compliments on her figure bursting out here and there, but no one suspects that in her bag is a submachine-gun, which, suddenly, will mow down four or five members of a patrol.[138]

Drif recounted the importance of this form of camouflage in her description of the famous attacks on the Milk Bar on place Bugeaud and the Cafeteria on rue Michelet, which Drif and her friends, Samia Lakhdari and Djamila Bouhired, carried out on September 30, 1956. In the weeks and days before the attack, the women engaged in strategic surveillance of important locales "at various moments of the day, taking great care not to be noticed" in order to "determine with precision the adequate place for hiding a bomb."[139] They also observed "the customers, the servers, as well as the girls who frequented [the cafeteria]: their clothes, the way of wearing them, their postures, their way of talking and comporting themselves,

their haircuts . . . everything, absolutely everything, with the goal of perfectly copying them on D Day."[140] In addition to study and observation,
they also "submitted to Samia's favorite exercise: repeat everything
beforehand by mimicking the gestures, expressions, and gait we would
adopt on Sunday, September 30."[141] On the day of the attacks, the women
put on European-style dresses and visited a European salon to get their
hair and makeup done to make sure "we would perfectly mix with the
European golden youth and even the most affluent of them." By completely transforming themselves into European women, they made it
"impossible for the Europeans, blinded by their racism, to see in us the
'Fatma' of their fantasies."[142] Far from being the passive, submissive, and
incapable woman constructed by the colonial imagination, Algerian
women demonstrated "courage, cold blood, and self-mastery."[143] Drif's
narrative shows that what appeared to be an affirmation of the colonizer's
value was, in fact, an effective instrument of anticolonial resistance.

In 1957, a new phase of the conflict resulted in a return of the veil. Note,
however, that Algerian women resumed the practice of veiling not in its
earlier form as an expression of resistance to colonial power but as a
"technique of camouflage."[144] Because some women combatants who had
been arrested by the colonial army had talked under torture, French authorities knew that in the cities, Europeanized Algerian women were the
primary agents of anticolonial violence. Moreover, the colonial authorities had also arrested European women who supported the fight for
Algerian independence. Faced with a complete collapse of categories
that had organized the colonial imagination—Algerian versus European
women, Algerian supporters of independence versus European supporters
of French Algeria—everyone became a suspect. Under these conditions,
Algerian women—as well as, evidently, some men[145]—resurrected the veil
as a useful means of concealing weapons and other gear. But veiling alone
was not enough. It was also necessary to sufficiently conform to the colonizer's image of Muslim women to avoid rousing suspicion in French
soldiers and police officers. This "historical dynamism of the veil" reveals
various configurations of the relationships among the veil, tradition, and
resistance, which were made possible and necessary by concrete material
conditions of the struggle.[146]

In addition to developing subversive practices of infiltration and strategic surveillance, Algerian combatants were confronted with the need to

respond to a massive colonial machinery of knowledge production and collection. We saw earlier that every piece of information recovered by agents of the colonial state was recorded and analyzed in a system of permanent registration in an attempt to prevent acts of terrorism. This presented somewhat of a catch-22 for the revolutionary leadership. On the one hand, successful anticolonial counterattack required "perfect knowledge of the Casbah and its smallest nooks," as well as of the position and actions of agents of the colonial state.[147] On the other hand, knowledge was dangerous because there was a constant risk that it might fall into the hands of colonial authorities through arrests or torture. As a consequence, it was desirable for combatants to know as little as possible. To negotiate the tension between the need for information and the danger knowledge posed to the mission, the FLN implemented a system of internal compartmentalization characterized by three principles.

The first was what the colonial army identified as a principle of mutual ignorance, according to which FLN members had very limited knowledge of other members.[148] The only other members they knew were those who were part of their mission and necessary for its success. Drif recounted, "At least in Algiers, the FLN was an organization simultaneously effective, extremely anchored in the people, but very compartmentalized. So I only knew . . . in the FLN Nabila, who was my friend Samia, Mourad, of whom I knew nothing, and the grocer, about whom I knew nothing either."[149]

The second was the principle of limitation of knowledge, which ensured that combatants had access only to information that was of direct relevance to them and their mission. As Drif succinctly put it, "The less you know, the better."[150]

The third principle enjoined strict rules of conduct in case of arrest and torture of combatants that were intended to prevent the colonial authorities from obtaining information about the organization or, if a victim talked, to make sure that any information obtained was worthless. For this purpose, one of the "holy rules" of the life of a combatant was to "break immediately with everything that an arrested person knew about the organization."[151] By staying away from members connected to and hideouts known by the arrested person, other combatants attempted to minimize the risk of being captured themselves. Further, arrested combatants were to "hang on for 48 hours without talking"[152] to buy the organization enough time to "take measures to ensure that any extracted information would no longer be of any value."[153] When the conditions of their arrest allowed, combatants also attempted to destroy as much evidence as possible. Take as an example Drif's account of her arrest by French paras in September 1957. Betrayed by a fellow combatant who had informed the paras of a secret shelter in which Drif and Yacef were hiding, the two combatants were unable to escape. Aware of the inevitability of their capture, Drif set fire to documents stored in the shelter to "let the fire do its salvific work of destruction of the documents, especially the list of names."[154] In sum, mutual ignorance, limited access to information, and strict rules of conduct in case of arrest served as an antidote to French military intelligence by preventing or at least minimizing the transfer of critical knowledge to colonial authorities.

These testimonies and analyses suggest that the frontists' mode of understanding discourses and practices of resistance differed in important ways from the French conceptualization of armed resistance as polemic terrorism. While for the colonial state, terrorism was a new phenomenon that dictated adequate tactics of counterinsurgency, Algerian combatants regarded armed resistance as a response to and wholly determined by a political system that effectively served as an instrument of a war that France had started in 1830. To put this more clearly, while the French colonial army appeared to reactivate practices of colonial war, particularly during the Battle of Algiers, it understood and justified these techniques in rather different ways. Indeed, it was the Algerian combatants who inscribed themselves in the nineteenth-century discourse of colonial war that the colonial state had introduced to defend war between distinct communities foreign to each other and threatening each other's survival.

Despite their differences, however, frontists and French forces inhabited the same conceptual framework and inscribed their practices in a distinctly biopolitical rationality. In fact, it was precisely by virtue of a shared epistemic and political space that the articulation of opposing positions in the conflict became possible. This was achieved by what Foucault described as the "tactical reversibility of the discourse," which requires the "regularity of the epistemological field" in order to allow the discourse "to be used in struggles that are extradiscursive." It is worth quoting Foucault at some length here:

The fact that this epistemic web is so tightly woven certainly does not mean that everyone is thinking along the same lines. It is in fact a precondition for not thinking along the same lines or for thinking along different lines; and it is that which makes the differences politically pertinent. If different subjects are to be able to speak, to occupy different tactical positions, and if they are to be able to find themselves in mutually adversarial positions, there has to be a tight field, there has to be a very tightly woven network to regularize historical knowledge. As the field of knowledge becomes more regular, it becomes increasingly possible for the subjects who speak within it to be divided along strict lines of confrontation, and it becomes increasingly possible to make the contending discourses function as different tactical units within overall strategies.[155]

Consider the following testimony given by Louisette Ighilahriz, a combatant and the first Algerian woman to give a detailed account of the violence suffered at the hands of French soldiers:

> I did not define myself as a terrorist nor did I feel like one; on the contrary: I had confidence that I was fighting for a noble cause. I was a simple *moujahida*. It was the French soldiers who regarded us as terrorists! I felt like an Algerian resistance fighter who had only one wish: that the racism, the humiliations, and the segregation between Algerians and French would stop.[156]

It is clear that Ighilahriz here accepts the colonizer's definition of terrorism, but she does so in order to deny that it adequately describes her actions. More important, however, this denial serves to legitimize armed resistance. If a terrorist is someone who fights for an ignoble cause, then Ighilahriz's fight against racism, humiliation, and segregation cannot possibly make her a terrorist. That is, rejecting French descriptions of Algerian combatants as false is not merely a matter of knowledge and truth but an operation of power that shapes the field of political and strategic possibilities. It is by virtue of a shared epistemic frame that these different strategies become intelligible and politically salient.

Competing evaluations of the conflict were firmly anchored in a biopolitical rationality. Even though the frontists inscribed themselves in a discourse of war between different populations that were foreign to each other, waging war was justified as necessary for the survival of the Algerian people. As Drif argued, armed resistance was required because "this kind of system does not leave you any other chance than to die in order to live in your country."[157] For France, Algeria's fate was equally a matter of national salvation, and it was this biopolitical concern that shaped the development of France's position on Algeria's status. We saw that in the nineteenth century, colonial war was justified as a precondition for the settlement of Algeria with Europeans and thus a means of realizing the regeneration of French society and securing France's political reputation. In the twentieth century, by contrast, military action was no longer justified as a method of subjugating a foreign population but as a way of maintaining internal order in the face of a terrorist threat.

Even the sudden shift in French policy toward Algeria after 1959 appealed to the salvation of the Republic. On the left, politicians and intellectuals began to oppose the effort to keep Algeria French, claiming that the means to do so (e.g., torture, internment, or collective punishment) threatened the Republic.[158] On the right, economic considerations and racist prejudice led to the conclusion that the costs of keeping Algeria French far outweighed the benefits.[159] As the historian Todd Shepard shows, between 1959 and 1962, France engaged in a rewriting of history that not only covered over the abrupt reversal of its position on Algerian independence but also allowed for the portrayal of decolonization as a historical necessity and its celebration as a victory of French republicanism.[160] This chapter has reconstructed a central aspect of this history, which provided the conditions of emergence of a set of novel and politically useful concepts and practices of terrorism and counterterrorism under conditions of imperial politics and settler colonialism. In chapter 5, I interrogate their persistence and examine the way in which the heterogeneous set of discourses, practices, norms, and experiences of terrorism excavated so far continues to shape our historical present.

5

REIMAGINING TERRORISM
AT THE END OF HISTORY

In addition to realizing Algerian independence, the Algerian Revolution had a lasting impact on political developments inside and outside the former French colony. In Algeria, the late 1980s saw the rise of new political forces that challenged the power of the FLN, the only party since 1962. In particular, the Front Islamique du Salut (FIS, Islamic Salvation Front), an Islamist political movement bent on establishing an Islamic state under sharia law in Algeria, was very successful in local elections in 1990 and the first round of parliamentary elections in 1991. In response, the Algerian army called off general elections in 1992, staged a military coup, declared a state of emergency, dissolved the FIS, and subjected FIS members to measures such as raids, torture, and internment. In 1993, the FIS called for armed resistance, and the country moved toward a civil war, which the government refused to identify as such.[1] Thus, Lazreg suggests that the years between 1992 and 2002 were an "uncanny repetition of history" in which "the hounded 'Muslim' of yesteryear was now in a position to hound the Islamist."[2] It was a "reenactment of history" in which the same drama played out, except with different characters.[3]

Outside Algeria, the legacy of the revolution was twofold. On the one hand, political figures like Yassir Arafat, Nelson Mandela, and Angela Davis regarded the Algerian Revolution as an exemplar of anticolonial struggle. On the other hand, the governments of Israel, apartheid South Africa, and the United States sought to learn its lessons. Interest in the

Algerian Revolution, in particular French counterterrorism during the Battle of Algiers, resurged in the early twenty-first century when the U.S. military was confronted with an insurgency after its invasion of Iraq in 2003. On August 27, 2003, the U.S. Pentagon put on a special screening of Gillo Pontecorvo's 1965 movie *The Battle of Algiers*, a dramatization of French counterterrorism against the FLN in Algeria's capital from 1956 to 1957.[4] The Pentagon advertised the movie as a cautionary tale of "how to win a battle against terrorism and lose the war of ideas":

> Children shoot soldiers at point blank range. Women plant bombs in cafes. Soon the entire Arab population builds to a mad fervor. Sound familiar? The French have a plan. It succeeds tactically, but fails strategically. To understand why, come to a rare showing of this film.[5]

Presumably, the Pentagon regarded the screening as an opportunity for U.S. troops to learn from France's mistakes. Although the French army was able to crush the uprising in the casbah, we saw in the previous chapter that French counterterrorism engendered new practices of resistance and failed, in the long run, to keep Algeria French. If the U.S. military wanted to succeed both tactically and strategically in the Middle East, it had to understand why the French had failed to win the war. It had to find a way to defeat the Iraqi insurgency without losing the ideological battle and jeopardizing stability and peace in the Middle East.

In hindsight, it is clear that the U.S. military learned only half the lesson. When a U.S. soldier was questioned about alleged mistreatment of Iraqis in 2005, he responded, "It's a little like the French colonel in 'The Battle of Algiers.' . . . You're all complaining about the tactics I am using to win the war, but that is what I am doing—winning the war."[6] But the U.S. army not only did not win the war but also did not really win the battle against the Iraqi insurgency. Instead, the U.S. occupation of Iraq led to a destabilization of the Middle East and an intensification of violence, both in the region and beyond. Not only had U.S. operations divided and destroyed the regional powers that had ensured order, but the army's actions had also created widespread opposition to the United States, from which movements such as al-Qaeda and Daesh draw support.[7]

Lazreg describes the taking up of the Algerian Revolution as a reference point in the U.S. invasion of Iraq as a redoubling of the repetition of history that occurred in 1990s Algeria. She identifies clear continuities between what she calls French state terrorism in Algeria and the United States' abuse of prisoners in the so-called war on terror: the war was not declared; the cited casus belli were mere pretexts; foreign territory was occupied; torture and detention were widely used; and terrorism was defined as a new kind of war. Lazreg holds that these similarities are "not fortuitous." Indeed, the Algerian Revolution served as "a source of information, if not inspiration, for the U.S. government."[8] That is, the techniques, methods, and devices used by the U.S. military in the Middle East were modeled on tactics of counterterrorism deployed by the French army in Algeria. In this way, French imperialism constituted a "primer for American imperial politics."[9]

In this chapter, I want to complicate this account of the continuities between past and present. Focusing on post-9/11 U.S. counterterrorism, I argue that we are not simply witnessing a repetition, reenactment, or replay of French counterterrorism in Algeria but a revision, rearrangement, and reworking of a much longer history of terrorism examined in preceding chapters. Following Kevin Olson's suggestion that we must look for forms of "creative improvisation" rather than mere repetition of past concepts and practices,[10] we might say that the present is not the same play enacted by a different cast but a different drama performed by a different cast on a different stage. Even though today's characters are well trained in the basic techniques of acting, they make them their own and adjust them to a different set. Moreover, and importantly, they also improvise. Improvisation is characterized by spontaneity and invention, but it requires a preexisting framework, as well as an understanding of the domain of improvisation. Accordingly, contemporary U.S. counterterrorism practices rely on creative extemporization at the same time as they take place and acquire stability within a historically formed dispositif of terrorism, in which charismatic, systemic, doxastic, identarian, strategic, criminal, and polemic terrorism coalesce in what I will call *synthetic terrorism*, which applies to tyrants and dictators, failed or rogue states, belief systems, racial identities, criminal actions, tactics of warfare, and types of war.

To say that terrorism today is synthetic is, crucially, not to say that it is the result of a continuous historical development. Nor is it to say that terrorism has a single, identifiable, and definable meaning. Rather, my claim is that the present moment makes possible the convergence of various historical discourses and practices, some of which I have examined in previous chapters, in a dispositif of terrorism. Consider as a helpful example Nietzsche's description of the concept of punishment in terms of a "synthesis of 'meanings'" in which the entire history of punishment "crystallizes in a sort of unity which is difficult to unravel, difficult to analyse, and ... completely *beyond definition*." But despite this unity, Nietzsche maintains, "one can still perceive how in each individual case the elements of the synthesis change their value and reorganize themselves accordingly, so that now one, now another element comes to the fore and dominates at the expense of the rest; even how under the right circumstances one element ... seems to cancel out all the others."[11]

Terrorism is in this way "overlaid with all sorts of uses."[12] It is a composite of loosely bound elements that can be distinguished as a matter of rationality, even if they often overlap on the register of acts, devices, methods, and tactics. To put this slightly differently, we might say that in archaeological terms, terrorism is polysemous, that is, a sign with multiple meanings. Genealogically, terrorism is best understood as the relation among a heterogeneous set of practices, discourses, institutions, laws, judgments, and strategies. In this sense, synthetic terrorism is a dispositif that serves the strategic function of establishing a pervasive network of power by responding to an imminent, ubiquitous, and amorphous terrorist threat. By uniting a variety of threats in a single frame, the dispositif of terrorism makes possible a multiplicity of mechanisms of social defense against threats including, but not limited to, violent aggression, immigration, limitations on free trade, oil depletion, violation of human rights, drug trafficking, and new diseases. However, while previously the dispositif of terrorism served to defend society or the nation from internal and external threats, what is defended today is not just a particular national or social body but also a specific notion of humanity.

The aim of this chapter is to examine the elaboration and stabilization of synthetic terrorism between the late 1980s and the early twenty-first century. I argue that the contemporary U.S. imagination of terrorism as a general security threat is not the cause of new global power relations but the correlate of a political rationality that gained influence in the late 1980s and posits the universalization of capitalism and liberal democracy as the end of historical development. September 11, 2001, was not a rupture or caesura that made necessary new forms of power but an occasion to implement a legal paradigm of executive prerogative and reshape the future according to the United States' vision. I consider the salience of terrorism in the production of a normative idea of citizenship and humanity and argue that the dispositif of terrorism that emerged after 9/11 serves as a means of social defense in a global economy of power that exercises the sovereign right to kill in the name of national security and humanitarianism.

THE END OF HISTORY

We saw in chapters 2, 3, and 4 that each historical context under examination gave rise to particular modes of understanding terrorism. After a brief episode of charismatic terrorism, the French revolutionary period was primarily marked by systemic and doxastic terrorism, while identarian terrorism as articulated by Babeuf—namely, as a political identity to be affirmed and cultivated—never really got off the ground. Late imperial and Bolshevik Russia, by contrast, featured a predominantly strategic concept of terrorism elaborated and endorsed by social revolutionaries and Bolshevik leaders. Finally, the Algerian Revolution gave rise to polemic terrorism, which developed out of a legal notion of criminal terrorism. Since the late 1980s, we have seen the formation of a notion of terrorism, namely, synthetic terrorism, that is not so much new as it is a blend of already-existing concepts mapped in previous chapters. How did terrorism become this composite term?

Synthetic terrorism has its historical and conceptual conditions of emergence in the rise to political prominence of American neoconservatism since the 1970s. American neoconservatism originated in a socialist critique of democratic foreign policy and draws heavily on a teleological view of history advanced by the philosophers Alexandre Kojève and Leo Strauss. Although Kojève and Strauss may not have endorsed many neoconservative claims and programs, their ideas entered political discourse and heavily influenced the development of American neoconservatism through a tight network of individuals connected by Albert Wohlstetter, a professor at the University of Chicago and former analyst for the Rand

Corporation.[13] Wohlstetter's students and friends are the who's who of post-9/11 foreign policy and include Paul Wolfowitz, Donald Rumsfeld, Richard Perle, and Zalmay Khalilzad.[14] The term *neoconservatism* describes a heterogeneous movement that is united by a shared set of policy principles, such as a minimal state; fiscal conservatism; individual liberty; traditional values such as "religion, the family, the 'high culture' of Western civilization"; an affirmation of equality of rights and a simultaneous rejection of egalitarianism; and a belief in the market as the most efficient solution for social, economic, and political problems.[15] Most important, with regard to foreign policy, neoconservatism holds that "American democracy is not likely to survive for long in a world that is overwhelmingly hostile to American values, if only because our transactions (economic and diplomatic) with other nations are bound eventually to have a profound impact on our own domestic economic and political system."[16] As a consequence, neoconservatism promotes the expansion of American values and free-market economics by any means necessary, including military force.

These claims are motivated by a belief in the end of history and an affirmation of American-style liberal democracy as the only viable posthistorical political model. The most systematic elaboration of this thesis was supplied by Francis Fukuyama in his 1989 article "The End of History?," which was based on a lecture Fukuyama delivered at the University of Chicago at the invitation of Strauss's and Kojève's student Allan Bloom. Fukuyama's central thesis is that the end of the Cold War signaled "the end of history as such: that is, the end point of mankind's ideological evolution and the universalization of Western liberal democracy as the final form of human government."[17] Endorsing Kojève's interpretation of Hegel, Fukuyama argues that "the basic *principles* of the liberal democratic state could not be improved upon," even though they had to be expanded spatially and extended to the entirety of human civilization.[18] The inevitable outcome is a politically and economically liberal "universal and homogeneous state," by which he means liberal democracy. Although Fukuyama claims that the elimination of challenges to and the imposition of liberal democracy and free markets should be achieved by force if necessary, as in the case of Germany or Japan, the key to the installation of the universal and homogeneous state is economic liberalization. In particular, Fukuyama argues that because the triumph of the

Western political model and the American way of life put an end to ideological conflicts, economic activity remained as the essentially exclusive object of political government. Thus, the spread of liberal economies would generate and stabilize liberal politics. As Fukuyama observes, "Political liberalism has been following economic liberalism . . . with seeming inevitability."[19]

Fukuyama elaborates on this argument in his 1992 book *The End of History and the Last Man*, in which he insists that economic liberalization alone does not necessarily result in liberal democracy. Indeed, there are several authoritarian regimes that outstrip many democratic societies in economic growth and productivity. Therefore, Fukuyama introduces the desire for recognition as a second necessary element for the establishment of the universal and homogeneous state. Drawing on Hegel's famous account of the struggle for recognition between master and slave, Fukuyama argues that the human desire to be recognized as a human being with value and dignity gives rise to an egalitarian political system in which all individuals are treated as free and autonomous human beings. Fukuyama concludes that at the international level, such reciprocal recognition of each other's equality significantly diminishes the threat of conflict and war. Indeed, Fukuyama notes that "there is substantial empirical evidence from the past couple of hundred years that liberal democracies do not behave imperialistically toward one another, even if they are perfectly capable of going to war with states that are not democracies and do not share their fundamental values."[20]

Although Fukuyama emphasizes the desire for recognition rather than a concern for security as the principal driving force of political liberalization, his claims may well be construed as an argument for imposing economic and political liberalism, by force if necessary. Specifically, if the universal and homogeneous state is crucial for international peace and national security, then military intervention in nonliberal and noncapitalist countries can be justified both as a peace-enforcing mission and as humanitarian intervention in pursuit of human dignity and reciprocal recognition.

A version of this argument underpins the United States' National Security Strategy (NSS). Established by the Goldwater-Nichols Department of Defense Reorganization Act of 1986, which subjected the Department of Defense and the U.S. armed forces to radical restructuring, the NSS is a periodic report prepared by the White House to provide a comprehensive description of the administration's approach to the nation's major security concerns. It is primarily a means of political communication intended to clarify the country's national security interests, establish consensus about foreign policy, and justify financial expenditures for its implementation, which, however, relies on supporting legislation.[21] Since its first installment under President Ronald Reagan in January 1987, the NSS has exhibited five main features that are characteristic of the neoconservative imagination outlined by Fukuyama and critical for understanding the elaboration of synthetic terrorism: (1) a teleological view of historical development; (2) an eschatological view of history as a struggle between liberal democracy and totalitarianism; (3) a firm belief that America is on the right side of this struggle; (4) the stipulation of American-style liberal democracy as the only political model; and (5) a strong economic understanding of freedom, peace, and prosperity.

Consider NSS 2002 as a particularly forceful statement of this view. Couched in a teleological language of historical progress, the document asserts that "the great struggles of the twentieth century between liberty and totalitarianism ended with a decisive victory for the forces of freedom—and a single sustainable model for national success: freedom, democracy, and free enterprise." But the language of universal values of freedom, democracy, and prosperity is underpinned by an economic understanding of these values that gives rise to an imperial strategy in the service of securing U.S. interests. As NSS 2002 notes, "We will actively work to bring the hope of democracy, free markets and free trade to every corner of the world. . . . The United States will work with individual nations, entire regions, and the entire global trading community to build a world that trades in freedom and therefore grows in prosperity."[22] Moreover, NSS 2002 defends economic freedom as a universal moral standard, stating that "the concept of 'free trade' arose as a moral principle even before it became a pillar of economics. If you can make something that others value, you should be able to sell it to them. If others make something that you value, you should be able to buy it. This is real freedom, the freedom for a person—or a nation—to make a living."[23]

On this view, then, worldwide peace and the preservation of American interests can be assured only if "the values of freedom [which] are right and true for every person, in every society," are implemented across the globe.[24] The importance of exporting freedom is anchored in a desire for security. In order to maintain global order, the American grand strategy is designed according to a logic by which poverty results in failed states, which in turn present a threat to the security and prosperity of the United States. In an interdependent world, the economy is not a zero-sum game. Rather, the already powerful depend on the growth and progress of disadvantaged and less economically successful states for the maintenance and expansion of their wealth. As a consequence, the freedom offered to failed, failing, and weak states is the freedom to participate in a system that is said to be the only way to prosperity. For those who are already successful—and of course, this success is measured by their own standards—freedom has no value in itself; it is useful only insofar as it is instrumental for economic growth. In short, freedom is a necessary condition for the smooth functioning of the market. As a consequence, America's apparent commitment to benefiting the poor and oppressed is actually an imperial strategy driven by the exclusive self-interest of major powers, dressed up as a humanitarian mission.[25]

Two key insights follow from this discussion. First, 9/11 was not a caesura that inaugurated a new political project but an occasion to reshape the future according to a global vision that had been elaborated since the 1970s. Indeed, NSS 2002 describes 9/11 as a "moment of opportunity to extend the benefits of freedom across the globe."[26] Therefore, and second, the inevitability of liberal democracy as the ideal political model made possible a threefold legitimation of the use of force against illiberal and undemocratic regimes: (1) as a strategy of national security and international peace; (2) as a humanitarian intervention intended to extend human rights and dignity to all humanity; and (3) as a means of accelerating history's progress toward its inexorable end.

This view, which is characteristic of American neoconservatism, shares key features of the political rationality of *raison d'État* discussed in chapter 2, albeit in modified form.[27] Recall that for *raison d'État*, there is nothing outside the state, whose existence must be guaranteed by any means necessary. Accordingly, the suspension of legality and the use of force are legitimate if they serve the purpose of founding or preserving the state. We saw that in times of crisis, *raison d'État* manifested itself in the form of a *coup d'État*, which suspended the law and authorized discretionary power unbound by legal procedure in order to save the state.

In the same vein, American neoconservatism is absolutely immanent in the political model of American-style liberal democracy and a free-market economy. As the universal and homogeneous state, American liberalism is without alternative and constitutes the only viable political model, toward which history inescapably progresses. What is more, while liberal democracies coexist in peaceful cooperation, illiberal and undemocratic regimes that do not share in free trade present a threat to national security and international peace. By violating universal principles of individual freedom and autonomy, they also deny fundamental human rights to their own populations. As a consequence, the use of force against such regimes is justified in the name of the health and survival of the United States and its citizens, as well as the realization of basic human rights. The neoconservative project is thus underwritten by a sort of imperial *raison d'État* that permits and requires the suspension of law and the use of force in defense of society at home and humanity abroad. To put this differently, the use of force against all kinds of threats to ostensibly universal values of freedom, democracy, and prosperity is best understood as an exercise of the old sovereign right to kill for the biopolitical purpose of ensuring the survival and well-being not only of the nation but also of humanity. We will see that in this context, synthetic terrorism emerged as a composite of various meanings and allowed for the formation of a surreptitious and versatile dispositif of social defense that made possible the global expansion of American sovereignty through a new legal paradigm of executive primacy.

EXECUTIVE PRIMACY

What I call imperial *raison d'État* is perhaps given its clearest expression in the legal paradigm of executive primacy.[28] Although the implementation of this paradigm under George W. Bush's presidency was certainly expedited by 9/11, its intellectual basis had been articulated half a decade earlier by John Yoo, a law professor at the University of California, Berkeley. In his 1996 article "The Continuation of Politics by Other Means: The Original Understanding of War Powers," Yoo advanced a textualist defense of presidential initiative in war and argued that the founders had intended the U.S. Constitution to preserve the structure of the British monarchy. In this way, they had invested the president with the power of the king and Congress with the rights and duties of Parliament. Accordingly, Yoo concluded that the president was a "king-in-the-making" and served as the protector of the people.[29] For this reason, he had ultimate powers of war, and any war initiated by the president was constitutional even without formal declaration or congressional approval.

Yoo had been regarded as "an eccentric figure at the periphery of legal thought" throughout the 1990s, but he rose to political prominence during the 2000 presidential election when he designed the Republican strategy to stop the recount of votes in Florida, thus helping Bush to victory.[30] Bush later appointed Yoo as deputy assistant U.S. attorney general in the Office of Legal Counsel in 2001, where his articulation of the paradigm of executive primacy became the foundation of foreign policy and the doctrinal basis for the administration's response to 9/11. The so-called 9/11 Resolution, drafted by Yoo and passed on September 18, 2001, authorized the use of U.S. armed forces against the perpetrators of the 9/11 attacks and placed constitutional authority to do so with the president, even, and crucially, in the absence of a formal declaration of war. In light of "acts of treacherous violence . . . committed against the United States and its citizens," the resolution approved the use of "all necessary and appropriate force against those nations, organizations, or persons [the President] determines planned, authorized, committed, or aided the terrorist attacks that occurred on September 11, 2001, or harbored such organizations or persons, in order to prevent any future acts of international terrorism against the United States by such nations, organizations or persons."[31] By failing to specify the kinds of actions that were to be considered necessary and appropriate, as well as the legitimate targets of such actions, the resolution gave President Bush essentially unlimited power. As Yoo explained in a memorandum issued on September 25, 2001, the president had broad constitutional authority to take both retaliatory and preemptive military action against persons, organization, and states "suspected of involvement in terrorist attacks on the United States," as well as states "suspected of harboring or supporting such organizations," regardless of "whether or not they can be linked to the specific terrorist incidents of September 11."[32] In other words, in the name of self-defense, national security, and the protection of U.S. citizens at home and abroad, the president was authorized to take any action whatever against anyone suspected of aiding and abetting terrorism. This included the use of military force; military tribunals; summary executions; apprehension, rendition, and detention of terrorist suspects; and enhanced interrogation techniques, or torture. Moreover, these practices were not justified only as a matter of foreign policy against noncitizens and other states; rather, the paradigm of executive primacy mandated the domestic use of such practices, as well as their implementation against U.S. citizens, when required for the protection of national security interests.[33] These broad powers of the president both permitted and required an equally broad understanding of the threat in defense against which executive primacy could be invoked. This threat took the form of synthetic terrorism.

SYNTHETIC TERRORISM

The formation of synthetic terrorism was made possible by the neoconservative belief in the universal and homogeneous state as the end of history and executive privilege as the legal paradigm intended to realize it. September 11, 2001, constituted an important moment in this development, even though the appearance of neoconservative politics preceded 9/11 by at least two decades. But the events of 9/11 provided an occasion to implement a neoconservative program, including executive primacy in foreign policy, that facilitated the stabilization of synthetic terrorism in its current form. Between the late 1980s and the contemporary post-9/11 moment, synthetic terrorism crystallized as the new enemy whose imminent and always present threat grounds the ostensible necessity of invasive and often illegal—or, perhaps, extralegal—techniques of state power. This process of stabilization can be traced in the transformation of terrorism in America's National Security Strategy since the late 1980s.

Between 1987 and 1993, synthetic terrorism emerged as a technique of American foreign policy that coalesced from four notions of terrorism identified in previous chapters: systemic, strategic, polemic, and doxastic terrorism. During this period, especially before 1991, terrorism was largely understood as a form of state policy (its systemic dimension) and was associated with communism and the Soviet Union (its doxastic element), as well as subversive forces and wars of national liberation (its strategic and polemic facets). Consider as an example NSS 1987, which established the effective combat of terrorism as "a major national security objective of the United States."[34] But the document failed to offer a clear definition of the term. Rather, the term *terrorism* was used to name a variety of phenomena, behaviors, and attitudes. Specifically, terrorism was understood in the following ways: a threat to national security "short of armed conflict;"[35] an "important aspect of Low Intensity Conflict;" a "subversive weapon;"[36] "an instrument of state policy, particularly by Syria, Lybia, and Iran;"[37] "state-sponsored terrorism," which represented a threat to the "stability of friendly governments;"[38] the actions of national liberation movements sponsored by the Soviet Union through "middle men" and "radical governments such as Cuba, North Korea, Nicaragua, Syria, and Lybia;"[39] and a strategy endorsed by "Marxist regimes."[40] NSS 1987 further posited a clear connection between the Soviet Union and terrorism, asserting that "the evidence of the relationship between the Soviet Union and the growth of worldwide terrorism is now conclusive."[41] Moreover, the document identified state-sponsored terrorism as a new "worldwide phenomenon" that "directly attacks our democratic values, undermines our diplomatic efforts for peaceful solutions to conflicts, and erodes the foundations of civilized societies."[42]

The characterization of terrorism offered in NSS 1987 illustrates with particular clarity the conflation of systemic, doxastic, strategic, and polemic conceptions of terrorism. Terrorism was a strategy deployed by the Soviet Union to threaten U.S. national interests, including the survival of the United States as a free and independent nation; a growing U.S. economy; a global expansion of freedom, democracy, and free markets; international stability; and strong political alliances. Soviet expansionism, in other words, had produced and relied on international terrorism as "an additional threat, which is particularly insidious in nature and growing in scope" and which was essentially "state-supported."[43] Terrorism was understood in terms of "state-sponsored terrorism,"[44] an "instrument of state policy,"[45] and state conduct on a par with hostage taking, arson, bombings, and armed assault.[46] Because of its use of such means of low-intensity warfare, terrorism thus also had an important polemic dimension. Its emerging association with opposition to civilized societies foreshadowed the function of the term as a humanitarian norm that distinguishes the civilized world from its ostensibly uncivilized, barbarian other.

The view of terrorism articulated in NSS 1987 came to underpin NSS discourse in subsequent years. NSS 1988, for instance, regarded state-sponsored terrorism as the primary threat to national security, even though it no longer identified the Soviet Union but rather Iran and its "terrorist surrogates in Lebanon," as well as Cuba, Libya, and Nicaragua, as the primary sponsor of international terrorism. NSS 1988 nevertheless insisted that Iran's actions "objectively benefit the Soviet Union globally"[47] by weakening governments fighting "radical and insurgent groups supported by the Soviets." This emphasis on state-sponsored terrorism was maintained in NSS 1990, which located the gravest threat of such conduct in the Middle East. In addition, both NSS 1988 and NSS 1990 diagnosed a new threat to U.S. interests in "increasing linkages between international terrorists and narcotics traffickers"[48] and asserted that "the twin scourges of international terrorism and narcotics trafficking also pose very high-priority, but non-traditional, intelligence requirements."[49] By 1991, these twin dangers had become unified in the new threat of "narco-terrorists."[50] NSS 1993 merely offered a brief statement on terrorism as one among many problems of national defense. Although its description of terrorism as a military problem and as state conduct foregrounded its polemic and systemic dimensions, NSS 1993 also drew on strategic and doxastic conceptions of terrorism by defining it in terms of "terrorist acts such as arson, bombings, and armed assaults"[51] that proliferated in the wake of "ethnic and aggressive nationalistic tensions around the world."[52]

Having identified the nature of the threat as a composite of systemic, strategic, doxastic, and polemic conceptions of terrorism, U.S. foreign policy in the late 1980s and early 1990s promoted the containment of Soviet expansionism as the most effective means of eliminating terrorism. "Increasingly frequent, indiscriminate" terrorism of the sort used by the Soviet Union and its vassals further resulted in calls for "specialized forces . . . configured to deal with terrorism,"[53] primarily by "deterring, preempting and effectively reacting to international terrorist incidents."[54] Given ostensibly "irrefutable evidence of Soviet expansionist aspirations," the United States sought to protect its interests by "arresting the spread of the Soviet Union's particular brand of totalitarianism and communism."[55] Moreover, the NSS affirmed the need for military operations, nontraditional forms of intelligence, and the targeted use of foreign aid as instruments of counterterrorism.

In sum, then, the period between 1987 and 1993 witnessed the formation of synthetic terrorism as a technique of U.S. foreign policy, which emerged as the effect of a political rationality whose main concern was the protection of national interests against Soviet-style communism and totalitarianism. As a consequence, certain nonstate groups like the Taliban, who are today considered terrorists, were then understood as "freedom fighters" who resisted the Soviet occupation of Afghanistan.[56] As the enemy of the United States' main enemy, the Taliban were friends who deserved support rather than terrorists. This changed in the years between 1994 and 2001, when the technique of synthetic terrorism gained prominence by being articulated against a new and more expansive target.

In the second half of the 1990s, the concept of terrorism underwent another series of transformations or, perhaps better, a process of radicalization such that by the end of the 1990s, the United States regarded itself as embattled in a "fight against terrorism."[57] This process was inaugurated by the loss of communism as the first and foremost threat to American national interests. NSS 1994 announced the end of the Cold War and the beginning of a new period "of great promise but also great uncertainty."[58] U.S. values were no longer under attack from a single enemy but "on many fronts at once."[59] The struggle between freedom and totalitarianism had not ended with the collapse of the Soviet Union but rather had transformed into a historical battle between those who endorsed American values and those who did not. NSS 1995 observed that what had to be defended was "an idea that comes under many names—democracy, liberty, civility, pluralism—but which together are the values of a society where leaders and governments preserve individual freedoms, and ensure opportunity and human dignity."

> As the President has said, "We face a contest as old as history—a struggle between freedom and tyranny; between tolerance and isolation. It is a fight between those who would build free societies governed by laws and those who would impose their will by force. Our struggle today, in a world more high-tech, more fast moving, more chaotically diverse than ever, is the age-old fight between hope and fear."[60]

Thus, instead of an easing of tension in light of America's proclaimed victory over the forces of Soviet-style totalitarianism, national security discourse in the second half of the 1990s was marked by a sense of uncertainty and acute new dangers. NSS 1994 warned that "violent extremists threaten fragile peace processes, from the Mideast to South Africa," and observed "a resurgence of militant nationalism as well as ethnic and religious conflict."[61] Put differently, the disintegration of the Soviet bloc gave rise to new, diverse and amorphous threats. Moreover, incidents such as the World Trade Center bombing in 1993 and Iraq's planned attempt to assassinate President Bush showed that terrorist threats loomed both within and outside the United States. As a consequence, NSS 1995 affirmed that "the line between our domestic and foreign policies is disappearing."[62] Accordingly, national security discourse in the mid-1990s conceived of terrorism not as a problem of military intervention, strictly speaking, but as a task for "intelligence, diplomatic and rule-of-law activities"—what I described in chapter 4 as a problem of peace enforcement.[63]

Drawing on Schmitt and Foucault, I argued there that after World War I, previously distinct spheres of internal order, or police power, and external peace, or military power, began to converge in a general peace-enforcing function of the state. As new forms of biopower began to take hold in Western societies, both internal and external enemies appeared as threats to the life and health of populations. As a consequence, they must equally be contained and eliminated. I further showed that a new form of polemic terrorism emerged during the 1950s in colonized Algeria as a functional requirement of the formation of the state's task of peace enforcement. Specifically, as Schmitt argued, the new peace-enforcing function of the state requires ideological phenomena that justify the use of escalating forms of state violence against internal and external enemies. In the same way, the transformation of synthetic terrorism during the second half of the 1990s should be understood as an effect of the collapse of the distinction between internal order and external peace and thus the advent of peace enforcement as the primary mode of American security policy. In addition, this peace-enforcing function was no longer limited to problems internal to the state and a matter of domestic policy, as in colonized Algeria, but was projected beyond its boundaries onto the register of international relations and foreign policy. Consequently, the extension of the concept of terrorism grew proportionately with the expansion of the scope of American peace-enforcing powers.

By the end of the 1990s, and no doubt because of the galvanizing effect of attacks on American embassies in Kenya and Tanzania perpetrated by al-Qaeda in 1998, terrorism was understood as a strategy of asymmetric or irregular warfare executed by a diverse set of actors, including states, who were united by their targeting of innocents and their hatred of democracy and American values. Consider, for instance, NSS 1998, which associates terrorism with "Osama bin Laden, perhaps the preeminent organizer and financier of international terrorism in the world today," as well as with "groups associated with bin Laden [that] come from diverse places, but share a hatred for democracy, a fanatical glorification of violence and a horrible distortion of their religion to justify the murder of innocents. They have made the United States their adversary precisely because of what we stand for and what we stand against."[64] At the close of the twentieth century, then, terrorism was predominantly understood as a strategy of irregular warfare used by groups associated with bin Laden in an ideological battle between America and so-called Islamic fundamentalism. This understanding exhibited elements of strategic, polemic, charismatic, and doxastic terrorism. In addition, the phenomenon continued to be portrayed as an instrument of state policy and was represented as a set of criminal actions under domestic and international law against which "all available legal mechanisms to punish international terrorists" ought to be exploited.[65]

Rather than providing a legal definition, however, U.S. counterterrorism law merely classified terrorism as a type of violent crime and specified offenses to be punished as acts of terrorism. The Omnibus Counterterrorism Act of 1995, for example, which was introduced to establish federal jurisdiction over international terrorism, describes terrorism in terms of "violent crime" and calls it a "serious and deadly problem" practiced and supported by states and organizations. However, it fails to stipulate a clear definition; instead, it provides a list of offenses, such as hostage taking, murder of internationally protected persons, aircraft piracy and sabotage, and conspiracy to destroy government buildings.[66] Repeating these offenses in its description of terrorism, the Antiterrorism and

Effective Death Penalty Act of 1996 asserts that terrorism is a threat to the "vital interests of the United States" and invokes the power of Congress to punish "crimes against the law of nations."[67]

The expansive notion of synthetic terrorism that emerged in the late 1980s and early 1990s served as a catalyst for the establishment of a new framework for national security and foreign policy during the second half of the 1990s that has all the hallmarks of our present system of counterterrorism. It bears emphasizing that the techniques typically understood as responses to 9/11 preceded the so-called war on terror.[68] NSS 2000, for instance, sums up counterterrorist practices deployed by the United States since 1993:

> Since 1993, a dozen terrorist fugitives have been apprehended overseas and rendered, formally or informally, to the United States to answer for their crimes. . . . Whenever possible, we use law enforcement, diplomatic, and economic tools to wage the fight against terrorism. But there have been, and will be, times when those tools are not enough. As long as terrorists continue to target American citizens, we reserve the right to act in self-defense by striking at their bases and those who sponsor, assist, or actively support them, as we have done over the years in different countries.[69]

Practices of counterterrorism, as well as laws and policies that facilitated a "new and more systematic approach to fighting the terrorist threat of the next century," were thus established throughout the 1990s as means of preempting and responding to terrorism.[70] Under the pretext of preventing terrorist attacks, the last years of the twentieth century, in particular, saw an increasingly "aggressive response to terrorism" that included "enhanced law enforcement and intelligence efforts; vigorous diplomacy and economic sanctions; and, when necessary, military force."[71] In addition, the United States emphasized joint databases and international cooperation in intelligence and law enforcement and established rendition, that is, formal and informal apprehension and transfer of terrorist suspects to the United States, as a main pillar of counterterrorism.[72]

These developments show that the infrastructure of the so-called war on terror was firmly in place before 9/11, even if the attacks on September 11 helped strengthen and expand state power. Thus, 9/11 did not constitute a caesura that radically transformed political discourse and practice; rather, it presented an occasion to expand and make permanent a form of American imperialism that had been in the works for at least two decades. Long-standing domestic and foreign policy concerns, such as the pacification of the Middle East, the suppression of the Taliban in Afghanistan, the toppling of Saddam Hussein, restrictions on immigration, an expansion of emergency systems, the suspension of basic rights, and increased surveillance, could now be justified by a broad notion of synthetic terrorism.

Synthetic terrorism is thus properly understood as an effect rather than the cause of particular political interests whose realization depends on new techniques of power. The justification of these techniques was made possible by a concept of terrorism that simultaneously described (1) premeditated, politically motivated violence against innocents; (2) illegitimate and intolerable behavior, akin to slavery, piracy, and genocide; (3) wanton destruction; (4) actions perpetrated by individuals who seek martyrdom in death; (5) the enemy of civilization; (6) state-sponsored violence; and (7) an attack on democratic values and the American way of life.

The deployment of all these conceptions of terrorism can be seen most clearly in NSS 2002, which justifies a war against terrorism in which "the enemy is not a single political regime or person or religion or ideology."[73] Rather, "the enemy is terrorism—premeditated, politically motivated violence perpetrated against innocents,"[74] on a par with "slavery, piracy, or genocide: behavior that no respectable government can condone or support and all must oppose."[75] Terrorism is further described both as state-sponsored violence[76] and as protected by its "statelessness." Its "avowed tactics are wanton destruction and the targeting of innocents," and "mass civilian casualties is the specific objective of terrorists."[77] Moreover, NSS 2002 explicitly associates terrorism with "the clash inside a civilization, a battle for the future of the Muslim world,"[78] and portrays terrorists as "enemies of civilization" who "seek martyrdom in death."[79] Finally, it presents the war against terrorism as a "war of ideas"[80] and a "struggle of ideas"[81] and inscribes terrorism in a moralizing discourse according to which America's "responsibility to history" is "to rid the world of evil"[82] and defend "our democratic values and way of life."[83]

To be sure, this brief overview of various conceptual uses of the term *terrorism* in NSS 2002 does not offer an exhaustive list of conceptions of terrorism that are operative in contemporary discourses about terrorism. Nevertheless, it serves to illustrate that terrorism today is at once criminal, strategic, identarian, doxastic, charismatic, systemic, and polemic. It is precisely the synthesis of all these different elements in one concept that gives terrorism its current political purchase.

TERRORISM AND CITIZENSHIP

To bring into view the salience of the dynamic of synthetic terrorism, it is helpful to consider its role in producing norms of citizenship and humanity. We saw in chapter 1 that a growing number of legal and political theorists are drawing attention to the role of terrorism in creating a particular image of citizenship and national identity by way of excluding ostensibly unruly and dangerous subjects from the social body. In particular, these scholars emphasize processes of racialization and perverse sexualization, which conflate terrorism with what Muneer Ahmad calls "the Muslim-looking person"[84] and Jasbir Puar refers to as "terrorist look-alikes."[85] Individuals perceived as terrorists are then disidentified as citizens, independently of their legal status. On this view, citizenship names a collective identity, or what Leti Volpp describes as "citizenship as a form of inclusion."[86] This notion of citizenship does not precede our understanding of terrorism, whose perpetrators are then excluded from the social body. Instead, the interpellation of certain subjects as terrorists serves to define citizenship negatively by marking who is not included in a notion of citizenship understood as a collective identity.[87] This is not simply an exclusion of the terrorist other from the fabric of citizenship but rather the simultaneous production of citizen and terrorist as "reciprocal and incompatible" identities.[88] Citizen and terrorist thus stand in a relationship that Colin Koopman describes as reciprocal incompatibility, in which contemporary notions of citizenship and terrorism—much like madness and reason, as well as freedom and power in Foucault's account of modernity—"presuppose one another"[89] at the same time as "they cannot admit of admixture with one another."[90]

Here I want to build on these claims to highlight the specific operation of synthetic terrorism in the production of citizenship. By considering the case of Dzokhar Tsarnaev, also known as the Boston Marathon bomber, I hope to illustrate the way in which the synthetic nature of contemporary terrorism is harnessed to articulate and implement a certain normative view of citizenship. I argue that although terrorism is predominantly associated with a racially and sexually inflected notion of Islam and the Muslim-looking person, other elements of the concept can be brought to the fore to identify perpetrators as terrorists even when they fail to conform to the Muslim-looking construct. In this way, it becomes possible to simultaneously be "one of us," that is, a citizen in both the legal and the inclusive sense, and a terrorist. This, in my view, is precisely what the notion of *domestic terrorism* is intended to capture. By selectively activating different dimensions of the synthetic concept of terrorism, a dispositif of terrorism can be deployed as a broad mechanism of social defense that protects society from a wide variety of threats, including crime, immigration, whistle blowing, and even doing math or reading Heidegger on an airplane.[91]

In 2013, Dzhokhar and his brother, Tamerlan Tsarnaev, detonated two bombs at the Boston Marathon, killing three people and injuring more than 250 others. After a shoot-out with Boston police, in which Tamerlan was killed, Dzhokhar was captured during an unprecedented manhunt in Boston's Watertown area. Before the identity of the perpetrators was confirmed, the FBI was investigating the incident as an act of terrorism, while President Obama cautioned that no one knew "who carried out this attack, or why; whether it was planned and executed by a terrorist organization, foreign or domestic, or was the act of a malevolent individual."[92] The day before the Tsarnaevs were identified, *Salon* columnist David Sirota expressed concern over the political fallout of the bombing. In a piece titled "Let's Hope the Boston Marathon Bomber Is a White American," Sirota argued that the identity of the bombers "will almost certainly dictate what kind of governmental, political and societal response we see in the coming weeks."

> That means regardless of your particular party affiliation, if you care about everything from stopping war to reducing the defense budget to protecting civil liberties to passing immigration reform, you should hope the bomber was a white domestic terrorist. Why? Because only in that case will privilege work to prevent the Boston attack from potentially undermining progress on those other issues.[93]

According to Sirota, perpetrators with white male privilege are usually treated as "lone wolves," while nonwhite suspects are typically regarded as representative of their communities. Recall, for example, Timothy McVeigh, a Persian Gulf War veteran, who detonated a bomb outside the Alfred P. Murrah Federal Building in Oklahoma City, killing 168 people and injuring more than 600 others. After the explosion and lacking information about the perpetrator, the government and the media described the bombing as a case of international terrorism and speculated that it had been perpetrated by the group responsible for the 1993 bombing at the World Trade Center in New York. CBS, ABC, the *Chicago Tribune*, and the *New York Post* all attributed the attack to Middle Eastern terrorists. The Department of Defense called in Arabic speakers to aid with the investigation, and numerous incidents of retaliation against the Muslim community followed. When it became clear that McVeigh was responsible for the attack, talk of terrorism subsided, and his actions were described as revenge against the use of deadly force by government agencies at Ruby Ridge and Waco. The federal government brought terrorism charges according to 18 U.S. Code Chapter 113B. McVeigh was convicted of use of a weapon of mass destruction, conspiracy to use a weapon of mass destruction, destruction with the use of explosives, and eight counts of first-degree murder and was sentenced to death by lethal injection.[94]

The case of McVeigh offers some support for Sirota's claim that the usual response to white perpetrators of acts of terrorism is to individualize their actions and prosecute them through legal means. Nonwhite perpetrators, by contrast, are often portrayed as acting out collective pathologies of particular groups, which are subsequently targeted by measures of social control. Under the pretext of terrorism, their actions tend to trigger an expansion of state power, as well as collective punishment of certain communities in the form of racial profiling and increased surveillance. This explains Sirota's belief that the political ramifications of the Boston Marathon bombing would have been less harmful for everyone had the perpetrator been a white American.

Once the Tsarnaevs' identity was released, however, responses were more complicated than Sirota had expected. Three pieces of information about the brothers seemed particularly difficult to reconcile. First, the brothers were of Chechen descent and thus white by the standards of the U.S. Census Bureau and the Office of Management and Budget. Second, the Tsarnaevs were Muslims. Third, Dzokhar was a naturalized citizen, while Tamerlan was a legal alien whose application for citizenship had been put on hold because of alleged ties to radical Islam. This put the brothers in a strange position between the white American who acts as a lone wolf, on the one hand, and the Muslim-looking person and potential terrorist, on the other. Accordingly, there were two different attempts to make sense of the bombing.

The first view referred to the Tsarnaevs' religion to deny that they were white and affirm that they were terrorists in the sense described by Muneer Ahmad as the fungibility of terrorism and the Muslim-looking person. Consider, for example, *Commentary* columnist Peter Wehner's claim that "despite the most fervent hopes of some writers over at Salon .com, the perpetrators of the Boston Marathon bombing are not 'white Americans'—a classification Salon used to exclude Islamists. . . . In fact, the accumulating evidence . . . points to two young men who were radicalized and became jihadists." For Wehner, the Tsarnaevs were not white Americans because they were Muslims. As such, they were part of the " 'root cause' of this age of terrorism," namely, "political Islam, abroad and increasingly at home."[95] Similarly, Senator Lindsey Graham demanded that the surviving brother, Dzhokhar, be treated as an enemy combatant, who should be held under the law of war. He argued, "You can't hold every person who commits a terrorist attack as an enemy combatant . . . but you have a right, with his radical Islamist ties and the fact that Chechens all over the world are fighting with Al Qaeda."[96] Graham's demand to try Tsarnaev as an enemy combatant required denying Dzokhar citizenship in the inclusive sense. Regardless of his legal status, Graham maintained that Tsarnaev was Muslim and Chechen and, therefore, an enemy combatant who was not protected by domestic and international legal frameworks. By virtue of a racialized identification of terrorists with the Muslim-looking person, Tsarnaev was disidentified as a white American citizen, and his actions were portrayed as terrorism. On this account, terrorism is defined by three necessary and sufficient features, according to which being a terrorist requires (1) engaging in certain criminal actions; (2) holding a particular ideological or religious view; and (3) not being a (white) American citizen in the inclusive sense.

By contrast, the second view, advanced by the U.S. government, affirmed that Tsarnaev was both white and an American citizen. Although this precluded his identification as a terrorist in the sense just discussed, he was nevertheless portrayed as a terrorist in a different, namely, criminal sense. The White House, for instance, argued that as an American citizen, Tsarnaev could not be treated as an enemy combatant and subject to trial by military commission.[97] CIA deputy director Philip Mudd argued that people were too quick to declare the attacks an act of terrorism. "If you look at some of those initial photos," he said, "you've got a kid with a hoodie and a cap."

> If he wants to obscure himself, the hoodie goes on, the cap forward. . . . This looks more to me like Columbine than it does al Qaeda. Two kids who radicalized between themselves in a closed circle go out and commit murder. I would charge these guys as murders, not terrorists.[98]

For U.S. law-enforcement agencies, in other words, Tsarnaev was a criminal, not an enemy combatant. Further, the FBI, which identified Dzokhar as white on its wanted poster, maintained that the Tsarnaevs were not connected to any terrorist organization. Nevertheless, federal prosecutors brought terrorism charges under federal law, including using and conspiring to use a weapon of mass destruction resulting in death, as well as malicious destruction of property resulting in death. This view is characterized by a rather different way of understanding terrorism, namely, as a set of criminal actions specified by law. The only condition for actions to constitute terrorism on this account is that they correspond to its legal definition. By bringing to the forefront the criminal element of synthetic terrorism, the U.S. government was able to affirm what Graham and others denied, namely, that it is possible to be both a white American citizen and a terrorist.

Moreover, we saw earlier that identifying someone as a terrorist in the criminal sense triggers a set of responses that differ sharply from those to classifying someone as a terrorist according to a racialized notion of terrorism in terms of the Muslim-looking construct. Criminal terrorism operates on the register of law; a racialized concept of terrorism serves as a justificatory mechanism for the exclusion of a perpetrator from the ambit of law and, further, collective punishment of entire communities by means of racial profiling, surveillance, and state-sanctioned violence. As Volpp explains, this is because a white American citizen is "one of us" and, therefore, "does not produce a discourse about good whites and bad whites, because we think of him as an individual deviant, a bad actor. We do not think of his actions as representative of an entire racial group. This is part and parcel of how racial subordination functions, to understand nonwhites as directed by group-based determinism but whites as individuals."[99] This differential treatment of terrorists draws our attention to a complex network of power relations that serve to defend society against dangers that threaten its health and survival. The differences between state responses to white and nonwhite perpetrators of violence throw into relief the kind of features, principles, and values that are regarded as worthy of protection. Specifically, they reflect the interests and strategies of a white supremacist political structure that treats white American or "domestic" terrorists as dangerous individuals who, nevertheless, are afforded basic legal rights, such as due process and a fair criminal trial. Nonwhites, by contrast, are portrayed as a collective threat to the social body to be restrained, suppressed, and eliminated.

TERRORISM AND HUMANITY

The analysis of terrorism's role in the production of citizenship at the domestic level must be extended to explain the operation of synthetic terrorism as an instrument of what I have called imperial *raison d'État*. As we saw in the discussion of U.S. national security strategy earlier in this chapter, U.S. foreign policy is underpinned by a humanitarian norm that posits freedom, democracy, and prosperity not only as a right and demand of human dignity but also as a requisite for the defense of American national interests. Terrorism plays an important role in justifying the pursuit of national interests by producing the very norm of humanity that is said to require protection. In other words, the dispositif of terrorism not only creates a particular notion of "citizenship as a form of inclusion," in Volpp's terminology, but also brings into being what might analogously be called "humanity as a form of inclusion." To put this more clearly, terrorism is not separate from universal human rights, which it threatens and whose protection demands that terrorism be fought. Rather, it is a functional requirement of an effort to universalize particular (American) values as requirements of human dignity. In other words, the identification of some subjects, worldviews, forms of government, and strategies with terrorism serves to single out and denounce as inhumane values, practices, or beliefs that are perceived as inimical to U.S. interests.

A version of this claim underpins feminist, queer, and postcolonial critiques of the so-called war on terror, which hold that emancipatory political principles have been hijacked to defend U.S. imperialism as a humanitarian mission to protect oppressed groups from uncivilized barbarians.[100] In what follows, I examine the work of a prominent representative of this view, Judith Butler, to illustrate the operation of terrorism in producing a humanitarian norm by disidentifying certain populations as fully human. Butler's main thesis is that ideas of civilization and humanity work "to produce the human differentially by offering a culturally limited norm for what the human is supposed to be."

> It is not just that some humans are treated as humans, and others are dehumanized; it is rather that dehumanization becomes the condition for the production of the human to the extent that a "Western" civilization defines itself over and against a population understood as, by definition, illegitimate, if not dubiously human.[101]

Butler argues that practices of detention and torture are key mechanisms in this process. Because both practices violate basic human rights and are prohibited by international legal frameworks, subjecting individuals to detention and torture requires that they be denied the legal standing of subjects to whom such rights accrue. That is, individuals must be understood as not fully human if they are to be detained indefinitely and exposed to what are euphemistically described as enhanced interrogation techniques. Portraying detainees as bestial and monstrous "killing machines" construes them as "something less than human," even though they assume human form.[102] Butler maintains, "The humans who are imprisoned in Guantánamo do not count as human; they are not subjects protected by international law. They are not subjects in any legal or normative sense."[103]

But Butler's claim is not only that detention and torture require prior dehumanization of their victims but also that these practices serve as mechanisms to produce a humanitarian norm by forcing terrorist suspects

to conform to preconceived ideas about ostensibly uncivilized and barbarian populations. Specifically, she argues that torture is not merely a
way to "shame and humiliate the prisoners of Abu Ghraib and Guantánamo
on the basis of their presumptive cultural formation" but also a means to
"coercively produce the Arab subject and the Arab mind. That means
that regardless of the complex cultural formations of the prisoners, they
were compelled to embody the cultural reduction described by the anthropological text."[104] On Butler's view, then, practices like detention and
torture function as means to test and ratify assumptions about cultural
and religious codes that its victims are forced to break. As a result, shame
and humiliation experienced by victims of torture exposed to a violation
of their bodily integrity are interpreted as a display of backward and barbarian sexual inhibitions and thus a lack of civilization—as if there is
even a remote possibility that torture might not be degrading and humili-
ating to ostensibly more progressive victims.[105]

Butler rightly concludes that in its production of the subhuman, torture
actually reveals, by means of projection, the "barbarism of the civilizational
mission."[106] This barbarism is justified in terms of imperial *raison d'État*
as a necessary means to defend humanity against dangerous threats. As
Butler notes, it is the particular philosophy of history typical of imperial
raison d'État that "positions 'the West' as articulating the paradigmatic
principle of the human." On this view, which posits the universal and
homogeneous state as the only viable posthistorical political model and
way of life, the victims of the so-called war on terror "belong either to a
time of cultural infancy or to a time that is outside time as we know it. It
follows from such a viewpoint that the destruction of such populations,
their infrastructures, their housing, and their religious and community
institutions, constitutes the destruction of what threatens the human, but
not of the human itself."[107] The historical narrative that underpins imperial *raison d'État* thus portrays individuals who are, as Fukuyama put it,
willing "to risk one's life for a purely abstract goal" as stuck in a "time
when history existed."[108] They are fair game in a war effort that presents
itself as an act of liberation on the path to the inevitable triumph of the
universal and homogeneous state.

From this vantage point, terrorism appears, in Butler's words, as "the
catchword of a self-defined Western perspective that considers itself
bound to certain versions of rationality and the claims that arise from

them."[109] Because of this association of terrorism with opposition to Western values, even the most inhumane acts of violence perpetrated by the United States and its "coalition of the willing" are exempt from constituting terrorism. Rather, they are elements in a dispositif of terrorism that legitimizes illegal violence in wars of aggression waged by the West under the pretext of defending society and humanity against terrorist threats.[110]

In conclusion, the consolidation of synthetic terrorism since the 1980s brings together a set of historical discourses and practices that form a flexible dispositif of terrorism that operates as a mechanism of social defense both at the domestic and the international level. It serves as a means of discriminating between citizens and noncitizens, as well as humans and subhumans, and puts into circulation a broad set of practices, methods, techniques, laws, institutions, and other devices that are said to be necessary to defend the American nation, as well as humanity as such, against a wide range of threats. To the extent that the dispositif of terrorism today allows for discrimination between who may live and who must die, it is a continuation of the history of terrorism traced in this book. Notice, however, that this continuation is not merely a repetition of contemporary terrorism's predecessors. Rather, what we are witnessing today is an expansion and modification of rationalities, modes of understanding, discourses, and practices of terrorism and counterterrorism as mechanisms of social defense.

We saw in previous chapters that since the eighteenth century, the social body to be defended has been articulated in terms of the nation or class as the universal subject of politics. Today, nation and class are supplemented—though, importantly, not replaced—by an understanding of humanity as the universal subject of political representation. By invoking human rights and dignity, imperial *raison d'État* portrays military aggression as humanitarian intervention and claims to represent the totality of humanity. The political model appropriate for this new subject of politics is the universal and homogeneous state. The realization of this model and the defense of the nation and humanity against a wide range of threats justify the exercise of the old sovereign right to kill, albeit in modified, namely, transnational or imperial form. The current war effort against terrorism is thus best understood as the globalization of techniques of sovereign, disciplinary, and regulatory power, which are projected beyond the boundaries of the state. Such a global extension of technologies of power traditionally associated with the state, be it bourgeois, socialist, or colonial, both permits and requires the invocation of an enemy that threatens not only a nation or class but also humanity as a whole. The requisite concept of enmity is found in synthetic terrorism, which is an effect and a functional prerequisite of a global economy of power that kills for humanitarian purposes.

6

TOWARD A CRITICAL THEORY
OF TERRORISM

Genealogy and Normativity

THE AIM OF GENEALOGY

I began this book by challenging the assertion that we seem to have a good sense of what terrorism is. I argued that various attempts to define *terrorism* on offer in the literature suffer from serious methodological flaws that hamper a nuanced, adequate, and politically productive understanding of terrorism as a complex phenomenon in social history. Specifically, I suggested that a definitional approach to objects of social reality runs the risk of importing incorrigible positions, which leads to a rarefied, impoverished, decontextualized, and ahistorical account of terrorism. In short, ostensibly objective and universal definitions of terrorism are divorced from the social world they describe because they ignore processes of historical change, conceptual transformation, contestations over political categories, resistances to hegemonic concepts, and the practices these concepts make possible.

The alternative approach I developed followed Foucault's practices of critical philosophy—archaeology and genealogy—in order to excavate the conditions under which a phenomenon like terrorism emerges. Such a project involves a choice of method that explicitly denies that terrorism is a primary given object and instead affirms that terrorism is made possible by historically contingent political rationalities and material conditions. As Foucault noted, "Instead of deducing concrete phenomena from universals, or instead of starting with universals as an obligatory grid of intelligibility for certain concrete practices, I would like to start with these concrete practices and, as it were, pass these universals through the grid of these practices."[1] Rather than performing an act of historicist reduction, by which contemporary modes of understanding terrorism are superimposed on the past, my aim was to bring into view the multiplicity of discourses, practices, and institutions that are organized around the phenomenon that ostensibly is terrorism. The critical advantage of such an approach is that it allows us to show "by what conjunctions a whole set of practices—from the moment they become coordinated with a regime of truth—was able to make what does not exist . . . nonetheless become something, something however that continues not to exist."[2] The result is a genealogy of terrorism as a historically specific and variable dispositif of social defense.

A potential worry about a critical project of this kind is that it appears bereft of normative power and constructive potential. Specifically, the worry is that although archaeological analysis maps the conceptual space of terrorism, it does not provide any reasons for favoring one or another of the concepts it excavates. In addition, one might object that even if genealogical critique shows us that things have been and so could be otherwise, it does not tell us anything about how they ought to be.

The usual way in which this challenge is put is to ask, "So, what should we do?" My response is to assert the problematizing rather than the problem-solving character of genealogy and to emphasize the importance of critique, both in its own right and as a preparatory condition of normative intervention. Following Colin Koopman's reading of Foucault, I understand problematization as the twofold attempt to show both that things commonly regarded as unproblematic are actually problematic and how these things became a problem.[3] Foucault insisted that the purpose of this mode of inquiry is not to contest or confirm certain practices but "to raise questions in an effective, genuine way, and to raise them with the greatest possible rigor, with the maximum complexity and difficulty so that a solution doesn't spring from the head of some reformist intellectual or suddenly appear in the head of a party's political bureau."

> The problems I try to pose . . . cannot be easily resolved. Years, decades, of work and political imagination will be necessary, work at the grass

roots, with the people directly affected, restoring their right to speak. Only then will we succeed, perhaps, in changing a situation that, with the terms in which it is currently laid out, only leads to impasses and blockages. I take care not to dictate how things should be. I try instead to pose problems, to make them active, to display them in such a complexity that they can silence the prophets and lawgivers, all those who speak for others or to others. In this way, it will be possible for the complexity of the problem to appear in its connection with people's lives; and, consequently, through concrete questions, difficult cases, movements of rebellion, reflections, and testimonies, the legitimacy of a common creative action can also appear. It's a matter of working through things little by little, of introducing modifications that are able if not to find solutions, at least to change the given terms of the problem.[4]

For Foucault, then, genealogy does not aim to deliver normative judgment about or a solution to a given situation, phenomenon, or practice but rather to problematize it in the double sense specified by Koopman: to reveal a seemingly innocuous phenomenon as problematic and to excavate how this phenomenon emerged as the problem it presently is.[5]

Consider briefly Foucault's account of neoliberalism as a paradigmatic example of this sort of historical-philosophical critique that engages empirical content to describe the conditions of possibility of modern economic practices. In *The Birth of Biopolitics*, Foucault sought to reveal the conditions that made it possible for neoliberals like Gary Becker and Lionel Stoléru to elaborate their economic projects. Foucault drew attention to a set of disparate and unrelated practices, techniques, institutions, and mechanisms, such as a biopolitical concern with the regulation and management of populations and practices of environmental modification. These practices of managing populations and intervening in their environment emerged in the seventeenth and eighteenth centuries, when a new art of governing modified prior practices connected with the Christian pastorate. Foucault thus not only described the intricacies of twentieth-century neoliberalism but also traced the accidents of history that made its articulation possible. Notice, however, that his aim was not to offer a defense or rejection of neoliberalism, as some commentators would have it.[6] Rather, Foucault sought to complicate seemingly unproblematic assumptions about neoliberalism by mapping the space in which

distinctions such as those between Left and Right, socialism and capitalism, and freedom and security become possible and meaningful in the
first place. Although it might make us uneasy that Foucault did not vo-
ciferously speak out against the neoliberal project in his lectures, his work
remains relevant and valuable precisely because it gives us a model of inquiry that can be taken up in our historical present to examine problematizations that might not have been perceptible in Foucault's time.

Despite his focus on empirically rigorous and historically specific critical inquiry, Foucault's reception in the humanities and social sciences
has largely taken two rather different forms. The first strand approaches
Foucault's work within the general framework of the history of philosophy and subjects his philosophical claims to hermeneutical interpretation. Among the best examples of this approach, to my mind, are the
important interventions of James Bernauer, Hubert Dreyfus and Paul
Rabinow, Thomas Flynn, and Gary Gutting.[7] A continuous stream of
posthumous publications of Foucault's work, as well as wider accessibil-
ity of his research notes, has generated new work on Foucault's thought
by scholars like Amy Allen, Stuart Elden, Ben Golder, Lynne Huffer, Mark
Kelly, Ladelle McWhorter, Martin Saar, and Tuomo Tiisala, to name just
a few.[8] These scholars have done much to advance our understanding of
Foucault's place in contemporary philosophy, the development of his
thought, the viability of his methodological innovations, and perceived
tensions between different periods of his intellectual production and
activist engagement.

A second strand of Foucault scholarship mobilizes emblematic concepts, like biopolitics, governmentality, or subjectivation, to shed light
on contemporary issues such as gender, war, (neo)liberalism, and security.[9] Although some of this work pays close attention to the historical
context out of which Foucault's concepts emerged, much of it bears only
conceptual resemblance to his work and therefore is actually in tension
with Foucault's careful historical and empirical approach.[10] As Koopman
rightly notes, whether discipline, biopower, or governmentality are operative in domains Foucault did not explore "is a question to be answered
through genealogical inquiry rather than decided in advance as a merely
conceptual matter."[11]

In contrast to these two major strands of Foucault scholarship, which
take the form of commentary on Foucault or application of his concepts

to contexts he did not investigate, a small share of thinkers has put Foucault to work in a different way, namely, by taking seriously his hope that his work will be used as "a sort of *tool-box* through which others can rummage to find a tool with which they can do what seems good to them, in their domain."[12] They have provided models for staying truthful to what Foucault did by being users of his work rather than merely readers and adapting his methods to analyses of sites not dealt with by Foucault himself. This mode of taking up Foucault is characterized by a rigorous deployment of his empirical practices, which often calls for a modification of his concepts and might even require the invention of new conceptualizations.

Among the thinkers who have been most influential for my use of Foucault are Santiago Castro-Gómez, Arnold Davidson, Andrew Dilts, Ian Hacking, Colin Koopman, Ladelle McWhorter, Kevin Olson, and Paul Rabinow.[13] Here I briefly consider Olson's work as an exemplary model of such methodological use of Foucault in a domain that was outside his own horizon. In *Imagined Sovereignties: The Power of the People and Other Myths of the Modern Age*, Olson problematizes the ostensibly obvious notion that political power rests in the people by revealing the complex historical process and concrete practices by which the people are collectively imagined—and thereby constituted, created, or invented—as the source of political power and normative force. Drawing on careful analysis of philosophical texts and archival materials of revolutionary France and the revolutionary Caribbean in the eighteenth and nineteenth centuries, he traces the slow and piecemeal emergence of a popular-universalist imaginary of the people as having unitary agency from which normative force derives.

Olson shows, for instance, that Rousseau's classical articulation of the people as a totality whose normative authority issues from its universal character relied on earlier conceptions of the people as a social class that was distinguished by destitution, on the one hand, and gave rise to Sieyès's famous positing of the Third Estate as the nation, on the other. Olson draws helpful analytic distinctions between these different conceptualizations of the people, but he also demonstrates that they all circulated simultaneously at the time. This resulted in an ambiguous and problematic concept of the people that was in constant need of clarification. These complexities were further exacerbated by the uptake of imaginaries of popular power in the colonial Caribbean, where a variety of social, racial, cultural, and geographic distinctions made an easy appeal to the people as a unified collective identity impossible. As a consequence, different collectivities relied on various strategies of popular politics to pursue their interests within a complicated framework of racial hierarchies.[14]

By using Foucault's methods rather than concepts like biopolitics or governmentality, Olson not only shows that current conceptions of popular power are less obvious than they seem but also how "our contemporary, relatively fixed and uncontroversial ideas about the power of the people" emerged out of a historically constituted field of problems.[15] His attention to political programs, philosophical treatises, artistic productions, emerging technologies of mass communication, performances of popular unity, constitutional debates and public deliberations, and *marronage* (escape from slavery) reveals that conceptual elaborations of popular power by philosophers, theorists, and political actors take up ideas that were already in circulation in a wide array of practices.

Particularly interesting in this regard is Olson's discussion of the tricolor cockade, a blue, red, and white ribbon that signaled allegiance to the Revolution. The archives of the French Revolution show that the cockade "originated as a sign by which revolutionaries could recognize one another, but went through a rapid evolution to take on much wider significance" both as a "sign of unity" and a "sign of difference."[16] To prevent modifications of the cockade that were seen as threats to national unity, a national standard was soon put in place that imposed regulations of style. Similarly, the archives of the Haitian Revolution highlight the role of the cockade as a symbol of revolutionary politics. Although there is reliable evidence that slaves began to imitate French use of the cockade, however, the archives contain no written records that shed light on the understanding slaves had of this symbol and the meaning they attributed to it. Nevertheless, Olson's perceptive analysis of the reactions of whites and elites of color that are represented in the archive suggests that "wearing the cockade *did something* in the public sphere," regardless of the specific intentions of the slaves who provoked them.[17] More generally, the slaves' practice of wearing the cockade throws into sharp relief that imaginations of popular politics take "material and symbolic forms." These may "simply be an artifact of what is available in this particular archive," but they could just as well be "an accurate representation of a sovereign imaginary that is at once performative, indeterminate, and underspecified."

> It may be the case that the Saint-Domingan revolutionaries did not have a carefully worked out, propositionally articulated set of political principles. We can try to discern their ideas in retrospect and from a distance, but we must be careful not to give those ideas more coherence than they actually had. This is an important caution. It suggests that a sovereign imaginary could be poorly elaborated, indeterminate, and partially inconsistent, yet have binding force and real-world importance.[18]

Olson's analysis of the tricolor cockade thus draws our attention to the fact that imaginaries of popular power can be both explicitly articulated in speech and implicit in political practices. Crucially, it is only by analyzing these practices through Foucault's methods, rather than passing them through his conceptual apparatus, that we can appreciate this point. Despite its different subject matter, Olson's work is therefore a model for the kind of engaged empirical critique elaborated in this book.

In what follows, I want to defend the viability and relevance of such a methodological use of Foucault in the context of contemporary problematizations of terrorism. To this end, I discuss arguments concerning whether the so-called Charleston church shooting was an act of terrorism with the aim of identifying a set of strategies of redefining terrorism. In keeping with the objections to definitional approaches to terrorism raised in chapter 1, my goal is to show that these strategies are ultimately unsuccessful because they are unmoored from careful empirical analysis. Therefore, they provide a useful foil against which the benefits of problematizing genealogy, as well as defensible strategies of transformation compatible with genealogical critique, will become clear.

REDEFINING TERRORISM

On June 17, 2015, Dylann Roof, a white American who admitted to being driven by racial hatred, killed nine African Americans during a prayer service at Emanuel African Methodist Episcopal Church in Charleston,

South Carolina. After the shooting, media outlets were quick to report that the incident was not an act of terrorism. Many commentators, however, insisted that Roof ought to be called a terrorist because it was "the same violence" and that the only reason that he was not identified as a terrorist was that he was "a white supremacist or apartheid sympathizer."[19] Had he been Muslim, his actions would certainly have been considered an act of terrorism. The idea, in short, is that the problematic use of the term *terrorism* ought to be contested by applying the word consistently to phenomenally identical acts of violence. I call this the *consistency-first* view.

As journalist Glenn Greenwald has argued, however, a consistency-first approach primarily serves critical or subversive purposes, since consistent application of the term to perpetrators of all backgrounds draws attention to the fact that terrorism "justifies everything *yet means nothing.*" By showing that members of majority groups, too, can be caught up in the consequences of being called a terrorist, it becomes clear that the word *terrorism* is "a completely malleable, manipulated, vapid term of propaganda that has no consistent application whatsoever." For Greenwald, applying a term without meaning to phenomenally similar acts of violence serves to show that it is actually inconsistent to hold both that terrorism has no single, stable meaning and that the concept of terrorism designates a particular, readily identifiable kind of violent behavior. Political consistency, in other words, comes at the expense of semantic inconsistency.[20]

Proponents of the consistency-first view might respond that such inconsistency is an acceptable price to pay for effective political strategies. But these kinds of conceptual questions about terrorism are not divorced from the social reality they seek to understand. Whether terrorism is, as Greenwald puts it, a "highly manipulated term of propaganda" without fixed meaning or a specific kind of "repulsive violence" is not just of philosophical interest but has important implications for how best to respond to terrorism.[21] If we seek to address the harmful effects of using *terrorism* as a propaganda term, we might very well want to extend its application, in an attempt to subvert its meaning, to individuals, groups, and actions usually not identified as terrorists or terrorism. By contrast, if we hope to end a kind of violence commonly called terrorism, our efforts will have to sincerely address the conditions that make such violence possible.

Another way to make sense of the claim that terrorism is both a propaganda term without meaning and a certain kind of violence is to insist that it is indeed both, but that we are using the word *terrorism* as a homonym. That is, we are not actually talking about the same thing in these cases, even if we are using the same word. I think that this is true, but I believe that it is important to flag these different meanings of the term *terrorism*, as I have done throughout this book, in order to avoid what Mary Beth Mader calls *sleights of reason* or *conceptual sleights*. According to Mader, concepts consist of various components, each of which can come to the fore and obscure other components, which nevertheless continue to operate invisibly and exert influence in the background.[22] The problem arises when we call these different components by the same name, that is, when we call certain behaviors, worldviews, systems of government, and strategies of warfare terrorism. The concept *terrorism* conceals that all these different elements work at the same time by implying that they are the same thing and obscuring the complexity of their interaction. This is not merely an abstract philosophical problem, given that human beings make sense of and engage with the world through concepts.

In addition to such theoretical objections to the consistency-first view, there are important practical objections to demands that the *terrorism* label be applied consistently to phenomenally identical acts of violence. Consider, for example, Russian-American journalist Masha Gessen's response to the Charleston church shooting. Gessen argues that even though Roof's actions clearly constitute an act of terrorism, calling him a terrorist and prosecuting him as such has considerable legal, extralegal, and rhetorical consequences that ought to be avoided. Since the governor of South Carolina had already called for the death penalty for Roof, transferring his case to federal jurisdiction as an act of terrorism punishable by death would not have served any pragmatic legal purpose. It would, however, have provided an occasion for the expansion of surveillance, torture, and a further dismantling of civil rights. Gessen suggests that because the term *terrorism* is meaningless, describing Roof's actions as terrorism prevents us from attaining a more nuanced understanding of what actually happened, and why. Consequently, we "would be better off retiring the word [*terrorism*] altogether."[23]

The view that we should stop using the word *terrorism* altogether because of the small- and large-scale consequences of attributions of terrorism might be described as *eliminativism*. To explicate this view and its implications, consider eliminativism about race, which holds that race is a main source of social injustice and that the abolition of social injustice requires the elimination of racial categories.[24] This claim is underpinned by the belief that the way we speak determines the way we act, or, in more Foucauldian terms, that discourse shapes practice. As critics of eliminativism about race have pointed out, however, this relationship is not as straightforward as eliminativists make it out to be. Although there certainly is some connection between our language and our actions, the elimination of race concepts does not necessarily eliminate social structures and institutional practices that perpetuate racial injustice.[25] A second, related objection to eliminativism about race is that it creates epistemic injustices against oppressed communities because it robs them of the conceptual framework to articulate the harms inflicted on them by systemic racism.[26]

These objections to eliminativism about race can also be raised in regard to eliminativism about terrorism. First, it is likely that the elimination of the concept of terrorism will not eliminate the political rationalities, interests, and structures that make it possible and necessary, but will instead generate different concepts that allow for the preservation of mechanisms of social control that are currently justified as necessary means to fight terrorism. If, as I have argued in this book, terrorism is indeed a functional requirement of relations of power that aim to produce a particular normative vision of the social body, then the elimination of terrorism will have to be part of a much broader project intended to transform the social, political, economic, and ideological conditions that rely on forms of social defense, including, but not limited to, racism, xenophobia, ableism, (hetero)sexism, homophobia, and transphobia. That is, terrorism must be tackled not merely at the discursive or conceptual level but on the register of a dispositif whose purpose is the maintenance of a particular idealized image of a social and political community.

Second, eliminativism about terrorism risks delegitimizing and even silencing claims of various oppressed groups that state and state-sanctioned violence against them constitutes terrorism.[27] It is important to keep in mind that the conceptual armature of terrorism provides a rich resource for marginalized communities to articulate and theorize the violence of a white supremacist power structure in diverse areas of their lives. To give just a few examples, consider the long tradition of understanding antiblack violence in the United States as terrorism. Shortly after emancipation, Southern black leaders noted that slavery had been replaced by a "system of terrorism and guerrilla warfare."[28] In her analysis of lynching, Ida B. Wells argued that the practice was not an exercise of extralegal justice against black rapists and criminals, as many whites claimed, but "an excuse to get rid of Negroes who were acquiring wealth and property and thus keep the race terrorized and 'keep the nigger down.'"[29] As a more recent example, consider rapper Jay-Z's description of the police as "Al'Qaeda to Black men."[30] We might argue that demands to identify white American shooters such as Dylann Roof as terrorists are in continuity with this tradition of naming white racial terrorism. Arguments that we should eliminate the concept of terrorism or that we should not call people like Dylann Roof terrorists because of the individual and social consequences of the rhetoric of terrorism run the risk of disabling interpretive resources available to oppressed communities to make sense of and adequately articulate their experiences.

In addition, we saw in previous chapters—in particular with regard to Gracchus Babeuf in chapter 2, Russian social revolutionaries in chapter 3, and members of the Algerian independence movement in chapter 4—that individuals and groups targeted by oppression and violence sometimes engage in subversive appropriation of the *terrorism* label. The elimination of the word would thus rob them of a potential means of resistance. Again, an analogy with racial terms helps illuminate this point. A common explanation of self-referential uses of racial slurs by marginalized communities holds that the appropriation of stigmatizing terms serves as a mechanism to turn derogation into affirmation and an expression of solidarity.[31] Appropriated uses, in other words, constitute different kinds of speech acts than derogatory uses. When out-group members object to appropriated uses of racial slurs, they fail to recognize this difference because they do not take into consideration conditions of community membership that grant or restrict access to different speech acts a term can be used to perform.[32] These claims suggest that eliminativism about terrorism generates similar consequences. It not only silences the voices of oppressed groups but also denies appropriation as a potential means of coping with stigmatization. It further ignores contextually specific rules of discourse and practice and assumes that all invocations of terrorism have the same meaning and function—a belief I hope I have debunked in this book.

TOWARD A STRATEGY OF TRANSFORMATION

This discussion throws into sharp relief the problems of normative responses to terrorism that are unmoored from its concrete historical context and highlights the importance of genealogical critique. For even though genealogy is not normatively ambitious in the sense that it seeks to supply concrete solutions to these problematizations, it is nevertheless normatively oriented insofar as it describes practices that are intolerable, to use Foucault's term, with the aim of making transformation possible.[33] The rationale for rigorous historical inquiry, on Foucault's view, is that the problems of the present "can be unmade, as long as we know how it was that they were made."[34] Consequently, genealogy "does not consist in a simple characterization of what we are" but is always geared toward opening up "the space of freedom understood as a space of concrete freedom, that is, of possible transformation."[35] Genealogy, in other words, traces the historical formation of present practices in response to past problematizations in order to provide the empirical material necessary to unmake these practices, "to imagine [the present] otherwise than it is, and to transform it not by destroying it but by grasping it in what it is."[36]

Following Foucault, then, I aim to supply the kind of nuanced, contextual, and historically informed understanding of terrorism required for defensible and productive strategies of transformation. As I hope I have made clear, not only is it neither feasible nor desirable to eliminate the concept of terrorism, but it is also impossible to apply it consistently in any meaningful way, given that terrorism today acquires its purchase precisely from its success at synthesizing a range of conceptual uses, some of which the genealogy of terrorism traced in this book sought to excavate. Any normative response to terrorism that seeks to open up a space for possible transformation must attend to this fact. While a fully fleshed-out defense of such a normative strategy far exceeds the scope of this final chapter, what remains to be done is to sketch how we might transform our understanding of and responses to terrorism in a way that is compatible with genealogy.

One promising view that aspires to a historically informed normative approach to terrorism is Mathias Thaler's ameliorative project. For Thaler, defensible conceptualizations of violence in general and terrorism in particular must be historically situated and used purposefully in order to achieve particular ends that are established by critical political judgment. The work of conceptual amelioration, in other words, must be based on and informed by a robust analysis of the historical formation of the concepts to be reconstructed. On his view, historical analysis allows us to reveal the contingency of concepts like terrorism and thereby open them up to contestation. Accordingly, Thaler suggests that we adopt object-focused definitions of terrorism—that is, definitions that regard terrorism as violence that targets innocent noncombatants—but simultaneously complicate such object-focused definitions by problematizing who counts as a noncombatant. Interestingly, he does this via a genealogy of innocence such that his ameliorative conceptualization of terrorism relies on a historical account of innocence as one of its components. Drawing on the work of Zehfuss and Kinsella, Thaler highlights the raced and gendered origins of the concept of innocence and deploys this insight not to reject object-focused definitions of terrorism but to supplement "the simplistic reference . . . to the identifying criterion of innocence . . . with an acknowledgment of the gendered history of its emergence." For Thaler, genealogy thus highlights the contingency and contestability of ostensibly unproblematic concepts like terrorism, even though it does not supply alternative conceptualizations.[37]

There is much to admire in Thaler's proposal, but my worry is that it does not go far enough in problematizing terrorism. Even though it certainly complicates ostensibly straightforward object-focused definitions of terrorism by revealing the hidden but operative origins of the concept of innocence, the key problem with Thaler's approach is that his ameliorative reconstruction of the concept of terrorism misses the mark of defensible conceptualizations he himself rightly emphasizes. Recall that for Thaler, genealogical critique serves to reveal the historical contingency of concepts like terrorism that he hopes to make available for ameliorative reconstruction. But rather than building his ameliorative concept of terrorism on a genealogy of terrorism, he accepts an object-focused concept of terrorism and problematizes it by pointing out the historical contingency of innocence as one of its components. As I have sought to demonstrate in previous chapters, however, object-focused definitions of terrorism are problematic and do not exhaust the conceptual space of terrorism. Even though Thaler's ameliorative conceptualization of terrorism is thus informed by the rich and problematic history of innocence as one key element in dominant definitions of terrorism, it is unmoored from the concrete historical formation of contemporary terrorism as a synthetic concept. In short, the crucial problem with Thaler's ameliorative approach to terrorism is that his reconstruction of the concept of terrorism relies on a genealogical diagnosis of innocence. A fully historicized, empirically rigorous, and thus defensible conceptualization of terrorism, however, must be informed by a diagnosis of terrorism as the object to be reconceptualized. Put differently, a normative reconstruction of the concept of terrorism must be compatible with its genealogy—that is, with a genealogy of terrorism. Nevertheless, even though Thaler's attempt at amelioration does not offer a modified concept of terrorism that is compatible with its genealogy, his call for normative reconstruction based on genealogical problematization promises to be productive once terrorism itself is subject to genealogical critique. My hope is that the genealogy of terrorism developed in this book may serve as a fruitful entry point into this discussion by supplying the diagnostic material on which successful reconstructive work can be brought to bear. In what follows, I outline how this might be done.

GENEALOGY AND THE PROBLEM OF NORMATIVITY

Two particularly insightful models of mobilizing genealogical diagnosis for normative political theory that inspire my thinking have been put forward by Amy Allen and Colin Koopman. In *The Politics of Our Selves: Power, Autonomy, and Gender in Contemporary Critical Theory*, Allen argues for a thoroughly contextualist form of normativity that harnesses the best insights of poststructuralism (in its Foucauldian form) and critical theory (in its Habermasian form). Traditionally, these philosophical traditions are seen as being in tension with each other, which arises from a historicized and contextualist view of the subject as constituted by variable relations of power attributed to Foucault, on the one hand, and a Kantian understanding of the subject as an autonomous agent with the capacity for self-constitution associated with Habermas, on the other. Allen's way out of this impasse is a robust philosophical synthesis of Foucault and Habermas that emphasizes Foucault's Kantian tendencies and deemphasizes Habermas's idea of context-transcendent validity claims in favor of a "principled form of contextualism that emphasizes our need *both* to posit context-transcending ideals *and* to continually unmask their status as illusions rooted in interest and power-laden contexts."[38]

Koopman objects to Allen's substantive reinterpretation of both Foucault and Habermas and instead argues for a more modest methodological reconciliation of genealogy and critical theory in a "dual-aspect conception of critical inquiry"[39] that he understands, following Seyla Benhabib, as comprising an "explanatory-diagnostic" and an "anticipatory-utopian" function.[40] On Koopman's account, "We should delegate to the genealogists the task of a diagnostic methodology for inquiry into problematizations, and to pragmatists and critical theorists we should delegate the task of deploying an anticipatory methodology for inquiry into the reconstruction of problematic situations."[41] This delegation of methodological tasks, he contends, avoids the need to offer substantive philosophical synthesis of the two traditions' core commitments, namely, contingency (Foucault) and universality (Habermas). Whereas contingency and universality and, by extension, genealogy and critical theory are usually presumed to be incompatible, Koopman argues that this is not so. Since contingency, like necessity, "specifies a modality and universality specifies a scope," it follows that universals can be inflected with either necessity, in which case they give rise to a notion of universalism that yields transcendental philosophy, or contingency, in which case we get "historicized forms of critical inquiry" that trace processes by which contingent phenomena are universalized.[42] Once universality is reconceived in terms of processes of contingent universalization rather than necessary transcendental universals, critical theory, or so Koopman seems to suggest, can commit itself to norms that are simultaneously context bound (contingent rather than necessary) and context-transcendent (universalizable rather than transcendental).

For Allen, however, it is not clear that such a modest methodological reconciliation of Foucauldian genealogy and Habermasian critical theory is possible. This is because of Habermas's metanormative commitments to a "so to speak transcendental constraint of unavoidable presuppositions of argumentation" on discourse, as well as his grounding of normativity in a backward-looking notion of history as the progressive realization of reason, which require a much more sweeping reinterpretation of Habermas than Koopman seems willing to grant.[43] As Allen argues in *The End of Progress: Decolonizing the Normative Foundations of Critical Theory*, a reconciliation of genealogy and critical theory requires a kind of metanormative contextualism that conflicts with Habermas's justification of norms as the outcome of a process of sociocultural development.[44] This is because genealogy reveals our first-order normative commitments as resting on historically contingent foundations. Nevertheless, Allen insists that such metanormative contextualism can be reconciled with critical theory's normative aspiration to develop justifiable responses to social problems. Such justifications must be grounded not in context-transcendent norms derived from a progressivist view of history as the realization of reason, à la Habermas, but in contingent and highly contextual normative foundations, à la Foucault.

Both Koopman and Allen convincingly make the case that a reconciliation of genealogy and critical theory is possible and that such reconciliation allows us to leverage genealogical critique for normative political theory, but I worry about the kinds of normative strategies their proposals entail. For Allen, genealogy enjoins critical theory to cultivate an attitude of epistemic humility toward its normative foundations. Allen does not elaborate on the kind of normative theory to which such a change might give rise. Without any substantive suggestions about how to reconcile genealogy and critical theory in a practice of inquiry that yields normative commitments that are compatible with genealogy, we can easily imagine that a change in our moral epistemology is entirely compatible with the perpetuation of currently dominant conceptualizations of and solutions to terrorism. Although we might be aware of their contingency, contextuality, and limitations, we can nevertheless accept concepts and practices we know are problematic. With regard to terrorism, Thaler's adoption of object-focused definitions, which he complicates via a genealogy of innocence, is a case in point. Thus, in addition to establishing that genealogy and critical theory can be reconciled in a practice of critical inquiry that delivers on both diagnosis and normative reconstruction, we need to say something about how such critical inquiry ought to be conducted.

Koopman answers this challenge by arguing for a delegation of the tasks of diagnostic problematization and normative reconstruction to genealogy and critical theory, respectively. His proposal, however, rests on the assumption that these are discrete philosophical moments. On his view, the genealogist supplies the material on which critical theorists can get to work to articulate normative projects. Although these two moments can no doubt be performed by one and the same theorist, many genealogists may insist that their empirically thorough and historically situated diagnoses of current problematizations are most effective when they inform political practice rather than normative theory. As Foucault maintained, "The project, the tactics and goals to be adopted are a matter for those who are fighting."

> What the intellectual can do is provide instruments of analysis, and at present this is the historian's essential role. What is effectively needed is a ramified penetrative perception of the present, one that makes it possible to locate lines of weakness, strong points, positions where the instances of power have secured and implanted themselves in a system of organisation dating back over a hundred and fifty years. In other words, a topological and geological survey of the battlefield—that is the intellectual's role. But as for saying, "Here is what you must do!", certainly not.[45]

Foucault, in other words, objected to an understanding of the intellectual's role as a prophet or lawgiver who imposes normative prescriptions about what is to be done on the practices of those who fight on the ground.[46] Rather, such norms should be articulated by activists in and for concrete political struggles. This leaves room for a mode of normative political theory that does not take the form of lawgiving but instead excavates, or helps excavate, norms from the practices of those who are fighting. In other words, the theorist can "illuminate a particular situation, social domain, or conjuncture" and bring "important elements to the perception and critique of things from which, if the people want this, a certain political choice can be deduced quite naturally."[47]

GENEALOGY AS ENGAGED CRITIQUE

The reason for Foucault's repudiation of the theorist as a lawgiver for political struggle lies in his conception of the relationship between theory and practice. He articulated this conception in a roundtable discussion from 1978 in which he resolutely rejected any claim to totality or universality of his theoretical interventions. Instead, he insisted, "what I say should be considered as proposals, 'games on offer' (*offres de jeu*) in which those who might be interested are invited to participate; they are not dogmatic assertions to be accepted as a whole."[48] This disavowal of universal and totalizing theory stems from Foucault's understanding of political transformation not as the necessary result of a theory, ideology, or program that is applied to political practice, but as the contingent effect of the interplay of a multiplicity of practices. This is not to deny the political efficaciousness of theories and programs, however. Foucault was clear that such denial would make sense only were one to think of theories as "ideal types" belonging to the order of pure ideas, uncontaminated by the "disorderly impurity of the real."[49] From the point of view of an analysis of regimes of practice, however, theory is just another kind of practice that interacts with other practices. As he stated in a discussion with Gilles Deleuze in 1972, "Theory does not express, translate, or apply a practice, it is a practice."[50] As such, theory "induce[s] a whole series of effects in the real," but it can bring about transformation only as one element in a network of actions—actions that can be theoretical or practical.[51] If reality is transformed, Foucault therefore maintained, "it will not be because a program for reform has been put into the head of social workers; it is when those, all of those, who have to deal with this reality will have clashed with each other and with themselves, when they will have encountered impasses, embarrassment, impossibility, when they will have overcome conflicts and affronts, when critique will have been played out in the real, and not when reformers will have realized their ideas."[52]

On Foucault's view, then, normative theorists who act as lawgivers misunderstand the relationship between theory and practice. By trying to impose norms on the sphere of practices, they fail to see that the theorist is engaged in different ways in the very relations of power that attribute to her the role of a truth teller or lawgiver.[53] Theory is thus a practice deployed in political struggles that can be used "in processes of conflict, affronts, attempts at refusal" to pose a "challenge in relation to that which is."[54] Rather than telling people what they ought to do, the theorist's role is therefore to show them "that they are much freer than they feel, that people accept as truth, as evidence, some themes which have been built up at a certain moment during history, and that this so-called evidence can be criticized and destroyed."[55]

As Foucault suggested, and as I hope I have illustrated throughout this book, genealogy serves precisely this theoretical function of problematizing what seems self-evident by revealing its complexity. It traces "connections, encounters, supports, blockages, plays of force, strategies, etc., which, in a given moment, have formed what will subsequently function as obviousness, universality, necessity"[56] in order to construct around an ostensibly unitary phenomenon a "'polyhedron of intelligibility' the number of whose sides is not determined in advance and can never properly be considered finished as a matter of law" (de plein droit).[57] In short, it brings about "causal multiplication" (démultiplication causale).[58] The result of such an analysis is that phenomena like madness, sexuality, criminality, and terrorism no longer appear as the necessary products of an anthropological constant or economic structure that constitutes their essence but as effects of a plurality of practices that are contingent, provisional, precarious, and contested.

A critical implication of this insight is that the causal multiplicity of seemingly obvious and singular problems revealed by genealogy both permits and requires a plurality of strategies of transformation that, moreover, must be local, specific, and open to revision. Foucault insisted this in a passage in his introductory volume to the *History of Sexuality* that is worth quoting in its entirety:

> There is not *one* place of great Refusal—soul of the revolt, focal point of all the rebellions, pure law of the revolutionary. But *a plurality* of resistances that are specific cases: possible, necessary, unlikely, spontaneous,

wild, solitary, concerted, sprawling, violent, irreconcilable, quick to settle, self-interested, or sacrificial. By definition, they can only exist within the strategic field of power relations. But this is not to say that they are nothing but the aftereffect, the hollow mark that forms, in relation to an essential domination, an underside that is ultimately always passive, destined for endless defeat. Resistances do not arise from a few heterogeneous principles, but they are not for all that a lure or promise necessarily betrayed. They are the other endpoint in power relations; they inscribe themselves in the latter as an irreducible counterpart [*l'irréductible vis-à-vis*]. They are, therefore, also distributed in irregular fashion: the points, nodes, focal points of resistance are disseminated with more or less density in time and space, sometimes training [*dressant*] groups or individuals in a definitive way, arousing certain parts of the body, certain moments of life, certain types of comportment. Great, radical ruptures, binary and massive divisions? Sometimes. But more often one has to do with mobile and transitory points of resistance, which introduce in a society cleavages that travel, that break up unities and give rise to regroupings, that run across individuals themselves, dissecting and reorganizing them, tracing in them, in their body and in their soul, irreducible regions. Just as the network of power relations ends up forming a thick fabric that traverses apparatuses [*les appareils*] and institutions, without being exactly localized in them, so a swarm of points of resistance traverses social stratifications and individual units. And it is without doubt the strategic coding of these points of resistance that makes a revolution possible, a little like the State rests on the institutional integration of relations of power.[59]

For Foucault, in short, resistances are as heterogeneous as the elements of a dispositif against which they are mobilized. These resistances can be excavated through "a series of historical inquiries that are as precise as possible" in order to highlight "very specific transformations that have proved to be possible" in a given domain of inquiry and "partial transformations that have been made in the correlation of historical analysis and the practical attitude."[60] Crucially, this excavation of resistances opens up theoretical possibilities for normative reconstruction that do not take the form of lawgiving but instead extract norms from the practices of those who are engaged in political struggles. The diagnostic function of genealogy is here tied to a reconstructive project in which theory serves as a relay among a plurality of concrete practices of resistance and transformation.[61] In sum, then, the kind of normativity that is compatible with such a project, and therefore with genealogy, is not that of prescriptive or speculative theory that articulates norms to be foisted on practices, but that of an empirical or historical form of critical inquiry that derives norms from the normative practices of those who are fighting.

TRANSFORMING TERRORISM

I conclude by outlining how the theorist can contribute to the kind of normative reconstruction just described. I find a promising model for a theoretical practice that serves as a relay for a plurality of concrete struggles in Gary Wilder's politics of radical literalism. Drawing on Adorno's "Aufzeichnungen zu Kafka," Wilder elaborates a principle of literalness (*Buchstäblichkeit*) that allows us to identify normative strategies of transformation that are fully immanent in a given problem.[62] To illustrate this idea, consider Wilder's discussion of Aimé Césaire's and Léopold Senghor's work on decolonization. He argues that rather than rejecting imperial formations outright, Césaire and Senghor attempted to reclaim and transform them by taking French claims about the colonies literally. That is, they asked what it would mean for colonies to really be French departments, as France said they were. For Césaire, for instance, departmentalization was more promising than national independence as a form of anticolonial liberation because it carried the possibility of a multinational democratic federation. If the colonies were made departments in the literal sense of the term, departmentalization would not only grant equal status to colonial subjects but also transform the French republic into a different political formation, namely, a decentralized multinational democratic federation. On Wilder's view, Césaire and Senghor thus focused on utopian potentialities and "transformative possibilities that may have been sedimented within existing arrangements."[63] Theirs was a strategy to construct alternative futures that might have been possible, even though they did not materialize in the end.

We can find similar practices of literalness in various attempts to subvert and rearticulate concepts and practices of terrorism surveyed in previous chapters. I conclude by briefly returning to Fanon's conceptualization of terrorism as a last resort of the colonized against the French colonial state. I argued in chapter 4 that for Fanon, frontist terrorism could not be understood unless it was properly situated within a context of French colonialism. On Fanon's view, terrorism was a legitimate form of counterattack against colonial war governed by the very norms that regulated French military action rather than an illegitimate use of force that was outside all norms. It was, in short, a response in kind to the actions of the colonial state. Fanon further criticized the disingenuousness of France's demonization of frontist violence by arguing that strategies of terrorism were taken straight from the playbook of the French Résistance against Nazi Germany. It was clear to him that the intentions driving these violent actions were the same in both cases, namely, resistance against an illegitimate occupation.[64]

Fanon's analysis of terrorism sought to highlight similarities between French and Algerian violence. He did not do this, however, to discredit the French discourse of terrorism by pointing out its hypocrisy or to legitimize Algerian resistance by showing that the French, too, had engaged in the same kind of actions. Rather, Fanon elaborated an understanding of terrorism as the only form of struggle appropriate for conditions of domination and occupation. On Fanon's view, that is, terrorism is a form of counterattack determined by material conditions of a prior conflict. This is why Fanon did not simply deny that frontist violence was terrorism but rather sought to reclaim and transform the colonial authorities' concept of terrorism by taking it more literally than they took it themselves.[65] Fanon accepted the French understanding of terrorism as a form of violence that is systematic, revolutionary, bent on overturning public order, directed against civilians, and extralegal, but he supplemented it with a broader account of the reasons that frontist terrorism exhibited these features. Most important, he argued that systematic revolutionary violence against a public order by way of targeting civilians was necessary because that order was a system of colonial domination that had been established by an illegal act of aggression, was maintained by the continued use of systematic violence for the benefit of European settlers, and excluded Algerians from political representation. Rather than draw a hard-and-fast distinction between state violence and terrorism, Fanon thus attempted to bring to light the underlying link between the violence of the colonial state and frontist terrorism. In doing so, he identified terrorism as an alienated form of defensive war for which the colonial state and the people in whose name it acted were responsible. His conception of terrorism must therefore be understood against the background of a larger project of anticolonial critique that challenges us to critically examine entrenched assumptions about state violence as the only legitimate form of violence, public order as lawful and peaceable, and civilians as innocent bystanders of colonial oppression. Despite its historical specificity and context boundedness, Fanon's attempt to reclaim and transform problematic notions of terrorism remains relevant precisely because his context is part of the background that shapes our contemporary understanding of terrorism.

No doubt, this book has examined only some of the historical dynamics that have made the present dispositif of terrorism possible, intractable, and powerful. Consequently, it points us to only some possible transformations that have been or have yet to be put to the test of reality. Other archives and other alternative futures lie in wait for those of us who refuse to accept as self-evident what seems natural, immobile, and fixed and who look for new ways of thinking and knowing. My point has not been to offer a better answer to the question what terrorism is but to loosen the rigidity of our thought and make us a little freer by rendering seemingly obvious answers a little less obvious.

NOTES

EPIGRAPH

1. Quoted in Zohra Drif, *Mémoires d'une combattante de l'ALN: Zone autonome d'Alger* (Alger: Chihab, 2013), 9.

2. Arlette Farge, *The Allure of the Archives*, trans. by Thomas Scott-Railton (New Haven, Conn.: Yale University Press, 2013), 123–24.

3. Michel Foucault, "Practicing Criticism," in *Politics, Philosophy, Culture: Interviews and Other Writings, 1977–1984*, ed. by Lawrence D. Kritzman (New York: Routledge, 1988), 154.

CHAPTER 1. THE TROUBLE WITH TERRORISM

1. Quoted in Jörg Friedrichs, "Defining the International Public Enemy: The Political Struggle Behind the Legal Debate on International Terrorism," *Leiden Journal of International Law* 19 (2006): 84.

2. E.g., Grégoire Chamayou, *A Theory of the Drone* (New York: New Press, 2015); Derek Gregory, "From a View to a Kill: Drones and Late Modern War," *Theory, Culture and Society* 28, nos. 7–8 (2011): 188–215, doi:10.1177/0263276411423027.

3. See Christine Hauser, "San Bernardino Shooting: The Investigation So Far," *New York Times*, December 2015, http://www.nytimes.com/2015/12/05/us/san-bernardino-shoot ing-the-investigation-so-far.html. Daesh is a transliteration of the Arabic acronym of the group's name, al-Dowla al-islaamiyya fii-il-i'raaq wa-ash-shaam, which means "Islamic State in Iraq and Syria" (ISIS). I use Daesh rather than IS, ISIS, or ISIL for reasons discussed by Alice Guthrie, "Decoding Daesh: Why Is the New Name for ISIS So Hard to Understand?," *Free Word*, February 19, 2015, https://www.freewordcentre .com/explore/daesh-isis-media-alice-guthrie; and Adam Hosein, "Is There an Islamic

State?," *Stockholm Centre for the Ethics of War and Peace*, September 4, 2015, http://stockholmcentre.org/is-there-an-islamic-state/.

4.   E.g., Abir Taha, *Defining Terrorism: The End of Double Standards* (London: Arktos Media, 2014).

5.   E.g., William Banks, ed., *New Battlefields/Old Laws: Critical Debates on Asymmetric Warfare* (New York: Columbia University Press, 2011); Robert J. Bunker, *Networks, Terrorism and Global Insurgency* (London: Routledge, 2005); Bard E. O'Neill, *Insurgency and Terrorism: Inside Modern Revolutionary Warfare* (Dulles: Brassey's, 2001); Colin Wight, *Rethinking Terrorism: Terrorism, Violence and the State* (London: Palgrave Macmillan, 2015).

6.   Tamar Meisels, "Defining Terrorism—A Typology," *Critical Review of International Social and Political Philosophy* 12, no. 3 (2009): 334.

7.   For an elaboration of this argument, see Lisa Stampnitzky, *Disciplining Terror: How Experts Invented "Terrorism"* (Cambridge: Cambridge University Press, 2013). Stampnitzky offers an excellent account of the emergence of terrorism studies and its attendant notion of terrorism since the 1960s. For a discussion of the role of gender in this development, see Amanda Third, *Gender and the Political: Deconstructing the Female Terrorist* (New York: Palgrave Macmillan, 2014).

8.   Anthony Richards, *Conceptualizing Terrorism* (Oxford: Oxford University Press, 2015), 18.

9.   I follow Sally Haslanger, "What Are We Talking About? The Semantics and Politics of Social Kinds," *Hypatia* 20, no. 4 (2005): 10–26, in her account of ameliorative approaches to conceptual analysis as attempts to generate concepts that allow us to achieve particular goals. I return to the question of amelioration in chapter 6.

10.   For a detailed critical engagement with definitional approaches to terrorism in the academic field of mainstream and critical terrorism studies, see Verena Erlenbusch, "How (Not) to Study Terrorism," *Critical Review of International Social and Political Philosophy* 17, no. 4 (2014): 470–91; Erlenbusch, "Terrorism: Knowledge, Power, Subjectivity," in *Critical Methods in Terrorism Studies*, ed. Jacob L. Stump and Priya Dixit (London: Routledge, 2016), 108–20; Mathias Thaler, *Critical Theory and the Engaged Imagination: The Politics of Torture, Genocide, and Terrorism* (New York: Columbia University Press, forthcoming).

11.   Foucault cites Wittgenstein, along with Austin, Searle, and Strawson, as influential for his approach to the study of power relations; see Michel Foucault, "La philosophie analytique de la politique," in *Dits et écrits*, vol. 3, *1976–1979*, ed. Daniel Defert and François Ewald (Paris: Gallimard, 1994), 534–51; and Foucault, "La vérité et formes juridiques," in *Dits et écrits*, vol. 2, *1970–1975*, ed. Daniel Defert and François Ewald (Paris: Gallimard, 1994), 538–646. On the relationship between Foucault and Wittgenstein, see also Arnold I. Davidson, "Structures and Strategies of Discourse: Towards a History of Foucault's Philosophy of Language," in *Foucault and His Interlocutors*, ed. Arnold I. Davidson (Chicago: University of Chicago Press, 1997), 1–22; Hubert L. Dreyfus and Paul Rabinow, *Michel Foucault: Beyond Structuralism and Hermeneutics* (Chicago: University of Chicago Press, 1983); Frédéric Gros and Arnold I. Davidson, eds.,

Foucault, Wittgenstein: De possibles rencontres (Paris: Kimé, 2011); Cressida J. Heyes, "Pictures of the Self: Wittgenstein and Foucault on Thinking Ourselves Differently," in *Self-Transformations: Foucault, Ethics, and Normalized Bodies* (Oxford: Oxford University Press, 2007), 15–37; Tuomo Tiisala, "Keeping It Implicit: A Defense of Foucault's Archaeology of Knowledge," *Journal of the American Philosophical Association* 1 (2015): 653–73; Tiisala, "Power and Freedom in the Space of Reasons" (Ph.D. diss., University of Chicago, 2016).

12. In my elaboration of a genealogy of terrorism, I also take inspiration from work in historical epistemology, genealogy, and critical theory in the tradition of Marx and the Frankfurt School. The following works have been especially important in developing my approach: Amy Allen, *The End of Progress: Decolonizing the Normative Foundations of Critical Theory* (New York: Columbia University Press, 2016); Walter Benjamin, "On the Concept of History," in *Selected Writings*, vol. 4, *1938–1940*, ed. Howard Eiland and Michael W. Jennings (Cambridge, Mass.: Harvard University Press, 2003), 389–400; Georges Canguilhem, *The Normal and the Pathological*, trans. Carolyn R. Fawcett (New York: Zone, 1991); Santiago Castro-Gómez, *La hybris del punto cero: Ciencia, raza e ilustración en la Nueva Granada (1750–1816)* (Bogotá: Pontificia Universidad Javeriana, 2005); Lorraine Daston, "Historical Epistemology," in *Questions of Evidence: Proof, Practice, and Persuasion Across the Disciplines*, ed. James K. Chandler, Arnold I. Davidson, and Harry D. Harootunian (Chicago: University of Chicago Press, 1994), 282–89; Arnold I. Davidson, *The Emergence of Sexuality: Historical Epistemology and the Formation of Concepts* (Cambridge, Mass.: Harvard University Press, 2004); Andrew Dilts, *Punishment and Inclusion: Race, Membership, and the Limits of American Liberalism* (New York: Fordham University Press, 2014); Stuart Elden, *The Birth of Territory* (Chicago: University of Chicago Press, 2013); Thomas R. Flynn, *Sartre, Foucault, and Historical Reason*, vol. 2, *A Poststructuralist Mapping of History* (Chicago: University of Chicago Press, 2010); Raymond Geuss, "Genealogy as Critique," *European Journal of Philosophy* 10, no. 2 (2002): 209–15; Ian Hacking, *Historical Ontology* (Cambridge, Mass.: Harvard University Press, 2004); Max Horkheimer, "Traditional and Critical Theory," in *Critical Theory: Selected Essays*, trans. Matthew J. O'Connell (New York: Continuum, 1972), 188–243; Colin Koopman, *Genealogy as Critique: Foucault and the Problems of Modernity* (Bloomington: Indiana University Press, 2013); Karl Marx and Friedrich Engels, *The German Ideology*, in *Collected Works*, vol. 5 (New York: International, 1976), 19–608; Ladelle McWhorter, *Racism and Sexual Oppression in Anglo-America: A Genealogy* (Bloomington: Indiana University Press, 2009); Friedrich Wilhelm Nietzsche, *On the Genealogy of Morals*, trans. Douglas Smith (Oxford: Oxford University Press, 1996); Kevin Olson, *Imagined Sovereignties: The Power of the People and Other Myths of the Modern Age* (Cambridge: Cambridge University Press, 2016); Sarah S. Richardson, *Sex Itself* (Chicago: University of Chicago Press, 2013); Martin Saar, *Genealogie als Kritik: Geschichte und Theorie des Subjekts nach Nietzsche und Foucault* (Frankfurt: Campus, 2007); Tiisala, "Keeping It Implicit."

13. Ludwig Wittgenstein, *Philosophical Investigations*, trans. G. E. M. Anscombe (Malden, Mass.: Blackwell, 2001), §316.

14. Hacking, *Historical Ontology*, 68. See also Davidson, *Emergence of Sexuality*.
15. Flavius Josephus, *The Wars of the Jews*, in *The Works of Josephus*, trans. William Whiston (Peabody, Mass.: Hendrickson, 1987), 625. The translation of *lēistai* as "robbers" follows Whiston's standard translation of Josephus. Some scholars have suggested that "bandits" is a more adequate translation. Although the etymology and legal history of this term are interesting and highly relevant for a comparative study of violence, neither *robbery* nor *banditry* seems to correspond well to our contemporary concept of terrorism. For legal histories of banditry and robbery, as well as outstanding accounts of banditry in the Roman Empire, see Bernard S. Jackson, "Some Comparative Legal History: Robbery and Brigandage," *Georgia Journal of International and Comparative Law* 1 (1970): 45–103; Brent Shaw, "Bandits in the Roman Empire," *Past and Present* 105 (1984): 3–52.
16. Josephus, *Wars of the Jews*, 614.
17. For discussions of the politics of naming, especially in the context of terrorism, see Michael Bhatia, "Fighting Words: Naming Terrorists, Bandits, Rebels and Other Violent Actors," *Third World Quarterly* 26, no. 1 (2005): 5–22, doi:10.1080/0143659042000322874; Bhatia, ed., *Terrorism and the Politics of Naming* (Abingdon: Routledge, 2008); Christopher J. Finlay, "How to Do Things with the Word 'Terrorist,'" *Review of International Studies* 35, no. 4 (2009): 751–74, doi:10.1017/S0260210509990167; Mahmood Mamdani, "The Politics of Naming: Genocide, Civil War, Insurgency," *London Review of Books* 29, no. 5 (2007): 5–8; Suthaharan Nadarajah and Dhananjayan Sriskandarajah, "Liberation Struggle or Terrorism? The Politics of Naming the LTTE," *Third World Quarterly* 26, no. 1 (2005): 87–100.
18. Bhatia, "Fighting Words," 8.
19. Michel Foucault, *The Punitive Society: Lectures at the Collège de France, 1972–1973*, ed. Bernard E. Harcourt, François Ewald, Alessandro Fontana, and Arnold I. Davidson, trans. Graham Burchell (Basingstoke: Palgrave Macmillan, 2015), 12; italics in original.
20. Rukmini Callimachi, "Islamic State Says 'Soldiers of Caliphate' Attacked in San Bernardino," *New York Times*, December 5, 2015, http://www.nytimes.com/2015/12/06/world/middleeast/islamic-state-san-bernardino-massacre.html.
21. For some representative accounts, see Giorgio Agamben, "Security and Terror," *Theory and Event* 5, no. 4 (2002): 1–2; Louise Amoore and Marieke de Goede, eds., *Risk and the War on Terror* (London: Routledge, 2008); Claudia Aradau and Rens van Munster, "Insuring Terrorism, Assuring Subjects, Ensuring Normality: The Politics of Risk After 9/11," *Alternatives: Global, Local, Political* 33, no. 2 (2008): 191–210; Aradau and Munster, "Taming the Future: The Dispositif of Risk in the War on Terror," in Amoore and Goede, *Risk and the War on Terror*, 23–40; Andreas Behnke, "Terrorising the Political: 9/11 Within the Context of the Globalisation of Violence," *Millennium—Journal of International Studies* 33, no. 2 (2004): 279–312; Didier Bigo and Anastassia Tsoukala, *Terror, Insecurity and Liberty: Illiberal Practices of Liberal Regimes After 9/11* (London: Routledge, 2008); Judith Butler, "Indefinite Detention," in *Precarious Life: The Powers of Mourning and Violence* (London: Verso, 2004), 50–100; Alejandro Colás and Richard

Saull, *The War on Terror and the American "Empire" After the Cold War* (London: Routledge, 2006); Elizabeth Dauphinée and Cristina Masters, eds., *The Logics of Biopower and the War on Terror: Living, Dying, Surviving* (New York: Palgrave Macmillan, 2006); François Debrix, *Tabloid Terror: War, Culture, and Geopolitics* (London: Routledge, 2008); Michael Dillon, "Governing Terror: The State of Emergency of Biopolitical Emergence," *International Political Sociology* 1, no. 1 (2007): 7–28; Brad Evans, *Liberal Terror: Global Security, Divine Power and Emergency Rule* (London: Routledge, 2012); Michael A. Genovese, *Presidential Prerogative: Imperial Power in an Age of Terrorism* (Stanford, Calif.: Stanford University Press, 2010); Richard Jackson, *Writing the War on Terrorism: Language, Politics and Counter-Terrorism* (Manchester: Manchester University Press, 2005); Bonnie Mann, *Sovereign Masculinity: Gender Lessons from the War on Terror* (New York: Oxford University Press, 2014); Stephen Morton and Stephen Bygrave, *Foucault in an Age of Terror: Essays on Biopolitics and the Defence of Society* (Basingstoke and New York: Palgrave Macmillan, 2008); Rens van Munster, "The War on Terrorism: When the Exception Becomes the Rule," *International Journal for the Semiotics of Law* 17, no. 2 (2004): 141–53; Andrew W. Neal, *Exceptionalism and the Politics of Counter-Terrorism: Liberty, Security, and the War on Terror* (Abingdon and New York: Taylor and Francis, 2010); Louiza Odysseos and Fabio Petito, eds., *The International Political Thought of Carl Schmitt: Terror, Liberal War and the Crisis of Global Order* (London: Routledge, 2007); Marc Redfield, *The Rhetoric of Terror: Reflections on 9/11 and the War on Terror* (New York: Fordham University Press, 2009); Julian Reid, *The Biopolitics of the War on Terror: Life Struggles, Liberal Modernity and the Defence of Logistical Societies* (Manchester: Manchester University Press, 2009); Ernesto Verdeja, "Law, Terrorism, and the Plenary Power Doctrine: Limiting Alien Rights," *Constellations* 9, no. 1 (2002): 89–97.

22.   For excellent analyses, see Muneer I. Ahmad, "A Rage Shared by Law: Post–September 11 Racial Violence as Crimes of Passion," *California Law Review* 92, no. 5 (2004): 1259–1330; Evelyn Alsultany, *Arabs and Muslims in the Media: Race and Representation After 9/11* (New York: New York University Press, 2012); Sean Brayton, "An American Werewolf in Kabul: John Walker Lindh, the Construction of 'Race,' and the Return to Whiteness," *International Journal of Media and Cultural Politics* 2, no. 2 (2006): 167–82; George N. Fourlas, "Being a Target: On the Racialization of Middle Eastern Americans," *Critical Philosophy of Race* 3, no. 1 (2015): 101–23, doi:10.5325/crit philrace.3.1.0101; Jasbir K. Puar, *Terrorist Assemblages: Homonationalism in Queer Times* (Durham, N.C.: Duke University Press, 2007); Jasbir K. Puar and Amit Rai, "Monster, Terrorist, Fag: The War on Terrorism and the Production of Docile Bodies," *Social Text* 20, no. 3 (2002): 117–48; Christopher Rivera, "The Brown Threat: Post-9/11 Conflations of Latina/os and Middle Eastern Muslims in the US American Imagination," *Latino Studies* 12, no. 1 (2014): 44–64; Victoria Sentas, *Traces of Terror: Counter-Terrorism Law, Policing, and Race* (Oxford: Oxford University Press, 2014); Falguni A. Sheth, *Toward a Political Philosophy of Race* (Albany: SUNY Press, 2009); Leti Volpp, "The Boston Bombers," *Fordham Law Review* 82, no. 5 (2014): 2209–20; Volpp, "The

Citizen and the Terrorist," *UCLA Law Review* 49, no. 5 (2012): 561–86; Michael Welch, *Scapegoats of September 11th: Hate Crimes and State Crimes in the War on Terror* (New Brunswick, N.J.: Rutgers University Press, 2006).

23. Muneer I. Ahmad, "Homeland Insecurities: Racial Violence the Day After September 11," *Social Text* 20, no. 3 (2002): 103. Falguni Sheth describes the racial reception of particular signifiers in terms of a "racial aesthetic." For her insightful discussion of the differential coding of the veil and the sari, see Falguni A. Sheth, "The Hijab and the Sari: The Strange and Sexy Between Colonialism and Global Capitalism," *Contemporary Aesthetics*, special volume 2 (2009). See also Alia al-Saji, "The Racialization of Muslim Veils: A Philosophical Analysis," *Philosophy and Social Criticism* 36, no. 8 (2010): 875–902.

24. M. I. Ahmad, "Rage Shared by Law," 1261.

25. Ibid., 1278–79. See also Rivera, "Brown Threat." As Lewis R. Gordon, "Falguni A. Sheth: Toward a Political Philosophy of Race," *Continental Philosophy Review* 44, no. 1 (2011): 119–30, reminds us, a more comprehensive discussion of the ways in which Muslims have been excluded in the United States must include an account of the experience of black Muslims. Gordon correctly points out that an understanding of American anti-Muslim racism in general and the historical relationship between Islam and terrorism in particular cannot be achieved without a careful consideration of the interlocking of anti-Muslim and antiblack racism. Specifically, an account of the interplay of antiblack racism and Islamophobia in the context of terrorism would have to include, for instance, a discussion of the invocation of terrorism by Malcolm X, as well as the representation of the Nation of Islam as a terrorist movement. Since it is impossible to do justice to these issues here, I flag them as topics for future research.

26. Volpp, "Citizen and the Terrorist," 581.

27. M. I. Ahmad, "Homeland Insecurities," 105.

28. Puar, *Terrorist Assemblages*, 14.

29. E.g., Natalie Cisneros, "'Alien' Sexuality: Race, Maternity, and Citizenship," *Hypatia* 28, no. 2 (2013): 290–306, doi:10.1111/hypa.12023; Cisneros, "The 'Illegal Alien': A Genealogical and Intersectional Approach" (Ph.D. diss., Vanderbilt University, 2012); Charles W. Mills, *The Racial Contract* (Ithaca, N.Y.: Cornell University Press, 1999); Joel Olson, *The Abolition of White Democracy* (Minneapolis: University of Minnesota Press, 2004).

30. See in particular Michel Foucault, *Abnormal: Lectures at the Collège de France, 1974–1975*, ed. Valerio Marchetti, Antonella Salomoni, François Ewald, Alessandro Fontana, and Arnold I. Davidson, trans. Graham Burchell (New York: Picador, 2004); Foucault, *The Birth of the Clinic: An Archaeology of Medical Perception*, trans. A. M. Sheridan (New York: Vintage, 1994); Foucault, *Discipline and Punish: The Birth of the Prison*, trans. Alan Sheridan (New York: Vintage, 1995); Foucault, *History of Madness*, ed. Jean Khalfa, trans. Jonathan Murphy (London: Routledge, 2006); Foucault, *The History of Sexuality*, vol. 1, *An Introduction*, trans. Robert Hurley (New York: Vintage, 1990); Foucault, *Psychiatric Power: Lectures at the Collège de France, 1973–1974*, ed. Jacques

Lagrange, François Ewald, Alessandro Fontana, and Arnold I. Davidson, trans. Graham Burchell (New York: Palgrave Macmillan, 2008).

31. Foucault, *History of Sexuality*, vol. 1, *Introduction*, 136.

32. Foucault, *Discipline and Punish*, 47–49.

33. Michel Foucault, *Security, Territory, Population: Lectures at the Collège de France, 1977–1978*, ed. Michel Senellart, François Ewald, Alessandro Fontana, and Arnold I. Davidson, trans. Graham Burchell (New York: Palgrave Macmillan, 2007), 108.

34. For critical engagements with Foucault's discussion of race, see Castro-Gómez, *Hybris del punto cero*; Dilts, *Punishment and Inclusion*; Ellen K. Feder, *Family Bonds: Genealogies of Race and Gender* (Oxford: Oxford University Press, 2007); Roderick A. Ferguson, *The Reorder of Things: The University and Its Pedagogies of Minority Difference* (Minneapolis: University of Minnesota Press, 2012); Brady Thomas Heiner, "Foucault and the Black Panthers," *City* 11, no. 3 (2007): 313–56; Grace Kyungwon Hong and Roderick A. Ferguson, eds., *Strange Affinities: The Gender and Sexual Politics of Comparative Racialization* (Durham, N.C.: Duke University Press, 2011); Mark Kelly, "Racism, Nationalism and Biopolitics: Foucault's *Society Must Be Defended*," *Contretemps* 4 (2004): 58–70; David Macey, "Rethinking Biopolitics, Race and Power in the Wake of Foucault," *Theory, Culture and Society* 26, no. 6 (2009): 186–205; Mary Beth Mader, "Modern Living and Vital Race: Foucault and the Science of Life," *Foucault Studies* 12 (2011): 97–112; McWhorter, *Racism and Sexual Oppression in Anglo-America*; Kim Su Rasmussen, "Foucault's Genealogy of Racism," *Theory, Culture and Society* 28, no. 5 (2011): 34–51; Sheth, *Toward a Political Philosophy of Race*; Ann Laura Stoler, *Race and the Education of Desire: Foucault's "History of Sexuality" and the Colonial Order of Things* (Durham, N.C.: Duke University Press, 1995); Chloë Taylor, "Race and Racism in Foucault's Collège de France Lectures," *Philosophy Compass* 6, no. 11 (2011): 746–56.

35. I discuss these in Verena Erlenbusch, "From Race War to Social Racism: Foucault's Second Transcription," *Foucault Studies* 22 (2017): 134–52, doi:http://dx.doi.org/10.22439/fs.v0i0.5239.

36. Foucault, *Abnormal*, 316.

37. Foucault, *History of Sexuality*, vol. 1, *Introduction*, 61.

38. The notion of social defense, specifically as it was articulated in criminal law in the early twentieth century, is a key theme of a series of lectures Foucault gave at the Catholic University of Louvain in 1981, published in English as *Wrong-Doing, Truth-Telling: The Function of Avowal in Justice*, ed. Fabienne Brion and Bernard E. Harcourt, trans. Stephen W. Sawyer (Chicago: University of Chicago Press, 2014).

39. For representative publications, see Kwame Anthony Appiah, "Racisms," in *Anatomy of Racism*, ed. David Goldberg (Minneapolis: University of Minnesota Press, 1990), 3–17; Lawrence Blum, "Racism: What It Is and What It Isn't," *Studies in Philosophy and Education* 21, no. 3 (2002): 203–18; Jorge Garcia, "The Heart of Racism," *Journal of Social Philosophy* 27, no. 1 (1996): 5–46; Garcia, "Current Conceptions of Racism: A Critical Examination of Some Recent Social Philosophy," *Journal of Social Philosophy* 28, no. 2 (1997): 5–42; Joshua Glasgow, "Racism as Disrespect," *Ethics* 120, no. 1 (2009): 64–93;

Lewis R. Gordon, *Bad Faith and Antiblack Racism* (Amherst, Mass.: Humanity, 1995); Charles W. Mills, "'Heart' Attack: A Critique of Jorge Garcia's Volitional Conception of Racism," *Journal of Ethics* 7, no. 1 (2003): 29–62; Tommie Shelby, "Ideology, Racism, and Critical Social Theory," *Philosophical Forum* 34, no. 2 (2003): 153–88.

40. Michel Foucault, "Le Jeu de Michel Foucault," in *Dits et écrits*, vol. 3, *1976–1979*, ed. Daniel Defert and François Ewald (Paris: Gallimard, 1994), 299. See also Foucault, "The Confession of the Flesh," in *Power/Knowledge: Selected Interviews and Other Writings, 1972–1977*, ed. Colin Gordon (New York: Random House, 1980), 194–228. Unless otherwise noted, all translations from French material in this book are mine.

41. Foucault, *Psychiatric Power*, 111.

42. "The National Security Strategy of the United States of America," 2002, 6–7, http://nssarchive.us/NSSR/2002.pdf.

43. E.g., Anna Sampaio, *Terrorizing Latina/o Immigrants: Race, Gender, and Immigration Policy Post-9/11* (Philadelphia: Temple University Press, 2015); Michael Welch, *Detained: Immigration Laws and the Expanding I.N.S. Jail Complex* (Philadelphia: Temple University Press 2002); Welch, "Ironies of Social Control and the Criminalization of Immigrants," *Crime, Law and Social Change* 39, no. 4 (2003): 319–37, doi:10.1023/A:1024068321783.

44. E.g., Neil Krishan Aggarwal, *Mental Health in the War on Terror: Culture, Science, and Statecraft* (New York: Columbia University Press, 2015).

45. E.g., Naomi Klein, *The Shock Doctrine: The Rise of Disaster Capitalism* (New York: Picador, 2007).

46. Michel Foucault, "What Is Enlightenment?," in *The Politics of Truth*, ed. Sylvère Lotringer (Los Angeles: Semiotext(e), 2007), 113–14.

47. When I describe the project I pursue in this book as a genealogy of terrorism, I take this to entail both an archaeological and a genealogical component. This is because archaeology and genealogy are intimately connected, rather than separate modes of analysis, one of which replaces the other. Indeed, Foucault explained in *Security, Territory, Population* that archaeology is a way of exploring discourse in order to "discover its guiding principles, the rules of formation of its concepts, its theoretical elements, and so on," whereas genealogy tries to "reconstruct the function of the text, not according to the rules of formation of its concepts, but according to its objectives, the strategies that govern it, and the program of political action it proposes" (35–36). Moreover, what makes an analysis distinctly genealogical rather than a work of history is that it is a history of the present. As Foucault put it in a 1984 interview with François Ewald, "I start off from a problem in the terms in which it presents itself at present and I try to do its genealogy. Genealogy means that I conduct the analysis beginning with a present-day question" (Foucault, "Le souci de la vérité," in *Dits et écrits*, vol. 4, *1980–1988*, ed. Daniel Defert and François Ewald [Paris: Gallimard, 1994], 674). See also Stuart Elden, *Foucault's Last Decade* (Malden, Mass.: Polity, 2016); Koopman, *Genealogy as Critique*.

48. I will develop the notion of *synthetic terrorism* in detail in chapter 5. I emphasize here that I understand the term *synthetic* not in its Kantian or Hegelian sense but rather in the sense intended by Friedrich Nietzsche when he described the concept of punish-

ment as a "synthesis of 'meanings'" by which "the whole history of punishment . . . crystallizes in a sort of unity which is difficult to unravel, difficult to analyse, and—a point which must be emphasized—completely *beyond definition*" (Nietzsche, *On the Genealogy of Morals*, 60).

49. For discussions of the term *enemy*, as well as some of its cognates, such as *tyrant*, *pirate, bandit*, and *partisan*, see Gil Anidjar, *The Jew, the Arab: A History of the Enemy* (Stanford, Calif.: Stanford University Press, 2003); Anidjar, "Terror Right," *CR: The New Centennial Review* 4, no. 3 (2004): 35–69; Vilho Harle, *The Enemy with a Thousand Faces: The Tradition of the Other in Western Political Thought and History* (Westport, Conn.: Praeger, 2000); Daniel Heller-Roazen, *The Enemy of All: Piracy and the Law of Nations* (New York: Zone, 2009); Eric Hobsbawm, *Bandits* (New York: Pantheon, 1981); Achille Mbembe, *Politiques de l'inimitié* (Paris: La Découverte, 2016); Sergei Prozorov, "Liberal Enmity: The Figure of the Foe in the Political Ontology of Liberalism," *Millennium* 35, no. 1 (2006): 75–99, doi:10.1177/03058298060350010801; William Rasch, "Lines in the Sand: Enmity as a Structuring Principle," *South Atlantic Quarterly* 104, no. 2 (2005): 253–62, doi:10.1215/00382876-104-2-253; Carl Schmitt, "The Concept of Piracy (1937)," *Humanity: An International Journal of Human Rights, Humanitarianism, and Development* 2, no. 1 (2011): 27–29; Schmitt, *The Nomos of the Earth in the International Law of Jus Publicum Europaeum*, trans. G. L. Ulmen (New York: Telos, 2006); Schmitt, *Theory of the Partisan: Intermediate Commentary on the Concept of the Political*, trans. G. L. Ulmen (New York: Telos, 2007).

50. Marnia Lazreg, *Torture and the Twilight of Empire: From Algiers to Baghdad* (Princeton, N.J.: Princeton University Press, 2007), 11.

51. For excellent critical discussions of these contexts, see André Barrinha, "The Political Importance of Labelling: Terrorism and Turkey's Discourse on the PKK," *Critical Studies on Terrorism* 4, no. 2 (2011): 163–80, doi:10.1080/17539153.2011.586203; Andrei Gómez-Suárez, *Genocide, Geopolitics and Transnational Networks: Con-Textualising the Destruction of the Unión Patriótica in Colombia* (London: Taylor and Francis, 2015); Derek Gregory, *The Colonial Present: Afghanistan, Palestine, Iraq* (Malden, Mass.: Blackwell, 2004); Gregory, "Palestine and the 'War on Terror,'" *Comparative Studies of South Asia, Africa and the Middle East* 24, no. 1 (2004): 183–95; Derek Gregory and Allan Pred, eds., *Violent Geographies: Fear, Terror, and Political Violence* (New York: Routledge, 2006); Adrian Guelke, "Irish Republican Terrorism: Learning from and Teaching Other Countries," *Studies in Conflict and Terrorism* 40, no. 7 (2017): 557–72, doi:10.1080/1057610X.2016.1237222; Maria Holt, "The Unlikely Terrorist: Women and Islamic Resistance in Lebanon and the Palestinian Territories," *Critical Studies on Terrorism* 3, no. 3 (2010): 365–82, doi:10.1080/17539153.2010.521640; C. L. R. James, *The Black Jacobins: Toussaint L'Ouverture and the San Domingo Revolution* (New York: Vintage, 1989); Nadarajah and Sriskandarajah, "Liberation Struggle or Terrorism?"; Ilan Pappe, "De-Terrorising the Palestinian National Struggle: The Roadmap to Peace," *Critical Studies on Terrorism* 2, no. 2 (2009): 127–46, doi:10.1080/17539150903021399; Joseba Zulaika and William Douglass, *Terror and Taboo: The Follies, Fables, and Faces of Terrorism* (New York: Routledge, 1996).

52. On the notion of the archive in Foucault, see in particular the chapter "The Historical a priori and the Archive" in Michel Foucault, *The Archaeology of Knowledge*, trans. A. M. Sheridan Smith (London: Routledge, 2002).

53. Frantz Fanon offers an excellent analysis of the revolutionary appropriation of the French language in "This Is the Voice of Algeria," chapter 2 of *A Dying Colonialism*, trans. Haakon Chevalier (New York: Grove, 1965).

54. Arlette Farge, *The Allure of the Archives*, trans. Thomas Scott-Railton (New Haven, Conn.: Yale University Press 2013), 30.

55. Ibid., 28.

56. Foucault, *Abnormal*, 8. I owe this point to Penelope Deutscher, who has aptly described this as "pluri-genealogy"; Penelope Deutscher, "Society Must Be Defended as Pluri-Genealogy" (paper presented at the Graduate Summer Institute in Rhetoric and Public Culture, Northwestern University, July 20, 2016).

57. On the completeness or incompleteness of genealogy, see Michel Foucault, "On the Ways of Writing History," in *Essential Works of Foucault, 1954–1984*, vol. 2, *Aesthetics, Method, and Epistemology*, ed. James D. Faubion (New York: New Press, 1998), 279–95.

CHAPTER 2. THE EMERGENCE OF TERRORISM

1. Bronislaw Baczko, *Ending the Terror: The French Revolution After Robespierre*, trans. Michel Petheram (Cambridge: Cambridge University Press, 1994), 49.

2. Immanuel Kant, "The Contest of Faculties," in *Political Writings*, ed. Hans Reiss (Cambridge: Cambridge University Press, 2009), 178–79. I owe this reference to Loren Goldman.

3. Piero Giordanetti, "Einleitung," in *Der Streit der Fakultäten*, by Immanuel Kant (Hamburg: Meiner, 2005), vii–xlv.

4. The popular movement consisted of the radical and militant sans-culottes, working-class people and urban laborers who did not wear the fashionable knee breeches of the nobility and upper middle classes, and the so-called *enragés*, a group of intellectuals who defended and gave voice to sans-culotte demands for popular power. Their main opponents were monarchists and royalists, who supported a monarchical system in general and Bourbon rule in particular. Political clubs included the Jacobin Club, in which radical Montagnards and more moderate Girondins vied for dominance; the Cordeliers, the most radical and decidedly populist club; and constitutional monarchist clubs such as the Society of 1789 and the Feuillants. For more information about key actors, factions, and events of the French Revolution, see François Furet and Mona Ozouf, eds., *A Critical Dictionary of the French Revolution* (Cambridge, Mass.: Harvard University Press, 1988).

5. The French Revolution remains a fiercely debated period of history among historians. For some key accounts, see Florin Aftalion, *The French Revolution: An Economic Interpretation* (Cambridge: Cambridge University Press, 1990); Thomas Carlyle, *The French Revolution: A History* (London: Chapman and Hall, 1888); Alfred Cobban, *The*

Social Interpretation of the French Revolution (Cambridge: Cambridge University Press, 1999); George C. Comninel, *Rethinking the French Revolution: Marxism and the Revisionist Challenge* (London: Verso, 1987); William Doyle, *The Oxford History of the French Revolution* (Oxford: Oxford University Press, 2003); Jonathan Israel, *Revolutionary Ideas: An Intellectual History of the French Revolution from "The Rights of Man" to Robespierre* (Princeton, N.J.: Princeton University Press, 2014); Georges Lefebvre, *The French Revolution*, vol. 1, *From Its Origins to 1793*, trans. Elizabeth Moss Evanson (New York: Columbia University Press, 1962); Lefebvre, *The French Revolution*, vol. 2, *From 1793 to 1799*, trans. John Hall Stewart and James Friguglietti (New York: Columbia University Press, 1964); George F. E. Rudé, *The French Revolution: Its Causes, Its History, and Its Legacy After 200 Years* (New York: Grove, 1988); Albert Soboul, *The French Revolution, 1787–1799: From the Storming of the Bastille to Napoleon*, trans. Alan Forrest and Colin Jones (Boston: Unwin Hyman, 1989).

6. My use of the term *doxastic terrorism*, from the Greek word *doxa* (belief or opinion), is inspired by the notion of "doxastic racism" elaborated by philosophers of race to articulate a conception of racism as a doctrine, dogma, or set of beliefs. See, for instance, Jorge Garcia, "Current Conceptions of Racism: A Critical Examination of Some Recent Social Philosophy," *Journal of Social Philosophy* 28, no. 2 (1997): 5–42.

7. Gerd van den Heuvel, "Terreur, Terroriste, Terrorisme," in *Handbuch Politisch-Sozialer Grundbegriffe in Frankreich, 1680–1820*, vol. 3, ed. Rolf Reichardt and Eberhard Schmitt (Munich: Oldenbourg, 1985), 89–132. See also Rudolf Walther, "Terror, Terrorismus," in *Geschichtliche Grundbegriffe: Historisches Lexikon zur politisch-sozialen Sprache in Deutschland*, vol. 6, ed. Otto Brunner, Werner Conze, and Reinhart Koselleck (Stuttgart: Klett-Kotta, 1990), 323–444.

8. Mikkel Thorup, *An Intellectual History of Terror: War, Violence and the State* (London: Routledge, 2010), 101.

9. Maximilien Robespierre, "On the Principles of Political Morality That Should Guide the National Convention in the Domestic Administration of the Republic," in *Robespierre: Virtue and Terror*, ed. Slavoj Žižek (London: Verso, 2007), 115.

10. E.g., Martha Crenshaw, "The Concept of Revolutionary Terrorism," *Journal of Conflict Resolution* 16, no. 3 (1972): 383–96.

11. Edgar Quinet, *La Révolution* (Paris: Belin, 1987), 502.

12. Quoted in Hugh Chisholm, ed., "Louvois, François Michel Le Tellier," in *The Encyclopaedia Britannica: A Dictionary of Arts, Sciences, Literature and General Information* 17 (Cambridge: Cambridge University Press, 1911): 69.

13. Quinet, *Révolution*, 503.

14. Ibid., 505.

15. Quoted in Antoine-Vincent Arnault, *Biographie nouvelle des contemporains, ou dictionnaire historique et raisonné de tous les hommes qui, depuis la Révolution française ont acquis de la célébrité par leurs actions, leurs écrits, leurs erreurs ou leurs crimes, soit en France, soit dans les pays étrangers* (Paris: Librairie Historique, 1825), 181.

16. Quoted in Pierre Sipriot, *Les cent vingt jours de Louis XVI, dit Louis Capet* (Paris: Plon, 1993), 48.

196 2. THE EMERGENCE OF TERRORISM

17. Damiens also makes an infamous appearance in the opening pages of Michel Foucault's *Discipline and Punish: The Birth of the Prison* (New York: Vintage, 1995).

18. Jules Michelet, *Histoire de la Révolution française* (Paris: Pilon, 1868), 236. Félix Montjoie observed a different genealogy and recounted rumors about a familial relationship between Damiens and Robespierre. Although Montjoie did not think that this widespread assumption deserved credence, "royalist writers . . . have made public that [Robespierre] was the nephew of Damien [*sic*], the assassin of Louis XV" (*Histoire de la conjuration de Maximilien Robespierre* [Paris: Maret, 1795], 10). In contrast to the continuity of practices of public torture noted by other writers, Montjoie's observation draws attention to a regicidal attitude that ostensibly connected Damiens and Robespierre.

19. Michel Foucault, *The Punitive Society: Lectures at the Collège de France, 1972–1973*, ed. Bernard E. Harcourt, François Ewald, Alessandro Fontana, and Arnold I. Davidson, trans. Graham Burchell (Basingstoke: Palgrave Macmillan, 2015), 8, 10.

20. Arnold I. Davidson, *The Emergence of Sexuality: Historical Epistemology and the Formation of Concepts* (Cambridge, Mass.: Harvard University Press, 2004), 3.

21. On this point, see Arno J. Mayer, *The Furies: Violence and Terror in the French and Russian Revolutions* (Princeton, N.J.: Princeton University Press, 2000).

22. For a discussion of the relationship between concepts and practices, see also Michel Foucault, "Table ronde du 20 mai 1978," in *Dits et écrits*, vol. 4, *1980–1988*, ed. Daniel Defert and François Ewald (Paris: Gallimard, 1994), 20–34; Colin Koopman, "Conceptual Analysis for Genealogical Philosophy: How to Study the History of Practices after Foucault and Wittgenstein," *The Southern Journal of Philosophy*, 55 (2017): 103–21.

23. Davidson, *Emergence of Sexuality*, 3.

24. On this point, see Michel Foucault, *The Archaeology of Knowledge*, trans. A. M. Sheridan Smith (London: Routledge, 2002); Tuomo Tiisala, "Keeping It Implicit: A Defense of Foucault's Archaeology of Knowledge," *Journal of the American Philosophical Association* 1 (2015): 653–73; Tiisala, "Power and Freedom in the Space of Reasons" (Ph.D. diss., University of Chicago, 2016).

25. By *episteme*, Foucault means the unconscious structures that make possible and regulate the formation of scientific knowledge in a particular time and place. Michel Foucault, *The Order of Things: An Archaeology of the Human Sciences* (New York: Vintage, 1994), xxiii–xxiv.

26. Michel Foucault, "L'intellectuel et les pouvoirs," in *Dits et écrits*, vol. 4, *1980–1988*, ed. Daniel Defert and François Ewald (Paris: Gallimard, 1994), 747–52.

27. Note that the notion of *raison d'État* itself is ripe for genealogical analysis. But while the genealogy of terrorism developed here intersects in important ways with a genealogy of *raison d'État*, the latter is beyond the scope of the account of terrorism developed in this book. A good place to start is Michel Foucault's further reflections on *raison d'État* in *The Hermeneutics of the Subject: Lectures at the Collège de France, 1981–1982*, trans. Graham Burchell (New York: Picador, 2005); and *On the Government of the Living: Lectures at the Collège de France, 1979–1980*, ed. Michel Senellart, François Ewald, Alessandro Fontana, and Arnold I. Davidson, trans. Graham Burchell (New York:

Palgrave Macmillan, 2014). For excellent discussions of *raison d'État*, see also Mark Neocleous, *Imagining the State* (Maidenhead: Open University Press, 2003); Sheldon Sanford Wolin, *Democracy Incorporated: Managed Democracy and the Specter of Inverted Totalitarianism* (Princeton, N.J.: Princeton University Press, 2010).

28. Michel Foucault, *Security, Territory, Population: Lectures at the Collège de France, 1977–1978*, ed. Michel Senellart, François Ewald, Alessandro Fontana, and Arnold I. Davidson, trans. Graham Burchell (New York: Palgrave Macmillan, 2007).

29. Ibid., 262.

30. Gabriel Naudé's treatise *Considérations politiques sur les coups d'état*, written in 1639 and discussed by Foucault as the paradigmatic text on the theory of *coup d'état*, was translated into English in 1711 and published as *Political Considerations upon Refin'd Politicks, and the Master-Strokes of State*, trans. William King (London: Clements, 1711).

31. Foucault, *Security, Territory, Population*, 262.

32. Ibid., 327.

33. Ibid., 340. See also Foucault, *Discipline and Punish*; Foucault, *Psychiatric Power: Lectures at the Collège de France, 1973–1974*, ed. Jacques Lagrange, François Ewald, Alessandro Fontana, and Arnold I. Davidson, trans. Graham Burchell (New York: Palgrave Macmillan, 2008).

34. Foucault noted that an effect of this new military-diplomatic technique was the establishment of a new juridical framework, in which war was separated from questions of justice and instead articulated as a political instrument. One no longer needed a just cause to wage war, but merely a diplomatic reason. Carl Schmitt describes this difference between medieval international law and the European public law in much detail, even though his analysis lacks the careful genealogical attention to historical forms of thought and practice that made this transformation both possible and necessary. I will return to Schmitt's analysis in chapter 4. On the history of contemporary international law since the nineteenth century, see Martti Koskenniemi, *The Gentle Civilizer of Nations: The Rise and Fall of International Law, 1870–1960* (Cambridge: Cambridge University Press, 2004).

35. Foucault, *Security, Territory, Population*, 15. In a later lecture, Foucault highlighted the importance of economic domination and colonization for the operation of a mercantilist system (ibid., 285–310). The relationship between colonialism and governmentality has been explored from a different perspective by David Scott, "Colonial Governmentality," *Social Text* 43 (1995): 191–220.

36. Foucault, *Security, Territory, Population*, 352.

37. Michel Foucault, *The Birth of Biopolitics: Lectures at the Collège de France, 1978–1979*, ed. Michel Senellart, François Ewald, Alessandro Fontana, and Arnold I. Davidson, trans. Graham Burchell (New York: Palgrave Macmillan, 2010), 15.

38. Ibid., 21.

39. For a discussion of the relationship between *raison d'État* and liberalism, see also Roberto Nigro, "From Reason of State to Liberalism: The Coup d'État as Form of Government," in *The Government of Life: Foucault, Biopolitics, and Neoliberalism*, ed. Vanessa Lemm and Miguel Vatter (New York: Fordham University Press, 2014), 127–40.

40. Foucault used the language of superimposition in *The History of Sexuality*, vol. 1, *An Introduction*, trans. Robert Hurley (New York: Vintage, 1990), 55, 106; *Security, Territory, Population*, 108; and *"Society Must Be Defended": Lectures at the Collège de France, 1975–1976*, ed. Mauro Bertani, Alessandro Fontana, François Ewald, and Arnold I. Davidson, trans. David Macey (New York: Picador, 2003), 249. The notion of superimposition is also operative in Nietzsche's work. In *On the Genealogy of Morals*, he took the example of punishment to show that over time, it has become "overlaid with all sorts of uses" (Friedrich Wilhelm Nietzsche, *On the Genealogy of Morals*, trans. Douglas Smith [Oxford: Oxford University Press, 1996], 61). For Nietzsche, it was precisely this layering of meanings onto a relatively enduring custom that was the object of the genealogist's work.

41. For a discussion of the debates between mercantilists and physiocrats, as well as their political influence in the years leading up to the Revolution, see David Andress, *The Terror: The Merciless War for Freedom in Revolutionary France* (New York: Farrar, Straus and Giroux, 2005), chap. 1.

42. Robespierre, "On the Principles of Political Morality," 115.

43. Maximilien Robespierre, "Extracts from 'On Subsistence,'" in *Robespierre: Virtue and Terror*, ed. Slavoj Žižek (London: Verso, 2007), 51.

44. Ibid., 49.

45. Ibid., 54.

46. Ibid., 52.

47. One of the first measures adopted by the Montagnards after Robespierre's putsch in June 1793 was the so-called Law of the Maximum (also known as the General Maximum or Jacobin Maximum), which limited food prices and allowed for those who bought or sold items for more than the maximum to be treated as counterrevolutionaries. See Margaret H. Darrow, "Economic Terror in the City: The General Maximum in Montauban," *French Historical Studies* 17, no. 2 (1991): 498–525; Robert B. Rose, "18th-Century Price-Riots, the French Revolution and the Jacobin Maximum," *International Review of Social History* 4, no. 3 (1959): 432–45; Eugene Nelson White, "The French Revolution and the Politics of Government Finance, 1770–1815," *Journal of Economic History* 55, no. 2 (1995): 227–55.

48. Israel, *Revolutionary Ideas*, 310.

49. E.g., Roger Barny, *Prélude idéologique à la Révolution francaise: Le Rousseauisme avant 1789* (Paris: Les Belles Lettres, 1985); Carol Blum, *Rousseau and the Republic of Virtue: The Language of Politics in the French Revolution* (Ithaca, N.Y.: Cornell University Press, 1989); Julien Boudon, *Les Jacobins: Une traduction des principes de Jean-Jacques Rousseau* (Paris: Librairie Générale de Droit et de Jurisprudence, 2006); Norman Hampson, *Will and Circumstance: Montesquieu, Rousseau and the French Revolution* (Norman: University of Oklahoma Press, 1983); Eli Sagan, *Citizens and Cannibals: The French Revolution, the Struggle for Modernity, and the Origins of Ideological Terror* (Lanham, Md.: Rowman and Littlefield, 2001). For alternative accounts, see Dan Edelstein, *The Terror of Natural Right: Republicanism, the Cult of Nature, and the French*

Revolution (Chicago: University of Chicago Press, 2010); Andrew Levine, "Robespierre: Critic of Rousseau," *Canadian Journal of Philosophy* 8 (September 1978): 543–57.

50. E.g., Denis Diderot, *Political Writings*, ed. John Hope Mason and Robert Wokler (Cambridge: Cambridge University Press, 2001); Paul Henri Thiry Holbach, *La politique naturelle; ou, Discours sur les vrais principes du gouvernement* (Hildesheim: Olms, 1971); Holbach, *Système social; ou, Principes naturels de la morale et de la politique* (Paris: Fayard, 1994).

51. On this point, see also Emilios Christodoulidis, "Political Trials as Events," in *Events: The Force of International Law*, ed. Fleur Johns, Richard Joyce, and Sundhya Pahuja (London: Routledge, 2010), 130–44; David P. Jordan, *The King's Trial: The French Revolution vs. Louis XVI* (Berkeley: University of California Press, 1979); Ruth Scurr, *Fatal Purity: Robespierre and the French Revolution* (New York: Owl, 2006); Slavoj Žižek, *In Defense of Lost Causes* (London: Verso, 2009).

52. Maximilien Robespierre, "On the Trial of the King," in *Robespierre: Virtue and Terror*, ed. Slavoj Žižek (London: Verso, 2007), 57–58. Robespierre, "On the Death Penalty: Speech at the Constituent Assembly, June 22, 1791," trans. Mitch Abidor, *Marxists.org*, 2004, https://www.marxists.org/history/france/revolution/robespierre/1791/death -penalty.htm, grounded his opposition to the death penalty in the injustice of judicial killing in a society. He was careful to distinguish between the right to kill an enemy in a state of nature and the killing of citizens in a state. In the state of nature, Robespierre maintained, one has only one's individual strength, and the law of natural defense justifies the killing of another when the alternative is to perish oneself. In society, however, the power of the state overawes the condemned and makes the death penalty neither necessary nor just. As we will see, this argument resurfaced in Robespierre's defense of the execution of Louis, whom he considered an enemy who was in a state of nature with regard to the people rather than a citizen.

53. Robespierre, "On the Trial of the King," 57–58. Robespierre here appropriated and extended Saint-Just's argument that Louis Capet was neither king nor citizen, and that his trial was a political act that founded the Republic; Louis-Antoine-Léon Saint-Just, "Discours concernant le jugement de Louis XVI," in *Oeuvres complètes*, ed. Charles Vellay (Paris: Librairie Charpentier et Fasquell, 1908), 364–72.

54. Robespierre, "On the Trial of the King," 59.

55. Ibid., 57.

56. Ibid., 64.

57. Jean-Jacques Rousseau, *On the Social Contract*, in *The Basic Political Writings*, trans. Donald A. Cress (Indianapolis: Hackett, 1987), 159–60.

58. For a similar interpretation of the Jacobin position on the trial of the king, see Foucault's discussion of Louis XVI in the context of the emergence of the figure of the juridical monster; Michel Foucault, *Abnormal: Lectures at the Collège de France, 1974–1975*, ed. Valerio Marchetti, Antonella Salomoni, François Ewald, Alessandro Fontana, and Arnold I. Davidson, trans. Graham Burchell (New York: Picador, 2004), 81–107. Here Foucault argued that because Louis had failed to enter into the social contract,

he was an enemy to the social body who had to be "crushed as one crushes an enemy or a monster" (95). For Foucault, the Jacobin articulation of the king as monster was the "general model" for psychiatric and legal conceptions of monstrosity in the nineteenth century (94). For a concise statement and contextualization of Foucault's reading, see also Stuart Elden, *Foucault's Last Decade* (Malden, Mass.: Polity, 2016), 15.

59.   Robespierre, "On the Principles of Political Morality," 115–16.

60.   Maximilien Robespierre, "On the Principles of Revolutionary Government," in *Robespierre: Virtue and Terror*, ed. Slavoj Žižek (London: Verso, 2007), 99.

61.   Robespierre, "On the Principles of Political Morality," 115.

62.   Ibid.

63.   In the original French, Montesquieu identified both *crainte* (fear) and *terreur* (terror) as principles of despotism (Charles de Montesquieu, *De l'ésprit des lois*, ed. Laurent Versini, vol. 1. [Paris: Gallimard, 1995], 130, 210, 228). It is plausible to assume that his understanding of terror forms part of a long tradition, for which terror was essentially synonymous with fear (e.g., Walther, "Terror, Terrorismus"). On the recent resurgence of the instrumentalization of fear, albeit in the context of liberal democratic rather than despotic governments, see Sara Ahmed, "The Politics of Fear in the Making of Worlds," *International Journal of Qualitative Studies in Education* 16, no. 3 (2003): 377–98; Benjamin R. Barber, *Fear's Empire: War, Terrorism, and Democracy* (New York: Norton, 2004); Ioannis D. Evrigenis, *Fear of Enemies and Collective Action* (Cambridge: Cambridge University Press, 2009); Frank Furedi, *Politics of Fear: Beyond Left and Right* (London: Bloomsbury Academic, 2005); Derek Gregory and Allan Pred, eds., *Violent Geographies: Fear, Terror, and Political Violence* (New York: Routledge, 2006); Brian Massumi, *Politics of Everyday Fear* (Minneapolis: University of Minnesota Press, 1993); Chris Sparks, "Liberalism, Terrorism and the Politics of Fear," *Politics* 23, no. 3 (2003): 200–206.

64.   Robespierre, "On the Principles of Political Morality," 115.

65.   See also David P. Jordan, "The Robespierre Problem," in *Robespierre*, ed. Colin Haydon and William Doyle (Cambridge: Cambridge University Press, 1999), 17–34.

66.   Robespierre, "On the Principles of Revolutionary Government," 100.

67.   Walter Benjamin examined the role of foundational and conservative violence in his classic text "Critique of Violence," in *Selected Writings*, vol. 1, *1913–1926*, ed. Michael W. Jennings (Cambridge, Mass.: Harvard University Press, 1996), 236–52. Here Benjamin developed a radical critique of the justification of violence in terms of means and ends that results from natural and positive law as ostensibly institutionalized forms of reason. The predicament created by such a constellation is that arbitrary violence can be justified either as a means to an allegedly just end or the unintended consequence of supposedly just procedures. Benjamin showed that rather than being an expression of justice, the law belongs to the order of natural necessity or fate. Fate reveals itself in myth in the form of an intervention of the gods that founds law. Law here appears as the institutionalized form of fate and natural necessity. The foundational or lawmaking violence that brings law into existence is conserved in the legal order as

law-preserving violence. Thus, every legal judgment and punishment is a repetition of mythical violence rather than a realization of justice.

68. Maximilien Robespierre, "Draft Declaration of the Rights of Man and of the Citizen," in *Robespierre: Virtue and Terror*, ed. Slavoj Žižek (London: Verso, 2007), 70.

69. Ibid., 69.

70. For accounts of the Thermidorian Reaction and its historical context, see Andress, *Terror*; Baczko, *Ending the Terror*; Howard G. Brown, *Ending the French Revolution: Violence, Justice, and Repression from the Terror to Napoleon* (Charlottesville: University of Virginia Press, 2007); Israel, *Revolutionary Ideas*; Robert R. Palmer, *Twelve Who Ruled: The Year of the Terror in the French Revolution* (New York: Atheneum, 1966).

71. Quoted in "Gazette Nationale N° 343 (3. VIII 1794)," in *Réimpression de l'ancien 'Moniteur': Seule histoire authentique et inaltérée de la Révolution Française depuis la réunion des États-Généraux jusqu'au consulat (Mai 1789–novembre 1799); avec des notes explicatives* (Paris: Plon, 1847), vol. 21, 613.

72. Ibid., 614.

73. Ibid., 613.

74. Ibid., 614.

75. Ibid., 615.

76. Ibid., 614.

77. Ibid., 615.

78. Ibid., 612.

79. Ibid.

80. Ibid., 612–13.

81. Ibid., 613.

82. Emmanuel Joseph Sieyès, "What Is the Third Estate?," in *Political Writings, Including the Debate Between Sieyès and Tom Paine in 1791*, ed. and trans. Michael Sonenscher (Indianapolis: Hackett, 2003), 92–162.

83. Quoted in "Gazette Nationale N° 343," 615.

84. Ibid., 613.

85. Ibid., 615.

86. Ibid.

87. Foucault offered a detailed discussion of the process by which law was transformed from an external constraint on governmental action in the system of *raison d'État* into liberalism's internal limitation of governmental power in the second lecture in *The Birth of Biopolitics*.

88. Quoted in Baczko, *Ending the Terror*, 184.

89. Gracchus Babeuf, "Journal de la Liberté de la Presse no. Ier," in *Journal de la Liberté de la Presse, an II–an III* (Milan: Galli Thierry), 3. Nos. 1–22 of Babeuf's pamphlets appeared as *Journal de la Liberté de la Presse* before he changed the title to *Le Tribun du Peuple, ou le défenseur des droits de l'homme; en continuation du journal de la liberté de la presse* (nos. 23–43). The pamphlets are collected in two volumes in the Galli Thierry edition. The first, *Journal de la liberté de la presse*, contains nos. 1–32; the second,

Le tribun du peuple, ou le défenseur des droits de l'homme, contains nos. 34–43. No. 33 was never published. All pamphlets up to and including no. 26 are individually paginated. Consecutive pagination begins with no. 27 on page 209. No page numbers are given for No. 4 of the *Journal* and No. 25 of the *Tribun.*

90. Ibid., 1.

91. Gracchus Babeuf, "Journal de la Liberté de la Presse no. 2," in *Journal de la Liberté de la Presse, an II–an III* (Milan: Galli Thierry, 1966), 2.

92. Gracchus Babeuf, "Journal de la Liberté de la Presse no. 18," in *Journal de la Liberté de la Presse, an II–an III* (Milan: Galli Thierry, 1966), 3. For the same argument, see Benjamin Constant, "On the Re-Establishment of Terror," in *Observations on the Strength of the Present Government of France, and Upon the Necessity of Rallying round It,* trans. James Losh (Bath: Cruttwell, 1797), 55–67.

93. Gracchus Babeuf, "Journal de la Liberté de la Presse no. 5," in *Journal de la Liberté de la Presse, an II–an III* (Milan: Galli Thierry, 1966), 4–5.

94. Gracchus Babeuf, "Journal de la Liberté de la Presse no. 6," in *Journal de la Liberté de la Presse, an II–An III* (Milan: Galli Thierry, 1966), 3.

95. Gracchus Babeuf, "Le Tribun du Peuple no. 23 (1)," in *Journal de la Liberté de la Presse, an II–an III* (Milan: Galli Thierry, 1966), 7–8.

96. Gracchus Babeuf, "Le Tribun du Peuple no. 32," in *Journal de la Liberté de la Presse, an II–an III* (Milan: Galli Thierry, 1966), 333.

97. Gracchus Babeuf, "Le Tribun du Peuple no. 27," in *Journal de la Liberté de la Presse, an II–An III* (Milan: Galli Thierry, 1966), 221.

98. Gracchus Babeuf, "Le Tribun du Peuple no. 25," in *Journal de la Liberté de la Presse, an II–an III* (Milan: Galli Thierry. 1966), 4.

99. Gracchus Babeuf, "Le Tribun du Peuple no. 36," in *Le Tribun du Peuple, ou Le Défenseur des Droits de l'Homme, an III–an IV* (Milan: Galli Thierry, 1966), 110.

100. Gracchus Babeuf, "Le Tribun du Peuple no. 30," in *Journal de la Liberté de la Presse, an II–an III* (Milan: Galli Thierry, 1966), 304.

101. Ibid., 308. Quinet agreed with Babeuf that "the system of extermination had changed hands, but it remained the same" (Quinet, *Révolution,* 624). He further argued that the Thermidorians had actually outdone the Jacobins in their efforts to eliminate their political opponents.

102. Babeuf, "Le Tribun du Peuple no. 30," 308.

103. Gracchus Babeuf, "Le Tribun du Peuple no. 31," in *Journal de la Liberté de la Presse, an II–an III* (Milan: Galli Thierry 1966), 311, 313.

104. Babeuf, "Le Tribun du Peuple no. 25," 4.

105. Baczko uses the expression "mode of thought" to refer to this conceptual use of the term terrorism (Baczko, *Ending the Terror,* 110).

106. For excellent discussions of the historical context, see Andress, *Terror;* Baczko, *Ending the Terror.*

107. Israel, *Revolutionary Ideas,* 604.

108. For a detailed account of the political struggles at the time, see Brown, *Ending the French Revolution.*

109. Quoted in Israel, *Revolutionary Ideas*, 610.

110. Soboul, *French Revolution*, 425–26. The term White Terror refers to violence exercised by ultraroyalist groups, who called themselves the Companions of Jehu, against Jacobins and their supporters. Acting in a manner reminiscent of the September Massacres, the Companions of Jehu murdered imprisoned terrorists (e.g., Alexandre Dumas, *The Companions of Jehu*, vol. 29 of *The Works of Alexandre Dumas* [New York: Collier, 1902]). On the White Terror, see Stephen Clay, "The White Terror: Factions, Reactions, and the Politics of Vengeance," in *A Companion to the French Revolution*, ed. Peter McPhee (Malden, Mass.: Blackwell, 2013), 359–77.

111. Babeuf, "Le Tribun du Peuple no. 30," 304.

112. Philippe Buonarroti, *Conspiration pour l'égalité dite de Babeuf: Suivie du procès auquel elle donna lieu, et des pièces justificatives* (Brussels: Librairie Romantique, 1828).

113. Gracchus Babeuf, "Le Tribun du Peuple, ou Le Défenseur des Droits de l'Homme no. 43," in *Le Tribun du Peuple, ou Le Défenseur des Droits de l'Homme, an III–an IV* (Milan: Galli Thierry, 1966), 304, 296.

114. Babeuf, "Le Tribun du Peuple no. 27," 211.

115. On this point, see also Heuvel, "Terreur, Terroriste, Terrorisme."

116. See Heuvel "Terreur, Terroriste, Terrorisme"; Walther, "Terror, Terrorismus."

117. Gracchus Babeuf, "Le Tribun du Peuple no. 34," in *Le Tribun du Peuple, ou Le Défenseur des Droits de l'Homme, an III–an IV* (Milan: Galli Thierry 1966), 49.

118. One is reminded of Ludwig Wittgenstein's claim in *Philosophical Investigations*, trans. G. E. M. Anscombe (Malden, Mass.: Blackwell, 2001), §43, that the meaning of a word is its use in linguistic practice.

119. Gracchus Babeuf, "Le Tribun du Peuple no. 38," in *Le Tribun du Peuple, ou Le Défenseur des Droits de l'Homme, an III–an IV* (Milan: Galli Thierry, 1966), 150.

120. Babeuf, "Le Tribun du Peuple no. 34," 17. For a historical account of ultraroyalist violence against Jacobins, see Quinet, *Révolution*, 623.

121. Quoted in François Victor Alphonse Aulard, *Recueil des actes du Comité de salut public avec la correspondance officielle des représentants en mission et le registre du Conseil exécutif provisoire*, vol. 28 (Paris: Imprimerie Nationale, 1951), 138.

122. Quoted in Ferdinand Brunot, *Histoire de la langue française des origines à 1900*, vol. 9, part 2, *La Révolution et l'empire: Les événements, les institutions et la langue* (Paris: Colin, 1937), 654.

123. "Gazette Nationale ou Le Moniteur Universel N°303 (21 Juillet 1795)," in *Réimpression de l'ancien "Moniteur": Seule histoire authentique et inaltérée de la Révolution française depuis la réunion des États-Généraux jusqu'au Consulat (mai 1789–novembre 1799); Avec des notes explicatives* 25 (Paris: Plon, 1847), 258.

124. Babeuf, "Le Tribun du Peuple no. 38," 154.

125. Ibid., 159.

126. Ibid., 160.

127. Babeuf's increasing radicalization, as well as his role in the Conspiracy of Equals, an attempt to subvert the government by insurrection and return to the Montagnard Constitution of 1793, led to a ban of Babeuf's journal and his arrest in May 1796. His

subsequent trial was conducted in exemplary fashion. Legal procedures were followed meticulously, and Babeuf had every chance to defend himself without interruption. Even so, he was convicted of conspiracy and sentenced to death on May 26, 1797, and was guillotined the following day. For accounts of these events, see Gracchus Babeuf, "The Defense of Gracchus Babeuf," in *The Defense of Gracchus Babeuf Before the High Court of Vendome*, ed. and trans. John Anthony Scott (New York: Schocken, 1972), 19–90; Ernest Belfort Bax, *The Last Episode of the French Revolution: Being a History of Gracchus Babeuf and the Conspiracy of the Equals* (Boston: Small, Maynard, 1911); Buonarroti, *Conspiration pour l'égalité dite de Babeuf*; Robert B. Rose, *Gracchus Babeuf: The First Revolutionary Communist* (Stanford, Calif.: Stanford University Press, 1978).

128.   Aulard, *Recueil des actes du Comité de salut public*, 567.

129.   Baczko, *Ending the Terror*, 29.

130.   Ibid., 109–10.

CHAPTER 3. STATE TERRORISM REVISITED

1.   Franz Neumann, *Behemoth: The Structure and Practice of National Socialism, 1933–1944* (Chicago: Dee, 2009).

2.   Hannah Arendt, *The Origins of Totalitarianism* (San Diego: Harcourt, 1973).

3.   Carl J. Friedrich and Zbigniew K. Brzezinski, *Totalitarian Dictatorship and Autocracy* (Cambridge, Mass.: Harvard University Press, 1965).

4.   For detailed accounts of Russian history in the late nineteenth and early twentieth centuries, see David Longley, *The Longman Companion to Imperial Russia, 1689–1917* (Abingdon: Routledge, 2000); Peter Waldron, *The End of Imperial Russia, 1855–1917* (New York: Palgrave Macmillan, 1997). On the philosophical and ideological landscape of late imperial Russia, see George Douglas Howard Cole, *A History of Socialist Thought*, vol. 1, *The Forerunners 1789–1850* (London: Macmillan, 1971); Cole, *A History of Socialist Thought*, vol. 2, *Marxism and Anarchism 1850–1890* (London: Macmillan, 1957); Cole, *A History of Socialist Thought*, vol. 3.1, *The Second International 1889–1914* (London: Macmillan, 1963); Cole, *A History of Socialist Thought*, vol. 3.2, *The Second International 1889–1914* (London: Macmillan, 1963); Cole, *A History of Socialist Thought*, vol. 4.1, *Communism and Social Democracy 1914–1931* (London: Macmillan, 1958); Cole, *A History of Socialist Thought*, vol. 4.2, *Communism and Social Democracy 1914–1931* (London: Macmillan, 1961); Cole, *A History of Socialist Thought*, vol. 5, *Socialism and Fascism 1931–1939* (London: Macmillan, 1961); Alexandre Koyré, *La philosophie et le problème national en Russie au début du XIXe siècle* (Paris: Champion, 1929); Georgiï Valentinovich Plekhanov, *Anarchism and Socialism*, trans. Eleanor Marx Aveling (Chicago: Kerr, 1909); Michael J. Schaack, *Anarchy and Anarchists: A History of the Red Terror and the Social Revolution in America and Europe* (Chicago: Schulte, 1889).

5.   Quoted in Franco Venturi, *Roots of Revolution. A History of the Populist and Socialist Movements in Nineteenth Century Russia* (London: Weidenfeld and Nicolson, 1964), 293.

6. Vladimir I. Lenin, "The Enemies of the People," in *Collected Works*, vol. 25, trans. Bernard Isaacs (Moscow: Progress, 1964), 57.

7. Karl Kautsky, *Terrorism and Communism: A Contribution to the Natural History of Revolution*, trans. W. H. Kerridge (Westport, Conn.: Hyperion, 1973).

8. Michel Foucault, *"Society Must Be Defended:" Lectures at the Collège de France, 1975–1976*, ed. Mauro Bertani, Alessandro Fontana, François Ewald, and Arnold I. Davidson, trans. David Macey (New York: Picador, 2003), 77.

9. Mary Beth Mader, "Modern Living and Vital Race: Foucault and the Science of Life," *Foucault Studies* 12 (2011): 97–112; Ladelle McWhorter, *Racism and Sexual Oppression in Anglo-America: A Genealogy* (Bloomington: Indiana University Press, 2009). See also Verena Erlenbusch, "From Race War to Social Racism: Foucault's Second Transcription," *Foucault Studies* 22 (2017): 134–52, doi:10.22439/fs.v0i0.5239.

10. Foucault, *Society Must Be Defended*, 60.

11. Note that Foucault is not alone in pointing out the origins of social classes in a hierarchy of races. Most notably, Cedric Robinson has criticized Western Marxism for its failure to account for the racial character of capitalism. Drawing on resources in the black radical tradition, Robinson argues that even before the colonization of Africa and the conquest of the Americas, processes of internal colonization, invasion, enslavement, and genocide created a racial hierarchy within Europe onto which class distinctions between proletariat and bourgeoisie were then grafted. Cedric J. Robinson, *Black Marxism: The Making of the Black Radical Tradition* (Chapel Hill: University of North Carolina Press, 2000).

12. Other examples of this view can be found in the writings of representatives of Narodnaia Volia (People's Will), a paramilitary organization formed in 1879. The group regarded the tsarist regime as illegitimate because its power derived from and, in fact, continued a long history of invasion, conquest, and war. Consider its political program, which stated, "The bourgeois excrescence in the form of a government sustains itself by mere brute force—by means of its military, police, and bureaucratic organization—in precisely the same way that the Mongols of Genghis Khan sustained themselves in Russia. It is not sanctioned by the people; it rules by arbitrary violence, and it adopts and enforces governmental and economic forms and principles that have nothing whatever in common with the people's wishes and ideals" ("Demands of the Narodnaia Volia," in *Imperial Russia: A Source Book, 1700–1917*, ed. Basil Dmytryshyn [Hinsdale, Ill.: Dryden, 1974], 310). See also Executive Committee, "Letter Sent by the Revolutionary Executive Committee to Alexander III at His Accession to the Throne," in *Early Writings on Terrorism*, ed. Ruth Kinna, (London: Routledge, 2006), 1:61–70; Figner, *Memoirs*; Nicolas Morozov, "The Terroristic Struggle," in *Violence in Politics. Terror and Political Assassination in Eastern Europe and Russia*, ed. Feliks Gross (The Hague: Mouton, 1972), 110–12; Sergei G. Nechaev, "The Catechism of the Revolutionary, 1968," in *Imperial Russia: A Source Book, 1700–1917*, ed. Basil Dmytryshyn (Hinsdale, Ill.: Dryden, 1974), 303–8; Stepniak, *Underground Russia* (London: Smith, Elder, 1883); G. Tarnovski, "Terrorism and Routine," in *Voices of Terror: Manifestos, Writings, and*

Manuals of Al Qaeda, Hamas, and Other Terrorists from Around the World and Throughout the Ages, ed. Walter Laqueur (Naperville: Sourcebooks, 2004), 83–87.

13. Lev Aleksandrovich Tikhomirov, *Russia: Political and Social*, trans. Edward Aveling (London: Swan Sonnenschein, Lowrey, 1888), 1:15. The original French version is Tikhomirov, Lev Aleksandrovich, *La Russie Politique et Sociale* (Paris: La Nouvelle Librairie Parisienne, 1886).

14. Tikhomirov, *Russia*, 1:15, translation modified.

15. Ibid., 1:108.

16. Ibid., 1:31–32.

17. For excellent historical analyses, see Isabel de Madariaga, *Ivan the Terrible* (New Haven, Conn.: Yale University Press, 2005); Andrei Pavlov and Maureen Perrie, *Ivan the Terrible* (Abingdon: Taylor and Francis, 2003).

18. Quoted in Tikhomirov, *Russia*, 1:236.

19. Ibid., 1:236–37.

20. Ibid., 1:243.

21. Ibid., 2:14–15.

22. Ibid., 1:251.

23. Ibid., 1:270.

24. Ibid., 1:272.

25. Ibid., 1:292.

26. Gracchus Babeuf, "Le Tribun du Peuple no. 34," in *Le Tribun du Peuple, ou Le Défenseur des Droits de l'Homme, an III–an IV* (Milan: Galli Thierry, 1966), 50.

27. Gracchus Babeuf, "The Defense of Gracchus Babeuf," in *The Defense of Gracchus Babeuf Before the High Court of Vendome*, ed. and trans. John Anthony Scott (New York: Schocken, 1972), 24–25.

28. François Victor Alphonse Aulard, *Paris pendant la réaction Thermidorienne et sous le Directoire: Recueil de documents pour l'histoire de l'ésprit publique à Paris*, vol. 5 (Paris: Cerf, 1902), 490.

29. On this point, see Howard G. Brown, *Ending the French Revolution: Violence, Justice, and Repression from the Terror to Napoleon* (Charlottesville: University of Virginia Press, 2007).

30. Edmund Burke, *Letters on a Regicide Peace*, in *Select Works of Edmund Burke*, vol. 3, ed. E.J. Payne (Indianapolis: Liberty Fund, 1999), 316–17.

31. Quoted in Rudolf Walther, "Terror, Terrorismus," in *Geschichtliche Grundbegriffe: Historisches Lexikon zur politisch-sozialen Sprache in Deutschland*, vol. 6, ed. Otto Brunner, Werner Conze, and Reinhart Koselleck (Stuttgart: Klett-Kotta, 1990), 359.

32. Matthias Metternich, "Rede am Feste des vierzehnten Julius in Mainz (1799)," in *Die Französische Revolution im Spiegel der deutschen Literatur*, ed. Claus Träger and Frauke Schäfer (Leipzig: Reclam, 1975), 575–76.

33. Walther, "Terror, Terrorismus," 379–80.

34. See Mikkel Thorup, *An Intellectual History of Terror: War, Violence and the State* (London: Routledge, 2010).

35.   See Johann Joseph Most, *The Science of Revolutionary Warfare* (El Dorado, Ark.: Desert, 1978).

36.   See Jay Bergman, "Vera Zasulich, the Shooting of Trepov and the Growth of Political Terrorism in Russia, 1878–1881," *Terrorism* 4, no. 1–4 (1980): 25–51; Lindsay Clutterbuck, "The Progenitors of Terrorism: Russian Revolutionaries or Extreme Irish Republicans?," *Terrorism and Political Violence* 16, no.1 (2004): 154–81; Marie Fleming, "Propaganda by the Deed: Terrorism and Anarchist Theory in Late Nineteenth-Century Europe," *Terrorism* 4, no. 1–4 (1980): 1–23; Anna Geifman, *Death Orders: The Vanguard of Modern Terrorism in Revolutionary Russia* (Santa Barbara, Calif.: Praeger, 2010); Deborah Hardy, *Land and Freedom: The Origins of Russian Terrorism, 1876–1879* (New York: Greenwood, 1987); Richard Bach Jensen, "Daggers, Rifles and Dynamite: Anarchist Terrorism in Nineteenth Century Europe," *Terrorism and Political Violence* 16, no. 1 (2004): 116–53; Richard Bach Jensen, *The Battle against Anarchist Terrorism: An International History, 1878–1934* (Cambridge: Cambridge University Press, 2015); David C. Rapoport, "The Four Waves of Modern Terrorism," in *Attacking Terrorism: Elements of a Grand Strategy*, ed. Audrey Kurth Cronin and James M. Ludes (Washington, D.C.: Georgetown University Press, 2004); Claudia Verhoeven, *The Odd Man Karakozov: Imperial Russia, Modernity, and the Birth of Terrorism* (Ithaca, N.Y.: Cornell University Press, 2009).

37.   For discussions of Russian radicalism and the student movement Young Russia, see James H. Billington, *Fire in the Minds of Men: Origins of the Revolutionary Faith* (New Brunswick, N.J.: Transaction, 1999); Abbott Gleason, *Young Russia: The Genesis of Russian Radicalism in the 1860s* (New York: Viking, 1980); Venturi, *Roots of Revolution*.

38.   Quoted in Billington, *Fire in the Minds*, 395.

39.   Quoted in Venturi, *Roots of Revolution*, 296.

40.   Quoted in Billington, *Fire in the Minds*, 395.

41.   Nechaev, "Catechism," 308.

42.   Ibid., 303.

43.   Ibid., 304.

44.   Figner, *Memoirs*, 70.

45.   Tarnovski, "Terrorism and Routine," 84. Romanenko was a member of Narodnaia Volia's Executive Committee. He published "Terrorism and Routine" in 1880 under his pseudonym Tarnovski. Excerpts of Romanenko's pamphlet are available in English translation in Laqueur, *Voices of Terror*. For the Russian original, see Gerasim Grigorevič Romanenko, *Terrorism i rutina* (London: Russkaâ Tipografiâ, 1880).

46.   Ibid., 83.

47.   Executive Committee, "Letter," 66.

48.   Tarnovski, "Terrorism and Routine," 83.

49.   Executive Committee, "Letter," 63.

50.   Quoted in Figner, *Memoirs*, 11.

51.   Morozov, "Terroristic Struggle," 111.

52.   Ibid., 110.

53. Ibid., 107.

54. Ibid., 106.

55. Ibid., 112.

56. Some relevant historiographical publications are Hans Brandenburg, *The Meek and the Mighty: The Emergence of the Evangelical Movement in Russia* (New York: Oxford University Press, 1977); Robert Francis Byrnes, *Pobedonostsev: His Life and Thought* (Bloomington: Indiana University Press, 1968); Gary M. Hamburg, *Politics of the Russian Nobility, 1881–1905* (New Brunswick, N.J.: Rutgers University Press, 1984); Max Hunterberg, *The Russian Mephistopheles* (Glasgow: Rae, 1909); Anatole Gregory Mazour, *Russia: Tsarist and Communist* (Princeton, N.J.: Van Nostrand, 1962); Manus I. Midlarsky, *Origins of Political Extremism: Mass Violence in the Twentieth Century and Beyond* (Cambridge: Cambridge University Press, 2011).

57. Konstantin P. Pobyedonostseff, *Reflections of a Russian Statesman*, trans. Robert Crozier Long (London: Richards, 1898), 94.

58. Ibid., 32.

59. Ibid., 33.

60. Ibid., 35.

61. Ibid., 49.

62. Thomas Hobbes, *Leviathan*, ed. Richard Tuck (Cambridge: Cambridge University Press, 2003).

63. Pobyedonostseff, *Reflections*, 85–86.

64. For a detailed account of this event, see Verhoeven, *Odd Man Karakozov*.

65. On this point, see Jonathan W. Daly, "On the Significance of Emergency Legislation in Late Imperial Russia," *Slavic Review* 54, no. 3 (1995): 602–29; Nicholas V. Riasanovsky, *A History of Russia* (New York: Oxford University Press, 2000); Peter Waldron, "States of Emergency: Autocracy and Extraordinary Legislation, 1881–1917," *Revolutionary Russia. Journal of the Study Group on the Russian Revolution* 8, no. 1 (1995): 1–25. Daly suggests an alternative interpretation of the state of emergency in which Russians lived from 1878 on. He argues that it was not a symbol of Russia's development toward a police state but rather indicated Russia's progression toward a modern constitutional state and the rule of law. He contends that the Security Law must be understood as the codification and limitation of the previous expansion of power through emergency measures. My emphasis here is on the government's concern with its loss of sovereignty, which is manifest in the implementation of the Security Law.

66. Riasanovsky, *History of Russia*, 392.

67. Waldron, "States of Emergency," 2.

68. Stepniak, *Underground Russia*, 35–37.

69. Max Weber, "Russia's Transition to Pseudo-Constitutionalism," in *The Russian Revolutions*, trans. Gordon C. Wells and Peter Baehr (Ithaca, N.Y.: Cornell University Press, 1995), 173.

70. Ibid., 229–30.

71. See also Sidney Harcave, *Count Sergei Witte and the Twilight of Imperial Russia: A Biography* (Armonk, N.Y.: Sharpe, 2004); Theodor von Laue, *Sergei Witte and the Industrialization of Russia* (New York: Columbia University Press, 1963); Howard D. Mehlinger and John M. Thompson, *Count Witte and the Tsarist Government in the 1905 Revolution* (Bloomington: Indiana University Press, 1972).

72. Weber, "Russia's Transition," 232.

73. Incidentally, Foucault regarded Trotsky as an exception to a common Marxist understanding of class struggle as a general principle of history. While other Marxists were silent on what exactly they meant by class struggle, Trotsky, along with Marx, understood struggle quite literally in terms of revolutionary war and state violence. See Michel Foucault, "Non Au Sexe Roi," in *Dits et écrits*, vol. 3, *1976–1979*, ed. Daniel Defert and François Ewald (Paris: Gallimard, 1994), 256–69; Foucault, "Le Jeu de Michel Foucault," in *Dits et écrits*, vol. 3, *1976–1979*, ed. Daniel Defert and François Ewald (Paris: Gallimard, 1994), 298–329.

74. Trotsky's theory of uneven and combined development has been influential in international relations theory, particularly in what is known as international historical sociology. For key interventions, see Sam Ashman, "Capitalism, Uneven and Combined Development and the Transhistoric," *Cambridge Review of International Affairs* 22, no. 1 (2009): 29–46, doi:10.1080/09557570802683896; John M. Hobson, "What's at Stake in the Neo-Trotskyist Debate? Towards a Non-Eurocentric Historical Sociology of Uneven and Combined Development," *Millennium—Journal of International Studies* 40, no. 1 (2011): 147–66, doi:10.1177/0305829811412653; Marcel van der Linden, "The 'Law' of Uneven and Combined Development: Some Underdeveloped Thoughts," *Historical Materialism* 15, no. 1 (2007): 145–65, doi:10.1163/156920607X171627; Justin Rosenberg, "Why Is There No International Historical Sociology?," *European Journal of International Relations* 12, no. 3 (2006): 307–40, doi:10.1177/1354066106067345; Ian D. Thatcher, "Uneven and Combined Development," *Revolutionary Russia* 4 no. 2 (1991): 235–58, doi:10.1080/09546549108575572.

75. Leon Trotsky, *History of the Russian Revolution*, trans. Max Eastman (Chicago: Haymarket, 2008).

76. Leon Trotsky, "The Bankruptcy of Terrorism," in *Against Individual Terrorism*, trans. Marilyn Vogt (New York: Pathfinder, 1974), 12.

77. Trotsky, "Bankruptcy of Terrorism," 11.

78. Leon Trotsky, "The Marxist Position on Individual Terrorism," in *Against Individual Terrorism*, trans. Marilyn Vogt and George Saunders (New York: Pathfinder, 1974), 7; italics in the original.

79. Leon Trotsky, "Terrorism and the Stalinist Regime in the Soviet Union," in *Against Individual Terrorism*, trans. Marilyn Vogt and George Saunders (New York: Pathfinder, 1974), 20.

80. Trotsky, "Marxist Position," 7.

81. Trotsky, "Terrorism and the Stalinist Regime," 20.

82. Trotsky, *History of the Russian Revolution*, xv.

83.   Ibid., 8.

84.   Ibid., 9.

85.   Ibid., 5. For a similar distinction between individual and systemic terrorism, as well as a critique of the former and endorsement of the latter, see Rosa Luxemburg, "Zur Frage des Terrorismus in Rußland," in *Gesammelte* Werke, vol. 1, *1893–1905* (Berlin: Dietz, 1972), 275–80.

86.   See Leon Trotsky, *Terrorism and Communism: A Reply to Karl Kautsky* (Ann Arbor, Mich.: University of Michigan Press, 1961).

87.   Vladimir I. Lenin, "Draft Programme of Our Party," in *Collected Works*, vol. 4, ed. Victor Jerome, trans. Joe Fineberg and George Hannah (Moscow: Progress, 1964), 238.

88.   Vladimir I. Lenin, "From the Defensive to the Offensive," in *Collected Works*, vol. 9, ed. George Hanna, trans. Abraham Fineberg and Julius Katzer (Moscow: Progress, 1964), 283; italics in the original.

89.   Vladimir I. Lenin, "Tasks of Revolutionary Army Contingents," in *Collected Works*, vol. 9, ed. George Hanna, trans. Abraham Fineberg and Julius Katzer (Moscow: Progress, 1964), 422.

90.   Vladimir I. Lenin, "The State and Revolution," in *Collected Works*, vol. 25, ed. Stepan Apresyan and Jim Riordan (Moscow: Progress, 1964), 397.

91.   See Friedrich Engels, "Herrn Eugen Dühring's Umwälzung der Wissenschaft ('Anti-Dühring')," in *Werke*, vol. 20, by Karl Marx and Friedrich Engels (Berlin: Dietz, 1962), 1–303.

92.   Lenin, "State and Revolution," 397.

93.   Ibid., 402–3.

94.   Ibid., 425.

95.   Ibid., 472.

96.   Ibid., 474.

97.   Vladimir I. Lenin, "Letter to American Workers," in *Collected Works*, vol. 28, ed. Jim Riordan (Moscow: Progress, 1964), 69.

98.   Ibid., 71.

99.   Nikolai Bukharin, *The Politics and Economics of the Transition Period*, trans. Oliver Field (London: Routledge and Kegan Paul, 1979), 165.

100. For a similar claim, see Eric D. Weitz, "Racial Politics without the Concept of Race: Reevaluating Soviet Ethnic and National Purges," *Slavic Review* 61, no. 1 (2002): 1–29, doi:10.2307/2696978. Weitz suggests that like its European counterparts, the Soviet state also relied on mechanisms of disciplinary and regulatory control in order to forge a particular vision of the Soviet nation. To achieve this end, he argues, the Soviet state deployed a historically specific form of racial politics distinct from, say, European or American racism in pursuit of what Trotsky described as a process of "radical reconstruction" by which man "will raise himself to a new level—to create a higher socio-biological type, an *Ubermensch*, if you will" (quoted in Nikolai Krementsov, *Revolutionary Experiments: The Quest for Immortality in Bolshevik Science and Fiction* [New York: Oxford University Press, 2013], 169). For critical engagements with Weitz's argument, see Francine Hirsch, "Race without the Practice of Racial Politics," *Slavic Review* 61, no. 1

(2002): 30–43; Alaina Lemon, "Without a 'Concept?' Race as Discursive Practice," *Slavic Review* 61, no. 1 (2002): 54–61; Amir Weiner, "Nothing but Certainty," *Slavic Review* 61, no. 1 (2002): 44–53.

101. Peter Holquist, "State Violence as Technique: The Logic of Violence in Soviet Totalitarianism," in *Landscaping the Human Garden: Twentieth-Century Population Management in a Comparative Framework*, ed. Amir Weiner (Stanford, Calif.: Stanford University Press, 2003), 25.

102. Quoted in Holquist, "State Violence as Technique," 29.

103. Quoted in George Leggett, *The Cheka: Lenin's Political Police* (Oxford: Clarendon Press, 1981), 114.

104. On this point, see Nikolai Krementsov, "Eugenics in Russia and the Soviet Union," in *The Oxford Handbook of the History of Eugenics*, ed. Alison Bashford and Philippa Levine (Oxford: Oxford University Press, 2010), 413–29.

105. Kautsky, *Terrorism and Communism*, 171; translation modified.

106. Holquist, "State Violence as Technique," 32, 31.

107. Kautsky, *Terrorism and Communism*, 113; translation modified.

108. Lenin, "Enemies of the People," 57.

CHAPTER 4. TERRORISM AND COLONIALISM

1. On this point, see Pamela Pilbeam, "The Economic Crisis of 1827–32 and the 1830 Revolution in Provincial France," *The Historical Journal* 32, no. 2 (1989): 319–38, doi:10.1017/S0018246X00012176.

2. See Louis Blanc, *The History of Ten Years*, trans. Walter K. Kelly (Philadelphia: Lea & Blanchard, 1848); François Pierre Guillaume Guizot, *France under Louis-Philippe: From 1841 to 1847*, in *Memoirs to Illustrate the History of My Time*, vol. 7 (London: Bentley. Reprint, New York: AMS, [1865] 1974), chap. 3; Alexis de Tocqueville, *Recollections*, trans. George Lawrence (Garden City, N.Y.: Doubleday, 1970).

3. François Pierre Guillaume Guizot, *Memoirs to Illustrate the History of My Time*, vol. 4, trans. J. W. Cole (London: Bentley. Reprint, New York: AMS, [1861] 1974), chap. 1.

4. Blanc, *History of Ten Years*; Gustave de Beaumont and Alexis de Tocqueville, *Du système pénitentiare aux Etats-Unis, et de son application en France* (Paris: Fournier Jeune, 1833); Alexis de Tocqueville, "Some Ideas about What Prevents the French From Having Good Colonies," in *Writings on Empire and Slavery*, ed. & trans. Jennifer Pitts (Baltimore: Johns Hopkins University Press, 2001), 1–4.

5. Blanc, *History of Ten Years*, 2:464. Similarly, the republican Alphonse de Lamartine declared in 1824 in the National Assembly that colonization was of utmost necessity because it "multiplies life" and "preserves the body politic" (quoted in Olivier Le Cour Grandmaison, *Coloniser, exterminer: Sur la guerre et l'état colonial* [Paris: Fayard, 2005], 13).

6. Ibid., 464–65.

7. Ibid., 466; translation modified.

8.   Guizot, *France under Louis-Philippe*, 117.

9.   Marnia Lazreg, *Torture and the Twilight of Empire: From Algiers to Baghdad* (Princeton, N.J.: Princeton University Press, 2007), 4.

10. Ibid., 7.

11. On this point, see also Frantz Fanon, "Une révolution démocratique," in *Écrits sur l'aliénation et la liberté*, ed. Jean Khalfa and Robert Young (Paris: La Découverte, 2015), 476–80.

12. "Constitution de 1848, IIe République," 1848, *Conseil Constitutionnel*, http://www.conseil-constitutionnel.fr/conseil-constitutionnel/francais/la-constitution/les-consti tutions-de-la-france/constitution-de-1848-iie-republique.5106.html.

13. On the history of colonized Algeria, see Mahfoud Bennoune, *The Making of Contemporary Algeria, 1830–1987: Colonial Upheavals and Post-Independence Development* (Cambridge: Cambridge University Press, 1988); William Gallois, *A History of Violence in the Early Algerian Colony* (Basingstoke: Palgrave Macmillan, 2013); Grandmaison, *Coloniser, exterminer*; Jennifer E. Sessions, *By Sword and Plow: France and the Conquest of Algeria* (Ithaca, N.Y.: Cornell University Press, 2011); Todd Shepard, *The Invention of Decolonization: The Algerian War and the Remaking of France* (Ithaca, N.Y.: Cornell University Press, 2006); Benjamin Stora, *Algeria, 1830–2000: A Short History*, trans. Jane Marie Todd (Ithaca, N.Y.: Cornell University Press, 2001).

14. John Stuart Mill, *On Liberty*, ed. Elizabeth Rapaport (Indianapolis: Hackett, 1978), 10.

15. Gustave de Beaumont and Alexis de Tocqueville, *On the Penitentiary System in the United States and Its Application in France*, trans. Francis Lieber (Carbondale: Southern Illinois University Press, 1964), 228.

16. See Jennifer Pitts, Introduction to *Writings on Empire and Slavery*, by Alexis de Tocqueville, ed. & trans. Jennifer Pitts (Baltimore: Johns Hopkins University Press, 2001), ix–xxxviii.

17. Alexis de Tocqueville, "Second Report on Algeria," in *Writings on Empire and Slavery*, ed. & trans. Jennifer Pitts (Baltimore: Johns Hopkins University Press, 2001), 180.

18. Ibid., 182.

19. Ibid., 180.

20. For the same argument, see Blanc, *History of Ten Years*, 2:466.

21. Alexis de Tocqueville, "First Report on Algeria," in *Writings on Empire and Slavery*, ed. & trans. Jennifer Pitts (Baltimore: Johns Hopkins University Press, 2001), 130.

22. Alexis de Tocqueville, "Second Letter on Algeria," in *Writings on Empire and Slavery*, ed. & trans. Jennifer Pitts (Baltimore: Johns Hopkins University Press, 2001), 19. For a discussion of assimilationism, associationism, and coexistence as models for organizing the relationship between Algerians and the French nation, see Shepard, *Invention of Decolonization*.

23. Alexis de Tocqueville, "Essay on Algeria," in *Writings on Empire and Slavery*, ed. & trans. Jennifer Pitts (Baltimore: Johns Hopkins University Press, 2001), 61.

24. Tocqueville, "Second Letter on Algeria," 21.

25. Tocqueville, "First Report on Algeria," 135.

26. Tocqueville, "Essay on Algeria," 83.

27. Ibid., 110.

28. Alexis de Tocqueville, "First Letter on Algeria," in *Writings on Empire and Slavery*, ed. & trans. Jennifer Pitts (Baltimore: Johns Hopkins University Press, 2001), 5–13. See also Le Cour Grandmaison, *Coloniser, exterminer*, 39; Le Cour Grandmaison, "The Exception and the Rule: On French Colonial Law," trans. Colin Anderson, *Diogenes* 53, no. 4 (2006): 34–53.

29. Ibid., 7.

30. Ibid., 10.

31. Tocqueville, "Essay on Algeria," 67.

32. Alexis de Tocqueville, "Notes on the Voyage to Algeria," in *Writings on Empire and Slavery*, ed. & trans. Jennifer Pitts (Baltimore: Johns Hopkins University Press, 2001), 37.

33. Foucault traced these developments in various places, most notably in Foucault, *Abnormal: Lectures at the Collège de France, 1974–1975*, ed. Valerio Marchetti, Antonella Salomoni, François Ewald, Alessandro Fontana, and Arnold I. Davidson, trans. Graham Burchell (New York: Picador, 2004); *The History of Sexuality*, vol. 1, *An Introduction*, trans. Robert Hurley (New York: Vintage, 1990); *The Order of Things: An Archaeology of the Human Sciences* (New York: Vintage, 1994); *Psychiatric Power: Lectures at the Collège de France, 1973–1974*, ed. Jacques Lagrange, François Ewald, Alessandro Fontana, and Arnold I. Davidson, trans. Graham Burchell (New York: Palgrave Macmillan, 2008); *"Society Must Be Defended": Lectures at the Collège de France, 1975–1976*, ed. Mauro Bertani, Alessandro Fontana, François Ewald, and Arnold I. Davidson, trans. David Macey (New York: Picador, 2003). For instructive discussions of the transformation of the concept of race in light of the science of biology, see Mary Beth Mader, "Modern Living and Vital Race: Foucault and the Science of Life," *Foucault Studies* 12 (2011): 97–112; Ladelle McWhorter, *Racism and Sexual Oppression in Anglo-America: A Genealogy* (Bloomington: Indiana University Press, 2009). For a critical analysis of the concept of development, see chapter 4, "Sleights of Development," in Mary Beth Mader, *Sleights of Reason: Norm, Bisexuality, Development* (Albany: State University of New York Press, 2011).

34. For recent discussions in critical theory of the normativity of European development in relation to empire and colonialism, see also Amy Allen, *The End of Progress: Decolonizing the Normative Foundations of Critical Theory* (New York: Columbia University Press, 2016); Gurminder K. Bhambra, *Rethinking Modernity: Postcolonialism and the Sociological Imagination* (Basingstoke: Palgrave Macmillan, 2007); Thomas McCarthy, *Race, Empire, and the Idea of Human Development* (Cambridge: Cambridge University Press, 2009).

35. For the sake of clarity and consistency, I will follow the nomenclature of French colonial law and use the term *Muslim* to refer to Algerians of Arab, Berber, and Kabyle origin except when citing source material.

36. See notably Olivier Le Cour Grandmaison, *De l'indigénat: Anatomie d'un "monstre" juridique; Le droit colonial en Algérie et dans l'empire français* (Paris: La Découverte, 2010).

37. On French colonial law, see Le Cour Grandmaison, "Exception and the Rule." On citizenship in French Algeria, see Shepard, *Invention of Decolonization*.

38. Tocqueville, "First Letter on Algeria," 11.

39. Tocqueville, "Essay on Algeria," 69.

40. Ibid., 70.

41. See Blanc, *History of Ten Years*, 2:474.

42. Tocqueville, "Essay on Algeria," 70.

43. Tocqueville, "First Report on Algeria," 135.

44. Ibid.

45. Ibid., 136.

46. Tocqueville, "Essay on Algeria," 111.

47. Ibid., 71.

48. Tocqueville, "First Report on Algeria," 136.

49. Tocqueville, "Essay on Algeria," 71.

50. Tocqueville, "First Report on Algeria," 138.

51. Michel Foucault, *Discipline and Punish: The Birth of the Prison*, trans. Alan Sheridan (New York: Vintage, 1995), 201.

52. Ibid., 197.

53. Frantz Fanon, *The Wretched of the Earth*, trans. Richard Philcox (New York: Grove, 2005), 3–5. For a discussion of sequestration, see also Michel Foucault, *The Punitive Society: Lectures at the Collège de France, 1972–1973*, ed. Bernard E. Harcourt, François Ewald, Alessandro Fontana, and Arnold I. Davidson, trans. Graham Burchell (Basingstoke: Palgrave Macmillan, 2015).

54. Tocqueville, "Essay on Algeria," 86, 76. For a discussion of a scientific practice of public hygiene in the colonies, see Olivier Le Cour Grandmaison, *L'empire des hygiénistes: Vivre aux colonies* (Paris: Fayard, 2014).

55. Tocqueville, "First Report on Algeria," 130.

56. Albert Sarrault, *Discours à l'ouverture des cours de l'École coloniale* (Paris: La Presse coloniale, 1923), 8.

57. Émile Larcher, *Trois années d'études algériennes, législatives, sociales, pénitentiaires et pénales* (Paris: Rousseau, 1902), 200.

58. The term *pied-noir*, literally "black-foot," initially served as a derogatory term for Algerians of North African descent (what the French from 1958 on called *français de souche nord-africaine* or FSNA) before it came to denote North African settlers of European descent (*français de souche européenne* or FSE). Here I use *pied-noir* in the latter sense. On the history and use of the term, see Guy Pervillé, "Comment appeler les habitants de l'Algérie avant la définition légale d'une nationalité algérienne?," *Cahiers de la Méditerranée*, 54 (1997), 55–60.

59. Estimates range from 1,000 to 45,000. See Alistair Horne, *A Savage War of Peace: Algeria 1954–1962* (New York: NYRB Classics, 2006).

60. For a detailed history of these developments, see Shepard, *Invention of Decolonization*.

61. Quoted in Ian Lustick, *Unsettled States, Disputed Lands: Britain and Ireland, France and Algeria, Israel and the West Bank-Gaza* (Ithaca, N.Y.: Cornell University Press, 1993), 110.

62. Quoted in Horne, *Savage War of Peace*, 98.

63. Quoted in Lustick, *Unsettled States*, 110.

64. The Battle of Dien Bien Phu during the First Indochina War in May 1954 ended in the Viet Minh's victory over the French colonial army and French withdrawal from Indochina. See Ivan Cadeau, *La guerre d'Indochine: de l'Indochine française aux adieux à Saigon, 1940–1956* (Paris: Tallandier, 2015); Bernard B. Fall, *Hell in a Very Small Place: The Siege of Dien Bien Phu* (Philadelphia: Lippincott, 1967).

65. Jacques Massu, *La vraie bataille d'Alger* (Paris: Plon, 1971), 32.

66. On the theory of revolutionary war, see, for instance, Lionel Max Chassin, *The Communist Conquest of China: A History of the Civil War, 1945–1949*, trans. Timothy Osato and Louis Gelas (Cambridge, Mass.: Harvard University Press, 1965); Roger Trinquier, *Guerre, subversion, révolution* (Paris: Laffont, 1968). For a detailed reconstruction of the theory, see Lazreg, *Torture and the Twilight of Empire*, 15–33.

67. Lazreg, *Torture and the Twilight of Empire*, 21.

68. Carl Schmitt, *The Leviathan in the State Theory of Thomas Hobbes: Meaning and Failure of a Political Symbol*, trans. George Schwab and Erna Hilfstein (Chicago: University of Chicago Press, 2008), 21. See also Schmitt, "The International Crime of the War of Aggression and the Principle 'Nullum Crimen, Nulla Poena Sine Lege,'" in *Writings on War*, ed. and trans. Timothy Nunan (Cambridge: Polity, 2011), 125–200.

69. Carl Schmitt, *The Nomos of the Earth in the International Law of Jus Publicum Europaeum*, trans. G. L. Ulmen (New York: Telos, 2006), 121.

70. Ibid., 321.

71. For a careful examination of discourses of terrorism in international law, see Ondrej Ditrych, *Tracing the Discourses of Terrorism: Identity, Genealogy and State* (Basingstoke: Palgrave Macmillan, 2014).

72. The French word *attentat* means a usually politically motivated attack on or assassination of a political figure. Jules Jacquin, a French citizen, had managed to flee to Belgium after an attempt to assassinate Napoléon III. He believed that he was protected from facing charges in France by the principle of nonextradition of political criminals provided for by Belgian law. When France demanded Jacquin's extradition, Belgium amended its extradition law and introduced the attentat clause, which declared attacks on foreign heads of government and their families outside the protection for political offenses. See Lassa Oppenheim, *International Law*, vol. 1, *Peace* (London: Longmans, Green, 1905); Christopher H. Pyle, *Extradition, Politics, and Human Rights* (Philadelphia: Temple University Press, 2001).

73. Ben Saul, *Defining Terrorism in International Law* (Oxford: Oxford University Press, 2008), 171.

74. Ibid.

75. Ibid., 172.

76. Ibid., 170.
77. Ibid., 172.
78. Let me emphasize that I use the term *polemic*, from the Greek word *polemos* (war), to describe a concept of terrorism as a new form of war. This is not to deny that the use of the term *terrorism* is always polemical in Carl Schmitt's sense that "all political concepts, images, and terms have a polemical meaning." For Schmitt, what makes a concept political is that it is "tied to a concrete situation, whose last consequence is a friend-enemy grouping (which manifests itself in war or revolution)." To understand its meaning, one has to know "who is to be affected, combated, refuted, or negated by such a term" (Carl Schmitt, *The Concept of the Political*, trans. George Schwab [Chicago: University of Chicago Press, 2007], 30–31; translation modified). Insofar as attributions of terrorism are acts of naming that reflect particular interests, interpretations, and perspectives, terrorism is a political concept in Schmitt's sense and, as such, has polemical meaning. But not all attributions of terrorism understand it in its polemic sense as a new form of insurrectional war. To flag this distinction, I use the term *polemic* only when I am referring to a concept of terrorism as a new kind of war. I employ the language of naming and the politics of naming when discussing the political, or what Christopher Finlay, "How to Do Things with the Word 'Terrorist,'" *Review of International Studies* 35, no. 4 (2009), 752, describes as a "'rhetorical,' self-serving and unprincipled usage of the term."
79. Massu, *Vraie bataille d'Alger*, 47.
80. Carl Schmitt, *Theory of the Partisan: Intermediate Commentary on the Concept of the Political*, trans. G. L. Ulmen (New York: Telos, 2007), 35.
81. Massu, *Vraie bataille d'Alger*, 47.
82. Ibid., 46.
83. Ibid., 47.
84. Ibid., 156. For discussions of the problematic nature of the distinction between combatants and noncombatants, as well as the value of innocence associated with the latter, see Helen M. Kinsella, "Gendering Grotius: Sex and Sex Difference in the Laws of War," *Political Theory* 34, no. 2 (2006): 161–91, doi:10.1177/0090591705279530; Kinsella, *The Image before the Weapon: A Critical History of the Distinction between Combatant and Civilian* (Ithaca, N.Y.: Cornell University Press, 2011); Maja Zehfuss, "Targeting: Precision and the Production of Ethics," *European Journal of International Relations* 17, no. 3 (2011): 543–66, doi:10.1177/1354066110373559; Zehfuss, "Killing Civilians: Thinking the Practice of War," *The British Journal of Politics & International Relations* 14, no. 3 (2012): 423–40, doi:10.1111/j.1467-856X.2011.00491.x.
85. Massu, *Vraie bataille d'Alger.*, 48.
86. Ibid., 47.
87. Ibid., 155.
88. Ibid., 158.
89. Ibid., 130. The term *hors-la-loi* (outlaw), along with the word *fellagha* (bandit), were preferred terms French authorities used to describe members of the ALN, who called

themselves *moujahidin* (fighters). In what follows, I use the term *frontist* to describe FLN members and *combatant* to refer to ALN fighters except when I represent the views of agents of the colonial state. This terminology is in keeping with the self-description of the men and women who were members of the FLN and the ALN. Although this is a break with the nomenclature of French historiography, according to which Algerians who fought the colonial state were terrorists, rebels, and insurgents, the purpose of this book is to show that these latter terms are problematic and must be understood as part of a political agenda. For a similar point, see Lazreg, *Torture and the Twilight of Empire*, 11.

90. Massu, *Vraie bataille d'Alger.*, 49.

91. Ibid., 48. Interestingly, the exceptional practices authorized by the colonial state under the pretext of nationalist terrorism were made permanent after 1958, when they were justified as necessary measures against what France then described as right-wing terrorism by the pro-French Algeria paramilitary organization Organisation de l'armée secrète. Even though France claimed that an extension of presidential authority was required to defend the Republic, it actually served to fundamentally alter the country's legal system. Although an adequate analysis of the transformation of the dispositif of terrorism from a means to justify military intervention to an instrument to redefine the Republic's legal tradition is far beyond the scope of this chapter, it supports the claim that terrorism is best understood by virtue of its strategic function in facilitating the pursuit of disparate political interests. See Anne-Marie Duranton-Crabol, *Le temps de l'OAS* (Bruxelles: Complexe, 1995); *Juger en Algérie, 1944–1962*, Genre humain (Paris: Seuil, 1997); Shepard, *Invention of Decolonization.*

92. Massu, *Vraie bataille d'Alger*, 49. For Giorgio Agamben, *State of Exception*, trans. Kevin Attell (Chicago: University of Chicago Press, 2005), the coming apart of law and force of law is the key feature of a state of exception. More recently, the legal scholar Frederick Schauer, *The Force of Law* (Cambridge, Mass.: Harvard University Press, 2015), has argued that coercive force distinguishes law from other social norms.

93. Massu, *Vraie bataille d'Alger*, 98–99.

94. Ibid., 29.

95. See Service historique de la défense (SHD), Vincennes, France, 1H 4054.

96. See SHD 1H 1159.

97. Massu, *Vraie bataille d'Alger*, 89.

98. Zohra Drif, *Mémoires d'une combattante de l'ALN: Zone autonome d'Alger* (Alger: Chihab, 2014), 77.

99. Ibid., 293.

100. Saadi Yacef, *Souvenirs de la bataille d'Alger, décembre 1956–septembre 1957* (Paris: Maillet, 1962), 35.

101. SHD 1H 1245.

102. Massu, *Vraie bataille d'Alger*, 89.

103. Ibid., 90.

104. Ibid., 101.

105. See in particular SHD 1H 1983 and SHD 1H 1022.

106. Paul Aussaresses, *The Battle of the Casbah: Terrorism and Counter-Terrorism in Algeria 1955–1957*, trans. Robert L. Miller (New York: Enigma, 2005), 16.

107. Roger Trinquier, *Modern Warfare: A French View of Counterinsurgency*, trans. Daniel Lee (Westport, Conn.: Praeger, 2006), 21.

108. Massu, *Vraie bataille d'Alger*, 163.

109. I owe this insight to Kevin Olson, "Epistemologies of Rebellion: The Tricolor Cockade and the Problem of Subaltern Speech," *Political Theory* 43, no. 6 (2014): 730–52, doi:10.1177/0090591714558425 and *Imagined Sovereignties: The Power of the People and Other Myths of the Modern Age* (Cambridge: Cambridge University Press, 2016), who theorizes the significance of the absence of material in the archive, as well as to Arlettte Farge's exhortation that we must remain "attentive to that which has fled, which has gone missing, which is noticeable by its absence," since "both presence and absence from the archive are signs we must interpret in order to understand how they fit into the larger landscape" (Arlette Farge, *The Allure of the Archives*, trans. Thomas Scott-Railton [New Haven, Conn.: Yale University Press, 2013], 71). On the lack of evidence for the success of torture in preventing violence, see Darius Rejali, *Torture and Democracy* (Princeton, N.J.: Princeton University Press, 2007).

110. SHD 1H 1570.

111. Marcel-Maurice Bigeard, *J'ai mal à la France* (Ostwald: Polygone, 2001), 186.

112. See Jean-Pierre Cômes, '*Ma' guerre d'Algérie et la torture: J'étais lieutenant dans les D.O.P* (Paris: L'Harmattan, 2002); Claude Dufresnoy, ed., *Des officiers parlent*, (Paris: Julliard, 1961); Jean-Charles Jauffret, *Ces officiers qui ont dit non à la torture, Algérie 1954–1962* (Paris: Autrement, 2005); Benoist Rey, *Les égorgeurs* (Paris: Monde Libertaire, 2000); Hélie de Saint Marc, *Mémoires* (Paris: Perrin, 1995); Benjamin Stora, *La gangrène et l'oubli: La mémoire de la guerre d'Algérie* (Paris: La Découverte, 1998); Pierre-Alban Thomas, *Les désarrois d'un officier en Algérie* (Paris: Seuil, 2002); Pierre Vidal-Naquet, ed., *Les crimes de l'armée française* (Paris: La Découverte, 2001); Jean-Pierre Vittori, *Confessions d'un professionnel de la torture* (Paris: Ramsay, 1980); Vittori, *On a torturé en Algérie* (Paris: Ramsay, 2000).

113. Henri Pouillot, *La villa susini* (Paris: Tirésias, 2001), 84–85.

114. SHD 1H 1571.

115. This is not to say that information did not play an important role. As Foucault maintained in *Discipline and Punish*, the meticulous collection of information and a system of permanent registration are central features of the disciplinary mechanism. They ensure, he argued, that "the formation of knowledge and the increase of power regularly reinforce one another in a circular process" (224). I will suggest in the pages that follow that this was true also for the system of colonial discipline established by the French colonial state in Algeria.

116. Drif, *Mémoires d'une combattante de l'ALN*, 303.

117. Pierre Leulliette, *St. Michael and the Dragon*, trans. John Edmonds (Boston: Houghton Mifflin, 1964), 296.

118. See, for instance, Lazreg, *Torture and the Twilight of Empire*; Shepard, *Invention of Decolonization*.

119. On this point, see also chapter 1, "On Violence," in Fanon, *Wretched of the Earth*.

120. For a monumental history of the FLN, see Gilbert Meynier, *Histoire intérieure du FLN: 1954–1962* (Paris: Fayard, 2002).

121. Quoted in Pauline Chambonnet, and Laure Cousin, "Attentat du Milk Bar: Rien, Zohra Drif, ne regrette rien," *Marianne*, April 1, 2012, http://www.marianne.net /Attentat-du-Milk-Bar-rien-Zohra-Drif-ne-regrette-rien_a216760.html.

122. Drif, *Mémoires d'une combattante de l'ALN*, 204. For a similar claim, see Frantz Fanon, "L'indépendance nationale, seule issue possible," in *Écrits sur l'aliénation et la liberté*, ed. Jean Khalfa and Robert Young (Paris: La Découverte, 2015), 461–66; Fanon, "Révolution démocratique."

123. Yacef, *Souvenirs de la bataille d'Alger*, 18–19.

124. Ibid., 19. See also Drif, *Mémoires d'une combattante de l'ALN*, 158.

125. Yacef, *Souvenirs de la bataille d'Alger*, 80.

126. Judith Butler, *Gender Trouble: Feminism and the Subversion of Identity* (New York: Routledge, 1990), offers an instructive discussion of the difference between repetition and subversion that inspires my reading here.

127. Frantz Fanon, "L'an V de la révolution algérienne," in *Oeuvres* (Paris: La Découverte, 2011), 290. The English translation of this text is *A Dying Colonialism*, trans. Haakon Chevalier (New York: Grove, 1965).

128. Fanon, *A Dying Colonialism*, 57.

129. Ibid., 55.

130. Drif, *Mémoires d'une combattante de l'ALN*, 201.

131. Ibid., 160.

132. Ibid., 173.

133. Zohra Drif, *La mort de mes frères* (Paris: Maspero, 1960), 8.

134. Fanon, "L'an V de la révolution algérienne," 276. For a discussion of Fanon's analysis of the veil in the context of terrorism in Algeria, see also Jeffrey Louis Decker, "Terrorism (Un) Veiled: Frantz Fanon and the Women of Algiers," *Culutral Critique* 17 (1990), 177–95.

135. Fanon, "L'an V de la révolution algérienne," 284.

136. Ibid., 288.

137. Ibid., 293. See also Yacef, *Souvenirs de la bataille d'Alger*, 28.

138. Fanon, L'an V de la révolution algérienne," 293.

139. Drif, *Mémoires d'une combattante de l'ALN,* 179.

140. Ibid., 180.

141. Ibid., 177.

142. Ibid., 182–83.

143. Ibid., 177.

144. Fanon, "L'an V de la révolution algérienne," 296.

145. Yacef, *Souvenirs de la bataille d'Alger*, 60.

146. Fanon, "L'an V de la révolution algérienne," 298. Note also the continuing relevance of Fanon's analysis of the veil as a means of resistance for accounts of contemporary forms of gendered racism in French debates about the veil. For excellent work on the complex interplay of racism, gender, and sexual politics, see Sharif Gemie, *French Muslims: New Voices in Contemporary France* (Cardiff: University of Wales Press, 2010); Maria Eleonora Sanna and Malek Bouyahia, eds., *La polysémie du voile: Politiques et mobilisations postcoloniales* (Paris: Éditions des archives contemporaines, 2013); Joan Wallach Scott, *The Politics of the Veil* (Princeton, N.J.: Princeton University Press, 2009); Fawzia Zouari, *Ce voile qui déchire la France* (Paris: Ramsay, 2004). For an analysis of the ways in which contemporary constructions of citizenship in France intersect with ideas about gender, sexuality, and race in the context of immigration, see Catherine Raissiguier, *Reinventing the Republic: Gender, Migration, and Citizenship in France* (Stanford, Calif.: Stanford University Press, 2010).

147. Yacef, *Souvenirs de la bataille d'Alger*, 38.

148. SHD 1H 1245. The dossier also contains a schematic representation of the organization of the "bomb network" (*réseau bombes*), which illustrates the rigid compartmentalization and lack of knowledge within the organizational structures of the FLN.

149. Drif, *Mémoires d'une combattante de* l'ALN, 154. Combatants often used aliases for reasons of security as well as symbolism. Zohra Drif was known as Farida; her friend Samia Lakhdari went by the name of Nabila.

150. Ibid.

151. Ibid., 557.

152. Ibid., 155.

153. Ibid. 457.

154. Ibid., 527.

155. Foucault, *Society Must Be Defended*, 208.

156. Louisette Ighilahriz, *Algérienne* (Paris: Fayard/Calmann-Lévy, 2001), 141.

157. Quoted in Chambonnet and Cousin, "Attentat du Milk Bar."

158. See Jean-Paul Sartre, *Critique of Dialectical Reason*, vol. 1, *Theory of Practical Ensembles*, ed. Jonathan Rée, trans. Alan Sheridan-Smith (London: Verso, 2004), Sartre, Preface to *The Wretched of the Earth*, by Frantz Fanon, trans. Richard Philcox (New York: Grove, 2005), xliii–lxii; Sartre, Preface to *The Question*, by Henri Alleg, trans. John Calder (Lincoln: University of Nebraska Press, 2006), xxvii–xliv; Sartre, *Colonialism and Neocolonialism*, trans. Azzedine Haddour (London: Routledge, 2006).

159. See Raymond Aron, *Mémoires: 50 ans de réflexion politique* (Paris: Julliard, 1983).

160. Shephard, *Invention of Decolonization*.

CHAPTER 5. REIMAGINING TERRORISM
AT THE END OF HISTORY

1. For an excellent analysis of political violence in Algeria in the 1990s, as well as the politics of naming this violence as civil war and the "antipolitics" of increasingly scientific

or, better, scientistic approaches to armed conflict, see Jacob Mundy, *Imaginative Geographies of Algerian Violence: Conflict Science, Conflict Management, Antipolitics* (Stanford, Calif.: Stanford University Press, 2015).

2. Marnia Lazreg, *Torture and the Twilight of Empire: From Algiers to Baghdad* (Princeton, N.J.: Princeton University Press, 2007), 256–57. On this point, see also Todd Shepard, *The Invention of Decolonization: The Algerian War and the Remaking of France* (Ithaca, N.Y.: Cornell University Press, 2006).

3. Lazreg, *Torture and the Twilight of Empire*, 259.

4. The movie was not the only source of inspiration for the U.S. government. In a 2007 interview, George W. Bush said that he was reading Alistair Horne's book *A Savage War of Peace*, which Henry Kissinger had recommended to him. Bush had also read Camus's *The Stranger* to gain insight into Muslim culture. See Maureen Dowd, "Aux Barricades!" *New York Times*, January 17, 2007, http://www.nytimes.com/2007/01/17/opinion/17dowd.html; Alistair Horne, *A Savage War of Peace: Algeria, 1954–1962* (New York: NYRB Classics, 2006); Michael T. Kaufman, "The World: Film Studies; What Does the Pentagon See in 'Battle of Algiers'?" *New York Times*, September 7, 2003, Week in Review sec, http://www.nytimes.com/2003/09/07/weekinreview/the-world-film-studies-what-does-the-pentagon-see-in-battle-of-algiers.html; Lazreg, *Torture and the Twilight of Empire*.

5. Quoted in Eqbal Ahmad, *The Selected Writings of Eqbal Ahmad*, ed. Carollee Bengelsdorf, Margaret Cerullo, and Yogesh Chandrani (New York: Columbia University Press, 2006), 85.

6. Thomas Ricks, "Commander Punished as Army Probes Detainee Treatment," *Washington Post*, April 4, 2004, http://www.washingtonpost.com/wp-dyn/articles/A50227-2004Apr4_2.html.

7. For discussions of the role of U.S. military intervention in the Middle East in the transformation of political violence in general and the formation of Daesh in particular, see Dan Glaister, "Campaign in Iraq Has Increased Terrorism Threat, Says American Intelligence Report," *Guardian*, September 25, 2006, World News sec., https://www.theguardian.com/world/2006/sep/25/usa.iraq; Joby Warrick, *Black Flags: The Rise of ISIS* (New York: Penguin Random House, 2015).

8. Lazreg, *Torture and the Twilight of Empire*, 10.

9. Ibid., 11.

10. Kevin Olson, *Imagined Sovereignties: The Power of the People and Other Myths of the Modern Age* (Cambridge: Cambridge University Press, 2016), 165.

11. Friedrich Wilhelm Nietzsche, *On the Genealogy of Morals*, trans. Douglas Smith (Oxford: Oxford University Press, 1996), 60–61.

12. Ibid., 61.

13. On Strauss, Kojève, and their political influence in the United States, see Shadia B. Drury, "The End of History and the New World Order," *International Journal* 48, no. 1 (1992): 80–99, doi:10.2307/40202821; Drury, *Alexandre Kojève: The Roots of Postmodern Politics* (New York: St. Martin's, 1994); Drury, *Leo Strauss and the American Right* (New York: St. Martin's, 1997); Drury, *The Political Ideas of Leo Strauss* (New York:

Palgrave Macmillan, 2005); Robert B. Pippin, "Being, Time, and Politics: The Strauss-Kojève Debate," *History and Theory* 32, no. 2 (1993): 138–61, doi:10.2307/2505349; Michael S. Roth, "A Problem of Recognition: Alexandre Kojève and the End of History," *History and Theory* 24, no. 3 (1985): 293–306, doi:10.2307/2505171.

14. For discussions of the origin and historical formation of neoconservatism, see Gary Dorrien, *Imperial Designs: Neoconservatism and the New Pax Americana* (New York: Routledge, 2013); John Ehrman, *The Rise of Neoconservatism: Intellectuals and Foreign Affairs, 1945–1994* (Ann Arbor, Mich.: Edwards, 1995); Brandon High, "The Recent Historiography of American Neoconservatism," *The Historical Journal* 52, no. 2 (2009): 475–491, doi:10.1017/S0018246X09007560; Justin Vaïsse, *Neoconservatism: The Biography of a Movement*, trans. Arthur Goldhammer (Cambridge, Mass.: Harvard University Press, 2010).

15. Irving Kristol, "What Is a 'Neoconservative?,' " in *The Neoconservative Persuasion. Selected Essays, 1942–2009*, ed. Gertrude Himmelfarb (New York: Basic Books, 2011), 149.

16. Ibid., 150.

17. Francis Fukuyama, "The End of History?," *The National Interest*, 1989, 4.

18. Ibid., 5.

19. Ibid., 10.

20. Francis Fukuyama, *The End of History and the Last Man* (New York: Free Press, 2006), xx.

21. For a detailed explanation of the National Security Strategy, its purposes, and the process of its formulation, see Don M. Snider, "The National Security Strategy: Documenting Strategic Vision," 1995, http://nssarchive.us/wp-content/uploads/2012/05/Snider.pdf.

22. "The National Security Strategy of the United States of America," 2002, http://nssarchive.us/NSSR/2002.pdf, president's introduction.

23. Ibid., 18.

24. Ibid., president's introduction.

25. On this point, see Danilo Zolo, *Invoking Humanity: War, Law and Global Order* (London: Continuum, 2002); Zolo, *Victors' Justice: From Nuremberg to Baghdad*, trans. M. W. Weir (London: Verso, 2009).

26. NSS 2002, president's introduction.

27. For a careful analysis of the relationship between the NSS and reason of state, see Sheldon Sanford Wolin, *Democracy Incorporated: Managed Democracy and the Specter of Inverted Totalitarianism* (Princeton, N.J.: Princeton University Press, 2010).

28. For discussions of this notion, see Giorgio Agamben, *State of Exception*, trans. Kevin Attell (Chicago: University of Chicago Press, 2005); Jess Bravin, *The Terror Courts: Rough Justice at Guantanamo Bay* (New Haven, Conn.: Yale University Press, 2013); Michael A. Genovese, *Presidential Prerogative: Imperial Power in an Age of Terrorism* (Stanford, Calif.: Stanford University Press, 2010); Joseph Margulies, *Guantanamo and the Abuse of Presidential Power* (New York: Simon and Schuster, 2006); John C. Yoo, "The Continuation of Politics by Other Means: The Original Understanding of War Powers,"

California Law Review 84, no. 2 (1996): 167; John Yoo and Robert J. Delahunty, "The President's Constitutional Authority to Conduct Military Operations Against Terrorist Organizations and the Nations That Harbor or Support Them," *Harvard Journal of Law and Public Policy* 25 (2002): 487–515.

29. Yoo, "The Continuation of Politics by Other Means," 174.

30. Bravin, *The Terror Courts*, 31.

31. The 9/11 Resolution, or Authorization for Use of Military Force Against Terrorists of 2001, is available at http://www.gpo.gov/fdsys/pkg/PLAW-107publ40/html/PLAW -107publ40.htm.

32. John C. Yoo, *The President's Constitutional Authority to Conduct Military Operations Against Terrorists and Nations Supporting Them: Memorandum Opinion for the Deputy Counsel to the President, Office of Legal Counsel*, 2001, https://www.justice.gov/olc /opinion/president%E2%80%99s-constitutional-authority-conduct-military -operations-against-terrorists-and.

33. For representative policies, see Legality of the Use of Military Commissions to Try Terrorists: OLC Memorandum to White House Counsel Alberto Gonzales, 2001, https://fas .org/irp/agency/doj/olc/commissions.pdf; Memorandum Regarding Constitutionality of Amending Foreign Intelligence Surveillance Act to Change the "Purpose" Standard for Searches, 2001, https://fas.org/irp/agency/doj/olc/amend-fisa.pdf.; Memorandum Regarding Authority for Use of Military Force to Combat Terrorist Activities within the United States, 2001, https://fas.org/irp/agency/doj/olc/milforce.pdf; Memorandum Regarding the President's Power as Commander in Chief to Transfer Captured Terrorists to the Control and Custody of Foreign Nations, 2002, https://fas.org/irp /agency/doj/olc/transfer.pdf; Memorandum Regarding Swift Justice Authorization Act, 2002, https://fas.org/irp/agency/doj/olc/swift-justice.pdf; Memorandum Regarding Determination of Enemy Belligerency and Military Detention, 2002, https://fas .org/irp/agency/doj/olc/belligerency.pdf; Memorandum Regarding Applicability of 18 U.S.C. § 4001(a) to Military Detention of United States Citizens, 2002, https://fas.org /irp/agency/doj/olc/detention.pdf; Application of 18 U.S.C. 2340–2340A to Certain Techniques That May Be Used in the Interrogation of a High Value Al Qaeda Detainee: Memorandum for John Rizzo, Acting General Counsel of the Central Intelligence Agency, 2005, https://fas.org/irp/agency/doj/olc/techniques.pdf.

34. "National Security Strategy of the United States," 1987, 7, http://nssarchive.us/NSSR /1987.pdf.

35. Ibid., 4.

36. Ibid., 34.

37. Ibid., 17.

38. Ibid., 5.

39. Ibid., 6.

40. Ibid., 13.

41. Ibid., 6.

42. Ibid., 7.

43. Ibid., 7.

44. Ibid., 5.

45. Ibid., 17.

46. See also "National Security Strategy of the United States," 1988, 29, http://nssarchive
    .us/NSSR/1988.pdf.

47. Ibid., 5.

48. Ibid., 6.

49. "National Security Strategy of the United States," 1990, 29, http://nssarchive.us/NSSR
    /1990.pdf.

50. "National Security Strategy of the United States," 1991, 8, http://nssarchive.us/NSSR
    /1991.pdf.

51. "National Security Strategy of the United States," 1993, 18, http://nssarchive.us/NSSR
    /1993.pdf.

52. Ibid., 13.

53. NSS 1987, 19.

54. Ibid., 34.

55. Ibid., 7.

56. Ibid., 11.

57. "A National Security Strategy for A New Century," 1999, 42, http://history.defense.gov
    /Portals/70/Documents/nss/nss1999.pdf?ver=2014-06-25-121300-170.

58. Ibid., 1.

59. "A National Security Strategy of Engagement and Enlargement," 1995, 1, http://
    nssarchive.us/NSSR/1995.pdf.

60. Ibid., 1–2.

61. Ibid., 1.

62. Ibid., i.

63. "A National Security Strategy of Engagement and Enlargement," 1994, 8, http://
    nssarchive.us/NSSR/1994.pdf.

64. "A National Security Strategy for A New Century," 1998, 16, http://nssarchive.us/NSSR
    /1998.pdf.

65. NSS 1994, 8.

66. Omnibus Counterterrorism Act of 1995. S.390—104th Congress (1995–1996), 1995,
    https://www.congress.gov/bill/104th-congress/senate-bill/390/text.

67. Antiterrorism and Effective Death Penalty Act of 1996. Pub. L. No. 104-132, 110 Stat. 1214,
    1996, https://www.gpo.gov/fdsys/pkg/PLAW-104publ132/html/PLAW-104publ132.htm.

68. On this point, see also Stuart Elden, *Terror and Territory: The Spatial Extent of Sover-
    eignty* (Minneapolis: University of Minnesota Press, 2009).

69. "A National Security Strategy for a New Century," 2000, 25, http://nssarchive.us/NSSR
    /2000.pdf.

70. NSS 1998, 15. The two main international conventions passed during this time were
    the aforementioned International Convention for the Suppression of Terrorist Bomb-
    ings, 1998, https://www.unodc.org/documents/treaties/Special/1997%20International%20
    Convention%20for%20the%20Suppression%20of%20Terrorist.pdf and International

Convention for the Suppression of the Financing of Terrorism, 1999, http://www.un
.org/law/cod/finterr.htm.

71. NSS 2000, 24.

72. On the practice of rendition, see also Alan Clarke, *Rendition to Torture* (New Brunswick, N.J.: Rutgers University Press, 2012); Stephen Grey, *Ghost Plane: The True Story
of the CIA Rendition and Torture Program* (New York: St. Martin's, 2006); "The Rendition Project," https://www.therenditionproject.org.uk/.

73. NSS 2002, 5.

74. Ibid.

75. Ibid., 6.

76. Ibid.

77. Ibid., 15.

78. Ibid., 31.

79. Ibid., 15.

80. Ibid., 6.

81. Ibid., 31.

82. Ibid., 5.

83. Ibid., 7.

84. Muneer I. Ahmad, "A Rage Shared by Law: Post–September 11 Racial Violence as
Crimes of Passion," *California Law Review* 92, no. 5 (2004), 1261.

85. Jasbir K. Puar, *Terrorist Assemblages: Homonationalism in Queer Times* (Durham,
N.C.: Duke University Press, 2007), 52, 72, 119, 136, 194.

86. Leti Volpp, "The Citizen and the Terrorist," *UCLA Law Review* 49, no. 5 (2012), 578. For
a related discussion of race and political membership, see Andrew Dilts, *Punishment
and Inclusion: Race, Membership, and the Limits of American Liberalism* (New York:
Fordham University Press, 2014); Joel Olson, *The Abolition of White Democracy* (Minneapolis: University of Minnesota Press, 2004).

87. On interpellation, see Louis Althusser, "Ideology and Ideological State Apparatuses,"
in *On Ideology*, trans. Ben Brewster (London: Verso, 2008), 1–60.

88. Michel Foucault, *History of Madness*, ed. Jean Khalfa, trans. Jonathan Murphy
(London: Routledge, 2006), 529.

89. Colin Koopman, *Genealogy as Critique: Foucault and the Problems of Modernity*
(Bloomington: Indiana University Press, 2013), 163.

90. Ibid., 157.

91. For discussions of these cases, see Hilary Hanson, "Flight Delayed After Woman Fears
Professor Doing Math Is a Terrorist," *Huffington Post*, May 7, 2016, http://www.huffington
post.com/entry/professor-math-terrorist-flight-delay_us_572e41e6e4b016f3789617f7;
Rick Jervis and Christopher Cooper, "Terrorists May Be Among Refugees Heading to
Europe," *Wall Street Journal*, July 5, 2002, News sec., http://www.wsj.com/articles
/SB1025818733332780560; Jason Seher, "Former NSA Chief Compares Snowden to
Terrorists," *CNN*, December 1, 2013, http://politicalticker.blogs.cnn.com/2013/12/
01/former-nsa-chief-compares-snowden-to-terrorists/; Volpp, "Citizen and the
Terrorist."

92. "President Obama's April 16 Speech on Boston Marathon Bombings," *Time*, April 16, 2013, http://swampland.time.com/2013/04/16/president-obamas-speech-on-boston -marathon-bombings-full-text/.

93. David Sirota, "Let's Hope the Boston Marathon Bomber Is A White American," *Salon*, April 17, 2013, http://www.salon.com/2013/04/16/lets_hope_the_boston_marathon _bomber_is_a_white_american/.

94. For relevant discussions, see Mark S. Hamm, *Apocalypse in Oklahoma: Waco and Ruby Ridge Revenged* (Boston: Northeastern University Press, 1997); Douglas Kellner, *Guys and Guns Amok: Domestic Terrorism and School Shootings from the Oklahoma City Bombing to the Virginia Tech Massacre* (Boulder, Colo.: Paradigm, 2008); Lou Michel and Dan Herbeck, *American Terrorist: Timothy McVeigh and the Oklahoma City Bombing* (New York: Harper, 2001); Jim Naureckas, "The Oklahoma City Bombing: The Jihad That Wasn't," *Fair! Fairness and Accuracy in Reporting*, July 1, 1995, http:// fair.org/extra-online-articles/the-oklahoma-city-bombing/. A similar, albeit non-American, incident took place in Norway in July 2011. Anders Behring Breivik, a Norwegian citizen, set off a car bomb in the government district in Oslo, killing eight people, and shot sixty-nine participants of a youth camp on the island of Utøya. Immediately after the attacks and without information about the identity of the bomber, the media reported acts of terrorism committed by fundamentalist jihadis and al-Qaeda. When it became evident that the culprit was a right-wing extremist, the rhetoric changed from terrorism to descriptions of the violence as shootings and bombings. Even though Breivik was convicted of committing an act of terrorism according to paragraph 147a of the Norwegian Criminal Code, he was generally portrayed as a mass killer, a shooter, a gunman, or a right-wing fanatic who, some commentators even suggested, had legitimate grievances. Likewise, in the United States, acts of gun violence perpetrated by white men are usually described in mainstream public discourse as mass shootings rather than acts of terrorism. I examine responses that such cases should equally be identified as terrorism in chapter 6 of this book. For discussions of Breivik, in particular, and the representation of mass shootings more generally, see Bruce Bawer, "Inside the Mind of the Oslo Murderer," *Wall Street Journal*, July 25, 2011, http://www.wsj.com/articles/SB10001424053111903999904576465801154130960; Alana Lentin and Gavan Titley, "Anders Behring Breivik Had No Legitimate Grievance," *Guardian*, July 26, 2011, http://www.theguardian.com/commentisfree/2011/jul/26 /anders-behring-breivik-multicultural-failure; Erin Steuter and Deborah Wills, *At War with Metaphor: Media, Propaganda, and Racism in the War on Terror* (Lanham, Md.: Lexington, 2009).

95. Peter Wehner, "The War Goes On," *Commentary*, April 23, 2014, http://www .commentarymagazine.com/2013/04/23/the-war-goes-on/. The same argument is put forward by Howard Portnoy, "Sorry, David Sirota: Looks Like Boston Bombing Suspects Not 'White Americans,'" *NewsBusters*, April 19, 2013, http://newsbusters.org /blogs/howard-portnoy/2013/04/19/sorry-david-sirota-looks-boston-bombing -suspects-not-white-americans.

96. Quoted in Rosenthal, Andrew, "What's the Difference Between McVeigh and Tsarnaev?," *Taking Note*, April 22, 2013, http://takingnote.blogs.nytimes.com/2013/04/22/whats-the-difference-between-mcveigh-and-tsarnaev/.

97. Ryan J. Reilly, "Dzhokhar Tsarnaev Will Not Be Treated as Enemy Combatant: White House," *Huffington Post*, April 22, 2013, http://www.huffingtonpost.com/2013/04/22/dzhokhar-tsarnaev-enemy-combatant_n_3132815.html. This claim is in tension with the fact that the United States captured and detained ninety-nine U.S. citizens in Afghanistan. Although many of them were detained without charge and also tortured in CIA and military custody, one of them, Yasser Hamdi, was held in Guantánamo. See, for instance, Melysa H. Sperber, "John Walker Lindh and Yaser Esam Hamdi: Closing the Loophole in International Humanitarian Law for American Nationals Captured Abroad While Fighting with Enemy Forces," *American Criminal Law Review* 40 (2003), 159–215.

98. Quoted in David Edwards, "Ex-CIA Deputy Director: Boston Bombing 'more like Columbine than Al Qaeda,'" *Raw Story*, April 21, 2013, http://www.rawstory.com/rs/2013/04/21/ex-cia-deputy-director-boston-bombing-more-like-columbine-than-al-qaeda/. For an analysis of the hoodie as a marker of criminality, see Chike Jeffers, "Should Black Kids Avoid Wearing Hoodies?," in *Pursuing Trayvon Martin: Historical Contexts and Contemporary Manifestations of Racial Dynamics*, ed. George Yancy and Janine Jones (Lanham, Md.: Lexington, 2012), 129–40.

99. Volpp, "Citizen and the Terrorist," 571.

100. For representative publications, see Roksana Bahramitash, "The War on Terror, Feminist Orientalism and Orientalist Feminism: Case Studies of Two North American Bestsellers," *Critique: Critical Middle Eastern Studies* 14, no. 2 (2005): 221–35; Gargi Bhattacharyya, *Dangerous Brown Men: Exploiting Sex, Violence and Feminism in the "War on the Terror"* (London: Zed Books, 2008); Judith Butler, *Frames of War: When Is Life Grievable?* (London: Verso, 2009); Krista Hunt and Kim Rygiel, eds., *(En)Gendering the War on Terror: War Stories and Camouflaged Politics* (Aldershot: Ashgate, 2008); Bonnie Mann, *Sovereign Masculinity: Gender Lessons from the War on Terror* (New York: Oxford University Press, 2014); Chandra Mohanty, Minnie Bruce Pratt, and Robin L. Riley, eds., *Feminism and War* (London: Zed Books, 2008); Puar, *Terrorist Assemblages*.

101. Judith Butler, *Precarious Life: The Powers of Mourning and Violence* (London: Verso, 2004), 91.

102. Ibid., 74.

103. Ibid., xvi.

104. Butler, *Frames of War*, 126.

105. For a harrowing account of torture inflicted on a French citizen during the Algerian Revolution, see Henri Alleg, *The Question*, trans. John Calder (Lincoln: University of Nebraska Press, 2006). See also Jean-Paul Sartre, Preface to *The Question*, by Henri Alleg, trans. John Calder (Lincoln: University of Nebraska Press, 2006), xxvii–xliv.

106. Butler, *Frames of War*, 132.

107. Ibid., 125.

108. Fukuyama, "End of History," 18.

109. Butler, *Frames of War*, 72.

110. It is worth emphasizing, as Jasbir Puar does, that the production of the terrorist sub-
      ject as subhuman and outside history does not serve only to justify the use of force and
      military aggression in the name of security. In her analysis of depictions of sexual
      shaming of detainees by American soldiers in the infamous Abu Ghraib photographs,
      Puar shows that the interlocking of race, gender, and sexuality in the construction of
      a racialized and perversely sexualized terrorist identity not only facilitates the pathol-
      ogization and "devitalization" of Muslim populations but also allows for the nor-
      malization, inclusion, and securitization of previously stigmatized identities (*Terrorist
      Assemblages*, xxxv). On the illegality of the invasion of Iraq, see "The Report of the
      Iraq Inquiry (Chilcot Report)," (London: House of Commons, 2016), http://www
      .iraqinquiry.org.uk/the-report/.

CHAPTER 6. TOWARD A CRITICAL THEORY OF TERRORISM

1. Michel Foucault, *The Birth of Biopolitics: Lectures at the Collège de France, 1978–1979*,
    ed. Michel Senellart, François Ewald, Alessandro Fontana, and Arnold I. Davidson,
    trans. Graham Burchell (New York: Palgrave Macmillan, 2010), 3.

2. Ibid., 19.

3. Colin Koopman, *Genealogy as Critique: Foucault and the Problems of Modernity*
    (Bloomington: Indiana University Press, 2013). This twofold focus on defamiliarization
    and explication of the historical emergence of present practices is what distinguishes
    Koopman's reading of Foucault's genealogy from interpretations that foreground de-
    naturalization. For examples of the latter approach, see, e.g., Judith Butler, *Gender
    Trouble: Feminism and the Subversion of Identity* (New York: Routledge, 1990);
    Thomas R. Flynn, *Sartre, Foucault, and Historical Reason*, vol. 2, *A Poststructuralist
    Mapping of History* (Chicago: University of Chicago Press, 2010); Johanna Oksala, *Fou-
    cault, Politics, and Violence* (Evanston, Ill.: Northwestern University Press, 2012);
    Martin Saar, *Genealogie als Kritik: Geschichte und Theorie des Subjekts nach Nietzsche
    und Foucaul.* (Frankfurt: Campus, 2007); Jana Sawicki, "Heidegger and Foucault:
    Escaping Technological Nihilism," in *Foucault and Heidegger: Critical Encounters*,
    ed. Alan Milchman and Alan Rosenberg (Minneapolis: University of Minnesota
    Press, 2003), 55–73.

4. Michel Foucault, "An Interview with Michel Foucault," in *Essential Works of Foucault,
    1954–1984*, vol. 3, *Power*, ed. James D. Faubion, trans. Robert Hurley (New York: New
    Press, 2001), 288.

5. As a mode of critique whose aim is not to articulate solutions to problems but to expli-
    cate problems and describe their historical formation, Foucault's genealogies can be
    contrasted with Nietzsche's subversive genealogy, which aims at undermining mod-
    ern moral practices that purport to express a will to truth, and Bernard Williams's

vindicatory genealogy, which seeks to support values and practices of truthfulness. Friedrich Wilhelm Nietzsche, *On the Genealogy of Morals*, trans. Douglas Smith (Oxford: Oxford University Press, 1996); Bernard Williams, *Truth and Truthfulness: An Essay in Genealogy* (Princeton, N.J.: Princeton University Press, 2002). See also Koopman, *Genealogy as Critique*.

6. See most prominently Daniel Zamora, ed., *Critiquer Foucault: Les années 1980 et la tentation néolibérale* (Saint-Gilles: Aden, 2014).

7. James Bernauer, *Michel Foucault's Force of Flight* (Atlantic Highlands, N.J.: Humanities, 1990); Hubert L. Dreyfus and Paul Rabinow, *Michel Foucault: Beyond Structuralism and Hermeneutics* (Chicago: University of Chicago Press, 1983); Flynn, *Sartre, Foucault, and Historical Reason*; Gary Gutting, *Michel Foucault's Archaeology of Scientific Reason* (Cambridge: Cambridge University Press, 1989).

8. Amy Allen, *The Politics of Our Selves: Power, Autonomy, and Gender in Contemporary Critical Theory* (New York: Columbia University Press, 2008); Stuart Elden, *Foucault's Last Decade* (Malden, Mass.: Polity, 2016); Stuart Elden, *Foucault: The Birth of Power* (Malden, Mass.: Polity, 2017); Ben Golder, *Foucault and the Politics of Rights* (Stanford, Calif.: Stanford University Press, 2015); Lynne Huffer, *Mad for Foucault: Rethinking the Foundations of Queer Theory* (New York: Columbia University Press, 2010); Mark Kelly, *The Political Philosophy of Michel Foucault* (New York: Routledge, 2009); Ladelle McWhorter, *Bodies and Pleasures: Foucault and the Politics of Sexual Normalization* (Bloomington: Indiana University Press, 1999); Saar, *Genealogie als Kritik*; Tuomo Tiisala, "Keeping It Implicit: A Defense of Foucault's Archaeology of Knowledge," *Journal of the American Philosophical Association* 1 (2015): 653–73.

9. Examples are Michael Dillon, *Biopolitics of Security: A Political Analytic of Finitude* (London: Routledge, 2015); Michael Dillon and Andrew Neal, eds., *Foucault on Politics, Security and War* (Basingstoke: Palgrave Macmillan, 2008); Michael Dillon and Julian Reid, *The Liberal Way of War: Killing to Make Life Live* (London: Routledge, 2009); Vanessa Lemm and Miguel Vatter, eds., *The Government of Life: Foucault, Biopolitics, and Neoliberalism* (New York: Fordham University Press, 2014); Julian Reid, *The Biopolitics of the War on Terror: Life Struggles, Liberal Modernity and the Defence of Logistical Societies* (Manchester: Manchester University Press, 2009); Jemima Repo, *The Biopolitics of Gender* (Oxford: Oxford University Press, 2015); Miguel Vatter, *The Republic of the Living: Biopolitics and the Critique of Civil Society* (New York: Fordham University Press, 2014).

10. Koopman, *Genealogy as Critique*, 6, aptly labels such conceptual borrowing that is unmoored from historical context "biopower-hunting." A paradigmatic example of this approach, in his view, is Giorgio Agamben's ontologization of Foucault's fully historically embedded analysis of biopolitics. See Colin Koopman, "Two Uses of Michel Foucault in Political Theory: Concepts and Methods in Giorgio Agamben and Ian Hacking," *Constellations* 22, no. 4 (2015): 571–85, doi:10.1111/1467-8675.12153.

11. Koopman, *Genealogy as Critique*, 7.

12. Michel Foucault, "Prisons et asiles dans le mécanisme du pouvoir," in *Dits et écrits*, vol. 2, *1970–1975*, ed. Daniel Defert and François Ewald (Paris: Gallimard, 1994), 523.

13. Santiago Castro-Gómez, *La hybris del punto cero: Ciencia, raza e ilustración en la Nueva Granada (1750–1816)* (Bogotá: Pontificia Universidad Javeriana, 2005); Arnold I. Davidson, *The Emergence of Sexuality: Historical Epistemology and the Formation of Concepts* (Cambridge, Mass.: Harvard University Press, 2004); Andrew Dilts, *Punishment and Inclusion: Race, Membership, and the Limits of American Liberalism* (New York: Fordham University Press, 2014); Ian Hacking, *The Taming of Chance* (Cambridge: Cambridge University Press, 1990); Colin Koopman, "How We Became Our Data: A Genealogy of the Informational Person," unpublished manuscript, 2017; Ladelle McWhorter, *Racism and Sexual Oppression in Anglo-America: A Genealogy* (Bloomington: Indiana University Press, 2009); Kevin Olson, *Imagined Sovereignties: The Power of the People and Other Myths of the Modern Age* (Cambridge: Cambridge University Press, 2016); Paul Rabinow, *French Modern: Norms and Forms of the Social Environment* (Cambridge, Mass.: MIT Press, 1991).

14. White plantation owners, for instance, pushed for "an autonomous slave state ruled by white planters," who invoked the rights of man for themselves while excluding slaves and free *gens de couleur* (people of color) from their scope of application (Olson, *Imagined Sovereignties*, 93). In response, free *gens de couleur*, some of whom were plantation owners with their own slaves, called for political equality with white plantation owners. This equality was grounded in the rights derived from property ownership guaranteed by the metropole. These *gens de couleur* thus sought to maintain slavery, which they rearticulated as a matter of social and economic class, while arguing for racial equality among property holders. Revolutionary slaves, by contrast, conceived of small-scale forms of collective self-organization, articulated as a demand for "three free days," which focused on an expansion of agricultural practices that ensured slaves' agrarian subsistence and economic independence. They also engaged in practices of *marronage*, often escaping from slavery for a few days to visit with family before returning to the plantation (*petit marronage*) or forming slave enclaves in remote parts of the colony (*grand marronage*).

15. Olson, *Imagined Sovereignties*, 93.

16. Ibid., 81.

17. Ibid., 129.

18. Ibid., 130.

19. Rick Gladstone, "Many Ask, Why Not Call Church Shooting Terrorism?," *New York Times*, June 18, 2015, http://www.nytimes.com/2015/06/19/us/charleston-shooting-terrorism-or-hate-crime.html.

20. Glenn Greenwald, "Refusal to Call Charleston Shootings 'Terrorism' Again Shows It's a Meaningless Propaganda Term," *Intercept*, June 19, 2015, https://theintercept.com/2015/06/19/refusal-call-charleston-shootings-terrorism-shows-meaningless-propaganda-term/.

21. Ibid.

22. Mary Beth Mader, *Sleights of Reason: Norm, Bisexuality, Development* (Albany: State University of New York Press, 2011).

23. Masha Gessen, "Why the South Carolina Shooting Suspect Should Not Be Called a Terrorist," *Reuters Blogs*, June 23, 2015, http://blogs.reuters.com/great-debate/2015/06/23/why-the-south-carolina-shooting-suspect-should-not-be-called-a-terrorist/.

24. For discussions of eliminativism, see Luvell Anderson, "Epistemic Injustice and the Philosophy of Race," in *The Routledge Handbook of Epistemic Injustice*, ed. Ian James Kidd, José Medina, and Gaile Polhaus Jr. (Abingdon: Routledge, 2017), 139–48; Bernard R. Boxill, "Two Traditions in African American Political Philosophy," in *African-American Perspectives and Philosophical Traditions*, ed. John Pittman (New York: Routledge, 1997), 119–35; Kathryn T. Gines, "A Critique of Postracialism: Conserving Race and Complicating Blackness Beyond the Black-White Binary," *Du Bois Review: Social Science Research on Race* 11, no. 1 (2014): 75–86, doi:10.1017/S1742058X1400006X; Joshua Glasgow, "Racism as Disrespect," *Ethics* 120, no. 1 (2009): 64–93.

25. See Eduardo Bonilla-Silva, *Racism without Racists: Color-Blind Racism and the Persistence of Racial Inequality in the United States* (Lanham: Rowman & Littlefield, 2006).

26. See Anderson, "Epistemic Injustice and the Philosophy of Race."

27. For articulations of this argument, as well as discussions of the notion of racial terrorism, see Cristina Beltrán, "On 'White Racial Terrorism,'" *The Trouble with Unity*, December 14, 2015, http://www.thetroublewithunity.com/the-trouble-with-unity/2015/12/on-white-racial-terrorism.html; Equal Justice Initiative, *Lynching in America: Confronting the Legacy of Racial Terror; Report Summary* (Montgomery, Ala.: Equal Justice Initiative, 2015); McWhorter, *Racism and Sexual Oppression*.

28. Leon F. Litwack, *Trouble in Mind* (New York: Vintage, 1998), 411.

29. Ida B. Wells, *Crusade for Justice: The Autobiography of Ida B. Wells*, ed. Alfreda M. Duster (Chicago and London: University of Chicago Press, 1970), 64.

30. Jay-Z. "A Ballad for the Fallen Soldier." *The Blueprint 2: The Gift & the Curse* (Roc-A-Fella/Def Jam, 2002).

31. Michelle Alexander, *The New Jim Crow: Mass Incarceration in the Age of Colorblindness* (New York: New Press, 2010).

32. Luvell Anderson, "Calling, Addressing, and Appropriation," in *Bad Words*, ed. David Sosa (Oxford: Oxford University Press, forthcoming).

33. On the notion of the intolerable, see Michel Foucault, "Je perçois l'intolérable," in *Dits et écrits*, vol. 2, *1970–1975*, ed. Daniel Defert and François Ewald (Paris: Gallimard, 1994), 203–5; Foucault, "Sur les prisons," in *Dits et écrits*, vol. 2, *1970–1975*, ed. Daniel Defert and François Ewald (Paris: Gallimard, 1994), 175–76; Foucault, "Enquête sur les prisons: Brisons les barreaux du silence," in *Dits et écrits*, vol. 2, *1970–1975*, ed. Daniel Defert and François Ewald (Paris: Gallimard, 1994), 176–82.

34. Michel Foucault, "Structuralism and Post-Structuralism," in *Essential Works of Foucault, 1954–1984*, vol. 2, *Aesthetics, Method, and Epistemology*, ed. James D. Faubion (New York: New Press, 1998), 450.

35. Ibid., 449–50.

36. Michel Foucault, "What Is Enlightenment?," in *The Politics of Truth*, ed. Sylvère Lotringer (Los Angeles: Semiotext(e), 2007), 108.

37. Thaler, Mathias. *Critical Theory and the Engaged Imagination: The Politics of Genocide, Torture, and Terrorism* (New York: Columbia University Press, forthcoming), chapter 4; Helen M. Kinsella, "Gendering Grotius: Sex and Sex Difference in the Laws of War," *Political Theory* 34, no. 2 (2006): 161–91, doi:10.1177/0090591705279530; Kinsella, *The Image Before the Weapon: A Critical History of the Distinction Between Combatant and Civilian* (Ithaca, N.Y.: Cornell University Press, 2011); Maja Zehfuss, "Killing Civilians: Thinking the Practice of War," *British Journal of Politics and International Relations* 14, no. 3 (2012): 423–40, doi:10.1111/j.1467-856X.2011.00491.x; Zehfuss, "Targeting: Precision and the Production of Ethics," *European Journal of International Relations* 17, no. 3 (2011): 543–66, doi:10.1177/1354066110373559.

38. Allen, *Politics of Our Selves*, 148.

39. Koopman, *Genealogy as Critique*, 218.

40. Seyla Benhabib, *Critique, Norm, and Utopia: A Study of the Foundations of Critical Theory* (New York: Columbia University Press, 1986), 142.

41. Koopman, *Genealogy as Critique*, 216.

42. Ibid., 229.

43. Jürgen Habermas, "A Genealogical Analysis of the Cognitive Content of Morality," in *The Inclusion of the Other: Studies in Political Theory*, ed. Ciaran Cronin and Pablo De Greiff (Cambridge, Mass.: MIT Press, 2000), 45.

44. For a careful development of this argument, see in particular chapters 1, 2, and 6 in Amy Allen, *The End of Progress: Decolonizing the Normative Foundations of Critical Theory* (New York: Columbia University Press, 2016).

45. Michel Foucault, "Body/Power," in *Power/Knowledge: Selected Interviews and Other Writings, 1972–1977*, ed. Colin Gordon (New York: Vintage, 1980), 62.

46. We can see this in definitional approaches to terrorism that abstract from the complexities of social reality to clarify what terrorism is with the aim of determining what ought to be done about it. Here the question of definition is important insofar as "the rights and wrongs of terrorist acts, and, for that matter, anti-terrorist responses, cannot be adequately addressed unless we are clear about what topic we are discussing" (C. A. J. "Tony" Coady, "Defining Terrorism," in *Terrorism: The Philosophical Issues*, ed. Igor Primoratz [London: Palgrave Macmillan, 2004], 3). The role of theory, on this view, is to find the truth of terrorism so that we may adapt our political responses accordingly.

47. Michel Foucault, "L'intellectuel et les pouvoirs," in *Dits et écrits*, vol. 4, *1980–1988*, ed. Daniel Defert and François Ewald (Paris: Gallimard, 1994), 727.

48. Michel Foucault, "Table ronde du 20 mai 1978," in *Dits et écrits*, vol. 4, *1980–1988*, ed. Daniel Defert and François Ewald (Paris: Gallimard, 1994), 21.

49. Ibid., 28. On this point see also Max Horkheimer's distinction between traditional and critical theory in his famous essay "Traditional and Critical Theory," in *Critical Theory: Selected Essays*, trans. Matthew J. O'Connell (New York: Continuum, 1972), 188–243. Horkheimer argues that while traditional theories present themselves as objective, disinterested, and pure thought rather than a social practice, critical theories

are self-reflectively aware of their being a practice embedded in concrete social, historical, political, and economic conditions.

50. Michel Foucault, "Les intellectuels et le pouvoir," in *Dits et écrits*, vol. 2, *1970–1975*, ed. Daniel Defert and François Ewald (Paris: Gallimard, 1994), 308. On this point, see also Louis Althusser's notion of a theoretical practice in *Philosophy and the Spontaneous Philosophy of the Scientists, and Other Essays*, trans. Gregory Elliott (London: Verso, 2011).

51. Foucault, "Intellectuels et le pouvoir," 29.

52. Ibid., 32–33. Thus, when asked about the impact of his work, Foucault expressed encouragement that psychiatric authorities bristled when confronted with his work, but he insisted that what really matters is "what happens on the ground" ("Table ronde du 20 mai 1978," 31). That is, the usefulness of his analyses is measured in relation to the actions they make possible for those who are struggling.

53. Take, again, the case of definitional approaches to terrorism that seek to provide the definitive account of terrorism to orient policy. David Rodin, for instance, proposes a "moral definition" of terrorism that is insulated from political contestations over meaning and use of the term while also allowing us to draw conclusions for policy. By elaborating this definition based on "the features of acknowledged core instances of terrorism which merit and explain the moral reaction which most of us have towards them," however, Rodin relies on implicit presuppositions about what terrorism is ("Terrorism Without Intention," *Ethics* 114, no. 4 [2004]: 753, doi:10.1086/383442). As I have tried to show throughout this book, such presuppositions reflect contextually specific modes of understanding terrorism, which are themselves effects of broader political rationalities. By claiming to evade political contestations over meaning and use of the term, such moral definitions thus merely conceal but do not avoid their implication in the politics of naming terrorism.

54. Foucault, "Intellectuels et le pouvoir," 32.

55. Michel Foucault, "Truth, Power, Self: An Interview with Michel Foucault," in *Technologies of the Self: A Seminar with Michel Foucault*, ed. Luther H. Martin, Huck Gutman, and Patrick H. Hutton (Amherst: University of Massachusetts Press, 1988), 10.

56. Foucault, "Table ronde du 20 mai 1978," 23.

57. Ibid., 24.

58. Ibid., 23.

59. Michel Foucault, *Histoire de la sexualité I: La volonté de savoir*, (Paris: Gallimard, 1976), 126–27.

60. Foucault, "What Is Enlightenment?," 114.

61. This notion of the theorist as a relay follows Deleuze's description of theory as a "relay from one practice to another" in Foucault, "Intellectuels et le pouvoir," 307.

62. Adorno, "Aufzeichnungen zu Kafka," in *Gesammelte Schriften*, vol. 10, *Kulturkritik und Gesellschaft*, part 1, *Prismen. Ohne Leitbild* (Frankfurt am Main: Suhrkamp, 2015), 262, cites the example of Kafka's use of psychoanalysis, which turns his works into an experiment in which he "studies what would happen if the results of psychoanalysis

were to apply not figuratively and mentally, but corporeally [*leibhaftig*]." This "exploding" of psychoanalysis by "taking it more literally than it takes itself" is Kafka's means "rather than to cure neurosis, to seek in neurosis itself healing power."

63. Gary Wilder, *Freedom Time: Negritude, Decolonization, and the Future of the World* (Durham and London: Duke University Press, 2015), xiii.

64. Frantz Fanon, *A Dying Colonialism*, trans. Haakon Chevalier (New York: Grove, 1965).

65. This is not to deny that there were Algerian combatants who denied that their acts of violence were terrorism. As we saw in chapter 4, Louisette Ighilahriz, for instance, insisted that she was not a terrorist but a *moujahida* who was fighting for a noble cause.

BIBLIOGRAPHY

ARCHIVES

Service historique de la défense, Vincennes, France. Series 1H: 1022; 1159; 1245; 1570; 1571; 1983; 4054.

REFERENCES

Adorno, Theodor W. "Aufzeichnungen zu Kafka." In *Gesammelte Schriften*, vol. 10, *Kulturkritik und Gesellschaft*, part 1, *Prismen. Ohne Leitbild*, 254–87. Frankfurt am Main: Suhrkamp, 2015.

Aftalion, Florin. *The French Revolution: An Economic Interpretation*. Cambridge: Cambridge University Press, 1990.

Agamben, Giorgio. "Security and Terror." *Theory and Event* 5, no. 4 (2002): 1–2.

——. *State of Exception*. Translated by Kevin Attell. Chicago: University of Chicago Press, 2005.

Aggarwal, Neil Krishan. *Mental Health in the War on Terror: Culture, Science, and Statecraft*. New York: Columbia University Press, 2015.

Ahmad, Eqbal. *The Selected Writings of Eqbal Ahmad*. Edited by Carollee Bengelsdorf, Margaret Cerullo, and Yogesh Chandrani. New York: Columbia University Press, 2006.

Ahmad, Muneer I. "Homeland Insecurities: Racial Violence the Day After September 11." *Social Text* 20, no. 3 (2002): 101–15.

——. "A Rage Shared by Law: Post–September 11 Racial Violence as Crimes of Passion." *California Law Review* 92, no. 5 (2004): 1259–1330.

Ahmed, Sara. "The Politics of Fear in the Making of Worlds." *International Journal of Qualitative Studies in Education* 16, no. 3 (2003): 377–98.

Alexander, Michelle. *The New Jim Crow: Mass Incarceration in the Age of Colorblindness*. New York: New Press, 2010.

Alleg, Henri. *The Question*. Translated by John Calder. Lincoln: University of Nebraska Press, 2006.

Allen, Amy. *The End of Progress: Decolonizing the Normative Foundations of Critical Theory*. New York: Columbia University Press, 2016.

——. *The Politics of Our Selves: Power, Autonomy, and Gender in Contemporary Critical Theory*. New York: Columbia University Press, 2008.

Alsultany, Evelyn. *Arabs and Muslims in the Media: Race and Representation after 9/11*. New York: New York University Press, 2012.

Althusser, Louis. "Ideology and Ideological State Apparatuses." In *On Ideology*. Translated by Ben Brewster. 1–60. London: Verso, 2008.

——. *Philosophy and the Spontaneous Philosophy of the Scientists, and Other Essays*. Translated by Gregory Elliott. London: Verso, 2011.

Amoore, Louise, and Marieke de Goede, eds. *Risk and the War on Terror*. London: Routledge, 2008.

Anderson, Luvell. "Calling, Addressing, and Appropriation." In *Bad Words*, edited by David Sosa. Oxford: Oxford University Press, forthcoming.

——. "Epistemic Injustice and the Philosophy of Race." In *The Routledge Handbook of Epistemic Injustice*, edited by Ian James Kidd, José Medina, and Gaile Polhaus Jr., 139–48. Abingdon: Routledge, 2017.

Andress, David. *The Terror: The Merciless War for Freedom in Revolutionary France*. New York: Farrar, Straus and Giroux, 2005.

Anidjar, Gil. *The Jew, the Arab: A History of the Enemy*. Stanford, Calif.: Stanford University Press, 2003.

——. "Terror Right." *CR: The New Centennial Review* 4, no. 3 (2004): 35–69.

Antiterrorism and Effective Death Penalty Act of 1996. Pub. L. No. 104-132, 110 Stat. 1214 (1996). https://www.gpo.gov/fdsys/pkg/PLAW-104publ132/html/PLAW-104publ132.htm.

Appiah, Kwame Anthony. "Racisms." In *Anatomy of Racism*, edited by David Goldberg, 3–17. Minneapolis: University of Minnesota Press, 1990.

Application of 18 U.S.C. 2340–2340A to Certain Techniques That May Be Used in the Interrogation of a High Value Al Qaeda Detainee: Memorandum for John Rizzo, Acting General Counsel of the Central Intelligence Agency. 2005. https://fas.org/irp/agency/doj/olc/techniques.pdf.

Aradau, Claudia, and Rens van Munster. "Insuring Terrorism, Assuring Subjects, Ensuring Normality: The Politics of Risk After 9/11." *Alternatives: Global, Local, Political* 33, no. 2 (2008): 191–210.

——. "Taming the Future: The Dispositif of Risk in the War on Terror." In *Risk and the War on Terror*, ed. Louise Amoore and Marieke de Goede, 23–40. London: Routledge, 2008.

Arendt, Hannah. *The Origins of Totalitarianism*. San Diego: Harcourt, 1973.

Arnault, Antoine-Vincent. *Biographie nouvelle des contemporains, ou dictionnaire historique et raisonné de tous les hommes qui, depuis la Révolution française ont acquis de la célébrité par leurs actions, leurs écrits, leurs erreurs ou leurs crimes, soit en France, soit dans les pays étrangers.* Paris: Librairie Historique, 1825.

Aron, Raymond. *Memoires: 50 ans de réflexion politique.* Paris: Julliard, 1983.

Ashman, Sam. "Capitalism, Uneven and Combined Development and the Transhistoric." *Cambridge Review of International Affairs* 22, no. 1 (2009): 29–46. doi:10.1080/09557570 802683896.

Aulard, François Victor Alphonse. *Paris pendant la réaction Thermidorienne et sous le Directoire: Recueil de documents pour l'histoire de l'ésprit publique à Paris.* Vol. 5. Paris: Cerf, 1902.

——. *Recueil des actes du Comité de salut public avec la correspondence officielle des représentants en mission et le registre du Conseil exécutif provisoire.* Vol. 28. Paris: Imprimerie Nationale, 1951.

Aussaresses, Paul. *The Battle of the Casbah: Terrorism and Counter-Terrorism in Algeria, 1955–1957.* Translated by Robert L. Miller. New York: Enigma, 2005.

Authorization for Use of Military Force Against Terrorists. S.J. Res. 23, 115 Stat. 224 (2001). http://www.gpo.gov/fdsys/pkg/PLAW-107publ40/html/PLAW-107publ40.htm.

Babeuf, Gracchus. "The Defense of Gracchus Babeuf." In *The Defense of Gracchus Babeuf Before the High Court of Vendome,* edited and translated by John Anthony Scott, 19–90. New York: Schocken, 1972.

——. "Journal de la Liberté de la Presse no. Ier." In *Journal de la Liberté de la Presse, an II–an III,* 1:1–8. Milan: Galli Thierry, 1966.

——. "Journal de la Liberté de la Presse no. 2." In *Journal de la Liberté de la Presse, an II–an III,* 1:1–8. Milan: Galli Thierry, 1966.

——. "Journal de la Liberté de la Presse no. 5." In *Journal de la Liberté de la Presse, an II–an III,* 1:1–8. Milan: Galli Thierry, 1966.

——. "Journal de la Liberté de la Presse no. 6." In *Journal de la Liberté de la Presse, an II–An III,* 1:1–8. Milan: Galli Thierry, 1966.

——. "Journal de la Liberté de la Presse no. 18." In *Journal de la Liberté de la Presse, an II–an III,* 1:1–8. Milan: Galli Thierry, 1966.

——. "Le Tribun du Peuple no. 23 (1)." In *Journal de la Liberté de la Presse, an II–an III,* 1:1–8. Milan: Galli Thierry, 1966.

——. "Le Tribun du Peuple no. 25." In *Journal de la Liberté de la Presse, an II–an III,* 1:1–8. Milan: Galli Thierry, 1966.

——. "Le Tribun du Peuple no. 27." In *Journal de la Liberté de la Presse, an II–An III,* 1:209–32. Milan: Galli Thierry, 1966.

——. "Le Tribun du Peuple no. 30." In *Journal de la Liberté de la Presse, an II–an III,* 1:187–310. Milan: Galli Thierry, 1966.

——. "Le Tribun du Peuple no. 31." In *Journal de la Liberté de la Presse, an II–an III,* 1:311–22. Milan: Galli Thierry, 1966.

——. "Le Tribun du Peuple no. 32." In *Journal de la Liberté de la Presse, an II–an III,* 1:323–38. Milan: Galli Thierry, 1966.

——. "Le Tribun du Peuple no. 34." In *Le Tribun du Peuple, ou Le Défenseur des Droits de l'Homme, an III–an IV*, 2:1–52. Milan: Galli Thierry, 1966.

——. "Le Tribun du Peuple no. 36." In *Le Tribun du Peuple, ou Le Défenseur des Droits de l'Homme, an III–an IV*, 2:109–28. Milan: Galli Thierry, 1966.

——. "Le Tribun du Peuple no. 38." In *Le Tribun du Peuple, ou Le Défenseur des Droits de l'Homme, an III–an IV*, 2:149–78. Milan: Galli Thierry, 1966.

——. "Le Tribun du Peuple, ou Le Défenseur des Droits de l'Homme no. 43." In *Le Tribun du Peuple, ou Le Défenseur des Droits de l'Homme, an III–an IV*, 2:296–308. Milan: Galli Thierry, 1966.

Baczko, Bronislaw. *Ending the Terror: The French Revolution After Robespierre.* Translated by Michel Petheram. Cambridge: Cambridge University Press, 1994.

Bahramitash, Roksana. "The War on Terror, Feminist Orientalism and Orientalist Feminism: Case Studies of Two North American Bestsellers." *Critique: Critical Middle Eastern Studies* 14, no. 2 (2005): 221–35.

Banks, William, ed. *New Battlefields/Old Laws: Critical Debates on Asymmetric Warfare.* New York: Columbia University Press, 2011.

Barber, Benjamin R. *Fear's Empire: War, Terrorism, and Democracy.* New York: Norton, 2004.

Barny, Roger. *Prélude idéologique à la Révolution francaise: Le Rousseauisme avant 1789.* Paris: Les Belles Lettres, 1985.

Barrinha, André. "The Political Importance of Labelling: Terrorism and Turkey's Discourse on the PKK." *Critical Studies on Terrorism* 4, no. 2 (2011): 163–80. doi:10.1080/17539153.2011.586203.

Bawer, Bruce. "Inside the Mind of the Oslo Murderer." *Wall Street Journal*, July 25, 2011. http://www.wsj.com/articles/SB10001424053111903999904576465801154130960.

Bax, Ernest Belfort. *The Last Episode of the French Revolution: Being a History of Gracchus Babeuf and the Conspiracy of the Equals.* Boston: Small, Maynard, 1911.

Beaumont, Gustave de, and Alexis de Tocqueville. *Du système pénitentiare aux Etats-Unis, et de son application en France.* Paris: Fournier Jeune, 1833.

——. *On the Penitentiary System in the United States and Its Application in France.* Translated by Francis Lieber. Carbondale: Southern Illinois University Press, 1964.

Behnke, Andreas. "Terrorising the Political: 9/11 Within the Context of the Globalisation of Violence." *Millennium—Journal of International Studies* 33, no. 2 (2004): 279–312.

Beltrán, Cristina. "On 'White Racial Terrorism.'" *The Trouble with Unity*, December 14, 2015. http://www.thetroublewithunity.com/the-trouble-with-unity/2015/12/on-white-racial-terrorism.html.

Benhabib, Seyla. *Critique, Norm, and Utopia: A Study of the Foundations of Critical Theory.* New York: Columbia University Press, 1986.

Benjamin, Walter. "Critique of Violence." In *Selected Writings*, vol. 1, *1913–1926*, edited by Michael W. Jennings, 236–52. Cambridge, Mass.: Harvard University Press, 1996.

——. "On the Concept of History." In *Selected Writings*, vol. 4, *1938–1940*, edited by Howard Eiland and Michael W. Jennings, 389–400. Cambridge, Mass.: Harvard University Press, 2003.

Bennoune, Mahfoud. *The Making of Contemporary Algeria, 1830–1987: Colonial Upheavals and Post-Independence Development.* Cambridge: Cambridge University Press, 1988.

Bergman, Jay. "Vera Zasulich, the Shooting of Trepov and the Growth of Political Terrorism in Russia, 1878–1881." *Terrorism* 4, nos. 1–4 (1980): 25–51.

Bernauer, James. *Michel Foucault's Force of Flight*. Atlantic Highlands, N.J.: Humanities, 1990.

Bhambra, Gurminder K. *Rethinking Modernity: Postcolonialism and the Sociological Imagination*. Basingstoke: Palgrave Macmillan, 2007.

Bhatia, Michael. "Fighting Words: Naming Terrorists, Bandits, Rebels and Other Violent Actors." *Third World Quarterly* 26, no. 1 (2005): 5–22. doi:10.1080/0143659042000322874.

——, ed. *Terrorism and the Politics of Naming*. Abingdon: Routledge, 2008.

Bhattacharyya, Gargi. *Dangerous Brown Men: Exploiting Sex, Violence and Feminism in the "War on the Terror."* London: Zed, 2005.

Bigeard, Marcel-Maurice. *J'ai mal à la France*. Ostwald: Polygone, 2001.

Bigo, Didier, and Anastassia Tsoukala. *Terror, Insecurity and Liberty: Illiberal Practices of Liberal Regimes After 9/11*. London: Routledge, 2008.

Billington, James H. *Fire in the Minds of Men: Origins of the Revolutionary Faith*. New Brunswick, N.J.: Transaction, 1999.

Blanc, Louis. *The History of Ten Years*. Translated by Walter K. Kelly. 2 vols. Philadelphia: Lea and Blanchard, 1848.

Blum, Carol. *Rousseau and the Republic of Virtue: The Language of Politics in the French Revolution*. Ithaca, N.Y.: Cornell University Press, 1989.

Blum, Lawrence. "Racism: What It Is and What It Isn't." *Studies in Philosophy and Education* 21, no. 3 (2002): 203–18.

Bonilla-Silva, Eduardo. *Racism Without Racists: Color-Blind Racism and the Persistence of Racial Inequality in the United States*. Lanham, Md.: Rowman and Littlefield, 2006.

Boudon, Julien. *Les Jacobins: Une traduction des principes de Jean-Jacques Rousseau*. Paris: Librairie Générale de Droit et de Jurisprudence, 2006.

Boxill, Bernard R. "Two Traditions in African American Political Philosophy." In *African-American Perspectives and Philosophical Traditions*, edited by John Pittman, 119–35. New York: Routledge, 1997.

Brandenburg, Hans. *The Meek and the Mighty: The Emergence of the Evangelical Movement in Russia*. New York: Oxford University Press, 1977.

Bravin, Jess. *The Terror Courts: Rough Justice at Guantanamo Bay*. New Haven, Conn.: Yale University Press, 2013.

Brayton, Sean. "An American Werewolf in Kabul: John Walker Lindh, the Construction of 'Race,' and the Return to Whiteness." *International Journal of Media and Cultural Politics* 2, no. 2 (2006): 167–82.

Brown, Howard G. *Ending the French Revolution: Violence, Justice, and Repression from the Terror to Napoleon*. Charlottesville: University of Virginia Press, 2007.

Brunot, Ferdinand. *Histoire de la langue française des origines à 1900*. Vol. 9, part 2, *La Révolution et l'empire: Les événements, les institutions et la langue*. Paris: Colin, 1937.

Bukharin, Nikolai. *The Politics and Economics of the Transition Period*. Translated by Oliver Field. London: Routledge and Kegan Paul, 1979.

Bunker, Robert J. *Networks, Terrorism and Global Insurgency*. London: Routledge, 2005.

Buonarroti, Philippe. *Conspiration pour l'égalité dite de Babeuf: Suivie du procès auquel elle donna lieu, et des pièces justificatives*. Brussels: Librairie Romantique, 1828.

Burke, Edmund. *Letters on a Regicide Peace*. In *Select Works of Edmund Burke*, edited by E. J. Payne. Vol. 3. Indianapolis: Liberty Fund, 1999.

Butler, Judith. *Frames of War: When Is Life Grievable?* London: Verso, 2009.

——. *Gender Trouble: Feminism and the Subversion of Identity*. New York: Routledge, 1990.

——. "Indefinite Detention." In *Precarious Life: The Powers of Mourning and Violence*, 50–100. London: Verso, 2004.

——. *Precarious Life: The Powers of Mourning and Violence*. London: Verso, 2004.

Byrnes, Robert Francis. *Pobedonostsev: His Life and Thought*. Bloomington: Indiana University Press, 1968.

Cadeau, Ivan. *La guerre d'Indochine: De l'Indochine française aux adieux à Saigon, 1940–1956*. Paris: Tallandier, 2015.

Callimachi, Rukmini. "Islamic State Says 'Soldiers of Caliphate' Attacked in San Bernardino." *New York Times*, December 5, 2015. http://www.nytimes.com/2015/12/06/world/middleeast/islamic-state-san-bernardino-massacre.html.

Canguilhem, Georges. *The Normal and the Pathological*. Translated by Carolyn R. Fawcett. New York: Zone, 1991.

Carlyle, Thomas. *The French Revolution: A History*. London: Chapman and Hall, 1888.

Castro-Gómez, Santiago. *La hybris del punto cero: Ciencia, raza e ilustración en la Nueva Granada (1750–1816)*. Bogotá: Pontificia Universidad Javeriana, 2005.

Chamayou, Grégoire. *A Theory of the Drone*. New York: New Press, 2015.

Chambonnet, Pauline, and Laure Cousin. "Attentat du Milk Bar: Rien, Zohra Drif, ne regrette rien." *Marianne*, April 1, 2012. http://www.marianne.net/Attentat-du-Milk-Bar-rien-Zohra-Drif-ne-regrette-rien_a216760.html.

Chassin, Lionel Max. *The Communist Conquest of China: A History of the Civil War, 1945–1949*. Translated by Timothy Osato and Louis Gelas. Cambridge, Mass.: Harvard University Press, 1965.

Chisholm, Hugh, ed. "Louvois, François Michel Le Tellier." In *The Encyclopaedia Britannica: A Dictionary of Arts, Sciences, Literature and General Information*, 17:69. Cambridge: Cambridge University Press, 1911.

Christodoulidis, Emilios. "Political Trials as Events." In *Events: The Force of International Law*, edited by Fleur Johns, Richard Joyce, and Sundhya Pahuja, 130–44. London: Routledge, 2010.

Cisneros, Natalie. "'Alien' Sexuality: Race, Maternity, and Citizenship." *Hypatia* 28, no. 2 (2013): 290–306. doi:10.1111/hypa.12023.

——. "The 'Illegal Alien': A Genealogical and Intersectional Approach." Ph.D. diss., Vanderbilt University, 2012.

Clarke, Alan. *Rendition to Torture*. New Brunswick, N.J.: Rutgers University Press, 2012.

Clay, Stephen. "The White Terror: Factions, Reactions, and the Politics of Vengeance." In *A Companion to the French Revolution*, edited by Peter McPhee, 359–77. Malden, Mass.: Blackwell, 2013.

Clutterbuck, Lindsay. "The Progenitors of Terrorism: Russian Revolutionaries or Extreme Irish Republicans?" *Terrorism and Political Violence* 16, no. 1 (2004): 154–81.

Coady, C. A. J. (Tony). "Defining Terrorism." In *Terrorism: The Philosophical Issues*, edited by Igor Primoratz, 3–14. London: Palgrave Macmillan, 2004.

Cobban, Alfred. *The Social Interpretation of the French Revolution.* Cambridge: Cambridge University Press, 1999.

Colás, Alejandro, and Richard Saull. *The War on Terror and the American "Empire" After the Cold War.* London: Routledge, 2006.

Cole, George Douglas Howard. *A History of Socialist Thought.* Vol. 1, *The Forerunners, 1789–1850.* London: Macmillan, 1971.

——. *A History of Socialist Thought.* Vol. 2. *Marxism and Anarchism, 1850–1890.* London: Macmillan, 1957.

——. *A History of Socialist Thought.* Vol. 3, *The Second International, 1889–1914.* 2 parts. London: Macmillan, 1963.

——. *A History of Socialist Thought.* Vol. 4, part 1, *Communism and Social Democracy, 1914–1931.* London: Macmillan, 1958.

——. *A History of Socialist Thought.* Vol. 4, part 2, *Communism and Social Democracy, 1914–1931.* London: Macmillan, 1961.

——. *A History of Socialist Thought.* Vol. 5, *Socialism and Fascism, 1931–1939.* London: Macmillan, 1961.

Cômes, Jean-Pierre. *"Ma" guerre d'Algérie et la torture: J'étais lieutenant dans les D.O.P.* Paris: L'Harmattan, 2002.

Comninel, George C. *Rethinking the French Revolution: Marxism and the Revisionist Challenge.* London: Verso, 1987.

Constant, Benjamin. "On the Re-Establishment of Terror." In *Observations on the Strength of the Present Government of France, and Upon the Necessity of Rallying round It,* translated by James Losh, 55–67. Bath: Cruttwell, 1797.

"Constitution de 1848, IIe République." 1848. *Conseil Constitutionnel.* http://www.conseil -constitutionnel.fr/conseil-constitutionnel/francais/la-constitution/les-constitutions-de -la-france/constitution-de-1848-iie-republique.5106.html.

Crenshaw, Martha. "The Concept of Revolutionary Terrorism." *Journal of Conflict Resolution* 16, no. 3 (1972): 383–96.

Daly, Jonathan W. "On the Significance of Emergency Legislation in Late Imperial Russia." *Slavic Review* 54, no. 3 (1995): 602–29.

Darrow, Margaret H. "Economic Terror in the City: The General Maximum in Montauban." *French Historical Studies* 17, no. 2 (1991): 498–525.

Daston, Lorraine. "Historical Epistemology." In *Questions of Evidence: Proof, Practice, and Persuasion Across the Disciplines,* edited by James K. Chandler, Arnold I. Davidson, and Harry D. Harootunian, 282–89. Chicago: University of Chicago Press, 1994.

Dauphinée, Elizabeth, and Cristina Masters, eds. *The Logics of Biopower and the War on Terror: Living, Dying, Surviving.* New York: Palgrave Macmillan, 2006.

Davidson, Arnold I. *The Emergence of Sexuality: Historical Epistemology and the Formation of Concepts.* Cambridge, Mass.: Harvard University Press, 2004.

——. "Structures and Strategies of Discourse: Towards a History of Foucault's Philosophy of Language." In *Foucault and His Interlocutors*, edited by Arnold I. Davidson, 1–22. Chicago: University of Chicago Press, 1997.

Debrix, François. *Tabloid Terror: War, Culture, and Geopolitics*. London: Routledge, 2008.

Decker, Jeffrey Louis. "Terrorism (Un)Veiled: Frantz Fanon and the Women of Algiers." *Culutral Critique* 17 (1990): 177–95.

Deutscher, Penelope. "Society Must Be Defended as Pluri-Genealogy." Paper presented at the Graduate Summer Institute in Rhetoric and Public Culture, Northwestern University, July 20, 2016.

Diderot, Denis. *Political Writings*. Edited by John Hope Mason and Robert Wokler. Cambridge: Cambridge University Press, 2001.

Dillon, Michael. *Biopolitics of Security: A Political Analytic of Finitude*. London: Routledge, 2015.

——. "Governing Terror: The State of Emergency of Biopolitical Emergence." *International Political Sociology* 1, no. 1 (2007): 7–28.

Dillon, Michael, and Andrew Neal, eds. *Foucault on Politics, Security and War*. Basingstoke: Palgrave Macmillan, 2008.

Dillon, Michael, and Julian Reid. *The Liberal Way of War: Killing to Make Life Live*. London: Routledge, 2009.

Dilts, Andrew. *Punishment and Inclusion: Race, Membership, and the Limits of American Liberalism*. New York: Fordham University Press, 2014.

Ditrych, Ondrej. *Tracing the Discourses of Terrorism: Identity, Genealogy and State*. Basingstoke: Palgrave Macmillan, 2014.

Dmytryshyn, Basil, ed. "Demands of the Narodnaia Volia." In *Imperial Russia: A Source Book, 1700–1917*, 309–13. Hinsdale, Ill.: Dryden, 1974.

Dorrien, Gary. *Imperial Designs: Neoconservatism and the New Pax Americana*. New York: Routledge, 2013.

Dowd, Maureen. "Aux Barricades!" *New York Times*, January 17, 2007. http://www.nytimes.com/2007/01/17/opinion/17dowd.html.

Doyle, William. *The Oxford History of the French Revolution*. Oxford: Oxford University Press, 2003.

Dreyfus, Hubert L., and Paul Rabinow. *Michel Foucault: Beyond Structuralism and Hermeneutics*. Chicago: University of Chicago Press, 1983.

Drif, Zohra. *Mémoires d'une combattante de l'ALN: Zone autonome d'Alger*. Alger: Chihab, 2014.

——. *La mort de mes frères*. Paris: Maspero, 1960.

Drury, Shadia B. *Alexandre Kojève: The Roots of Postmodern Politics*. New York: St. Martin's, 1994.

——. "The End of History and the New World Order." *International Journal* 48, no. 1 (1992): 80–99. doi:10.2307/40202821.

——. *Leo Strauss and the American Right*. New York: St. Martin's, 1997.

——. *The Political Ideas of Leo Strauss*. New York: Palgrave Macmillan, 2005.

Dufresnoy, Claude, ed. *Des officiers parlent*. Paris: Julliard, 1961.

Dumas, Alexandre. *The Companions of Jehu*. Vol. 29 of *The Works of Alexandre Dumas*. New York: Collier, 1902.

Duranton-Crabol, Anne-Marie. *Le temps de l'OAS*. Bruxelles: Complexe, 1995.

Edelstein, Dan. *The Terror of Natural Right: Republicanism, the Cult of Nature, and the French Revolution*. Chicago: University of Chicago Press, 2010.

Edwards, David. "Ex-CIA Deputy Director: Boston Bombing 'more like Columbine than Al Qaeda.'" *Raw Story*, April 21, 2013. http://www.rawstory.com/rs/2013/04/21/ex-cia-deputy-director-boston-bombing-more-like-columbine-than-al-qaeda/.

Ehrman, John. *The Rise of Neoconservatism: Intellectuals and Foreign Affairs, 1945–1994*. Ann Arbor, Mich.: Edwards, 1995.

Elden, Stuart. *The Birth of Territory*. Chicago: University of Chicago Press, 2013.

——. *Foucault's Last Decade*. Malden, Mass.: Polity, 2016.

——. *Foucault: The Birth of Power*. Malden, Mass.: Polity, 2017.

——. *Terror and Territory: The Spatial Extent of Sovereignty*. Minneapolis: University of Minnesota Press, 2009.

Engels, Friedrich. "Herrn Eugen Dühring's Umwälzung der Wissenschaft ('Anti-Dühring')." In *Werke*, by Karl Marx and Friedrich Engels, 20:1–303. Berlin: Dietz, 1962.

Equal Justice Initiative. *Lynching in America: Confronting the Legacy of Racial Terror; Report Summary*. Montgomery, Ala.: Equal Justice Initiative, 2015.

Erlenbusch, Verena. "From Race War to Social Racism: Foucault's Second Transcription." *Foucault Studies* 22 (2017): 134–52. doi:http://dx.doi.org/10.22439/fs.v0i0.5239.

——. "How (Not) to Study Terrorism." *Critical Review of International Social and Political Philosophy* 17, no. 4 (2014): 470–91.

——. "Terrorism: Knowledge, Power, Subjectivity." In *Critical Methods in Terrorism Studies*, edited by Jacob L. Stump and Priya Dixit, 108–20. London: Routledge, 2016.

Evans, Brad. *Liberal Terror: Global Security, Divine Power and Emergency Rule*. London: Routledge, 2012.

Evrigenis, Ioannis D. *Fear of Enemies and Collective Action*. Cambridge: Cambridge University Press, 2009.

Executive Committee. "Letter Sent by the Revolutionary Executive Committee to Alexander III at His Accession to the Throne." In *Early Writings on Terrorism*, edited by Ruth Kinna, 1:61–70. London: Routledge, 2006.

Fall, Bernard B. *Hell in a Very Small Place: The Siege of Dien Bien Phu*. Philadelphia: Lippincott, 1967.

Fanon, Frantz. *L'an V de la révolution algérienne*. In *Oeuvres*, 259–418. Paris: La Découverte, 2011.

——. *A Dying Colonialism*. Translated by Haakon Chevalier. New York: Grove, 1965.

——. "L'indépendance nationale, seule issue possible." In *Écrits sur l'aliénation et la liberté*, edited by Jean Khalfa and Robert Young, 461–66. Paris: La Découverte, 2015.

——. "Une révolution démocratique." In *Écrits sur l'aliénation et la liberté*, edited by Jean Khalfa and Robert Young, 476–80. Paris: La Découverte, 2015.

——. *The Wretched of the Earth*. Translated by Richard Philcox. New York: Grove, 2005.

Farge, Arlette. *The Allure of the Archives*. Translated by Thomas Scott-Railton. New Haven, Conn.: Yale University Press, 2013.

Feder, Ellen K. *Family Bonds: Genealogies of Race and Gender*. Oxford: Oxford University Press, 2007.

Ferguson, Roderick A. *The Reorder of Things: The University and Its Pedagogies of Minority Difference*. Minneapolis: University of Minnesota Press, 2012.

Figner, Vera. *Memoirs of a Revolutionist*. New York: International, 1927.

Finlay, Christopher J. "How to Do Things with the Word 'Terrorist.'" *Review of International Studies* 35, no. 4 (2009): 751–74. doi:10.1017/S0260210509990167.

Fleming, Marie. "Propaganda by the Deed: Terrorism and Anarchist Theory in Late Nineteenth-Century Europe." *Terrorism* 4, nos. 1–4 (1980): 1–23.

Flynn, Thomas R. *Sartre, Foucault, and Historical Reason*. Vol. 2, *A Poststructuralist Mapping of History*. Chicago: University of Chicago Press, 2010.

Foucault, Michel. *Abnormal: Lectures at the Collège de France, 1974–1975*. Edited by Valerio Marchetti, Antonella Salomoni, François Ewald, Alessandro Fontana, and Arnold I. Davidson. Translated by Graham Burchell. New York: Picador, 2004.

——. *The Archaeology of Knowledge*. Translated by A. M. Sheridan Smith. London: Routledge, 2002.

——. *The Birth of Biopolitics: Lectures at the Collège de France, 1978–1979*. Edited by Michel Senellart, François Ewald, Alessandro Fontana, and Arnold I. Davidson. Translated by Graham Burchell. New York: Palgrave Macmillan, 2010.

——. *The Birth of the Clinic: An Archaeology of Medical Perception*. Translated by A. M. Sheridan. New York: Vintage, 1994.

——. "Body/Power." In *Power/Knowledge: Selected Interviews and Other Writings, 1972–1977*, edited by Colin Gordon, translated by Colin Gordon, Leo Marshall, John Mepham, and Kate Soper, 55–62. New York: Pantheon Books, 1980.

——. "The Confession of the Flesh." In *Power/Knowledge: Selected Interviews and Other Writings, 1972–1977*, edited by Colin Gordon, translated by Colin Gordon, Leo Marshall, John Mepham, and Kate Soper, 194–228. New York: Pantheon Books, 1980.

——. *Discipline and Punish: The Birth of the Prison*. Translated by Alan Sheridan. New York: Vintage, 1995.

——. "Enquête sur les prisons: Brisons les barreaux du silence." In *Dits et écrits*, vol. 2, *1970–1975*, edited by Daniel Defert and François Ewald, 176–82. Paris: Gallimard, 1994.

——. *The Hermeneutics of the Subject: Lectures at the Collège de France, 1981–1982*. Edited by Frédéric Gros, François Ewald, Alessandro Fontana, and Arnold I. Davidson. Translated by Graham Burchell. New York: Picador, 2005.

——. *Histoire de la sexualité I: La volonté de savoir*. Paris: Gallimard, 1976.

——. *History of Madness*. Edited by Jean Khalfa. Translated by Jonathan Murphy. London: Routledge, 2006.

——. *The History of Sexuality*. Vol. 1, *An Introduction*. Translated by Robert Hurley. New York: Vintage, 1990.

——. "L'intellectuel et les pouvoirs." In *Dits et écrits*, vol. 4, *1980–1988*, edited by Daniel Defert and François Ewald, 747–52. Paris: Gallimard, 1994.

——. "Les intellectuels et le pouvoir." In *Dits et écrits*, vol. 2, *1970–1975*, edited by Daniel Defert and François Ewald, 306–15. Paris: Gallimard, 1994.

——. "An Interview with Michel Foucault." In *Essential Works of Foucault, 1954–1984*, vol. 3, *Power*, edited by James D. Faubion, translated by Robert Hurley, 239–97. New York: New Press, 2001.

——. "Je perçois l'intolérable." In *Dits et écrits*, vol. 2, *1970–1975*, edited by Daniel Defert and François Ewald, 203–5. Paris: Gallimard, 1994.

——. "Le jeu de Michel Foucault." In *Dits et écrits*, vol. 3, *1976–1979*, edited by Daniel Defert and François Ewald, 298–329. Paris: Gallimard, 1994.

——. "Non au sexe roi." In *Dits et écrits*, vol. 3, *1976–1979*, edited by Daniel Defert and François Ewald, 256–69. Paris: Gallimard, 1994.

——. *On the Government of the Living: Lectures at the Collège de France, 1979–1980*. Edited by Michel Senellart, François Ewald, Alessandro Fontana, and Arnold I. Davidson. Translated by Graham Burchell. New York: Palgrave Macmillan, 2014.

——. "On the Ways of Writing History." In *Essential Works of Foucault, 1954–1984*, vol. 2, *Aesthetics, Method, and Epistemology*, edited by James D. Faubion, 279–95. New York: New Press, 1998.

——. *The Order of Things: An Archaeology of the Human Sciences*. New York: Vintage, 1994.

——. "La philosophie analytique de la politique." In *Dits et écrits*, vol. 3, *1976–1979*, edited by Daniel Defert and François Ewald, 534–51. Paris: Gallimard, 1994.

——. "Practicing Criticism." In *Politics, Philosophy, Culture: Interviews and Other Writings, 1977–1984*. Edited by Lawrence D. Kritzman. 152–156. New York: Routledge, 1988.

——. "Prisons et asiles dans le mécanisme du pouvoir." In *Dits et écrits*, vol. 2, *1970–1975*, edited by Daniel Defert and François Ewald, 521–25. Paris: Gallimard, 1994.

——. *Psychiatric Power: Lectures at the Collège de France, 1973–1974*. Edited by Jacques Lagrange, François Ewald, Alessandro Fontana, and Arnold I. Davidson. Translated by Graham Burchell. New York: Palgrave Macmillan, 2008.

——. *The Punitive Society: Lectures at the Collège de France, 1972–1973*. Edited by Bernard E. Harcourt, François Ewald, Alessandro Fontana, and Arnold I. Davidson. Translated by Graham Burchell. Basingstoke: Palgrave Macmillan, 2015.

——. *Security, Territory, Population: Lectures at the Collège de France, 1977–1978*. Edited by Michel Senellart, François Ewald, Alessandro Fontana, and Arnold I. Davidson. Translated by Graham Burchell. New York: Palgrave Macmillan, 2007.

——. *"Society Must Be Defended": Lectures at the Collège de France, 1975–1976*. Edited by Mauro Bertani, Alessandro Fontana, François Ewald, and Arnold I. Davidson. Translated by David Macey. New York: Picador, 2003.

——. "Le souci de la vérité." In *Dits et écrits*, vol. 4, *1980–1988*, edited by Daniel Defert and François Ewald, 668–78. Paris: Gallimard, 1994.

——. "Structuralism and Post-Structuralism." In *Essential Works of Foucault, 1954–1984*, vol. 2, *Aesthetics, Method, and Epistemology*, edited by James D. Faubion, 433–58. New York: New Press, 1998.

——. "Sur les prisons." In *Dits et écrits*, vol. 2, *1970–1975*, edited by Daniel Defert and François Ewald, 175–76. Paris: Gallimard, 1994.

——. "Table ronde du 20 mai 1978." In *Dits et écrits*, vol. 4, *1980–1988*, edited by Daniel Defert and François Ewald, 20–34. Paris: Gallimard, 1994.

——. "Truth, Power, Self: An Interview with Michel Foucault." In *Technologies of the Self: A Seminar with Michel Foucault*, edited by Luther H. Martin, Huck Gutman, and Patrick H. Hutton, 9–15. Amherst: University of Massachusetts Press, 1988.

——. "La vérité et les formes juridiques." In *Dits et écrits*, vol. 2, *1970–1975*, edited by Daniel Defert and François Ewald, 538–646. Paris: Gallimard, 1994.

——. "What Is Enlightenment?" In *The Politics of Truth*, edited by Sylvère Lotringer, 97–120. Los Angeles: Semiotext(e), 2007.

——. *Wrong-Doing, Truth-Telling: The Function of Avowal in Justice*. Edited by Fabienne Brion and Bernard E. Harcourt. Translated by Stephen W. Sawyer. Chicago: University of Chicago Press, 2014.

Fourlas, George N. "Being a Target: On the Racialization of Middle Eastern Americans." *Critical Philosophy of Race* 3, no. 1 (2015): 101–23. doi:10.5325/critphilrace.3.1.0101.

Friedrich, Carl J., and Zbigniew K. Brzezinski. *Totalitarian Dictatorship and Autocracy*. Cambridge, Mass.: Harvard University Press, 1965.

Friedrichs, Jörg. "Defining the International Public Enemy: The Political Struggle Behind the Legal Debate on International Terrorism." *Leiden Journal of International Law* 19 (2006): 69–91.

Fukuyama, Francis. "The End of History?" *National Interest*, no. 16 (1989): 3–18.

——. *The End of History and the Last Man*. New York: Free Press, 2006.

Furedi, Frank. *Politics of Fear: Beyond Left and Right*. London: Bloomsbury Academic, 2005.

Furet, François, and Mona Ozouf, eds. *A Critical Dictionary of the French Revolution*. Cambridge, Mass.: Harvard University Press, 1988.

Gallois, William. *A History of Violence in the Early Algerian Colony*. Basingstoke: Palgrave Macmillan, 2013.

Garcia, Jorge. "Current Conceptions of Racism: A Critical Examination of Some Recent Social Philosophy." *Journal of Social Philosophy* 28, no. 2 (1997): 5–42.

——. "The Heart of Racism." *Journal of Social Philosophy* 27, no. 1 (1996): 5–46.

"Gazette Nationale N° 343 (3. VIII 1794)." In *Réimpression de l'ancien 'Moniteur': Seule histoire authentique et inaltérée de la Révolution Française depuis la réunion des États-Généraux jusqu'au consulat (Mai 1789–novembre 1799); avec des notes explicatives*, vol. 21, 612–616. Paris: Plon, 1847.

"Gazette Nationale ou Le Moniteur Universel N°303 (21 Juillet 1795)." In *Réimpression de l'ancien "Moniteur": Seule histoire authentique et inaltérée de la Révolution française depuis la réunion des États-Généraux jusqu'au Consulat (mai 1789–novembre 1799); Avec des notes explicatives*, vol. 25, 257–59. Paris: Plon, 1862.

Geifman, Anna. *Death Orders: The Vanguard of Modern Terrorism in Revolutionary Russia*. Santa Barbara, Calif.: Praeger, 2010.

Gemie, Sharif. *French Muslims: New Voices in Contemporary France*. Cardiff: University of Wales Press, 2010.

Genovese, Michael A. *Presidential Prerogative: Imperial Power in an Age of Terrorism*. Stanford, Calif.: Stanford University Press, 2010.

Gessen, Masha. "Why the South Carolina Shooting Suspect Should Not Be Called a Terror-ist." *Reuters Blogs*, June 23, 2015. http://blogs.reuters.com/great-debate/2015/06/23/why-the -south-carolina-shooting-suspect-should-not-be-called-a-terrorist/.

Geuss, Raymond. "Genealogy as Critique." *European Journal of Philosophy* 10, no. 2 (2002): 209–15.

Gines, Kathryn T. "A Critique of Postracialism: Conserving Race and Complicating Blackness Beyond the Black-White Binary." *Du Bois Review: Social Science Research on Race* 11, no. 1 (2014): 75–86. doi:10.1017/S1742058X1400006X.

Giordanetti, Piero. "Einleitung." In *Der Streit der Fakultäten*, by Immanuel Kant, vii–xlv. Hamburg: Meiner, 2005.

Gladstone, Rick. "Many Ask, Why Not Call Church Shooting Terrorism?" *New York Times*, June 18, 2015. http://www.nytimes.com/2015/06/19/us/charleston-shooting-terrorism-or -hate-crime.html.

Glaister, Dan. "Campaign in Iraq Has Increased Terrorism Threat, Says American Intelligence Report." *Guardian*, September 25, 2006, World News sec. https://www.theguardian.com /world/2006/sep/25/usa.iraq.

Glasgow, Joshua. "Racism as Disrespect." *Ethics* 120, no. 1 (2009): 64–93.

——. *A Theory of Race*. New York: Routledge, 2009.

Gleason, Abbott. *Young Russia: The Genesis of Russian Radicalism in the 1860s*. New York: Vi-king, 1980.

Golder, Ben. *Foucault and the Politics of Rights*. Stanford, Calif.: Stanford University Press, 2015.

Gómez-Suárez, Andrei. *Genocide, Geopolitics and Transnational Networks: Con-Textualising the Destruction of the Unión Patriótica in Colombia*. London: Taylor and Francis, 2015.

Gordon, Lewis R. *Bad Faith and Antiblack Racism*. Amherst, Mass.: Humanity, 1995.

——. "Falguni A. Sheth: Toward a Political Philosophy of Race." *Continental Philosophy Review* 44, no. 1 (2011): 119–30.

Greenwald, Glenn. "Refusal to Call Charleston Shootings 'Terrorism' Again Shows It's a Meaningless Propaganda Term." *Intercept*, June 19, 2015. https://theintercept.com/2015/06 /19/refusal-call-charleston-shootings-terrorism-shows-meaningless-propaganda-term/.

Gregory, Derek. *The Colonial Present: Afghanistan, Palestine, Iraq*. Malden, Mass.: Blackwell, 2004.

——. "From a View to a Kill: Drones and Late Modern War." *Theory, Culture and Society* 28, nos. 7–8 (2011): 188–215. doi:10.1177/0263276411423027.

——. "Palestine and the 'War on Terror.'" *Comparative Studies of South Asia, Africa and the Middle East* 24, no. 1 (2004): 183–95.

Gregory, Derek, and Allan Pred, eds. *Violent Geographies: Fear, Terror, and Political Violence*. New York: Routledge, 2006.

Grey, Stephen. *Ghost Plane: The True Story of the CIA Rendition and Torture Program*. New York: St. Martin's Griffin, 2006.

Gros, Frédéric, and Arnold I. Davidson, eds. *Foucault, Wittgenstein: De possibles rencontres*. Paris: Kimé, 2011.

Guelke, Adrian. "Irish Republican Terrorism: Learning from and Teaching Other Countries." *Studies in Conflict and Terrorism* 40, no. 7 (2017): 557–72. doi:10.1080/1057610X.2016.1237222.

Guizot, François Pierre Guillaume. (1865) 1974. *France under Louis-Philippe: From 1841 to 1847.* In *Memoirs to Illustrate the History of My Time.* Vol. 7. London: Bentley. Reprint, New York: AMS. Citations refer to the AMS edition.

——. (1861) 1974. *Memoirs to Illustrate the History of My Time.* Translated by J.W. Cole. Vol. 4. London: Bentley. Reprint, New York: AMS. Citations refer to the AMS edition.

Guthrie, Alice. "Decoding Daesh: Why Is the New Name for ISIS So Hard to Understand?" *Free Word*, February 19, 2015. https://www.freewordcentre.com/explore/daesh-isis-media -alice-guthrie.

Gutting, Gary. *Michel Foucault's Archaeology of Scientific Reason.* Cambridge: Cambridge University Press, 1989.

Habermas, Jürgen. "A Genealogical Analysis of the Cognitive Content of Morality." In *The Inclusion of the Other: Studies in Political Theory*, edited by Ciaran Cronin and Pablo de Greiff, 3–46. Cambridge, Mass.: MIT Press, 2000.

Hacking, Ian. *Historical Ontology.* Cambridge, Mass.: Harvard University Press, 2004.

——. *The Taming of Chance.* Cambridge: Cambridge University Press, 1990.

Hamburg, Gary M. *Politics of the Russian Nobility, 1881–1905.* New Brunswick, N.J.: Rutgers University Press, 1984.

Hamm, Mark S. *Apocalypse in Oklahoma: Waco and Ruby Ridge Revenged.* Boston: Northeastern University Press, 1997.

Hampson, Norman. *Will and Circumstance: Montesquieu, Rousseau and the French Revolution.* Norman: University of Oklahoma Press, 1983.

Hanson, Hilary. "Flight Delayed After Woman Fears Professor Doing Math Is a Terrorist." *Huffington Post*, May 7, 2016. http://www.huffingtonpost.com/entry/professor-math -terrorist-flight-delay_us_572e41e6e4b016f3789617f7.

Harcave, Sidney. *Count Sergei Witte and the Twilight of Imperial Russia: A Biography.* Armonk, N.Y.: Sharpe, 2004.

Hardy, Deborah. *Land and Freedom: The Origins of Russian Terrorism, 1876–1879.* New York: Greenwood, 1987.

Harle, Vilho. *The Enemy with a Thousand Faces: The Tradition of the Other in Western Political Thought and History.* Westport, Conn.: Praeger, 2000.

Haslanger, Sally. "What Are We Talking About? The Semantics and Politics of Social Kinds." *Hypatia* 20, no. 4 (2005): 10–26.

Hauser, Christine. "San Bernardino Shooting: The Investigation So Far." *New York Times*, December 2015. http://www.nytimes.com/2015/12/05/us/san-bernardino-shooting-the -investigation-so-far.html.

Heiner, Brady Thomas. "Foucault and the Black Panthers." *City* 11, no. 3 (2007): 313–56.

Heller-Roazen, Daniel. *The Enemy of All: Piracy and the Law of Nations.* New York: Zone, 2009.

Heuvel, Gerd van den. "Terreur, Terroriste, Terrorisme." In *Handbuch politisch-sozialer Grundbegriffe in Frankreich, 1680–1820*, vol. 3, edited by Rolf Reichardt and Eberhard Schmitt, 89–132. Munich: Oldenbourg, 1985.

Heyes, Cressida J. "Pictures of the Self: Wittgenstein and Foucault on Thinking Ourselves Differently." In *Self-Transformations: Foucault, Ethics, and Normalized Bodies*, 15–37. Oxford: Oxford University Press, 2007.

High, Brandon. "The Recent Historiography of American Neoconservatism." *Historical Journal* 52, no. 2 (2009): 475–491. doi:10.1017/S0018246X09007560.

Hirsch, Francine. "Race Without the Practice of Racial Politics." *Slavic Review* 61, no. 1 (2002): 30–43.

Hobbes, Thomas. *Leviathan*. Edited by Richard Tuck. Cambridge: Cambridge University Press, 2003.

Hobsbawm, Eric. *Bandits*. New York: Pantheon, 1981.

Hobson, John M. "What's at Stake in the Neo-Trotskyist Debate? Towards a Non-Eurocentric Historical Sociology of Uneven and Combined Development." *Millennium—Journal of International Studies* 40, no. 1 (2011): 147–66. doi:10.1177/0305829811412653.

Holbach, Paul Henri Thiry. *La politique naturelle; ou, Discours sur les vrais principes du gouvernement*. Hildesheim: Olms, 1971.

——. *Système social: ou, Principes naturels de la morale et de la politique*. Paris: Fayard, 1994.

Holquist, Peter. "State Violence as Technique: The Logic of Violence in Soviet Totalitarianism." In *Landscaping the Human Garden: Twentieth-Century Population Management in a Comparative Framework*, edited by Amir Weiner, 23–45. Stanford, Calif.: Stanford University Press, 2003.

Holt, Maria. "The Unlikely Terrorist: Women and Islamic Resistance in Lebanon and the Palestinian Territories." *Critical Studies on Terrorism* 3, no. 3 (2010): 365–82. doi:10.1080/1753 9153.2010.521640.

Hong, Grace Kyungwon, and Roderick A. Ferguson, eds. *Strange Affinities: The Gender and Sexual Politics of Comparative Racialization*. Durham, N.C.: Duke University Press, 2011.

Horkheimer, Max. "Traditional and Critical Theory." In *Critical Theory: Selected Essays*, translated by Matthew J. O'Connell, 188–243. New York: Continuum, 1972.

Horne, Alistair. *A Savage War of Peace: Algeria, 1954–1962*. New York: NYRB Classics, 2006.

Hosein, Adam. "Is There an Islamic State?" Stockholm Centre for the Ethics of War and Peace. September 4, 2015. http://stockholmcentre.org/is-there-an-islamic-state/.

Huffer, Lynne. *Mad for Foucault: Rethinking the Foundations of Queer Theory*. New York: Columbia University Press, 2010.

Hunt, Krista, and Kim Rygiel, eds. *(En)Gendering the War on Terror: War Stories and Camouflaged Politics*. Aldershot: Ashgate, 2008.

Hunterberg, Max. *The Russian Mephistopheles*. Glasgow: Rae, 1909.

Ighilahriz, Louisette. *Algérienne*. Paris: Fayard/Calmann-Lévy, 2001.

International Convention for the Suppression of Terrorist Bombings. 1998. https://www.unodc .org/documents/treaties/Special/1997%20International%20Convention%20for%20 the%20Suppression%20of%20Terrorist.pdf.

International Convention for the Suppression of the Financing of Terrorism. 1999. http://www .un.org/law/cod/finterr.htm.

Israel, Jonathan. *Revolutionary Ideas: An Intellectual History of the French Revolution from "The Rights of Man" to Robespierre*. Princeton, N.J.: Princeton University Press, 2014.

Jackson, Bernard S. "Some Comparative Legal History: Robbery and Brigandage." *Georgia Journal of International and Comparative Law* 1 (1970): 45–103.

Jackson, Richard. *Writing the War on Terrorism: Language, Politics and Counter-Terrorism.* Manchester: Manchester University Press, 2005.

James, C. L. R. *The Black Jacobins: Toussaint L'Ouverture and the San Domingo Revolution.* New York: Vintage, 1989.

Jauffret, Jean-Charles. *Ces officiers qui ont dit non à la torture, Algérie, 1954–1962.* Paris: Autrement, 2005.

Jay-Z. "A Ballad for the Fallen Soldier." *The Blueprint 2: The Gift & the Curse.* Roc-A-Fella/Def Jam, 2002.

Jeffers, Chike. "Should Black Kids Avoid Wearing Hoodies?" In *Pursuing Trayvon Martin: Historical Contexts and Contemporary Manifestations of Racial Dynamics,* edited by George Yancy and Janine Jones, 129–40. Lanham, Md.: Lexington, 2012.

Jensen, Richard Bach. *The Battle Against Anarchist Terrorism: An International History, 1878–1934.* Cambridge: Cambridge University Press, 2015.

——. "Daggers, Rifles and Dynamite: Anarchist Terrorism in Nineteenth Century Europe." *Terrorism and Political Violence* 16, no. 1 (2004): 116–53.

Jervis, Rick, and Christopher Cooper. "Terrorists May Be Among Refugees Heading to Europe." *Wall Street Journal,* July 5, 2002, News sec. http://www.wsj.com/articles/SB1025 818733332780560.

Jordan, David P. *The King's Trial: The French Revolution vs. Louis XVI.* Berkeley: University of California Press, 1979.

——. "The Robespierre Problem." In *Robespierre,* edited by Colin Haydon and William Doyle, 17–34. Cambridge: Cambridge University Press, 1999.

Josephus, Flavius. *The Wars of the Jews.* In *The Works of Josephus,* translated by William Whiston, 543–772. Peabody, Mass.: Hendrickson, 1987.

Juger en Algérie, 1944–1962. Genre humain. Paris: Seuil, 1997.

Kant, Immanuel. "The Contest of Faculties." In *Political Writings,* edited by Hans Reiss, 176–90. Cambridge: Cambridge University Press, 2009.

Kaufman, Michael T. "The World: Film Studies; What Does the Pentagon See in 'Battle of Algiers'?" *New York Times,* September 7, 2003, Week in Review sec. http://www.nytimes.com/2003/09/07/weekinreview/the-world-film-studies-what-does-the-pentagon-see-in-battle-of-algiers.html.

Kautsky, Karl. *Terrorism and Communism: A Contribution to the Natural History of Revolution.* Translated by W. H. Kerridge. Westport, Conn.: Hyperion, 1973.

Kellner, Douglas. *Guys and Guns Amok: Domestic Terrorism and School Shootings from the Oklahoma City Bombing to the Virginia Tech Massacre.* Boulder, Colo.: Paradigm, 2008.

Kelly, Mark. *The Political Philosophy of Michel Foucault.* New York: Routledge, 2009.

——. "Racism, Nationalism and Biopolitics: Foucault's *Society Must Be Defended.*" *Contretemps* 4 (2004): 58–70.

Kinsella, Helen M. "Gendering Grotius: Sex and Sex Difference in the Laws of War." *Political Theory* 34, no. 2 (2006): 161–91. doi:10.1177/0090591705279530.

———. *The Image Before the Weapon: A Critical History of the Distinction Between Combatant and Civilian.* Ithaca, N.Y.: Cornell University Press, 2011.

Klein, Naomi. *The Shock Doctrine: The Rise of Disaster Capitalism.* New York: Picador, 2007.

Koopman, Colin. "Conceptual Analysis for Genealogical Philosophy: How to Study the History of Practices after Foucault and Wittgenstein," *The Southern Journal of Philosophy,* 55 (2017): 103–21.

———. *Genealogy as Critique: Foucault and the Problems of Modernity.* Bloomington: Indiana University Press, 2013.

———. "How We Became Our Data: A Genealogy of the Informational Person." Unpublished manuscript, 2017.

———. "Two Uses of Michel Foucault in Political Theory: Concepts and Methods in Giorgio Agamben and Ian Hacking." *Constellations* 22, no. 4 (2015): 571–85. doi:10.1111/1467-8675 .12153.

Koskenniemi, Martti. *The Gentle Civilizer of Nations: The Rise and Fall of International Law, 1870–1960.* Cambridge: Cambridge University Press, 2004.

Koyré, Alexandre. *La philosophie et le problème national en Russie au début du XIXe siècle.* Paris: Champion, 1929.

Krementsov, Nikolai. "Eugenics in Russia and the Soviet Union." In *The Oxford Handbook of the History of Eugenics,* edited by Alison Bashford and Philippa Levine, 413–29. Oxford: Oxford University Press, 2010.

———. *Revolutionary Experiments: The Quest for Immortality in Bolshevik Science and Fiction.* New York: Oxford University Press, 2013.

Kristol, Irving. "What Is a 'Neoconservative?'" In *The Neoconservative Persuasion: Selected Essays, 1942–2009,* edited by Gertrude Himmelfarb, 148–50. New York: Basic Books, 2011.

Laqueur, Walter, ed. *Voices of Terror: Manifestos, Writings, and Manuals of Al Qaeda, Hamas, and Other Terrorists from Around the World and Throughout the Ages.* New York: Reed, 2004.

Larcher, Émile. *Trois années d'études algériennes, législatives, sociales, pénitentiaires et pénales.* Paris: Rousseau, 1902.

Laue, Theodor von. *Sergei Witte and the Industrialization of Russia.* New York: Columbia University Press, 1963.

Lazreg, Marnia. *Torture and the Twilight of Empire: From Algiers to Baghdad.* Princeton, N.J.: Princeton University Press, 2007.

Le Cour Grandmaison, Olivier. *Coloniser, exterminer: Sur la guerre et l'état colonial.* Paris: Fayard, 2005.

———. *De l'indigénat: Anatomie d'un "monstre" juridique; Le droit colonial en Algérie et dans l'empire français.* Paris: La Découverte, 2010.

———. *L'empire des hygiénistes: Vivre aux colonies.* Paris: Fayard, 2014.

———. "The Exception and the Rule: On French Colonial Law." Translated by Colin Anderson. *Diogenes* 53, no. 4 (2006): 34–53.

Lefebvre, Georges. *The French Revolution.* Vol. 1, *From Its Origins to 1793.* Translated by Elizabeth Moss Evanson. New York: Columbia University Press, 1962.

——. *The French Revolution.* Vol. 2, *From 1793 to 1799.* Translated by John Hall Stewart and James Friguglietti. New York: Columbia University Press, 1964.

Legality of the Use of Military Commissions to Try Terrorists: OLC Memorandum to White House Counsel Alberto Gonzales. 2001. https://fas.org/irp/agency/doj/olc/commissions.pdf.

Leggett, George. *The Cheka: Lenin's Political Police.* Oxford: Clarendon Press, 1981.

Lemm, Vanessa, and Miguel Vatter, eds. *The Government of Life: Foucault, Biopolitics, and Neoliberalism.* New York: Fordham University Press, 2014.

Lemon, Alaina. "Without a 'Concept?' Race as Discursive Practice." *Slavic Review* 61, no. 1 (2002): 54–61.

Lenin, Vladimir I. "Draft Programme of Our Party." In *Collected Works,* edited by Victor Jerome, translated by Joe Fineberg and George Hannah, 4:227–54. Moscow: Progress, 1964.

——. "The Enemies of the People." In *Collected Works,* translated by Bernard Isaacs, 25:57–58. Moscow: Progress, 1964.

——. "From the Defensive to the Offensive." In *Collected Works,* edited by George Hanna, translated by Abraham Fineberg and Julius Katzer, 9:283–85. Moscow: Progress, 1964.

——. "Letter to American Workers." In *Collected Works,* edited by Jim Riordan, 28:62–75. Moscow: Progress, 1964.

——. "The State and Revolution." In *Collected Works,* edited by Stepan Apresyan and Jim Riordan, 25:381–532. Moscow: Progress, 1964.

——. "Tasks of Revolutionary Army Contingents." In *Collected Works,* edited by George Hanna, translated by Abraham Fineberg and Julius Katzer, 9:420–26. Moscow: Progress, 1964.

Lentin, Alana, and Gavan Titley. "Anders Behring Breivik Had No Legitimate Grievance." *Guardian,* July 26, 2011. http://www.theguardian.com/commentisfree/2011/jul/26/anders-behring-breivik-multicultural-failure.

Leulliette, Pierre. *St. Michael and the Dragon.* Translated by John Edmonds. Boston: Houghton Mifflin, 1964.

Levine, Andrew. "Robespierre: Critic of Rousseau." *Canadian Journal of Philosophy* 8 (September 1978): 543–57.

Linden, Marcel van der. "The 'Law' of Uneven and Combined Development: Some Underdeveloped Thoughts." *Historical Materialism* 15, no. 1 (2007): 145–65. doi:10.1163/156920607X171627.

Litwack, Leon F. *Trouble in Mind.* New York: Vintage, 1998.

Longley, David. *The Longman Companion to Imperial Russia, 1689–1917.* Abingdon: Routledge, 2000.

Lustick, Ian. *Unsettled States, Disputed Lands: Britain and Ireland, France and Algeria, Israel and the West Bank–Gaza.* Ithaca, N.Y.: Cornell University Press, 1993.

Luxemburg, Rosa. "Zur Frage des Terrorismus in Rußland." In *Gesammelte Werke,* vol. 1, *1893–1905,* 275–80. Berlin: Dietz, 1972.

MacAskill, Ewen. "Julian Assange like a Hi-Tech Terrorist, Says Joe Biden." *Guardian,* December 19, 2010. https://www.theguardian.com/media/2010/dec/19/assange-high-tech-terrorist-biden.

Macey, David. "Rethinking Biopolitics, Race and Power in the Wake of Foucault." *Theory, Culture and Society* 26, no. 6 (2009): 186–205.

Madariaga, Isabel de. *Ivan the Terrible*. New Haven, Conn.: Yale University Press, 2005.

Mader, Mary Beth. "Modern Living and Vital Race: Foucault and the Science of Life." *Foucault Studies* 12 (2011): 97–112.

——. *Sleights of Reason: Norm, Bisexuality, Development*. Albany: State University of New York Press, 2011.

Mamdani, Mahmood. "The Politics of Naming: Genocide, Civil War, Insurgency." *London Review of Books* 29, no. 5 (2007): 5–8.

Mann, Bonnie. *Sovereign Masculinity: Gender Lessons from the War on Terror*. New York: Oxford University Press, 2014.

Margulies, Joseph. *Guantanamo and the Abuse of Presidential Power*. New York: Simon and Schuster, 2006.

Marx, Karl, and Friedrich Engels. *The German Ideology*. In *Collected Works*, vol. 5, 19–608. New York: International, 1976.

Massu, Jacques. *La vraie bataille d'Alger*. Paris: Plon, 1971.

Massumi, Brian. *Politics of Everyday Fear*. Minneapolis: University of Minnesota Press, 1993.

Mayer, Arno J. *The Furies: Violence and Terror in the French and Russian Revolutions*. Princeton, N.J.: Princeton University Press, 2000.

Mazour, Anatole Gregory. *Russia: Tsarist and Communist*. Princeton, N.J.: Van Nostrand, 1962.

Mbembe, Achille. *Politiques de l'inimitié*. Paris: La Découverte, 2016.

McCarthy, Thomas. *Race, Empire, and the Idea of Human Development*. Cambridge: Cambridge University Press, 2009.

McWhorter, Ladelle. *Bodies and Pleasures: Foucault and the Politics of Sexual Normalization*. Bloomington: Indiana University Press, 1999.

——. *Racism and Sexual Oppression in Anglo-America: A Genealogy*. Bloomington: Indiana University Press, 2009.

Mehlinger, Howard D., and John M. Thompson. *Count Witte and the Tsarist Government in the 1905 Revolution*. Bloomington: Indiana University Press, 1972.

Meisels, Tamar. "Defining Terrorism—A Typology." *Critical Review of International Social and Political Philosophy* 12, no. 3 (2009): 331–51.

Memorandum Regarding Applicability of 18 U.S.C. § 4001(a) to Military Detention of United States Citizens. 2002. https://fas.org/irp/agency/doj/olc/detention.pdf.

Memorandum Regarding Authority for Use of Military Force to Combat Terrorist Activities within the United States. 2001. https://fas.org/irp/agency/doj/olc/milforce.pdf.

Memorandum Regarding Constitutionality of Amending Foreign Intelligence Surveillance Act to Change the "Purpose" Standard for Searches. 2001. https://fas.org/irp/agency/doj/olc/amend-fisa.pdf.

Memorandum Regarding Determination of Enemy Belligerency and Military Detention. 2002. https://fas.org/irp/agency/doj/olc/belligerency.pdf.

Memorandum Regarding the President's Power as Commander in Chief to Transfer Captured Terrorists to the Control and Custody of Foreign Nations. 2002. https://fas.org/irp/agency/doj/olc/transfer.pdf.

Memorandum Regarding Swift Justice Authorization Act. 2002. https://fas.org/irp/agency/doj/olc/swift-justice.pdf.

Metternich, Matthias. "Rede am feste des vierzehnten Julius in Mainz (1799)." In *Die Französische Revolution im Spiegel der deutschen Literatur*, edited by Claus Träger and Frauke Schäfer, 572–80. Leipzig: Reclam, 1975.

Meynier, Gilbert. *Histoire intérieure du FLN: 1954–1962*. Paris: Fayard, 2002.

Michel, Lou, and Dan Herbeck. *American Terrorist: Timothy McVeigh and the Oklahoma City Bombing*. New York: Harper, 2001.

Michelet, Jules. *Histoire de la Révolution française*. Paris: Pilon, 1868.

Midlarsky, Manus I. *Origins of Political Extremism: Mass Violence in the Twentieth Century and Beyond*. Cambridge: Cambridge University Press, 2011.

Mill, John Stuart. *On Liberty*. Edited by Elizabeth Rapaport. Indianapolis: Hackett, 1978.

Mills, Charles W. "'Heart' Attack: A Critique of Jorge Garcia's Volitional Conception of Racism." *Journal of Ethics* 7, no. 1 (2003): 29–62.

——. *The Racial Contract*. Ithaca, N.Y.: Cornell University Press, 1999.

Mohanty, Chandra, Minnie Bruce Pratt, and Robin L. Riley, eds. *Feminism and War*. London: Zed, 2008.

Montesquieu, Charles de. *De l'ésprit des lois*. Edited by Laurent Versini. Vol. 1. Paris: Gallimard, 1995.

Montjoie, Félix. *Histoire de la conjuration de Maximilien Robespierre*. Paris: Maret, 1795.

Morozov, Nicolas. "The Terroristic Struggle." In *Violence in Politics: Terror and Political Assassination in Eastern Europe and Russia*, edited by Feliks Gross, 110–12. The Hague: Mouton, 1972.

Morton, Stephen, and Stephen Bygrave. *Foucault in an Age of Terror: Essays on Biopolitics and the Defence of Society*. New York: Palgrave Macmillan, 2008.

Most, Johann Joseph. *The Science of Revolutionary Warfare*. El Dorado, Ark.: Desert, 1978.

Mundy, Jacob. *Imaginative Geographies of Algerian Violence: Conflict Science, Conflict Management, Antipolitics*. Stanford, Calif.: Stanford University Press, 2015.

Munster, Rens van. "The War on Terrorism: When the Exception Becomes the Rule." *International Journal for the Semiotics of Law* 17, no. 2 (2004): 141–53.

Nadarajah, Suthaharan, and Dhananjayan Sriskandarajah. "Liberation Struggle or Terrorism? The Politics of Naming the LTTE." *Third World Quarterly* 26, no. 1 (2005): 87–100.

"A National Security Strategy of Engagement and Enlargement." 1994. http://nssarchive.us/NSSR/1994.pdf.

"A National Security Strategy of Engagement and Enlargement." 1995. http://nssarchive.us/NSSR/1995.pdf.

"A National Security Strategy for A New Century." 1998. http://nssarchive.us/NSSR/1998.pdf.

"A National Security Strategy for A New Century." 1999. http://history.defense.gov/Portals/70/Documents/nss/nss1999.pdf?ver=2014-06-25-121300-170.

"A National Security Strategy for a New Century." 2000. http://nssarchive.us/NSSR/2000.pdf.

"National Security Strategy of the United States." 1987. http://nssarchive.us/NSSR/1987.pdf.

"National Security Strategy of the United States." 1988. http://nssarchive.us/NSSR/1988.pdf.

"National Security Strategy of the United States." 1990. http://nssarchive.us/NSSR/1990.pdf.

"National Security Strategy of the United States." 1991. http://nssarchive.us/NSSR/1991.pdf.

"National Security Strategy of the United States." 1993. http://nssarchive.us/NSSR/1993.pdf.

"The National Security Strategy of the United States of America." 2002. http://nssarchive.us /NSSR/2002.pdf.

Naudé, Gabriel. (1639) 1993. *Considérations politiques sur les coups d'état*. Edited by F. Charles-Daubert. Rome: G. N. P., Reprint, Hildesheim: Olms. Citations refer to the Olms edition.

——. *Political Considerations Upon Refin'd Politicks, and the Master-Strokes of State*. Translated by William King. London: Clements, 1711.

Naureckas, Jim. "The Oklahoma City Bombing: The Jihad That Wasn't." *Fair! Fairness and Accuracy in Reporting*, July 1, 1995. http://fair.org/extra-online-articles/the-oklahoma-city -bombing/.

Neal, Andrew W. *Exceptionalism and the Politics of Counter-Terrorism: Liberty, Security, and the War on Terror*. Abingdon and New York: Taylor and Francis, 2010.

Nechaev, Sergei G. "The Catechism of the Revolutionary, 1868." In *Imperial Russia: A Source Book, 1700–1917*, edited by Basil Dmytryshyn, 303–8. Hinsdale, Ill.: Dryden, 1974.

Neocleous, Mark. *Imagining the State*. Maidenhead: Open University Press, 2003.

Neumann, Franz. *Behemoth: The Structure and Practice of National Socialism, 1933–1944*. Chicago: Dee, 2009.

Nietzsche, Friedrich Wilhelm. *On the Genealogy of Morals*. Translated by Douglas Smith. Oxford: Oxford University Press, 1996.

Nigro, Roberto. "From Reason of State to Liberalism: The Coup d'État as Form of Government." In *The Government of Life: Foucault, Biopolitics, and Neoliberalism*, edited by Vanessa Lemm and Miguel Vatter, 127–40. New York: Fordham University Press, 2014.

Odysseos, Louiza, and Fabio Petito, eds. *The International Political Thought of Carl Schmitt: Terror, Liberal War and the Crisis of Global Order*. London: Routledge, 2007.

Oksala, Johanna. *Foucault, Politics, and Violence*. Evanston, Ill.: Northwestern University Press, 2012.

Olson, Joel. *The Abolition of White Democracy*. Minneapolis: University of Minnesota Press, 2004.

Olson, Kevin. "Epistemologies of Rebellion: The Tricolor Cockade and the Problem of Subaltern Speech." *Political Theory* 43, no. 6 (2014): 730-52, doi:10.1177/0090591714558425.

——. *Imagined Sovereignties: The Power of the People and Other Myths of the Modern Age*. Cambridge: Cambridge University Press, 2016.

Omnibus Counterterrorism Act of 1995. S.390—104th Congress (1995–1996) (1995). https:// www.congress.gov/bill/104th-congress/senate-bill/390/text.

O'Neill, Bard E. *Insurgency and Terrorism: Inside Modern Revolutionary Warfare*. McLean, VA: Brassey's, 2001.

Oppenheim, Lassa. *International Law*. Vol. 1, *Peace*. London: Longmans, Green, 1905.

Palmer, Robert R. *Twelve Who Ruled: The Year of the Terror in the French Revolution*. New York: Atheneum, 1966.

Pappe, Ilan. "De-Terrorising the Palestinian National Struggle: The Roadmap to Peace." *Critical Studies on Terrorism* 2, no. 2 (2009): 127–46. doi:10.1080/17539150903021399.

Pavlov, Andrei, and Maureen Perrie. *Ivan the Terrible*. Abingdon: Taylor and Francis, 2003.

Pervillé, Guy. "Comment appeler les habitants de l'Algérie avant la définition légale d'une nationalité algérienne?" *Cahiers de la Méditerranée* 54 (1997): 55–60.

Pilbeam, Pamela. "The Economic Crisis of 1827–32 and the 1830 Revolution in Provincial France." *Historical Journal* 32, no. 2 (1989): 319–38. doi:10.1017/S0018246X00012176.

Pippin, Robert B. "Being, Time, and Politics: The Strauss-Kojève Debate." *History and Theory* 32, no. 2 (1993): 138–61. doi:10.2307/2505349.

Pitts, Jennifer. Introduction to *Writings on Empire and Slavery*, by Alexis de Tocqueville, edited and translated by Jennifer Pitts, ix–xxxviii. Baltimore: Johns Hopkins University Press, 2001.

Plekhanov, Georgiĭ Valentinovich. *Anarchism and Socialism*. Translated by Eleanor Marx Aveling. Chicago: Kerr, 1909.

Pobyedonostseff, Konstantin P. *Reflections of a Russian Statesman*. Translated by Robert Crozier Long. London: Richards, 1898.

Portnoy, Howard. "Sorry, David Sirota: Looks Like Boston Bombing Suspects Not 'White Americans.'" *NewsBusters*, April 19, 2013. http://newsbusters.org/blogs/howard-portnoy /2013/04/19/sorry-david-sirota-looks-boston-bombing-suspects-not-white-americans.

Pouillot, Henri. *La villa susini*. Paris: Tirésias, 2001.

"President Obama's April 16 Speech on Boston Marathon Bombings." *Time*, April 16, 2013. http://swampland.time.com/2013/04/16/president-obamas-speech-on-boston-marathon -bombings-full-text/.

Prozorov, Sergei. "Liberal Enmity: The Figure of the Foe in the Political Ontology of Liberalism." *Millennium* 35, no. 1 (2006): 75–99. doi:10.1177/03058298060350010801.

Puar, Jasbir K. *Terrorist Assemblages: Homonationalism in Queer Times*. Durham, N.C.: Duke University Press, 2007.

Puar, Jasbir K., and Amit Rai. "Monster, Terrorist, Fag: The War on Terrorism and the Production of Docile Bodies." *Social Text* 20, no. 3 (2002): 117–48.

Pyle, Christopher H. *Extradition, Politics, and Human Rights*. Philadelphia: Temple University Press, 2001.

Quinet, Edgar. *La Révolution*. Paris: Belin, 1987.

Rabinow, Paul. *French Modern: Norms and Forms of the Social Environment*. Cambridge, Mass.: MIT Press, 1991.

Raissiguier, Catherine. *Reinventing the Republic: Gender, Migration, and Citizenship in France*. Stanford, Calif.: Stanford University Press, 2010.

Rapoport, David C. "The Four Waves of Modern Terrorism." In *Attacking Terrorism: Elements of a Grand Strategy*, edited by Audrey Kurth Cronin and James M. Ludes. 46–73. Washington, D.C.: Georgetown University Press, 2004.

Rasch, William. "Lines in the Sand: Enmity as a Structuring Principle." *South Atlantic Quarterly* 104, no. 2 (2005): 253–62. doi:10.1215/00382876-104-2-253.

Rasmussen, Kim Su. "Foucault's Genealogy of Racism." *Theory, Culture and Society* 28, no. 5 (2011): 34–51.

Redfield, Marc. *The Rhetoric of Terror: Reflections on 9/11 and the War on Terror*. New York: Fordham University Press, 2009.

Reid, Julian. *The Biopolitics of the War on Terror: Life Struggles, Liberal Modernity and the Defence of Logistical Societies*. Manchester: Manchester University Press, 2009.

Reilly, Ryan J. "Dzhokhar Tsarnaev Will Not Be Treated as Enemy Combatant: White House." *Huffington Post*, April 22, 2013. http://www.huffingtonpost.com/2013/04/22/dzhokhar -tsarnaev-enemy-combatant_n_3132815.html.

Rejali, Darius. *Torture and Democracy*. Princeton, N.J.: Princeton University Press, 2007.

"The Rendition Project." Accessed July 4, 2016. https://www.therenditionproject.org.uk/.

Repo, Jemima. *The Biopolitics of Gender*. Oxford: Oxford University Press, 2015.

"The Report of the Iraq Inquiry (Chilcot Report)." London: House of Commons, 2016. http:// www.iraqinquiry.org.uk/the-report/.

Rey, Benoist. *Les égorgeurs*. Paris: Monde Libertaire, 2000.

Riasanovsky, Nicholas V. *A History of Russia*. New York: Oxford University Press, 2000.

Richards, Anthony. *Conceptualizing Terrorism*. Oxford: Oxford University Press, 2015.

Richardson, Sarah S. *Sex Itself*. Chicago: University of Chicago Press, 2013.

Ricks, Thomas. "Commander Punished as Army Probes Detainee Treatment." *Washington Post*, April 4, 2004. http://www.washingtonpost.com/wp-dyn/articles/A50227-2004Apr4 _2.html.

Rivera, Christopher. "The Brown Threat: Post-9/11 Conflations of Latina/os and Middle Eastern Muslims in the US American Imagination." *Latino Studies* 12, no. 1 (2014): 44–64.

Robespierre, Maximilien. "Draft Declaration of the Rights of Man and of the Citizen." In *Robespierre: Virtue and Terror*, edited by Slavoj Žižek, 66–72. London: Verso, 2007.

——. "Extracts from 'On Subsistence.'" In *Robespierre: Virtue and Terror*, edited by Slavoj Žižek, 49–56. London: Verso, 2007.

——. "On the Death Penalty: Speech at the Constituent Assembly, June 22, 1791." Translated by Mitch Abidor. *Marxists.org*. 2004. https://www.marxists.org/history/france/revolution /robespierre/1791/death-penalty.htm.

——. "On the Principles of Political Morality That Should Guide the National Convention in the Domestic Administration of the Republic." In *Robespierre: Virtue and Terror*, edited by Slavoj Žižek, 108–25. London: Verso, 2007.

——. "On the Principles of Revolutionary Government." In *Robespierre: Virtue and Terror*, edited by Slavoj Žižek, 98–107. London: Verso, 2007.

——. "On the Trial of the King." In *Robespierre: Virtue and Terror*, edited by Slavoj Žižek, 57–65. London: Verso, 2007.

Robinson, Cedric J. *Black Marxism: The Making of the Black Radical Tradition*. Chapel Hill: University of North Carolina Press, 2000.

Rodin, David. "Terrorism Without Intention." *Ethics* 114, no. 4 (2004): 752–71. doi:10.1086 /383442.

Romanenko, Gerasim Grigorevič. *Terrorism i rutina*. London: Russkaâ Tipografiâ, 1880.

Rose, Robert B. "18th-Century Price-Riots, the French Revolution and the Jacobin Maximum." *International Review of Social History* 4, no. 3 (1959): 432–45.

——. *Gracchus Babeuf: The First Revolutionary Communist*. Stanford, Calif.: Stanford University Press, 1978.

Rosenberg, Justin. "Why Is There No International Historical Sociology?" *European Journal of International Relations* 12, no. 3 (2006): 307–40. doi:10.1177/1354066106067345.

Rosenthal, Andrew. "What's the Difference Between McVeigh and Tsarnaev?" *Taking Note*, April 22, 2013. http://takingnote.blogs.nytimes.com/2013/04/22/whats-the-difference-between-mcveigh-and-tsarnaev/.

Roth, Michael S. "A Problem of Recognition: Alexandre Kojève and the End of History." *History and Theory* 24, no. 3 (1985): 293–306. doi:10.2307/2505171.

Rousseau, Jean-Jacques. *On the Social Contract*. In *The Basic Political Writings*, translated by Donald A. Cress, 141–227. Indianapolis: Hackett, 1987.

Rudé, George F. E. *The French Revolution: Its Causes, Its History, and Its Legacy After 200 Years*. New York: Grove, 1988.

Saar, Martin. *Genealogie als Kritik: Geschichte und Theorie des Subjekts nach Nietzsche und Foucault*. Frankfurt: Campus, 2007.

Sagan, Eli. *Citizens and Cannibals: The French Revolution, the Struggle for Modernity, and the Origins of Ideological Terror*. Lanham, Md.: Rowman and Littlefield, 2001.

Saint-Just, Louis-Antoine-Léon de. "Discours concernant le jugement de Louis XVI." In *Oeuvres complètes*, edited by Charles Vellay, , 364–372. Paris: Librairie Charpentier et Fasquell, 1908.

Saint Marc, Hélie de. *Mémoires*. Paris: Perrin, 1995.

Saji, Alia al-. "The Racialization of Muslim Veils: A Philosophical Analysis." *Philosophy and Social Criticism* 36, no. 8 (2010): 875–902.

Sampaio, Anna. *Terrorizing Latina/o Immigrants: Race, Gender, and Immigration Policy Post-9/11*. Philadelphia: Temple University Press, 2015.

Sanna, Maria Eleonora, and Malek Bouyahia, eds. *La polysémie du voile: Politiques et mobilisations postcoloniales*. Paris: Éditions des archives contemporaines, 2013.

Sarrault, Albert. *Discours à l'ouverture des cours de l'École coloniale*. Paris: La Presse coloniale, 1923.

Sartre, Jean-Paul. *Colonialism and Neocolonialism*. Translated by Azzedine Haddour. London: Routledge, 2006.

——. *Critique of Dialectical Reason*. Vol. 1, *Theory of Practical Ensembles*. Edited by Jonathan Rée. Translated by Alan Sheridan-Smith. London: Verso, 2004.

——. Preface to *The Question*, by Henri Alleg, translated by John Calder, xxvii–xliv. Lincoln: University of Nebraska Press, 2006.

——. Preface to *The Wretched of the Earth*, edited by Frantz Fanon, translated by Richard Philcox, xliii–lxii. New York: Grove, 2005.

Saul, Ben. *Defining Terrorism in International Law*. Oxford: Oxford University Press, 2008.

Sawicki, Jana. "Heidegger and Foucault: Escaping Technological Nihilism." In *Foucault and Heidegger: Critical Encounters*, edited by Alan Milchman and Alan Rosenberg, 55–73. Minneapolis: University of Minnesota Press, 2003.

Schaack, Michael J. *Anarchy and Anarchists: A History of the Red Terror and the Social Revolution in America and Europe*. Chicago: Schulte, 1889.

Schauer, Frederick. *The Force of Law*. Cambridge, Mass.: Harvard University Press, 2015.

Schmitt, Carl. "The Concept of Piracy (1937)." Translated by Daniel Heller-Roazen. *Humanity: An International Journal of Human Rights, Humanitarianism, and Development* 2, no. 1 (2011): 27–29.

———. *The Concept of the Political*. Translated by George Schwab. Chicago: University of Chicago Press, 2007.

———. "The International Crime of the War of Aggression and the Principle 'Nullum Crimen, Nulla Poena Sine Lege.'" In *Writings on War*, edited and translated by Timothy Nunan, 125–200. Cambridge: Polity, 2011.

———. *The Leviathan in the State Theory of Thomas Hobbes: Meaning and Failure of a Political Symbol*. Translated by George Schwab and Erna Hilfstein. Chicago: University of Chicago Press, 2008.

———. *The Nomos of the Earth in the International Law of Jus Publicum Europaeum*. Translated by G. L. Ulmen. New York: Telos, 2006.

———. *Theory of the Partisan: Intermediate Commentary on the Concept of the Political*. Translated by G. L. Ulmen. New York: Telos, 2007.

Scott, David. "Colonial Governmentality." *Social Text* 43 (1995): 191–220.

Scott, Joan Wallach. *The Politics of the Veil*. Princeton, N.J.: Princeton University Press, 2009.

Scurr, Ruth. *Fatal Purity: Robespierre and the French Revolution*. New York: Owl, 2006.

Seher, Jason. "Former NSA Chief Compares Snowden to Terrorists." *CNN*, December 1, 2013. http://politicalticker.blogs.cnn.com/2013/12/01/former-nsa-chief-compares-snowden-to -terrorists/.

Sentas, Victoria. *Traces of Terror: Counter-Terrorism Law, Policing, and Race*. Oxford: Oxford University Press, 2014.

Sessions, Jennifer E., *By Sword and Plow: France and the Conquest of Algeria*. Ithaca, N.Y.: Cornell University Press, 2011.

Shaw, Brent. "Bandits in the Roman Empire." *Past and Present* 105 (1984): 3–52.

Shelby, Tommie. "Ideology, Racism, and Critical Social Theory." *Philosophical Forum* 34, no. 2 (2003): 153–88.

Shepard, Todd. *The Invention of Decolonization: The Algerian War and the Remaking of France*. Ithaca, N.Y.: Cornell University Press, 2006.

Sheth, Falguni A. "The Hijab and the Sari: The Strange and Sexy Between Colonialism and Global Capitalism." *Contemporary Aesthetics*, special volume 2 (2009).

———. *Toward a Political Philosophy of Race*. Albany: SUNY Press, 2009.

Sieyès, Emmanuel Joseph. "What Is the Third Estate?" In *Political Writings, Including the Debate Between Sieyès and Tom Paine in 1791*, edited and translated by Michael Sonenscher, 92–162. Indianapolis: Hackett, 2003.

Sipriot, Pierre. *Les cent vingt jours de Louis XVI, dit Louis Capet*. Paris: Plon, 1993.

Sirota, David. "Let's Hope the Boston Marathon Bomber Is A White American." *Salon*, April 17, 2013. http://www.salon.com/2013/04/16/lets_hope_the_boston_marathon_bomber _is_a_white_american/.

Snider, Don M. "The National Security Strategy: Documenting Strategic Vision." 1995. http:// nssarchive.us/wp-content/uploads/2012/05/Snider.pdf.

Soboul, Albert. *The French Revolution, 1787–1799: From the Storming of the Bastille to Napoleon*. Translated by Alan Forrest and Colin Jones. Boston: Unwin Hyman, 1989.

Sparks, Chris. "Liberalism, Terrorism and the Politics of Fear." *Politics* 23, no. 3 (2003): 200–206.

Sperber, Melysa H. "John Walker Lindh and Yaser Esam Hamdi: Closing the Loophole in International Humanitarian Law for American Nationals Captured Abroad While Fighting with Enemy Forces." *American Criminal Law Review* 40 (2003): 159–215.

Stampnitzky, Lisa. *Disciplining Terror: How Experts Invented "Terrorism."* Cambridge: Cambridge University Press, 2013.

Stepniak. *Underground Russia.* London: Smith, Elder, 1883.

Steuter, Erin, and Deborah Wills. *At War with Metaphor: Media, Propaganda, and Racism in the War on Terror.* Lanham, Md.: Lexington, 2009.

Stoler, Ann Laura. *Race and the Education of Desire: Foucault's "History of Sexuality" and the Colonial Order of Things.* Durham, N .C.: Duke University Press, 1995.

Stora, Benjamin. *Algeria, 1830-2000: A Short History.* Translated by Jane Marie Todd. Ithaca: Cornell University Press, 2001.

——. *La gangrène et l'oubli: La mémoire de la guerre d'Algérie.* Paris: La Découverte, 1998.

Taha, Abir. *Defining Terrorism: The End of Double Standards.* London: Arktos Media, 2014.

Tarnovski, G. "Terrorism and Routine." In *Voices of Terror,* edited by Walter Laqueur, 83–87. Naperville, Ill.: Sourcebooks, 2004.

Taylor, Chloë. "Race and Racism in Foucault's Collège de France Lectures." *Philosophy Compass* 6, no. 11 (2011): 746–56.

Thaler, Mathias. *Critical Theory and the Engaged Imagination: The Politics of Genocide, Torture, and Terrorism.* New York: Columbia University Press, forthcoming.

Thatcher, Ian D. "Uneven and Combined Development." *Revolutionary Russia* 4, no. 2 (1991): 235–58. doi:10.1080/09546549108575572.

Third, Amanda. *Gender and the Political: Deconstructing the Female Terrorist.* New York: Palgrave Macmillan, 2014.

Thomas, Pierre-Alban. *Les désarrois d'un officier en Algérie.* Paris: Seuil, 2002.

Thorup, Mikkel. *An Intellectual History of Terror: War, Violence and the State.* London: Routledge, 2010.

Tiisala, Tuomo. "Keeping It Implicit: A Defense of Foucault's Archaeology of Knowledge." *Journal of the American Philosophical Association* 1 (2015): 653–73.

——. "Power and Freedom in the Space of Reasons." Ph.D. diss., University of Chicago, 2016.

Tikhomirov, Lev Aleksandrovich. *Russia: Political and Social.* Translated by Edward Aveling. 2 vols. London: Swan Sonnenschein, Lowrey, 1888.

——. *La Russie politique et sociale.* Paris: La Nouvelle Librairie Parisienne, 1886.

Tocqueville, Alexis de. "Essay on Algeria." In *Writings on Empire and Slavery,* edited and translated by Jennifer Pitts, 59–116. Baltimore: Johns Hopkins University Press, 2001.

——. "First Letter on Algeria." In *Writings on Empire and Slavery,* edited and translated by Jennifer Pitts, 5–13. Baltimore: Johns Hopkins University Press, 2001.

——. "First Report on Algeria." In *Writings on Empire and Slavery,* edited and translated by Jennifer Pitts, 129–73. Baltimore: Johns Hopkins University Press, 2001.

——. "Notes on the Voyage to Algeria." In *Writings on Empire and Slavery,* edited and translated by Jennifer Pitts, 36–58. Baltimore: Johns Hopkins University Press, 2001.

——. *Recollections.* Translated by George Lawrence. Garden City, N.Y.: Doubleday, 1970.

——. "Second Letter on Algeria." In *Writings on Empire and Slavery*, edited and translated by Jennifer Pitts, 14–26. Baltimore: Johns Hopkins University Press, 2001.

——. "Second Report on Algeria." In *Writings on Empire and Slavery*, edited and translated by Jennifer Pitts, 174–98. Baltimore: Johns Hopkins University Press, 2001.

——. "Some Ideas About What Prevents the French From Having Good Colonies." In *Writings on Empire and Slavery*, edited and translated by Jennifer Pitts, 1–4. Baltimore: Johns Hopkins University Press, 2001.

Trinquier, Roger. *Guerre, subversion, révolution*. Paris: Laffont, 1968.

——. *Modern Warfare: A French View of Counterinsurgency*. Translated by Daniel Lee. Westport, Conn.: Praeger, 2006.

Trotsky, Leon. "The Bankruptcy of Terrorism." In *Against Individual Terrorism*, translated by Marilyn Vogt, 10–14. New York: Pathfinder, 1974.

——. *History of the Russian Revolution*. Translated by Max Eastman. Chicago: Haymarket, 2008.

——. "The Marxist Position on Individual Terrorism." In *Against Individual Terrorism*, translated by Marilyn Vogt and George Saunders, 5–9. New York: Pathfinder, 1974.

——. *Terrorism and Communism: A Reply to Karl Kautsky*. Ann Arbor: University of Michigan Press, 1961.

——. "Terrorism and the Stalinist Regime in the Soviet Union." In *Against Individual Terrorism*, 15–21. New York: Pathfinder, 1974.

Vaïsse, Justin. *Neoconservatism: The Biography of a Movement*. Translated by Arthur Goldhammer. Cambridge, Mass.: Harvard University Press, 2010.

Vatter, Miguel. *The Republic of the Living: Biopolitics and the Critique of Civil Society*. New York: Fordham University Press, 2014.

Venturi, Franco. *Roots of Revolution. A History of the Populist and Socialist Movements in Nineteenth Century Russia*. London: Weidenfeld and Nicolson, 1964.

Verdeja, Ernesto. "Law, Terrorism, and the Plenary Power Doctrine: Limiting Alien Rights." *Constellations* 9, no. 1 (2002): 89–97.

Verhoeven, Claudia. *The Odd Man Karakozov: Imperial Russia, Modernity, and the Birth of Terrorism*. Ithaca, N.Y.: Cornell University Press, 2009.

Vidal-Naquet, Pierre, ed. *Les crimes de l'armée française*. Paris: La Découverte, 2001.

Vittori, Jean-Pierre. *Confessions d'un professionnel de la torture*. Paris: Ramsay, 1980.

——. *On a torturé en Algérie*. Paris: Ramsay, 2000.

Volpp, Leti. "The Boston Bombers." *Fordham Law Review* 82, no. 5 (2014): 2209–20.

——. "The Citizen and the Terrorist." *UCLA Law Review* 49, no. 5 (2012): 561–86.

Waldron, Peter. *The End of Imperial Russia, 1855–1917*. New York: Palgrave Macmillan, 1997.

——. "States of Emergency: Autocracy and Extraordinary Legislation, 1881–1917." *Revolutionary Russia: Journal of the Study Group on the Russian Revolution* 8, no. 1 (1995): 1–25.

Walther, Rudolf. "Terror, Terrorismus." In *Geschichtliche Grundbegriffe: Historisches Lexikon zur politisch-sozialen Sprache in Deutschland*, vol. 6, edited by Otto Brunner, Werner Conze, and Reinhart Koselleck, 323–444. Stuttgart: Klett-Cotta, 1990.

Warrick, Joby. *Black Flags: The Rise of ISIS*. New York: Penguin Random House, 2015.

Weber, Max. "Russia's Transition to Pseudo-Constitutionalism." In *The Russian Revolutions*, translated by Gordon C. Wells and Peter Baehr, 148–240. Ithaca, N.Y.: Cornell University Press, 1995.

Wehner, Peter. "The War Goes On." *Commentary*, April 23, 2014. http://www.commentarymagazine .com/2013/04/23/the-war-goes-on/.

Weiner, Amir. "Nothing but Certainty." *Slavic Review* 61, no. 1 (2002): 44–53. doi:10.2307/2696980.

Weitz, Eric D. "Racial Politics without the Concept of Race: Reevaluating Soviet Ethnic and National Purges." *Slavic Review* 61, no. 1 (2002): 1–29. doi:10.2307/2696978.

Welch, Michael. *Detained: Immigration Laws and the Expanding I.N.S. Jail Complex*. Philadelphia: Temple University Press, 2002.

——. "Ironies of Social Control and the Criminalization of Immigrants." *Crime, Law and Social Change* 39, no. 4 (2003): 319–37. doi:10.1023/A:1024068321783.

——. *Scapegoats of September 11th: Hate Crimes and State Crimes in the War on Terror*. New Brunswick, N.J.: Rutgers University Press, 2006.

Wells, Ida B. *Crusade for Justice: The Autobiography of Ida B. Wells*. Edited by Alfreda M. Duster. Chicago: University of Chicago Press, 1970.

White, Eugene Nelson. "The French Revolution and the Politics of Government Finance, 1770–1815." *Journal of Economic History* 55, no. 2 (1995): 227–55.

Wight, Colin. *Rethinking Terrorism: Terrorism, Violence and the State*. London: Palgrave Macmillan, 2015.

Wilder, Gary. *Freedom Time: Negritude, Decolonization, and the Future of the World*. Durham, N.C.: Duke University Press, 2015.

Williams, Bernard. *Truth and Truthfulness: An Essay in Genealogy*. Princeton, N.J.: Princeton University Press, 2002.

Wittgenstein, Ludwig. *Philosophical Investigations*. Translated by G. E. M. Anscombe. Malden, Mass.: Blackwell, 2001.

Wolin, Sheldon Sanford. *Democracy Incorporated: Managed Democracy and the Specter of Inverted Totalitarianism*. Princeton, N.J.: Princeton University Press, 2010.

Yacef, Saadi. *Souvenirs de la bataille d'Alger, décembre 1956–septembre 1957*. Paris: Maillet, 1962.

Yoo, John C. "The Continuation of Politics by Other Means: The Original Understanding of War Powers." *California Law Review* 84, no. 2 (1996): 167–305.

——. *The President's Constitutional Authority to Conduct Military Operations Against Terrorists and Nations Supporting Them: Memorandum Opinion for the Deputy Counsel to the President, Office of Legal Counsel*. 2001. https://www.justice.gov/olc/opinion/president%E2%80%99s -constitutional-authority-conduct-military-operations-against-terrorists-and.

Yoo, John C., and Robert J. Delahunty. "The President's Constitutional Authority to Conduct Military Operations Against Terrorist Organizations and the Nations That Harbor or Support Them." *Harvard Journal of Law and Public Policy* 25 (2002): 487–515.

Zamora, Daniel, ed. *Critiquer Foucault: Les années 1980 et la tentation néolibérale*. Saint-Gilles: Aden, 2014.

Zehfuss, Maja. "Killing Civilians: Thinking the Practice of War." *British Journal of Politics and International Relations* 14, no. 3 (2012): 423–40. doi:10.1111/j.1467-856X.2011.00491.x.

——. "Targeting: Precision and the Production of Ethics." *European Journal of International Relations* 17, no. 3 (2011): 543–66. doi:10.1177/1354066110373559.

Žižek, Slavoj. *In Defense of Lost Causes*. London: Verso, 2009.

Zolo, Danilo. *Invoking Humanity: War, Law and Global Order*. London: Continuum, 2002.

——. *Victors' Justice: From Nuremberg to Baghdad*. Translated by M. W. Weir. London: Verso, 2009.

Zouari, Fawzia. *Ce voile qui déchire la France*. Paris: Ramsay, 2004.

Zulaika, Joseba, and William Douglass. *Terror and Taboo: The Follies, Fables, and Faces of Terrorism*. New York: Routledge, 1996.

INDEX

polemic terrorism (*continued*)
17, 94, 113–17, 121, 148; as outside of law
and protections of law, 115–17; and
polemic, as term, 216n78; in twentieth
century, 144–45, 145–46, 149
police: and *raison d'État*, evolution of role,
29–31; role in Tallien's view of
revolutionary government, 42
police powers, merging with military power:
in French revolutionary war theory, 108;
in twentieth century, 108–10; in U. S.
counterterrorism after 9/11, 148–49. *See
also* peace-enforcement function of state
Polish invasion of Russia, 58–59
political or religious identity, terrorism
associated with. *See* identarian terrorism
political strategy, terrorism as. *See* strategic
terrorism
political transformation: genealogical
critique and, 173; as goal of this work, 20.
See also normative political theory
The Politics of Ourselves (Allen), 175–76
politics of radical literalism: Kafka and,
233–34n62; and normative responses to
terrorism, 182–84
politiques, and *raison d'État*, 28, 29
Pontecorvo, Gillo, 134
poststructuralism, combining with critical
theory, in normative political theory,
175–78
power. *See* technologies of power
*The Power of the People and Other Myths of
the Modern Age* (Olson), 166–68
president of U.S., power under executive
primacy doctrine, 143–44
prostitution, dispositif of, 12
Puar, Jasbir, 8, 152, 228n110
The Punitive Society (Foucault), 26

Quinet, Edgar, 25, 26

Rabinow, Paul, 165, 166
race, critique of eliminativist view of, 171

race war, and racial mix in Russian society,
Pobyedonostseff on, 75–76
race war, transition to class struggle:
Foucault on, 56–57, 64; Narodnaia Volia
on, 205n12; Robinson on, 205n11;
Russian revolutionaries and, 69, 70,
71–72, 90; Tikhomirov on, 57–59, 62, 64
racialization of terrorism, 6–8, 152–57,
226n94
racial justifications of colonialism, in
Tocqueville, 97–101; biological concept
of race in, 99–100; and race as marker of
development, 100
racial profiling of Muslims: African
American and Latina/o support of, 7–8;
and degrading of citizenship status, 7–8
racism: definition of, 10; Foucault's
definition of, 9–10
raison d'État: coexistence with *raison
économique* at time of French
Revolution, 31, 42–43; genealogy of,
196–97n27; and military-diplomatic
apparatus to balance states, 29, 30,
197n34; replacement of sovereign model
by, 28–29; and rise of *raison économique*,
30–31; Robespierre and, 37–38; role of
law and police in, 29–31, 37–38; survival
of state as sole goal of, 29, 37–38; and
U.S. foreign policy, 141, 142, 157–61
raison économique: coexistence with *raison
d'État* at time of French Revolution, 31,
42–43; Foucault on rise of, 30–31; and
rise of biopower, 30–31; of Russian
revolutionary movement, 63–64; and
subservience of sovereign to economic
law, 30; Tallien's revolutionary
government as product of, 42
Reagan, Ronald W., 140
recognition, desire for, as impetus toward
egalitarian political systems, 139
Reflections of a Russian Statesman
(Pobyedonostseff), 74–76
Reign of Terror. *See* French Reign of Terror

Russian revolutionary movement (*continued*)
54–55, 71, 80, 81; origins of, 55, 56;
transition to systemic terror of
Bolshevik state, 16, 56, 83, 90
Russian Revolution of 1905, Weber on, 78–79
Russian ruling class: counterproductivity
of repressive measures by, 78–80;
revolutionaries on foreign origin of,
57–59, 62–63, 69, 70, 71–72; and rule of
law, 205n65; and terrorism as justification
for repressive measures, 74, 76–79
Rychkov, 87–88

Saar, Martin, 165
San Bernardino shooting (2015), 2, 6
sans-culottes, 194n4; attachment of terrorist
label to, 48, 49; radical, National
Convention and, 47, 48
Sarraut, Albert, 105
A Savage War of Peace (Horne), 221n4
Schmitt, Carl, 108–9, 114, 148, 216n78
"Second Report on Algeria" (Tocqueville,
1947), 97
Security, Territory, Population (Foucault),
28–31, 192n47
Senghor, Léopold, 182
9/11 Resolution (2001), 143
September 11th terrorist attacks: and
development of synthetic terrorism
concept, 144; and transformation of
global political landscape, 6, 7. *See also*
United States counterterrorism after 9/11
Shepard, Todd, 132
sicarii, 4–5, 188n15
Sieyès, Abbé de, 41, 62, 166
Sirota, David, 153–54
Soboul, Albert, 47–48
social control, terrorism as mechanism of, 8
social defense. *See* Algeria, French conquest
of, and dispositif of social defense;
biopolitical model of social defense;
exclusion of deviant and dangerous
persons; mechanisms of social defense;

modern dispositif of terrorism;
terrorism as dispositif of social defense
socialist racism, Foucault on, 57
"Society Must Be Defended" (Foucault), 56–57
Society of 1789, 194n4
"Some Ideas About What Prevents the
French from Having Good Colonies"
(Tocqueville), 97
South Africa, 133
sovereign right to kill: biopolitical model of
social defense and, 9–10, 55, 57, 109–10,
142, 160; Foucault on, 8–9; modern
dispositif of terrorism and, 137, 142, 160;
and state power as peace enforcement,
109–10; terrorism as dispositif of social
defense and, 15, 24, 51, 52, 76, 90
sovereignty, in Russia: counterproductivity
of repressive measures, 78–80; encounter
with biopower, 76–77; Pobyedonostseff
on, 74–76; and terrorism as justification
for repressive measures, 76–79
sovereignty model: Foucault on, 8–9;
Hobbes on, 75–76; race war models'
undermining of, 56–57; Robespierre and,
24, 32, 35–38; severing of connection to
divine order, 28
sovereignty's encounter with biopolitical
model: evolution of terrorism concept
and, 15; in French Revolution, 9, 24, 31,
52, 76; in Russian Revolution, 76–77
Soviet Union. *See* Bolshevik state
The Spirit of the Laws (Montesquieu), 37,
200n63
Stalin, Josef, 82
"The State and Revolution" (Lenin), 84–85
state's peace-enforcement function,
merging of internal and external forms
of, 108–10
state violence as terrorism. *See* systemic
terrorism
Statute on Measures to Safeguard State
Security and Public Order (Russia,
1881), 77

GPSR Authorized Representative: Easy Access System Europe, Mustamäe tee
50, 10621 Tallinn, Estonia, gpsr.requests@easproject.com

www.ingramcontent.com/pod-product-compliance
Lightning Source LLC
Chambersburg PA
CBHW032119020426
42334CB00016B/1002